Matthew P. Berg, Maria Mesner (Eds.)

After Fascism: European Case Studies in Politics, Society, and Identity since 1945

After Fascism: European Case Studies in Politics, Society, and Identity since 1945

edited by

Matthew P. Berg and Maria Mesner

LIT

Gedruckt mit Unterstützung des Bundesministeriums
für Wissenschaft und Forschung in Wien

Bibliographic information published by the Deutsche Nationalbibliothek
The Deutsche Nationalbibliothek lists this publication in the Deutsche Nationalbibliografie; detailed bibliographic data are available in the Internet at http://dnb.d-nb.de.

ISBN 978-3-643-50018-2

A catalogue record for this book is available from the British Library

Krotenthallergasse 10/8
A-1080 Wien
Tel. +43 (0) 1-409 56 61
Fax +43 (0) 1-409 56 97
e-Mail: wien@lit-verlag.at
http://www.lit-verlag.at

LIT VERLAG Dr. W. Hopf
Berlin 2009
Fresnostr. 2
D-48159 Münster
Tel. +49 (0) 2 51-620 32 22
Fax +49 (0) 2 51-922 60 99
e-Mail: lit@lit-verlag.de
http://www.lit-verlag.de

Distribution:

In Germany: LIT Verlag Fresnostr. 2, D-48159 Münster
Tel. +49 (0) 2 51-620 32 22, Fax +49 (0) 2 51-922 60 99, e-Mail: vertrieb@lit-verlag.de

In Austria: Medienlogistik Pichler-ÖBZ GmbH & Co KG
IZ-NÖ, Süd, Straße 1, Objekt 34, A-2355 Wiener Neudorf
Tel. +43 (0) 22 36-63 53 52 90, Fax +43 (0) 22 36-63 53 52 43, e-Mail: mlo@medien-logistik.at

In Switzerland: B + M Buch- und Medienvertriebs AG
Hochstr. 357, CH-8200 Schaffhausen
Tel. +41 (0) 52-643 54 30, Fax +41 (0) 52-643 54 35, e-Mail: order@buch-medien.ch

In the UK by: Global Book Marketing, 99B Wallis Rd, London, E9 5LN
Phone: +44 (0) 20 8533 5800 – Fax: +44 (0) 1600 775 663
http://www.centralbooks.co.uk/html

In North America by:

Transaction Publishers
New Brunswick (U.S.A.) and London (U.K.)

Transaction Publishers
Rutgers University
35 Berrue Circle
Piscataway, NJ 08854

Phone: +1 (732) 445 - 2280
Fax: + 1 (732) 445 - 3138
for orders (U. S. only):
toll free (888) 999 - 6778
e-mail: orders@transactionpub.com

Table of Contents

Preface

We first began to think about a project on the transition of European societies to democracy "after fascism" in the summer of 2003. At the time we were working together on a volume that explored how Austrian Social Democrats dealt with the fact that major groups of Austrians, political élites included, had been involved in Hitler's NSDAP from the early 1930s until the defeat of National Socialism in May 1945. The further we investigated this theme, the more interested we became in broadening our perspective to consider various European countries and other factors relevant to the analysis of societies "after fascism," whether they had their own dominant indigenous fascist movements or experienced occupation by the German military. In order to bring together scholars with similar interests, we convened a conference in May 2005, which coincided nearly with the sixtieth anniversary of the end of World War II. On the basis of the strength of panel presentations and lively discussion on the campus of the University of Vienna, we determined that assembling a collection of conference contributions in extended essay form would make for a stimulating volume and a meaningful contribution to ongoing scholarly debate.

Between the initial concept and submission of the manuscript to Manchester University Press in July 2008, a number of fine people and helpful organizations have assisted us in our efforts. Without them we could not have been successful. The Stiftung Bruno Kreisky Archiv and the Renner-Institut, above all its director Karl A. Duffek were instrumental in providing logistical support and the financial basis for the conference in Vienna, and the Federal Bank of Austria contributed generously to the conference's budget. We thank all the participants of the conference in May 2005 for sharing with us their insightful contributions and a wide range of exciting research and conceptual frameworks. We are particularly indebted to the contributors to this volume who readily accepted the challenge to reconsider and revise their drafts; their patience and dedication made the realization of this project possible. Finally, we are grateful that LIT took on our endeavor and helped shepherd it into print.

We hope that the volume will initiate further intellectual debate and efforts to investigate and think through the transition to democracy "after fascism."

Matthew P. Berg

Maria Mesner

Introduction

The conference that was the starting point for the volume was organized to coincide with the sixtieth anniversary of the end of fascist hegemony over continental Europe. Two thousand five provided an occasion for a considerable number of projects in Europe and North America—conferences, exhibitions, monographs, and collections of essays treating 1945 and its immediate aftermath[1]—but the experiences of Europeans after fascism was certainly not a novel focus for scholarly research at this commemorative moment. Rich and diverse, such studies have tended to take as their foci specific country case studies, unified methodological approaches, or a common theme.[2] *After Fascism* takes what might be considered a synthetic approach. It provides examples of recent scholarship that offer insights into how particular European societies that had either experienced indigenous fascist rule or National Socialist hegemony "came to terms with"—or, alternatively, resolved to suppress—the ways that their experiences cast shadows over social dynamics, popular culture, democratization, and identity after 1945.

"Coming to terms with the past" may have started as a call for enlightenment after fascism but has become little more than a pious exhortation. Its decline can be traced to the basic ambivalence of the German source word: *Vergangenheitsbewältigung*. The word has one set of connotations: it points to finality—terms are reached to end a siege, pay off a debt, complete studies; in psychobabble coming to terms with loss means "letting go in order to move on." Applied to postwar democracy this points to the kind of view developed by Hermann Lübbe in a famous and controversial defense of "communicative silencing" as functionally necessary for postwar West German democracy.[3] Tony Judt extends the argument to all of occupied Europe in his recent study when he argues "[I]n 1945 much was to be gained by behaving as though the past was indeed dead and buried."[4] The contrasting connotations are indicated by the alternative English translation: "confronting the past" points less towards release than to the process of engagement, to facing the unvarnished truth; for this courage and honesty is needed, in this perspective "breaking free of the past" is a dangerous illusion.[5]

Much depends, of course, on how the negotiations are organized, determined, or constrained. Specifically, in what sense was 1945 a genuinely new beginning? Martin Conway dismisses debates about whether there was a *Stunde Null* as "rather redundant" and prefers to speak of "a complex amalgam of restoration and renewal."[6] Neal Ascherson, by contrast, has written in a review of Judt's study of "Europe's buried Revolution 1943-48" of what we might consider a "missing book" in postwar Europe, one which would tell the story of "the revolutionary consensus on postwar change which arose in all the Resistance movements, East and West, and how that consensus sank under the floods of Stalinism and Cold War mobilisation."[7] The idea that there was a window of opportunity before East-West division became entrenched is also indicated by Aristotle Kallis, when he observes

> [T]he post-fascist order was predicated on the paramount moral need to castigate and eradicate fascism. As, however, antagonism between the West and the Soviet Union escalated in the second half of the 1940s, it soon became clear that each side of the victorious wartime coalition understood this need in fundamentally different ways. For the west, post-fascist Europe should be edified on an unequivocal commitment to exactly those values that fascism had defiled—liberalism, democracy, freedom and respect for individual rights. For the Soviet Union, however, transcending fascism entailed a much wider project of radical social transformation.[8]

Whether these differences were always irreconcilable is hard to assess in the abstract. Social and political trajectories varied widely across Europe, reflecting the diversity of experiences of fascism itself.

The definition of the term fascism itself has always been highly contested. A reasonable point of departure is Juan J. Linz's argument that "fascism as an ideology and a movement" can be defined "by what it rejects"—i.e., a liberal socioeconomic order, political pluralism and parliamentary government, the failure to advance a vigorous national agenda. Linz also acknowledges that fascism's "negative appeals, however, had a kind of distorted positive counterpart" in the form of a new, dynamic order, that Paxton describes as "ongoing mass mobilization."[9] Other scholars, such as Roger Eatwell and Roger Griffin focus less on negative appeals and more on what they refer to as the "regenerative" message of fascist movements (restoration of lost pride, fulfillment of national destiny despite experiences of collective frustration or humiliation).[10] Such a message stood in direct contrast, contends Griffin, to liberal democratic society's alleged tendencies to allow for those whom fascists maintained did not have the nation's interests at heart—or represented ostensibly foreign elements in the national body—to rise to prominence. "Not only does the pluralism of such a society guarantee considerable political space in which competing ideological movements can develop," he concludes, "but liberalism's commitment to such values as materialism, internationalism, party politics and racial tolerance means that it can more easily be equated by ultra-nationalists with a corrupt, decadent system needing to be destroyed and replaced."[11] Stanley Payne elaborates on the point, qualifying it as

> a significant phenomenon only in certain relatively new countries during the period in which they were just making, or had very recently made, the initial transition to a liberal democracy that was as yet unconsolidated. Simultaneously, and again seemingly paradoxically, conditions approxi-

> mating liberal democracy were in fact necessary for fascist movements to develop and flourish.[12]

Following from Griffin and Payne that the absence of an adequate consensus on liberal values was an important precondition for the success of fascism—certainly in cases such as Germany, Austria, Italy, Hungary, or Spain—we can appreciate the enormity of the challenges faced in these societies after 1945.

In the end however, as Robert Paxton is careful to note, "[D]efinitions are inherently limiting. They frame a static picture of something better perceived in movement, and they perceive as 'frozen statuary' something that is better understood as a process."[13] In that sense this volume does not attempt to find a uniform definition that encompasses the complexity of the European experiences in Eastern and Western European societies. Rather, it collects a range of individual insights from a broad spectrum of historiographical and methodological interests. Each of them explores, in their own fashion, the possibilities and limits to Kallis's "post-fascist order." Because fascist parties as movements (and later as governments) had been clear about their worldviews and rather unambiguous about their goals, because the relationship between ideology, propaganda, and policy had been so closely linked, and because complicity or silence had been so widespread, once Nazi hegemony or indigenous regimes collapsed the establishment of democratic structures and (re-)creation of civil society faced novel challenges.[14]

Cynicism and resignation rather than optimism were prevailing sentiments, and liberal values could scarcely find a warmer reception in the wake of the Second World War after they seemed to have been discredited by circumstances following the first. The myth of the immediate postwar years as a *Stunde Null* could hardly have been taken as a regenerative movement by many apart from dedicated communists or democrats not dissuaded by recent political experience. Yet, as Kallis reminds us "[f]or the west, post-fascist Europe should be edified on an unequivocal commitment to exactly those values that fascism had defiled—liberalism, democracy, freedom and respect for individual rights."[15]

In a way, the body of historiography presented in this volume is related to the trajectory that "Vergangenheitsbewältigung" took in postwar societies. In terms of geographical range, a core group of contributions focuses on the area that had been the "Third Reich"—i.e., Germany and Austria—between 1938-45, indicating the richness of recent research into the consequences of National Socialism. Here occupation regimes that set the parameters for future social and political developments carefully monitored them into the early Cold War years, and provided vital reconstruction aid. Without their presence it is difficult to imagine that West German and Austrian society would have begun to accept such values as quickly as they did. Social reconstruction in the wake of fascism brought new challenges to identity. These included: the extent to which older traditions could be reclaimed, free of association with now outlawed political organizations and their claims to have championed fundamental cultural norms or deeply-rooted "national values"; the impact of (re-)establishing democratic political culture through legislative, educational, even housing reform; and the ways in which individuals understood their own choices and experiences in light of new realities. An Italian case study complements this core "European Axis" focus.

Outside this core, Denmark and the Netherlands were part of the territories Nazi Germany occupied during its drive for expansion. Narratives of national resistance dominated public discourse. Only recently have collaboration on the part of Danish and Dutch citizens and their share in the maintenance of National Socialist control become issues for historical research. Finally, the Hungarian approach to the past offers a glimpse into what in western scholarship has been a rather neglected dimension of the Cold War. Its inclusion in this volume is a step towards the dissolution of a lingering Cold War-influenced dichotomy in our understanding of historical perceptions and the framing of narrative. In addition to nationally-centered case studies, the collection presents contributions in the burgeoning and dynamic area of transnational histories, whether "entangled" on a bi-national level or applying a trans-European perspective.

Moreover, the studies assembled in this volume not only reflect geographical diversity and disparities in experience, but also a number of more recent methodological developments. The so-called cultural turn provided political history with tools to explore hitherto neglected aspects of social experience. Dense interpretation of both popular and profoundly personal statements undertaken in these case studies—letters, interviews, school magazines, petitions—has drawn from approaches in fields ranging from literary criticism to anthropology and content analysis, and thereby contributes to our understanding of the complexity of identity formation and identity transformation. Including textual, visual, and material cultures into historical research—hitherto the domain of a cultural studies field all too often insensitive or indifferent to historical context—challenges our understanding of existing historiography and expand the limits of what can be subjected to historical analysis. The range of methodological approaches and foci represented here—including everyday life experiences, political culture, education reform, family history and memory, international politics, and a case study involving an economic institution—points to the complexities facing individuals and institutions as they tried to find their bearings in the immediate or longer term aftermath of fascist domination.

Tony Judt has noted that after the fall of the Nazi regime in Germany the population "had little sense of the way the rest of the world saw them."[16] Valerie Hébert illustrates this point in her chapter examining the intense, morally indignant West German lobbying campaign on behalf of war criminals in U.S. custody (in the German press, the term war criminals was almost invariably prefixed with "so-called" or the term itself was swathed in inverted commas). She focuses not on the usual issues of collective psychology (repression or displacement), but on a more banal but nonetheless vital problem: lack of resources. Quite simply, the U.S. authorities were not prepared to finance enough German language translations of their well-documented case against their prisoners. In effect, they were not prepared to take on German public opinion in order to make clear "how the world saw them." Hébert takes a grain of comfort in the fact that the lobbying for clemency adopted "democratic" means (letter-writing rather than storming the walls of Landsberg prison), and the fact that, though most were released early, "their criminal records were not erased." Nevertheless her conclusion is bleak: the American authorities "squandered whatever opportunity they might have possessed to convince the German people under their administration of the legitimacy of the trials' judgments and reconcile them to their recent traumatic past."

On the central issue of antisemitism, Christoph Jahr traces West German discussions about the possibilities of proscription through legislation, which echo current debates about the so-called "Auschwitz-lie law" and the treatment of "Holocaust denial." In postwar Germany, he notes, Jewish DPs were more visible in some areas (e.g., in parts of Bavaria) than Jews had been before the Holocaust. To many they appeared to be, in the words of an American observer "the *corpus delicti*." In contrast to the casuistry of later Holocaust deniers, postwar antisemites had not yet learned how to encode their prejudice. But how should or could such "expressions of opinion" be reconciled with the democratic emphasis on free speech? Some "anti-antisemitic decrees" implemented by the Allies found resonance in Federal Republic legal codes—for example, the Bavarian law "against Racial Fanaticism and Hatred of other Peoples." But the Basic Law did not explicitly incriminate "incitement to racial hatred." The editors of the *Süddeutsche Zeitung* defended the decision to publish an antisemitic letter on the grounds that "a tactic of hushing up or calming [reality] can never by the right way to fight antisemitism." On the face of it, the argument appears more applicable to the stable democracy that contemporary Germany has become than the "house of the hangman" it was in 1949. Here and more widely, as Jahr notes, Jews were conspicuous by their absence. Apart from some notable exceptions (e.g., social democratic leader Kurt Schumacher) politicians tended not to mention them by name, much less see them as worthy of specific protection because of what they had suffered. Combating antisemitism—where it was seen as necessary—was supported for utilitarian, political reasons that had "very little if anything at all, to do with empathy for the victims." Cold War exigencies polarized and diverted attention from West Germany's democratic deficit; accusations from the East allowed some West German politicians to blame antisemitic outbreaks on "communist *agents provocateurs*."

In Austria there was not even this limited debate. Even if the country did not, as sometimes claimed, receive its liberated status "on a platter," it is clear that Western Allies adopted a much more *laissez-faire* stance there than in West Germany. As a result, the terms of rehabilitation and reintegration of Nazi party members were largely negotiated between and within the two pillars of Austria's Grand Coalition, Social Democrats (SPÖ) and the Catholic-conservative People's Party (ÖVP).[17] Matthew Berg looks here at the SPÖ, re-established in their Viennese stronghold after twelve years of suppression. Paxton's study of fascism urges us to look beyond the pageantry of rallies and marches; "conventional images of fascism ... omit the solid texture of everyday experience and the complicity of ordinary people in the establishment and functioning of fascist regimes. Fascist movements could never grow without the help of ordinary people, even conventionally good people." He adds:

> The excesses of fascism in power also required wide complicity among members of the establishment: magistrates, police officials, army officers, businessmen. To understand how fascist regimes worked, we must dig down to the level of ordinary people and examine the choices they made in their ordinary routines.[18]

Berg's chapter scrutinizes the way the party organization dealt with the thousands of former Nazi party members who applied for rehabilitation, and draws on petitions and affidavits that provide a measure of insight into "the texture of everyday experience" and "complicity of ordinary people" Paxton exhorts us to consider. Many applicants had, like members of the illegal Nazi party, been persecuted by Austria's pre-war authoritarian clerical regime; some had joined the Nazi party before, many more after the Anschluss. Their pleas to join—or rejoin—the social democratic fold and the justifications for their choices centered on "economic hardship," fear, and their failure to understand the "true" nature of National Socialism. In analyzing the response of the party's leadership, Berg distinguishes between two groups: those "whose resentment towards indigenous fascists outweighed virulent antipathy towards the Third Reich" and those "who understood former National Socialists as the greatest threat to the Second Republic." Chancellor Karl Renner led the first group and argued "one cannot demand heroism from every [socialist] party member." This false antithesis (from a leader whose own response to the Anschluss had been anything but heroic) was one of several common rhetorical strategies whose success in Austria resulted in the fact that "meaningful efforts towards *Vergangenheitsbewältigung* were deferred to subsequent generations."[19]

One aspect of that deferral—restitution and compensation—is illuminated by Sonja Niederacher and Stefan Lütgenau's analysis of the Vienna's Dorotheum auction house. The Dorotheum had been a major hub for the purchase and sale of "aryanized" property after the Anschluss. Postwar in-house histories covered up this role "under a layer of both repression and self-victimization" which paralleled national evasions. The Dorotheum case study sheds light on Paxton's interest in the way that "fascism redrew the frontiers between private and public, sharply diminishing what had once been untouchably private" as does Alexandra Staub's chapter on housing, below.[20] Niederacher and Lütgenau provide a striking illustration of the continuity between Nazi and post-Nazi circumstances when they show how the Dorotheum continued auctioning "aryanized" property well into 1946. The property had come from a range of financial and state institutions and no instructions had been received from them rescinding earlier commissions. This legalism contrasts starkly with the failure of the Dorotheum (shared by many other Austrian institutions and individuals) to comply effectively with a law requiring the registration of all property of dubious provenance..[21]

The case of Hungary, as discussed by Bela Rásky, was in some ways similar to Austria: widespread participation in a fascist regime with little real resistance. But unlike Austria there was no legal exoneration clause since the country had been an ally of Nazi Germany, even if the full-blooded fascist Arrow Cross regime did not take over until October 1944. Rásky sees a brief window of opportunity after the war; elements of "a social and political revolution" in which critical "scholarly" engagement with the past and some "painful but helpful debates" were briefly possible. A prominent example was the writer and politician István Bibo who "tried to analyze the complexity of Hungarian history and the need for a radical democratization." In his work on "the Jewish Question" he produced an "uncompromising reckoning with Hungarian antisemitism." However this kind of critical unflinching analysis was silenced by the imposition of Zhdanovite orthodoxy, centered on a "progressive lower class that had always fought for democracy and national values." One result was that Jewish victims were "written out" of Hungary's national narrative. After this view of the immediate postwar—which he concedes might appear over-optimistic—Rásky gives a sober account of what followed, the antisemitic purges of Stalinism and the evasions of Kadarism. After 1948 Auschwitz and Mauthausen "were never present in the public discourse." After the 1956 uprising (described by Rásky as an enormous failed democratization project) the Kadar regime based its legitimation on "dehistoricization" and the "myth of Hungary as the happiest barrack in the socialist camp."

The Austrians and Hungarians were not uniquely duplicitous vis-à-vis rejection of perpetrators status and the responsibilities it would entail; all across Europe material self-interest, public policy and antisemitism (in varying proportions) restricted the scope of restitution and protected memory from uncomfortable scrutiny.[22] The related phenomenon of assimilating Jewish victims into national or class categories was also Europe-wide. Here Daniel Cohen's examination of the International Refugee Organization shows, perhaps surprisingly, an exception. The IRO did see Jewish survivors as "paradigmatic victims" and "unique targets of racial and political persecution warranting historical recognition."

But Cohen also makes clear that this occurred within a context of widespread "dilution of Jewish suffering." Furthermore, by the late 1940s the central image of the victim of Nazism had been displaced by the victim of communism as "ideal types of political refugees who deserved legal, material, and historical recognition." Nevertheless, Cohen's basic argument is quite upbeat: a new readiness to make victimhood the criteria for assessing refugee status was part of a "human rights revolution" and a "democratic turn" in which "the rights of individuals against the prerogatives of states" were explicitly recognized.

There is little sign of a missed chance in David Messenger's account of French attitudes towards Spanish republicans, who had optimistically—or, perhaps, foolishly—crossed back over the border in the hope of toppling the Franco regime, were promptly arrested, and in many cases sentenced to death. Nevertheless, values had changed in French society since the 1930s, and Messenger shows how a sense of debt towards those who had been often at the forefront of French resistance, combined with guilt—or embarrassment—about the prewar French policy of non-intervention to fuel a campaign to "persuade" Franco to commute the death sentences. Their cases touched a deep nerve of French opinion, which even extended to the *Quai d'Orsay* where diplomats, despite reservations, gave some support for sanctions. The campaign for clemency was only partially successful, and in February 1946 twelve republicans were executed—including the prominent resistance leader Cristino Garcia. Meanwhile, the Cold War was taking policymakers in London and Washington in the opposite direction; the French minister in Madrid described their assumption that Franco's police force, "while reprehensible or repugnant in its procedures, nonetheless . . . maintained order."

Molly Tambor focuses on the phenomenon, that in Italy, a new democratic understanding of the role of women was evident in the debates of the Constitutional Assembly after World War II. As she argues, there was common idealistic ground between left and right that "centered on a spirit of solidarity, a distrust of unlimited capitalism and consumer culture, and a sense that the destinies of equal individuals and democracy were interdependent." The corollary to this position was that the state should lead reform—not just reflect society as it presently existed—and the constitution should be a tool for enforcing the destruction of fascism and advancing the establishment of democracy. Debates about the role of the family in the constitution and women's participation as full citizens via suffrage were seen as an essential guarantee of a definitive break with the Fascist regime. The resulting constitution enshrined "solidarity, community responsibility and social citizenship." However, the change was much more modest than the women MPs Tambor discusses had hoped for, and the resulting constitution retained important aspects of fascist understandings of the family and the role of women. For example, women continued to be barred from becoming judges or magistrates.

Over the following decades, despite the ideological mobilization affected by the Cold War, much of Western Europe experienced a conservative value shift, reflecting what Judt calls "a deep longing for normality." [23] Alexandra Staub's discussion of West German housing shows how this longing was channeled into pursuit of the "dream of a nation of homeowners." She follows two tracks: housing legislation that privileged home ownership in the hope that it would "root the population to the soil," and visual images of "ideal" and actual houses that "became powerful tools in furthering the concepts of "home" and home ownership." Staub illustrates this development with the example of the kitchen: the older *Wohnküche* had already been supplanted by the smaller, working kitchen in the interwar period. Now "films reinforced the message that in a bourgeois household there were serving and served spaces, and the kitchen was to be kept out of view." Another example was the *Diele*—a vestibule/entrance hall whose roots went back to the thirteenth century, but which had mutated in the nineteenth century into a sub-Wagnerian bourgeois space, with entrance to the office below and secluded family rooms above, a dual staircase, and an ornate fireplace. In one pre-fabricated version the *Diele* was "little more than a tiny entry hallway" but the designation was a marketing tool. Both moving images of "ideal" houses and print images "helped establish the conservative political and social climate of the Adenauer years," as well as anchor "the Federal Republic in the capitalist system of the West." Proper consumer choices for the private citizen had profound consequences, then, for the broader public.[24]

Within the conservative turn in Adenauer's West Germany there are nonetheless glimpses of a pre-history to the turbulent 1960s. Of course, the road to 1968 was far from straightforward. In reference to antisemitism, Jahr refers to a "non-linear learning process." Nevertheless, he concludes "long before 1968 West Germans were beginning to re-establish the foundations for a more wide-ranging dispute about the Nazi past" which "paved the way for the emergence of a civil society with a greater sense of ownership and responsibility in a democratic process that had previously been considered primarily a concern of the State."

If Lübbe's "communicative silencing" had ever been "functionally" necessary—an assertion that could be roundly debated—by the 1960s it surely ceased to be so.25 Sabine Manke focuses on a moment in West German history where this silence was rudely interrupted: the Bundestag debate on the Christian Social Union vote of no confidence facing Chancellor Willy Brandt in the wake of the first phase of Ostpolitik. Within nine days the chancellor's office received tens of thousands of letters, postcards, and telegrams, two-thirds of them on the day of the vote itself (27 April 1972). Manke discusses only a handful, but her close reading shows how much unfinished business there was within West German society; her analysis is also an antidote to any neat division of the West German population into enlightened anti-Nazi sheep and unreconstructed post-Nazi goats. The letters in support of Brandt show a quasi-religious tone which express "redemptive expectations" for an unacknowledged historical burden, and in that sense are even more revealing than the crude direct attacks of the Bayern Kurier (implicitly equating Brandt with Hitler). Manke concludes that because of his biography, but also because of the ambivalence associated with him, Brandt "offered German society a huge associative space." Overall, the ultimately unsuccessful no confidence vote amounted to "one of the most profound processes of democratization in the history of the Federal Republic."

After the fall of the Iron Curtain the terms were re-negotiated again, and the process what Judt calls a "deeply asymmetrical" European memory was exposed. In the West, the Holocaust has become the center of an official, ritualized memory. In a sense the recognition of Jews as "paradigmatic victims," which Cohen sees in the postwar refugee regime has now become the mainstream. The recent wave of interest in "aryanization" and restitution is one aspect of this. However, there are also dangers inherent to this form of memory, including what Judt calls a "new layer of mis-memory"—that is the illusion that the fate of Jews was central to most people's wartime experience of the war.[26] Isabella Matauschek examines this very point within individual families, in her revealing analysis of intergenerational discussions in Denmark and Holland. After the war "the dominant postwar narrative turned everyone into a hero," she observes. The subsequent "rediscovery" of the Jews came through the media—not through family accounts—and with it came emotive identification of older family members with the victim. To adapt the title of an influential book on German memory, not only was "granddad not a Nazi"; he probably risked his life to save Jews from the Nazis.[27]

By contrast, in much of the former communist East public memory seems dominated by the perception of equivalence between fascism or Nazis on the one side and communism on the other, with the significant twist that, as Judt puts it, to many it seems that communism "not only lasted longer but did far more harm than its Nazi predecessor."[28] The creation of Budapest's House of Terror (*Terrorhaza*) is a well-known, controversial example of an instance where little or no distinction has been made between Arrow Cross fascists and postwar Communists, and the extermination of Hungary's Jews is marginalized. Rásky adds his voice to other critics[29] who see in the *Terrorhaza* evidence of Hungary's return to "old, worn-out national myths." He also notes that, while there are numerous honest and moving memorials in Hungary, the "staging of memory remains quite superficial." Sometimes it resembles "the working off of a debt and almost burdensome duty, in order to prove that Hungary conforms to the standards and expectations of the European Union." The desire to work off a debt, not just in Hungary but in many of the other countries discussed in this collection, recalls Adorno's discussion of West Germany in the early 1960s:

One wants to break free from the past: rightly, because nothing at all can live in its shadow, and because there will be no end to the terror as long as guilt and violence are repaid with guilt and violence; wrongly, because the past that one would like to evade is still very much alive.[30]

Notes

[1] Berndt-A. Rusinek ed., *Kriegsende 1945: Verbrechen, Katastrophen, Befreiungen in nationaler und internationaler Perspektive* (Göttingen: Wallstein Verlag, 2004); Norbert Frei, *1945 und wir: das dritte Reich im bewusstsein der Deutschen* (Munich: Beck, 2005); Dagmar Herzog, *Sex After Fascism: Memory and Morality in Twentieth-Century Germany* (Princeton: Princeton University Press, 2005); Tony Judt, Postwar: *A History of Europe since 1945* (London: Pimlico, 2005); Peter Süß ed., *1945: Befreiung und Zusammenbruch. Erinnerungen aus sechs Jahrzehnten* (Munich: Deutscher Taschenbuchverlag, 2005); Richard Ned Lebow, Wulf Kansteiner and Claudio Fogu eds., *The Politics of Memory in Postwar Europe* (Durham and London: Duke University Press, 2006); Götz Aly, *Hitlers Volksstaat: Raub, Rassenkrieg und nationaler Sozialismus* (Fischer: Frankfurt/Main, 2006).

[2] Among the most compelling collections with a specific regional focus, see Robert Moeller ed., *West Germany under Construction: Politics, Society, and Culture in the Adenauer Era* (Ann Arbor: University of Michigan Press, 1997). For thematic studies treating indigenous fascist and Nazi legacies, see István Deák, Jan T. Gross, and Tony Judt eds., *The Politics of Retribution in Europe: World War II and its Aftermath* (Princeton: Princeton University Press, 2000); Jan-Werner Müller ed., *Memory & Power in Post-War Europe: Studies in the Presence of the Past* (Cambridge and New York: Cambridge University Press, 2002); Pieter Lagrou, *The Legacy of Nazi Occupation: Patriotic Memory and National Recovery in Europe, 1945-1965* (Cambridge and New York: Cambridge University Press, 2000); and Richard Bessel and Dirk Schumann eds., *Life after Death: Approaches to a Cultural and Social History of Europe during the 1940s and 1950s* (Cambridge and New York: Cambridge University Press, 2003). Klaus-Dietmar Henke and Hans Woller eds., *Politische Säuberung in Europa: Die Abrechnung mit Faschismus und Kollaboration nach dem Zweiten Weltkrieg* (Munich: Deutscher Taschenbuchverlag, 1991) provides a comparative study of state institutions and legal measures brought to bear in the adjudication of fascists and collaborators.

[3] Hermann Lübbe, "Der Nationalsozialismus im politischen Bewußtsein der Gegenwart," in *Deutschlands Weg in die Diktatur. Internationale Konferenz zur nationalsozialistischen Machtübernahme*, (Berlin: Siedler, 1983), 329-49. See also the criticism by Gesine Schwan, *Politics and Guilt: The Destructive Power of Silence* (London: University of Nebraska Press, 2001).

[4] Judt, 61-2.

[5] See Theodor Adorno, "Was bedeutet: Aufarbeitung der Vergangenheit," in Adorno, *Eingriffe. Neun kritische Modelle*, (Frankfurt/Main: Suhrkamp, 1963), 125. Here Adorno uses the term "critical reappraisal" ("Aufarbeitung") of the past.

[6] Martin Conway, "The Rise and Fall of Western Europe's Democratic Age," *Contemporary European History,* 13, 1 (2004): 67-88. By way of contrast see Robert Moeller's

reflections on this point in West German historiography in *West Germany under Construction*, 3-11.
[7] Neal Ascherson, "The Atlantic Gap," *London Review of Books*, 17 November 2005: 7.
[8] Aristotle A. Kallis, *The Fascism Reader* (London and New York: Routledge, 2003), 6.
[9] Juan J. Linz, *Totalitarian and Authoritarian Regimes* (Boulder CO and London: Lynne Rienner Publishers, 2000), 220. Linz links fascism with an "exacerbated nationalism"—and assumes thereby the existence of a normative nationalism. See also Paxton, 13.
[10] Eatwell, 172-73; Roger Griffin, *The Nature of Fascism* (London and New York: Routledge, 1993), 32-33. Griffin understands the notion of regeneration in fascist ideology as "a generic term for the vision of a radically *new* beginning which follows a period of destruction or perceived dissolution" (33, emphasis in the original). Central to the concept of social transformation is what George Mosse referred to as "a virile activism" associated with revolutionary youth [. . .] asserting the primacy of ideology"; see Mosse, "The Genesis of Fascism" in *International Fascism 1920-1945*: *Journal of Contemporary History* 1 (1966): 19.
[11] Griffin, 210-211.
[12] Stanley Payne, *A History of Fascism, 1914-1945* (Madison: University of Wisconsin Press, 1995), 490.
[13] Robert O. Paxton, *The Anatomy of Fascism* (New York: Knopf, 2004), 14.
[14] On the persistence of mentalities linked to National Socialist values, see for example, Josef Foschepoth, "German Reactions to Defeat and Occupation and Frank Stern, "The Historic Triangle: Occupiers, Germans, and Jews in Postwar Germany" in *West Germany under Construction*, 73-89 and 199-229, respectively. On National Socialist values and German (or Austrian) society, see Claudia Koonz, The Nazi Conscience (Cambridge MA and London: The Belknap Press of Harvard University Press, 2003). On the relationship between fascist ideology and propaganda and their connection to totalistic claims for recasting social order in a broader sense, see Roger Eatwell, "Towards a New Model of Generic Fascism," *Journal of Theoretical Politics* 2 (1992): 172-73. Paxton cautions us, however, to be mindful that "what fascists *did* tells us at least as much as what they *said*" [emphasis added] and reminds us that even as we acknowledge their rhetoric and program statements, these things alone do not necessarily explain fascist movements' appeal—certainly not beyond the initial core of supporters during the early years of struggle. Even once they came to power, fascist rhetoric tended to be selective; for example, Paxton points to widespread anti-capitalist or antireligious rhetoric within fascist movements, but in practice property was confiscated from political opponents, foreigners, or certain regime-identified state enemies (e.g., Jews in Nazi-led Germany), and arrangements were reached with the Vatican or Protestant churches. Paxton, 10.
[15] Kallis, op cit.
[16] Judt,, 61.
[17] See Maria Mesner ed, *Entnazifizierung zwischen politischem Anspruch, Parteienkonkurrenz und Kaltem Krieg: Das Beispiel der SPÖ*, (Vienna: Oldenbourg, 2005);
Robert Knight, "Denazification and Integration in the Austrian Province of Carinthia," *Journal of Modern History* 79 (2007): 572–612.
[18] Paxton, 13-14.
[19] See Matthew Paul Berg, "Commemoration versus *Vergangenheitsbewältigung*: Contextualizing Austria's *Gedenkjahr* 2005." *German History* 26 (2008) No. 1: 47-71.
[20] Paxton, 11.

[21] See Clemens Jabloner et. al., *Schlussbericht der Historikerkommission der Republik Österreich: Vermögensentzug während der NS-Zeit sowei Rückstellungen und Entschädigungen seit 1945 in Österreich. Zusammenfassung und Einschätzungen* (Vienna: Oldenbourg, 2004).
[22] See Martin Dean, Constantin Goschler and Philipp Ther ed., *The Conflict over Jewish Property in Europe*, (Oxford and New York: Berghahn, 2007).
[23] Judt, 82.
[24] On the relationship between the public and private spheres, gender, class, and consumption during the Adenauer years and continuities/discontinuities with the Nazi era, see also Erica Carter, "Alice in the Consumer Wonderland: West German Case Studies in Gender and Consumer Culture" and Uta G. Poiger, "Rock 'n' Roll, Female Sexuality, and the Cold War Battle over German Identities" in *West Germany under Construction*, 347-71 and 373-410, respectively.
[25] The phrase comes from Lübbe, op cit.
[26] Judt, 821.
[27] Sabine Moller, Karoline Tschuggnall, and Harald Welzer ed., Opa war kein Nazi: Nationalsozialismus im Familiengedächtnis (Frankfurt/Main: Fischer, 2002).
[28] Judt, 826-28.
[29] Mark Pittaway, "The Politics of Legitimacy and Hungary's Postwar Transition," *Contemporary European History*, 13.4 (2004): 453-75; for historiography see Ulf Brunnbauer ed., *(Re)Writing History: Historiography in Southeast Europe after Socialism*, (Münster: Litverlag, 2004).
[30] Adorno, op cit. Translated citation from Theodor W. Adorno, *Critical Models: Interventions and Catchwords*, Translated by Henry W. Pickford (New York: Columbia University Press, 1998), 89.

I. Transnational Experiences

"Who is a Refugee?" Managing Displacement in the Aftermath of World War Two

G. Daniel Cohen

Among the many illusions shattered by the Second World War was the idea that the proper place for citizens is within the territory of their state. The millions of displaced persons found by the Allies in 1945 (an unprecedented case of mass displacement on the European continent) provided a vivid illustration of this new possibility. If the liberation of Europe announced a long awaited return to at least partial normalcy, it also plunged the continent into a chaos of population movements. The magnitude of post-hostilities displacement did not come as a surprise to the Western liberators. As early as October 1939, Franklin D. Roosevelt predicted that "when this ghastly war ends, there may be not one million but ten million or twenty million men, women and children belonging to many races [...] who will enter into the wide picture—the problem of the human refugee." Similarly, wartime British anticipations foresaw a dramatic "movement of people larger than any that history has seen in the modern time." As one British expert summarized in 1943, "one may well say that as soon as the war is over most of the people of continental Europe will wish to move."[1] Particularly sensitive to refugee problems and their significance for the modern world, Hannah Arendt was another voice warning of unprecedented upheaval. The end of the war in Europe, Arendt wrote in April 1945, "will not automatically return thirty to forty million exiles to their homes"; instead, she estimated, "a very large proportion will regard repatriation as deportation and will insist on retaining their statelessness."[2] As rightly predicted, between ten to twenty million European civilians found themselves on the move in the spring and summer of 1945, although five to six million were already repatriated home by the autumn. In Germany, former soldiers, slave laborers, and concentration camp survivors emerging from captivity formed a heterogeneous mass of "displaced persons," initially a military expression encompassing all the civilians encountered in combat areas by advancing Allies armies.[3] Bulging with displaced foreigners, German roads were compared by a contemporary witness to "swollen mountain torrents in the spring, a Babel of people and languages, all former slaves of the Third Reich."[4] As one historian observed, postwar Germany unexpectedly became "the unlikely, unloved, and reluctant host to hundreds of thousand of its former victims", including Jews, concentration camps inmates, and forced laborers mostly concentrated in the British and American occupation zones.[5] The displaced persons, in short, turned out to be one of the most prominent groups spawned by the aftermath of the war. Between the years 1945 and 1951, for a few months or a few years, millions of individuals in Europe were categorized by the abbreviated Anglo-Saxon neologism "DP."

The history of displaced persons is generally divided into two distinct phases: "repatriation" (attempts made by the West to return refugees to their East European home countries, forcibly in the case of Soviet DPs) and "resettlement" (the organized emigration of the remaining DPs to new countries in Europe and the New World). Repatriation operations were carried out in 1945/46 under the aegis of the United Nations Relief and Rehabilitation Agency (UNRRA) and the occupying armies. For the Allies, repatriation was a pragmatic way to swiftly undo the population disorder created by Nazi racial and forced labor policies. Close to six million DPs were returned by the Allies after May 1945. Yet the pace of voluntary repatriation dramatically dwindled in 1946, when it became clear that most of the remaining DPs refused to go home. As one of the first historians of displaced persons pointed out, it then "dawned upon Allied authorities that repatriation would no longer be acceptable for this group."[6] In 1947, the International Refugee Organization (IRO) was mandated by the United Nations to find resettlement solutions for the DPs. Free from military control, the IRO was a modern agency staffed by American, British and French international civil servants. As opposed to UNRRA, which was terminated in 1947, the IRO viewed DPs as political and humanitarian refugees more than "displaced" individuals. In Germany, the IRO assumed responsibility for nearly a million refugees—largely Poles, Jews, Ukrainian, and Baltic peoples who refused or were simply unable to return "home." Many factors accounted for this refusal: for Jewish Holocaust survivors, it was the resurgence of antisemitism in Poland and a desire to "divorce themselves from Europe"; for Baltic and Ukrainian DPs, the fear of Soviet retribution and the persistence of strong nationalist feelings dominated; for Poles, anti-communism as well as straightforward economic motives played a decisive role; and in all cases, one might point to the continuation of a East-West migration trend generations in the making.[7]

In this essay, I suggest that the administration of displaced persons in occupied Germany offers a unique vantage point to examine the issue of "democracy after fascism" from an international perspective. To what extend did the international treatment of the "refugee question" reflect a commitment to the liberal-democratic values trumpeted in the West after 1945? For many advocates of displaced persons, democracy had in fact little to do with the postwar refugee system. For them, DPs were victims, more than beneficiaries, of Western humanitarian politics. Defenders of particular groups initially targeted as suspicious, such as Ukrainians or Baltic nationals, resented the "arbitrariness" of screening procedures; in Western Europe, public intellectuals denounced the treatment of DPs as a "scandal" and viewed the DP camps (regularly visited by representatives of countries eagerly searching for manpower) as a reincarnation of "slave markets." Refugees themselves emphasized the dehumanization inherent to the DP condition, at times in poetic fashion: "Would you please excuse that I nothing know," rhymed the satirical author of a *DP's Song of the*

Songs, "for I am only a number in the long IRO row." Yet the extraterritorial universe of DP camps in Germany can be seen, especially under the civilian administration of the IRO, as a reflection of a distinctive Western democratic ethos: a conception of democracy inherently linked to the aftermath of World War Two and the nascent Cold War. Antifascism, and especially after 1948, anticommunism, evolved into political norms that defined a "true" refugee in the eyes of the West. In this context, wartime victims of Nazism and postwar victims of communism emerged as ideal types of political refugees who deserved legal, material, and historical recognition.

It may certainly seem paradoxical to argue that the spectacle of hundreds of thousands of DPs confined to regimented camp life reflected the advent of new democratic values on the Western side of the Iron Curtain. Indeed, many contemporary observers, such as a French military doctor touring occupied Germany in 1947, described the network of DP camps as sites of rigorous surveillance: "The DPs enjoy full freedom of movement," he reported ironically, "within a five miles radius". In 1953, a refugee expert emphasized the prominent role played by central authority in the lives of displaced persons: "The great majority of refugees lived for years in camps where a paternal administration drew up the menu, fixed meals and curfew times, chose the cinema films, allocated accommodation, repaired footwear, washed linen, and provided toothpaste, cigarettes, and chocolate according to carefully worked out scales".[8] Indeed, the idea that refugees in camps should always remain carefully monitored was one of the institutional legacies of the DP years, as a UNESCO publication from 1955 testifies: "It is usually regarded as useful or necessary that refugees, as aggrieved and rootless people, should be kept under a centralized and mobile control, and should not be allowed to forget their special status until those in control decide that it is advisable."[9] Since then, several scholars have argued that postwar displaced persons were the guinea pigs of a nefarious form of "humanitarian governmentality," still traceable today in the functioning of UNHCR.[10] Nonetheless, and despite its propensity to bureaucratic surveillance, the management of displacement in occupied Germany reflected a democratic turn in three different ways. First, the postwar refugee system explicitly recognized the rights of individuals against the prerogatives of states; it also performed a unique function of historical recognition by acknowledging the victim status of prominent groups of refugees, Jewish survivors in particular; and it ultimately construed the "political dissident" as a distinctive persecuted migrant who ought to be protected by international law.

In order to assess the democratic nature of refugee governance in the postwar years, I will first locate the displaced persons within an important shift in international law, one that saw the advent of a new relationship between individuals and states already theorized in international legal thinking and by refugee advocates in the 1930s. Against the League of Nation's narrow definition of refugees as "stateless," internationalists stressed persecution as the key identifier of modern refugees. For them, exposure to political violence was the primary feature of refugeehood. Internationalists also believed that the recognition of a group as refugees was tantamount to a formal charge by the international community that a state was engaging in persecution. European think tanks, such as the Institute of International Law at The Hague, strongly advocated this shift of emphasis. In their view, undoubtedly shaped by the plight of victims of European fascism, statelessness could no longer constitute the sole feature of the refugee condition.[11]

In the aftermath of World War Two, the reinforcement of persecution as a predominant element in the determination of refugees was accompanied by the individualization of international law. The fact that individuals could be equal to states as true subjects of international law—a debate opposing Kantian proponents of natural rights to "statist" Hegelian legal scholars since the late 19th century—was overwhelmingly recognized in the postwar years. For one internationalist, what broke down in 1945 was nothing less than "Hegel's apotheosis, the state is God on earth."[12] The new prominence of individuals in international law was also observed by Hersch Lauterpacht, a distinguished Cambridge legal scholar who played a prominent role in the drafting of the 1948 Universal Declaration of Human Rights. In 1950, Lauterpacht concluded "the individual has now acquired a status and a stature which have transformed him from an object of international compassion into a subject of international right. The time is now ripe for assessing the significance of these changes (...) in the functioning of international society."[13] As a vivid example of this new mindset, the system of individual eligibility established to screen displaced persons in occupied Germany between 1945 and 1951 reflected both the Western sensitivity to persecution and the final emergence of refugees as individual subjects of law.

However, the recognition of the individual's rights against the omnipotence of the state—one of the key human rights principles of the postwar era—was at first blatantly violated by Western powers. Under the UNRRA (1945/46)—an agency subordinated to military occupation controls—the overall policy was to repatriate all (non-Jewish) DPs to their country of origin as a mean to swiftly eliminate the effects of the Second World War by bringing order to the world again. Repatriation was supposed to be voluntary, but due to Grand Alliance considerations, Soviet nationals (most of them prisoners of war) were targeted for forcible return "home," where they more often than not faced execution, deportation, or retribution.[14] The policy of forcible return eventually subsided with the rise of Cold War tensions, and by 1946 repatriation was offered freely to all DPs, though overwhelmingly rejected on political grounds. Even if claimed by their countries of origin—to be punished and/or pressed into reconstruction efforts—DPs found in the myriad of UNRRA camps in Germany a relatively protective environment. For instance, even when Polish communist "repatriation missions" were allowed in DP camps, they could be opposed—at times violently—by refugees determined to remain in Germany with hopes to emigrate elsewhere.[15]

The formal recognition by the West of the DPs' right to not to return home did not prevent the establishment of a rigorous selection process, of course. Between 1945 and 1952, the UNRRA and the IRO grappled with one fundamental question: who was a victim of political persecution? The democratic tenets of refugee management, therefore, revolved around a rigorous separation of the wheat ("authentic" victims of oppression) from the chaff (e.g., former collaborators, applicants of ethnic German descent, suspected economic migrants). The identification of true and false refugees (through hearings, testimonies and the review of personal documents) was the primary task of screeners touring the camps, eager to recognize deserving victims and to hound out usurpers of DP status. One international jurist compared this approach to selective "net fishing" by the Western Powers. The West, argued Roger Nathan-Chapotot in 1949, was now "fishing chosen individuals among masses of refugees and displaced persons. This fishnet bears the name Allies/United Nations."[16]

Initially, screening procedures were based on strong "antifascist" criteria: suspicion of collaboration and assistance to the Nazi regime prevented admission into the DP community. Czech or Polish refugees unfortunate enough to bear German-sounding family names were arbitrarily scrutinized as potential ethnic Germans "expellees", a category deemed "not within the mandate" of the IRO. Similarly, a large number of Ukrainians and Balts were turned down by the UNRRA—despite their insistence (at times with proof) that their enrollment into the *Wehrmacht* was coerced. This "atmosphere of perpetual screening" elicited bitterness and resentment. "Such screenings," lamented American advocates of Ukrainian refugees, "bring real terror to displaced persons."[17] Other observers of refugee hearings in the camps noted "each and every question sets a trap."[18] The selection of displaced persons clearly reproduced the norms of the "victors' justice," with its share of arbitrariness and inconsistencies. Yet the governance of displaced persons recognized the right of individuals to oppose the will of their former states, insofar as rejected applicants to DP status were simply left to care for themselves or handed over to West German welfare organizations; it also fostered historical recognition by acknowledging, in no ambivalent terms, the victim status of "displaced persons" eventually granted DP status.

The place of Holocaust survivors in the postwar refugee system is quite revealing in this context. Much has been recently written on the initial mistreatment of survivors following the liberation of the concentration camps. From being handled by American authorities "just like Nazis treated Jews, except that we do not exterminate them" (to quote the scathing report written by Truman's envoy Earl Harrison in the summer of 1945), Jews evolved into a protected and distinctive refugee population, accommodated in specific Jewish camps. Jewish survivors gradually became recognized by the actors of refugee governance in their unique dimension of genocide victims, in stark contrast with the dilution of Jewish suffering into the all-encompassing category of "victims of fascism" in both Western and Eastern Europe after the war. This recognition process was not entirely unique to the refugee system. For instance, the International Tribunal at Nuremberg has been described as the first distinctive effort "outside of Jewish circles to grasp the awful significance of the murder of European Jews."[19] However, the international protection of refugees concretely made Jewish survivors into paradigmatic victims (Jews did not have to undergo screening) before anticommunist dissidents became the new symbols of persecution following the Communist takeover in East-Central Europe.

This symbolic "vindication" of Jews was first a matter of status, as survivors were automatically accepted as DPs once liberated from concentration camps or when they reached the American zone coming from Eastern Europe. Jews were not merely perceived as "war victims" deserving of humanitarian relief but also as unique targets of racial and political persecution warranting historical recognition. To be sure, occasional harassment by the British or American military or the persistence of racial stereotypes (Jewish DPs as "black marketers") remained features of the lives of Holocaust survivors in occupied Germany. Yet the institutional recognition of Jewish victimization had crucial political consequences: entitled with specific migratory and "resettlement" rights, it was as displaced refugees that Jews were ultimately "nationalized" as a people entitled to self-determination. As Dan Diner pointed out in relation to Jewish DP camps in Bavaria, "it is arguable that the immediate founding of the State of Israel had its beginnings in southern Germany."[20]

The elevation of Jewish survivors to the rank of primary victims between 1945 and 1948 was followed by the rise of the political dissident as the most desirable type of refugees. This process took shape under the administration of the IRO. An entirely civilian organization, the IRO was a modern bureaucracy aiming at the rational treatment of refugee problems, such as uniform guidelines, casework management, standard camp administration, and a professed commitment to due process.[21] IRO field workers constantly feared that waves of unaccounted intruders had illegally found their way into the protected DP universe. One official voiced this concern: "How many managed to slip into our camps without being entitled to do so? And how many sought shelter in DP camps, merely to hide and escape retribution at home?"[22] Besides suspected "collaborators," however, the IRO also sought to track down economic "adventurers" among the DPs. With a limited budget and life expectancy, the IRO wanted to restrict its mandate to what it considered "genuine" political refugees only. This emphasis on political persecution in the determination of DP status coincided with the growing influence of Cold War considerations on refugee selection. The contours of the DP population started to change in 1948 with the arrival of anticommunist refugees from East-Central Europe. In particular, following the 1948 Prague Coup, "escapees" from Czechoslovakia trickled into

Germany in search of a safe haven. These so-called "post-hostilities" refugees from behind the Iron Curtain were now screened by professionally trained IRO reviewers of refugee status (Americans, British, and in few cases, French nationals), who were asked to evaluate new claims of "political dissidence." The Cold War strongly impinged on the politicization of the IRO: "This humanitarian organization (...) took on a political character which was to become even more marked as streams of refugees continued to arrive from Eastern Europe."[23] As opposed to the old stock of DPs (individuals forcibly displaced during the war), the claims of persecution presented by this new generation of refugees were no longer determinable with reference to "wartime events." Rather, what was at stake after 1948 was the evaluation of individual "dissidence," a term already used in the late 1930s by refugee advocates to define persons with genuine political conviction contrary to that of their government. After 1948, political dissidents—whether or not they had suffered persecution under the Nazis—were solely evaluated on behalf of a personal narrative of postwar persecution. An IRO official summarized this new policy thus: "If a refugee comes from Eastern Europe, he is required to prove that the abandonment of his country of origin was forced upon him by the fear of racial, religious or political persecution."

One important feature of contemporary refugee hearings was being created in the DP camps of occupied Germany: the obligation for asylum seekers to solely bear the burden of proof in their claim of "genuine" political persecution. Like a magic formula, the adjective "genuine" opened the gates of the West to a new breed of refugees fleeing the Soviet bloc. The ideal-type of dissenter was assumed to have "genuine" political creeds as well as "genuine" reasons to fear persecution. Moreover, the political convictions that led to persecution in the home country had to be assertive and resolute, coherently argued and publicly harbored: "The absence of agreement with a regime is not sufficient. For example, the mere fact of not being Communist is not adequate for valid political objections to a country with a Communist government."[24] Since interviewers in DP camps sought to detect clear signs of political objection, opposition to a regime had to be evidenced by religious or political grounds, or by "proven membership to a political party (...) known to be subject of persecution."[25] IRO "Eligibility Guidelines" stressed the necessity for refugees to argue in clear terms their opposition to a political regime, to make a positive impression upon their interviewers, and to prove beyond reasonable doubt some significant degree of political involvement.

The Cold War context thus provided strong incentives for refugees to define themselves politically, or to couch their life stories in exclusive political terms. The emphasis on the specificity of political migration posited a qualitative difference between political and economic migrants. The IRO viewed displaced persons (and any future refugee) as a purely political group, and it did so by heralding the supremacy of the "dissident" over the ordinary migrant with regard to political asylum. Some examples can concretely illustrate the search for true dissidents among Czech refugees who fled to Germany following the 1948 Prague Coup. In a fashion reminiscent of today's general suspicion against abusers of asylum procedures, the IRO assumed that a large number of Czechs were mere "adventurers" yearning for a better material existence in Western Europe or preferably in North America. Refugee advocates, for their part, vigorously stressed the political identity of Czech emigrants, "martyrs of democracy who escaped tyranny voluntarily" and who were not merely displaced by material hardship.[26] Yet suspicious allegations made in the course of interviews reinforced the belief of refugee screeners that it was, in fact, economic hardship that drove many young Czechoslovak refugees out of their home country. The case of 28 year-old Jan Izolt, for instance, is emblematic of the incriminating potential of economic arguments expressed in refugee narratives. Applying for DP status, this refugee mentioned "his refusal to join a Work Brigade" as the main reason for his flight. After further investigation, screeners concluded that work brigades were not instruments of coercion *per se*; as civilian bodies, the brigades were set up by the Communist Party to enroll young workers in compulsory hard labor necessitated by postwar reconstruction. For the IRO, refusal to join such "brigades" merely meant that this particular refugee preferred to flee to Germany to improve his material situation. "It was undoubtedly felt," they concluded, "that he left for economic reasons."[27]

Similar cases illustrate how the IRO was wary of claims of political fears disguising economic woes. A young Czech waiter, for example, stated that he escaped to Germany "because his father, during a birthday celebration, expressed anticommunist sentiments and was denounced. Two days later, he was informed that the police had sought him and fled to Germany." His story was not considered convincing, probably also because this DP shared "that his salary of 600 Kcs was insufficient for his needs."[28] Similarly, Frantisek Zalesak was "warned by a friend that because of his democratic convictions" he would be arrested. He nonetheless failed to convince his interviewers "that his anticommunist convictions were such as to make his arrest imminent."[29] The same reasoning was applied to Alois Janak. A student at an agricultural college in Prague, he failed his "political examination" and feared employment discrimination, since, as he put it, "a politically ignorant can expect work only in mines or in the forest." The IRO disagreed: "Dismissal for failure to pass an examination in a subject, however tendentious, cannot be considered political persecution."[30] Greater leniency toward suspected economic motivations was noticeable by 1949, however; due to American pressure to accept large numbers of anticommunist refugees, "the policy of the IRO was to reject only the few who are naive enough to admit that they are economic emigrants."[31] This less suspicious attitude was also triggered by the sharp decrease in Czechoslovak applicants to DP status: the crossing of the border into the US occupation zone in Germany had become increasingly difficult, and the cost of buying exit permits was too exorbitant to have been used "as a method of escape by any other than the genuine political refugees whose situation is desperate."[32]

The end of IRO operations in Germany in 1952—and the closing of most DP camps after the overseas resettlement of the vast majority of postwar refugees—coincided with the signature of the 1951 Geneva Convention on Refugees by most Western powers (except the United States). In many respects, the Convention solidified in international law the overall experience of postwar displacement, with still important consequences for asylum seekers today. In keeping with the revival of natural rights in international law, the 1951 Geneva Convention defined refugees as "any person who owing to well-founded fear of being persecuted for reasons of race, religion, nationality, membership of a particular social group or political opinion, is outside the country of his nationality (...)"; in a Eurocentric manner, it initially pertained to "refugees in Europc" only, excluding from its scope other categories of displaced in the Middle East or Asia—as well as potential refugees from the colonial world. However, above all it contained a strong prohibition on *refoulement*—i.e. sending back refugees to places where they face persecution. This marked a radical departure from the pre-1945 period and the tragic lot of forcefully returned refugees, in Europe as in the United States. Decried today by many refugee advocates as a document that now excludes the majority of the world's involuntary migrants—European nations turn down most asylum seekers on the ground that they are in fact "economic" migrants in disguise—the 1951 Geneva Convention nonetheless reflected a democratic turn in the treatment of refugees in the postwar period. Despite its improvised, selective, and at times arbitrary nature, Western management of displacement reflected an international commitment to counteract political violence by defending individuals against oppressive states. As such, the history of political refugees in Europe after fascism is part and parcel of the imperfect, ambivalent yet pathbreaking human rights revolution of the 1940s.

Notes

[1] Kenneth G. Brooks, "The Re-Establishment of Displaced Persons" in *When Hostilities Cease. Papers on Relief and Reconstruction Prepared For the Fabian Society* (Victor Gollancz Ltd: London, 1944), 99-123.

[2] Hannah Arendt, "The Stateless People," *Contemporary Jewish Record* 8 (1945): 137-153.

[3] Malcolm Proudfoot, "Anglo-American Displaced Persons Program for Germany and Austria", *The American Journal of Economics and Sociology* 6 (1946): 33-54.

[4] Alexander Donat, *The Holocaust Kingdom. A Memoir* (New York: Holt, Rinehart, 1965), 318.

[5] Atina Grossmann, "Victims, Villains, and Survivors: Gendered Perceptions and Self-Perceptions of Jewish Displaced Persons in Occupied Post-War Germany," *Journal of the History of Sexuality* 11 (2002), 291-318.

[6] Wolfgang Jacobmeyer, "The Displaced Persons Problem: Repatriation and Resettlement" in Johannes-Dieter Steinert and Inge Weber-Newth, *European Immigrants in Britain 1933-1950* (Munich: K.G Saur, 2003), 137-149.
[7] The standard account of the DP experience is Mark Wyman, *DPs: Europe's Displaced Persons 1945-1951* (Ithaca: Cornell University Press, 1998).
[8] Jacques Vernant, *The Refugee in the Post-War World* (New Haven: Yale University Press, 1953), 162.
[9] H.B.M Murphy, *Flight and Resettlement*, (UNESCO: Paris, 1955), 58.
[10] Liisa H. Malkki Refugees and Exile: From Refugee Studies to the National Order of Things, *Annual Review of Anthropology* 24 (1995): 495-523; Jennifer Hyndman, *Managing Displacement. Refugees and the Politics of Humanitarianism* (Minneapolis: University of Minnesota Press, 2000).
[11] Sir John Hope Simpson's 1939 European refugee survey testifies to this shift in emphasis from *statelessness* to *persecution*: "Other features of the existence of the refugee, such as the absence of national status may be incidental but are not *essential* to his quality as refugee." See Sir John Hope Simpson, *The Refugee Problem: Report of a Survey* (London: Oxford University Press, 1939), 4.
[12] Eduard Reut-Nicolussi, *Displaced Persons and International Law* (The Hague: Institute of International Law, 1948), 64.
[13] Hersch Lauterpacht, *International Law and Human Rights* (New York: F.A Praeger, 1950), 4.
[14] Pavel Polian, *Deportiert nach Hause. Sowjetische Kriegsgefangene im "Dritten Reich" und ihre Repatriierung* (Munich: Oldenburg, 2001).
[15] Some 5,800,000 DPs were repatriated between May and October 1945; only 500,000 in 1946; and insignificant numbers afterwards, when 1,200,000 DPs became "permanent refugees" refusing to go home.
[16] Roger Nathan-Chapotot, *Les Nations-Unies et les réfugiés. Le maintien de la paix et le conflit des qualifications entre l'Ouest et l'Est* (Paris: A.Pedone, 1949).
[17] Walter Dushnyck and William J. Gibbons, *Refugees Are People. The Plight of Europe's Displaced Persons* (New York: n.p., 1947).
[18] Léon Richard, "Le problème peut-il être résolu?" in *Personnes Déplacées* (Paris : Chemins du Monde, 1948), 338.
[19] Michael Marrus, *The Nuremberg War Crimes Trial 1945-46: A Documentary History* (Boston: Bedford Books, 1997), 254.
[20] Dan Diner, "Elemente des Subjektwerdung: Jüdische DPs in historischem Kontext" in *Jahrbuch zur Geschichte und Wirkung des Holocaust* (1997): 229-248.
[21] Louise Holborn, *The International Refugee Organization. A Specialized Agency of the United Nations. Its History and Work, 1946-1952* (London : Oxford University Press, 1956).
[22] René Ristelhueber, *Au secours des réfugiés. L'oeuvre de l'Organisation Internationale des Réfugiés* (Paris: Plon, 1951), 141.
[23] René Ristelhueber, "The International Refugee Organization" in *International Conciliation*, April 1951, 180.
[24] IRO, *Eligibility Guidelines*, 1949.
[25] Ibid.
[26] Council of Free Czechoslovakia, *In Seach of Haven: The Story of Czechoslovak Refugees* (Washington, DC: Council of Free Czechoslovakia, 1950).
[27] Archives Nationales (Paris), IRO Archives, AJ43/141.

[28] Ibid., *Case 15 723*.
[29] Ibid., *Case 15 713*.
[30] Ibid., *Case 15 716*.
[31] AN, AJ43/574, *Review Board. Semetrial Report to the Director General, First Semester 1949*.
[32] Ibid.

Exporting Republicanism: The French Government's Defense of Political Prisoners in Franco's Spain after France's Liberation

David A. Messenger

The aftermath of France's Liberation from Nazi occupation and the Vichy regime that had collaborated with Hitler, seemed to harken the beginning of a "new politics," one symbolized by governments that conceived of issues as "moral engagements."[1] Jean-Pierre Rioux has written, "the Right had collapsed with Vichy, and the Left, invested with all the moral authority of the Resistance, was now the natural spokesman for the national interest."[2] Yet despite the prevalence of such sentiments, both Henri Rousso and Rioux argue that it did not change politics, citing, for instance, the fact that a new "Party of the Resistance" was unable to be created.[3] In Rousso's words, "the postwar citizen clung to the reassuring image of a resisting France, but the desire for a return to normalcy and the wish to forget the exceptional circumstances of the Occupation stood in the way of any real consecration of the Resistance."[4] Was there really any practical evidence that a new political environment had been forged in postwar France? Was there ever a moment where one could say that the Resistance inspired a "new politics" in the aftermath of fascism and collaboration that was of any influence? The question has been examined more recently with reference to the immediate postwar trials and purges targeting collaborators, most notably by Alice Kaplan who has argued that the 1945/46 purge in France was intended "to rebuild a nation and restore its dignity."[5] It is also a question worth examining in the context of other policies and proposals related to the connection between justice and the national "dignity" of France. Kaplan and others suggest that such arguments had the capacity to influence debates about how to organize society and govern differently than the decision-makers of the wartime era had.[6] In France, more than just collaboration was discussed in this way. The case of relations with Francisco Franco's Spanish regime was similarly striking in its capacity to think about the implications of making government policy after fascism.

The question of relations with Spain provoked strong reactions inside France that reflected its own experience of Resistance and Collaboration. The war had been fought to liberate France and other European nations from fascism, to replace fascism and Nazism with democracy. In Spain there remained a government with ties, direct and indirect, to the Axis states.[7] Within weeks of France's own liberation, the campaign to end the reign of Francisco Franco began. On 7 September 1944, *Combat*—a leading daily produced clandestinely under Nazi occupation and continued after Liberation as a voice of the Resistance unaffiliated with any political party—reminded readers that, "this European war that began in Spain, eight years ago, cannot end without Spain."[8] In Toulouse *La*

République du Sud-Ouest wrote that the Franco regime was "a monstrous anachronism in a world liberated from fascism."[9]

Such calls for action against Spain occurred not only in France. At the founding conference of the United Nations in San Francisco, France joined Britain and the United States in support of a resolution excluding Spain from membership in the world body, and this sentiment was repeated by Britain, the US, and the Soviet Union at Potsdam in August 1945. Yet with the exception of the Soviet Union, none of the powers considered a complete break with Spain; rhetorical condemnation was considered sufficient. Veterans of the French Resistance and other activists sought a more aggressive policy in France, especially as the government of Charles De Gaulle followed the policy of its Allies and continued to have representation in Madrid that led to a significant trade agreement in September 1945.[10] A number of different groups became involved in the French debate about diplomatic relations with Franco's Spain, none of whose members were necessarily exclusive. First, there were the non-party resistance organizations such as the *Mouvement de Libération Nationale* (MLN), formerly known as the *Mouvement Unifié de Résistance* (MUR). This organization was represented in Paris by its daily newspaper *Franc-Tireur.* In the region of Toulouse, where the Spanish issue attracted significant interest, the MLN published the daily *La République du Sud-Ouest* and also assisted an umbrella organization of Spanish exiles, the *Junta Espanola de Liberación*, with the publication of a French language newspaper dedicated to the Republican cause, *l'Espagne Républicaine.* The second set of concerned organization were the political parties, most importantly the three parties that dominated France's first postwar parliaments: Communists (PCF), Socialists (SFIO) and Christian Democrats (organized in the newly formed *Mouvement Républicaine Populaire*, or MRP). Finally, new associations concerned solely with the Spanish question emerged, the most important of which was the *Association France-Espagne*, a multi-party pressure group organized at departmental and national levels. The involvement of these groups in the debate about relations with Franco's Spain primarily took place in public, with various points of view expounded upon in meetings of the National Assembly, in organizational congresses, and particularly in the press.

In terms of specific policies to be pursued internationally, the Resistance emphasized the principle of democratic policy-making and democratic goals above all. In contrast to General Charles de Gaulle's desire to return to France a place of "*grandeur*" on the world stage as one of the Great Powers, Resistance ideas of foreign policy saw greatness as a result of "proclaiming democratic principles and international solidarity, and supporting all tentatives with the aim of applying these principles [...]."[11] Moreover, France's own history reinforced recent experience and suggested the broad outline of a foreign policy based on principle. Writing in the Socialist *Populaire de Paris*, Charles Dumas emphasized:

> because [France] has so suffered and because French civilization is made of moderation, wisdom, justice and humanity, and also revolutionary boldness, she can ask of others to sacrifice sovereignty, to renounce ambitions of dominance or national egotism, and tell them that humanity disturbed by an unparalleled storm is no longer able to delay in these ruts...[12]

To apply such rhetoric to the Spanish case was easy enough, due to its dictatorial nature and wartime ties with the Axis. At the end of May 1945, the pressure of various individuals and organizations resulted in the Foreign Affairs Commission of the Constituent National Assembly unanimous vote to pass a resolution that called for France to end diplomatic relations with Franco's Spain.[13] The resolution was renewed in August.[14] Those concerned with the Spanish case in other countries used much of the same general rhetoric about democracy and anti-fascism. The real difference between French and Anglo-American anti-Franco activists was in the ability of the French to draw upon images and themes unique to their own experience with fascism. Furthermore, it was through this appeal that the French Resistance made its mark on France's postwar policy toward the Franco regime, one that saw a fairly consistent policy of intervening in Spanish internal affairs, most especially concerning political prisoners, and one that resulted in the imposition of economic and other sanctions against Spain by 1946. Neither the French government nor the foreign ministry originated such policies; rather, they came from public pressure. Yet in their application, the same sentiments of liberal republican values and humanitarianism that inspired calls for change also motivated government action. In this manner, it is possible to see the influence of Resistance ideas, especially republican conceptions of justice, in French policy toward Spain.

France's unique debt to Spanish Republicans was the most common theme found in the Resistance press when it came to assessing the need for change in French-Spanish relations. Debt extended back to the French experience of the Spanish Civil War. The Popular Front government's 1936 decision not to aid the Spanish Republic, made in order to avoid replicating a similar division between Left and Right at home and to conform with the British position of non-intervention, worked only to the benefit of Franco and against the Republic.[15] An editorialist in *Combat* confessed that "many of us, since 1938, have been unable to think of this fraternal country without a secret shame [...] we must not recommit the same errors."[16] At the end of 1945, in an interview with *L'Espagne Républicaine*, Albert Camus said that, "for nine years men of my generation have lived the life of Spain. It is like a wound that will not close."[17]

This debt was of course one shared by many on the left in Europe and elsewhere. What extended the debt in France was the legacy of the Spanish Civil War. In January and February 1939, approximately 500,000 Spanish Republican exiles entered France, including many former members of the Republican Army.[18] Most were interned in camps under harsh conditions. As the French republic collapsed and a new political order emerged, first under Vichy and then under full German occupation, numerous Spanish Republicans joined the French Resistance in a variety of capacities. The most significant single group was the 4,000 troops of the Communist-dominated *Union Nacional Espanola* (UNE), later called the *Agrupacion de Guerilleros espanoles* (AGE), based in the southwest and part of the French Resistance organization *Franc Tireurs et Partisans (FTP) - Main d'Oeuvre Immigrant (MOI).*[19] Many Spaniards joined French Resistance organizations and became veterans of the *Forces Françaises de l'Intérieur* (FFI).[20] Still others were arrested and placed in concentration camps, or aided the Resistance in less obvious ways. The most recent estimate of active Spanish participation in the armed French Resistance is somewhere near 10,000.[21]

This was a debt to Spanish Republicans borne by liberated France alone and proved to form the basis of the most effective anti-Franco propaganda used by the Resistance and French left-wing political parties. Reviewing France's non-intervention in the Spanish Civil War and the internment of Spanish refugees in 1939, *La Voix du Midi* remarked with awe that after the defeat of France the Spanish refugees "rose, in the thousands, forgetting the past, without rifles" just as the French people had, and "with us, they fought, and they were killed when necessary with us."[22] François Donnez in *L'Espagne Républicaine* described Spanish participation in the Resistance as "instinct, because they come from a people always taken with liberty and always oppressed; they joined with Frenchmen who wanted to reconquer their country and with [French] Republicans who wanted to reconquer their Republic."[23] Madelaine Braun of the Communist Party and Vice President of the *Association France-Espagne*, compared Spanish Republicans in the French Resistance to foreigners who had joined the International Brigades against Franco in the Spanish Civil War, both attempting to "restore the Republic."[24]

What did such a debt mean for France? How was it to be repaid? From Toulouse, the Communist daily *La Voix du Midi* reported that "the hour of [Spanish] liberation will sound; the UNE asks the French people to give a fraternal hand and France gives its heart, knowing that its own liberation will not be definitive until the last Hitlerian has been chased off."[25] The official policy of the UNE after France's liberation was to attempt to instigate a revolt against Franco in northern Spain. Border crossings from France on the part of armed Spanish Republicans were common in 1944, and continued through 1945, albeit in smaller numbers. As early as 2 September 1944, the Spanish Government complained about the influence and activities of Spanish Republican units on the French side of the Pyrenees.[26] A French military report dated 1 October 1944 concluded that, "a veritable Spanish Republican army," consisting of anywhere from 20,000 to 30,000 men, existed on the north side of the Pyrenees. At least half of these forces were commanded by the UNE.[27] This figure was likely an exaggeration, and a document prepared by a *guerrillero* member put the actual number of Spanish *maquis* organized into eleven battalions throughout the southwest at 12,000.[28] Nonetheless, the situation was troubling, as it was clear that the leadership of the UNE—as well as of many other Spanish Republican groups—viewed the reconquest of Spain as the next step, after French Liberation, in the war against fascism.[29] The most significant attempt to instigate a new phase in the political history of Spain came when Spanish guerrillas invaded the frontier region of Val d'Aran on 19 October 1944. The night of 18-19 October 1944, between 3,500 and 4,000 members of seven UNE divisions crossed into the valley and, between 19 October and 28 October, some 7,000 Spanish Republicans were in the Aran at various times fighting with forces from the Spanish Army. They withdrew only when it was clear that the national revolution they hoped to provoke was not forthcoming.[30]

Within France there was never any thought of overt military support, or active French intervention in Spain. "We have no intention of intervening in Spain," editorialized *Combat*. "We are also of the feeling that the Republicans must wait for the right moment to move with certainty. But we know that it will be necessary for Allied diplomatic pressure to guarantee the fall of Franco and to avoid the flow of the most generous blood in Europe."[31] Indeed, the various Spanish Republican groups active in France made it clear to French politicians that they did not seek any form of military intervention, but desired a diplomatic initiative above all; *L'Espagne Républicaine*, the official organ of the *Junta Espanola de Liberación*, called for a French economic boycott of key Spanish exports such as oranges, pyrites, and tungsten.[32]

As noted, the French government had no intention of shutting off its economic and other ties to Spain. In a series of analyses written in early December 1945 by the European Section of the Quai d'Orsay, an effort was made to assess the relationship between the Provisional Government of the Republic and its authoritarian neighbor to the south. Since the Liberation, France had been content to ally itself with Great Britain and the United States in their approach to Spain's government under General Francisco Franco. Like the Anglo-Americans, French officials acknowledged that the Franco regime was incompatible with the emerging democratic order in the west, and that the Generalissimo had clearly favored the Axis powers for most of the war. For these reasons, France agreed with its western allies that the regime should be morally condemned and excluded from the United Nations. Despite the defeat of Nazi Germany and Fascist Italy, however, Franco remained in power, and was essentially unchallenged at home. Since the end of the war in Europe, the French Mission in Madrid, under Jacques Truelle and then Bernard Hardion, had renewed commercial relations with Spain and defended French citizens living in Spain. As Britain and the United States were similarly pursuing political and economic advantage within Spain and rhetorical condemnation on the international stage, there was little reason for France to act differently.[33] The only possibility for action against Franco was in alignment with Great Britain and the United States, neither of which seemed inclined to dramatic action at the moment. Any unilateral action by France would only "risk the inconveniences of rupture [but would not] have a decisive influence on the evolution of the situation in Spain [unless] accompanied by a similar measure on the part of the United States and Great Britain."[34]

Quite clear in this assessment, the French Foreign Ministry nonetheless could not ignore domestic criticism and thus approached the British and American embassies in Paris on 12 December 1945 with the suggestion to open a discussion on the possibility of a change of policy toward Spain. The note proposed that only one avenue of action was open if the intention was in fact to topple Franco: a joint diplomatic rupture with Spain on the part of France, Great Britain, and the United States.[35] France could not, and would not, act on its own. Georges Bidault reinforced the cautious tone of the French note to the Foreign Affairs Commission of the Assembly. "The policy of the French government," he said, "is a bit of a policy of *attentisme* [...] It is from the French Government and myself that came the proposition of rupture with Franco. We will see what the other [powers] do."[36] An internal memo prepared for Bidault confirms that the French hopes were exactly as he expressed: the possibility of a rupture or other sanction was accepted, but only if the other western powers agreed. The note of 12 December represented only "a polling" of France's allies.[37]

Even before this moment in time, however, there was one policy that the government did use to demonstrate both its desire to respond to its critics and its shared sympathies with their arguments about morality and democracy as a necessary motive behind international policy. After the UNE's failed invasion of the Val d'Aran in October 1944, most Spanish Republicans dismissed major armed interventions in Spain as a viable method of overthrowing Franco. Still, clandestine border crossings continued on a much smaller and much less organized scale. A typical example was one near Tolosa, Spain in April 1945 when 20 Republicans encountered a Spanish army patrol and two were killed.[38] More likely than not, Spanish Republicans were not killed but arrested in the course of such instances. Thus, many Spanish veterans of the French Resistance found themselves political prisoners under Franco. One of the most direct ways in which France repaid its debt to Spanish Republicans was through its involvement in the cases of such individuals who had been part of the French Resistance, had subsequently returned clandestinely to Spain, and were arrested and facing death sentences there. Intervention in an effort to commute death sentences in Spain became a sustained, important, and overlooked government policy, one that responded to a public demand that postwar France make foreign policy more democratic, more humanitarian, more republican.

Repression under General Francisco Franco was not new. As Michael Richards has written, immediately following the end of the Spanish Civil War in 1939 repression had assumed an important place in Spain as part of Franco's victorious "purification" of the nation and related installation of military, authoritarian, and autarchic culture.[39] Between 1939 and 1944, almost 200,000 people were executed in Spain by the Franco regime; those targeted by the state first and foremost were those deemed incompatible with Franco's conception of the nation as nationalistic, militaristic, and Catholic—i.e., Republicans, unionists, and freemasons above all.[40] Franco's systematic repression of opponents never ceased, lasting well into the last days of his regime in the 1970s, yet the changes in the course of the Second World War in France mark an important moment in the history of this repression. In late 1944, as small groups of armed Spanish Republicans entered Spain from the relative safety of liberated France, the Spanish police reinvigorated authoritarian practices. The Spanish fascist party, the Falange wrote in its organ *Arriba* that France had lost control of its borders to Spanish "Reds" and that the Spanish Army would respond if necessary.[41] French authorities based in Bordeaux learned that previously released political prisoners in Spain were being re-arrested in the aftermath of French liberation, as well as those who had crossed the border from France.[42] France inevitably was drawn in to the circumstances of this particular round of repression inside Spain.

When the *Comité France-Espagne* formed in Toulouse in 1944, one of its primary activities was to pressure French and Allied governments to do all they could in order to prevent executions of Spanish Republicans.[43] The growth of similar local and regional committees across France led to the creation of a national *Association France-Espagne* by June 1945. As noted, there were many groups in France, and especially in the French press, that advocated a different approach to Franco's Spain than that taken by the government in Paris. The importance of the *Association France-Espagne* was that while it shared the general belief that France should rupture all diplomatic ties to Spain, it largely dedicated itself to advocating that France use the ties it had in Spain to advocate for the commutation of death sentences imposed on Spanish Republicans with ties to France. Led by the academic Jean Cassou, this group organized petitions and held rallies opposing the imposition and execution of death sentences inside Spain; it created a commission of jurists to review such cases in order to demonstrate the lack of a rule of law in Spain; it involved other groups such as the *Ligue des Droits de l'Homme* in the cause; and it called energetically for French and Allied intervention. The *Association* also published a memoir of a former political prisoner in Spain, Ramon Via.[44] From these non-governmental efforts an activist and Resistance-inspired government policy emerged.

The *Association* was successful in getting the government to intervene for a number of reasons. Naturally, its advocacy of intervention picked up on the general arguments made by those who wanted France to adopt a firm anti-Franco policy, and thus increased pressure on the government. Moreover, the *Association* had significant membership among members in the Constituent National Assembly that crossed party lines. Vice presidents of the organization included Madelaine Braun, a member of the Communist Party and Deputy Speaker in the Assembly, as well as Charles d'Aragon, member of Foreign Minister Bidault's Christian Democratic movement, the MRP.

The March 1945 execution of sixteen political prisoners by the Franco government led to the first major petition campaign organized by the *Association*, based in Toulouse, in April. The petition sent to President de Gaulle condemned the executions for targeting those who merely wanted to "make a democratic Republic in Spain to be a friend of liberated France," and demanded that the French Government urge Franco to end the executions and allow French delegations to visit prisons inside Spain. It was signed by a number of prominent Toulousians, including the former Resistance General Riquelme and by the editors of every newspaper in the city.[45]

The first significant intervention by the French Mission in Madrid came in April 1945. That month José Vitini, a former FFI commander with three years of wartime service, was executed in Madrid. Protests and petitions aimed at President de Gaulle followed, and in Toulouse every newspaper once again condemned the execution and demanded French action.[46] On April 29, 1945, the head of the French Mission in Madrid, Jacques Truelle, was directed by the foreign ministry to personally approach the Spanish foreign minister in order to forcefully emphasize that the execution of the Resistance hero Vitini was an "unfriendly gesture" toward France that "risked seriously affecting" French-Spanish relations.[47]

The second major case to gain significant publicity in France was that of FFI veterans Santiago Alvarez and Sebastián Zapirain who were sentenced to death in September 1945. Both the French Socialist Party (SFIO) and the *Conseil National de la Resistance* made requests to the Quai d'Orsay to intervene with the Franco government and demand commutation.[48] A Paris rally in favor of commutation that featured exiled Spanish Commuist Dolores Iaburruri was the subject of a counter-protest by the Spanish Mission in France that threatened French-Spanish relations if the French government "persisted in their lamentable attitudes towards such public meetings."[49] By October, the French government was willing to investigate the possibility that the two might be taken in by another country, but this idea seems to have been dropped when no reply came from Madrid.[50]

The *Association France-Espagne* and various parliamentarians met with Foreign Minister Bidault on November 26, 1945 to ask for his assistance in a number of cases, including Alvarez and Zapirain, former FFI member Ventura Marquez (who had a French wife), twenty-two trade union members held in Cadiz, and five former FFI veterans held in Barcelona, including Cristino García, a former FFI commander. Bidault agreed that France had an obligation to intervene in these cases on principle.[51] By autumn 1945, French interventions were a regular feature of the diplomatic activity of French Minister in Madrid Bernard Hardion. The campaign within France continued to expand to such a degree that by 1946 requests for intervention to the government involved multiple organizations. One representative example from December 1946 involved the case of Agustin Zoroa Sànchez, and came at the request of the Federation of Spaniards in France, the Spanish Communist Party in Exile, the Veterans of the FFI Resistance, the National Association of Deportees, the French Socialist Party, the CGT trade union, the Union of French Women, and the Communist Party of France. Later, a number of members of the National Assembly, including the leaders of the *Association France-Espagne*, added their concerns to those directed to the government.[52]

From Madrid, Hardion insisted in each case of speaking directly with Spanish Foreign Minister Martin Artajo, seen by many as a moderate within the Franco regime. Despite the fact that by late November 1945 both French and Spanish officials welcomed a sharp decrease in armed border crossings and incidents likely to lead to arrest,[53] French officials did not cease their monitoring of the Spanish legal system when it came to political prisoners. In addition to intervening in specific cases, French representatives in Spain kept a close watch on the Franco government's alleged amnesty program for political prisoners returning from exile. As early as June 1945, the French consul in Barcelona, Jacques Coiffard, reported that the amnesty was more rhetorical than real; after two to three weeks of relative freedom, most exiles who had returned from France found themselves in prison for additional interrogations and eventual charges.[54] Between April 1945 and January 1946, Bernard Hardion intervened in sixty-two cases. The demand for interventions came from the foreign ministry in Paris, from groups like the *Association France-Espagne* via the foreign ministry, or directly to Hardion from families of the accused. Hardion emphasized that even in cases where a French intervention had not resulted in a death sentence commutation, it had bought time for the accused, as none of the individuals the French had spoken for had yet been executed.[55] A sense of success, then, contributed to the longevity of the policy of intervention.

Eventually the optimism associated with French interventions and the injustice of Franco's regime led Hardion to expand efforts beyond assistance to those Spanish Republicans who had direct ties to the French Resistance. At a trial in Alcala de Henares in December 1945, fifteen of twenty-five Republican activists found guilty of political crimes received death sentences. Families of the accused visited Hardion and pleaded for French intervention. Although Hardion noted that these individuals had no ties to France, he responded "I did not believe that I could refuse that which struck my most elemental humanitarian sentiments."[56] The French delegation did indeed intervene in the weeks following the sentences and successfully pushed for the commutation of nine death sentences. Similarly, at the request of the Spanish Socialist Party in exile (PSOE), an observer from the French Mission in Madrid attended the February 1946 trial of thirty-seven Socialists in Alcala de Henares. Their crime had been to try to re-establish the PSOE as an underground organization. Although most had no direct ties to France, the French Mission decided to intervene with the foreign ministry as well as to attend the trial, and the result was a series of relatively "moderate" sentences, ranging from six months to twelve years in jail. The PSOE credited France's involvement as a major factor in the outcome.[57] In Barcelona, the clandestine lodge of the Freemasons (heavily persecuted by the Franco regime) contacted French Consul Jean Coiffard and asked that French diplomatic mail be used to allow the Masons to report on conditions inside Spain to Spanish exile groups in France and to French Masons. This was subsequently done, as it was also for a series of clandestine Catalan groups and the Spanish Human Rights League.[58] Of the sixty-two cases in which France was involved by January 1946, only about fifty percent had some connection to France and the French Resistance.[59] This activity on the part of French officials in Spain coincided with the facilitation of a series of contacts between anti-Franco forces clandestinely organized in Spain and their compatriots in France aimed to create an alternative government.[60]

Thanks to press reports, the petitions of groups like the *Association France-Espagne*, and ties the Government had with the Spanish exile community in France, officials at the Quai d'Orsay in Paris regularly made inquiries to their Mission in Madrid about particular cases and about the Francoist justice system generally.[61] In autumn 1946, Hardion intervened in six specific cases brought to his attention by officials in Paris. In these instances Hardion noted the value of research done in Paris to authenticate direct ties to the French Resistance, arguing that his rate of success would be greater if a French role could be undeniably demonstrated.[62] Thus, the importance of cooperation between the Mission in Madrid and government officials in Paris was made clear. Moreover, Spanish groups in France began to regularly contact the Quai d'Orsay in order to thank the French government for interventions, raise awareness of new political trials, and to make connection between France's efforts, a general commitment to justice, and the cause of Spanish Republicanism.[63] In one specific case, Georges Bidault even arranged for a French lawyer to represent one Republican detainee and the government went to work in order to facilitate his entry to Spain.[64]

What arguably is most striking about the intervention policy was in fact the consistency of language used by Spanish Republicans, by their supporters from the French Resistance, and by officials within the foreign ministry. Government officials who did not want to see an end to French-Spanish relations surprisingly echoed the language of the exile and Resistance press in France. Writing of his efforts to help the families of political prisoners with no ties to France, Bernard Hardion stated that their approach to him was "witness to the confidence certain sectors of the Spanish people put in our country and of the radiance beyond our borders of our liberal and humane traditions."[65] Hardion underlined that he never intervened as part of a diplomatic negotiation or bargaining ploy; his actions and words always motivated "strictly by humanitarianism."[66] Foreign Minister Georges Bidault, in December 1945 testimony to the Foreign Affairs Commission of the Constituent National Assembly, called the question of interventions in Spanish trials as one of his ministry's "most passionate" issues.[67]

In short, it is clear that the motivation behind French action was more than a simple need to respond to public pressure, even if that was, in fact, a consideration in the early days of intervention policy. There was clearly a sense of justice behind the rhetoric of French government officials involved. Although inspired by the Resistance and the Left as part of a general policy that advocated an end to relations with Spain, those in the government who maintained that relations with Spain should not be broken because of ideology shared the sentiments behind such action. The ideals of justice in the republican and liberal sense inspired this policy once it was undertaken. In that sense, the attitudes of officials, of Resistance veterans, and expressed in the left-wing press were remarkably similar, and arguably they suggest evidence that a Resistance-inspired vision for a new foreign policy was being implemented.

France's commitment to intervention in individual cases in Spain had profound consequences for its overall policy towards the Franco regime. First, despite these efforts, criticism of French foreign policy toward Franco did not let up. Second, and most significantly, the very fact that France did intervene in so many cases increased the stakes among organized critics and among the general public when such interventions were ignored by the Franco regime. French policy was fundamentally altered as a result. In part because of activism concerning political prisoners, the Spanish issue grew in importance in France. The government's December 1945 effort to consult with its Allies on Spain was not enough; the National Assembly's Foreign Affairs Commission greeted the French proposal with a motion that encouraged the French government to "prepare and realize" its own break with Franco, regardless of the Allied response, and this motion was subsequently passed by the entire Constituent National Assembly in January, 1946.[68] The resignation of Charles de Gaulle from the head of the French government on 20 January 1946 complicated matters and gave way to a coalition government in which agreement of the parties involved included a reference to examining and implementing the resolutions of the National Assembly on Spain hitherto ignored by the Quai d'Orsay.[69] The constant pressure from many sides, and the publicity given to the interventions by France in favor of political prisoners, combined to create the situation that led to the

French issue becoming, in the words of John Young, nearly "the most important issue" in foreign affairs by late 1945.[70]

In February 1946, Franco's government executed twelve Spanish Republicans. One of the condemned was Cristino García, who had played a major role in the French Resistance as a commander of the UNE's 3rd Division which had been actively engaged in the liberation of Nîmes.[71] García was the first notable case where an execution occurred despite French intervention. Moreover, his case had received the most publicity of any in France, and Hardion intervened with the Spanish foreign ministry on more than one occasion, the final instance coming less than two weeks before García's death.[72] Thus, his execution on 21 February 1946 had a profound effect on France and French policy in Spain.

The García case came to the public's attention due primarily to the efforts of the Communist Party; he was a member of the Spanish Communist Party (PCE) which was largely supported, financially and otherwise, by the PCF. The PCF's main organ, *L'Humanité*, was the major force in organizing opinion concerning the García case. It reminded its readers that García, "a Spanish patriot, we know, is equally a soldier in the liberation of our own country," a man who embodied the comprehensive "spirit of sacrifice required in the antifascist war for democracy."[73] The newspaper reported in detail the vast number of CGT sections, local PCF cadres and other groups that held meetings and passed resolutions calling for government intervention in the García case and diplomatic break with and trade sanctions against Spain.[74] Other groups were also involved. It was the *Association France-Espagne* and the Young Socialists of the Gard that formally brought the case to the attention of the foreign ministry.[75] The *Association* also publicized the case by distributing 500,000 pamphlets.[76] In February and March alone, political parties, local committees of the *Association France-Espagne*, and trade unions were responsible for forty-nine petitions in favor of diplomatic rupture, municipal councils for twenty-three motions in twelve different regions, and eleven cities had significant public protests.[77] Mobilization by these forces led the Quai d'Orsay to urge Hardion to emphasize to the Spanish that the case was a "most pressing" issue in the context of French-Spanish relations as a whole and prompted a statement from the President, Socialist Felix Gouin, who spoke of the many letters received urging intervention.[78] Gouin repeated the themes long cherished by the Resistance when it came to Spain, for his words gave expression of a sense of debt as well as to a hope that the true democratic nature of the Spanish people would permit them a better future. His decision to publicly intervene in the García case, he stated, was due to "the gratitude of the French people" toward García and his colleagues, "and the promise of a fruitful understanding with the Spanish people."[79]

Once Cristino García was executed, the call for action became almost universal. The pressure to take a diplomatic initiative against Franco out of debt to García was now intensified, for his execution was seen as a sign of Franco's defiance toward France and its ideals. "It is the last card," wrote Charles Dumas in *Le Populaire de Paris*.[80] In Toulouse, *La Voix du Midi* exclaimed "France must avenge this affront [...] it is an act of defiance against the civilized world. It is before anything a slap in the fact to France, who especially intervened for these artists of its own liberation."[81] In the *Franc-Tireur*, the execution was used once again to cast the Spanish question in terms of its parallels to the fight for French liberation, most especially in terms of the debt owed by France to Spanish Republicans involved in that battle:

> It is our fault [that Franco remained in power]; Have we forgotten that fascism exists at out border; Was it not against all fascisms that Cristino García and thousands of our Spanish brothers fought with us on our soil? Did they not fall beside us, as at the Eysses prisons, under the same Nazi bullets, for France? And today will we disown their sacrifice, their blood and their martyrdom because the fight against fascism has moved to the other side of the Pyrénées? No, thank you![82]

Franc-Tireur claimed that "the immense majority" of the French public felt as it did, and wanted severance of diplomatic relations and the imposition of economic sanctions.[83] The Assembly immediately passed a motion condemning the assassination and calling for diplomatic rupture.[84] Former FFI veterans rallied outside the Spanish embassy in Paris, and most importantly, the CGT and its affiliated unions announced that it would suspend all traffic and communications with Spain.[85]

The Quai d'Orsay, despite shared sentiments with these emotions, was vehemently opposed to the idea of unilateral diplomatic rupture, for it continued to believe that the potential economic losses that would result from such an act would be significant and—most importantly—the Quai continued to believe that France alone could not topple Franco through sanctions.[86] This was the position that Georges Bidault took into a heated meeting of the French Council of Ministers on 26 February, two days after the National Assembly had once again voted for rupture. The result of that meeting was a decision to close the border between France and Spain to all commercial and personal traffic and communication. France's diplomatic representatives were to remain in Madrid, however —the Council's lone concession to Bidault. At the time, Spanish and American officials saw the decision as a result of pressure imposed on the government by the Communists and the CGT.[87] Bidault later revealed that pressure came from all sides of the Council table, not only the communist side. It was all he could do to propose the border closure as the only way to maintain some semblance of the Quai's position (not a unilateral rupture) while giving government ministers and the public something of what they wanted: a gesture "sufficiently spectacular to satisfy their unchained passions."[88]

Built upon the images associated with France's own Resistance experience, the passions invoked in the Spanish case were applied in a way that linked the fates of Republican France and Republican Spain, seen most dramatically in the defense of certain political prisoners inside Spain. Such sentiments were not unique to veterans and organizations associated with the Resistance, for the foreign ministry and its officials had become passionate advocates of political prisoners facing the death sentence in Spain. Indeed, even after the border closure, the French Mission in Madrid continued to track Franco's political arrests, intervene with Spanish officials in a number of trials, and generally build on the record established in 1945.[89] Such interventions represented to the Quai d'Orsay one of the benefits of maintaining diplomatic relations with Franco, despite what had occurred in the García case. Again this is striking, for despite what had happened with the border closure, those involved in French policymaking embraced the language and imagery of a noble Republicanism in the case of interventions while arguing against the Resistance's preferred policy of completely severing all diplomatic ties with Spain. Long after the García case exploded, Bernard Hardion consistently argued that any sort of spectacular action such as a diplomatic break would only harm Spanish Republicans, for the majority of French interventions had proved to be successful in saving lives. He saw his work driven by the same humanitarian values as those of the Resistance, but within the framework of quiet diplomacy rather than public action:

> If this Delegation is to exercise an effective protection in favor of Republican elements here, it is with appeal to discrimination and prudence; to record all information given to us by the families of the detainees and the groups they belong to; to have the presence of our observers in the audience of military trials; to make official approaches to the many authorities who sentence. This patient work, without the glare [of publicity], is the only one that will have a chance of success, given the heavy psychological state of Spaniards.[90]

Following García's death, the French government continued to intervene in a number of specific cases involving political prisoners in Spain. In a report prepared for incoming President Leon Blum, who had tortured memories of his failure to arm the Spanish Republic in the 1930s, the Quai d'Orsay indicated that since 1945 interventions had been made on behalf of some 110 individuals, most in an effort to reduce a sentence from death to something milder—although many interventions began before a trial and continued through sentencing.[91] Evidence about the outcome of each case is sketchy, although it does appear that the record of commutations of death sentences was less successful after March 1946 than before García's death.[92] Hardion continued to describe France's role as one of a "moral supporter" of political prisoners in Spain.[93]

However, for many on the Left and from the Resistance the policy of intervention remained important, but not equal to the impact that they envisioned cutting ties with Spain would have had.

It is interesting to note the differences that developed between France and its Anglo-American allies concerning the policy of intervention. In 1945, the initial phase of intervention, Hardion had reached out to his American and British colleagues with the hope that it would be highly unlikely that the Spanish Government would risk antagonizing all three western missions by ignoring requests for commutation.[94] Indeed, many of the same groups inside France that petitioned the Quai d'Orsay to act in specific cases also petitioned the United State Embassy in Paris to take similar action.[95] Moreover, American and British interventions occurred alongside French ones, although they were fewer in number. The Americans and British limited themselves to specific cases where detailcd evidence about a clear violation of due process could be demonstrated.[96] Nonetheless, the perspective that motivated such actions was arguably similar to that which existed in France. Throughout 1945, anti-Franco sentiment seemed strong among a number of US decision-makers, most prominently President Truman.[97] Both British representatives and Norman Armour, American Ambassador to Spain throughout 1945, repeatedly expressed their governments' disappointment at the lack of political and institutional reform in Franco's Spain after the war, most notably in his July 1945 *Fuero de los Espanoles*.[98] Moreover, when Armour left Spain and Truman declined to replace him with an ambassador-level appointment, the issue of political prisoners and postwar justice was a prominent factor in the decision.[99] Similarly, Prime Minister Clement Attlee drew attention to García's execution at a meeting of Cabinet on 25 February 1946 and received Cabinet approval to review Britain's policy towards Spain, including consideration of "further steps" in order to "expedite a change in the present political regime in Spain."[100] Clearly, then, anti-Franco sentiment existed within both American and British societies and governments, and many saw the issue of political prisoners in particular as an important one.

However, just as the García case drove French policy on Spain to a level that went beyond rhetorical condemnation, officials in the Anglo-American governments backed away from being too critical of the regime in Madrid. A joint American-British-French statement on Spain issued on 4 March 1946 condemned Franco, but did not prescribe any action against him or his regime.[101] More important in the long run was the fact that, as French action moved towards a policy of sanctions directly connected to the history of interventions on behalf of political prisoners, a number of policymakers in the State Department and Foreign Office increasingly came to view Spanish policy in light of the emerging conflict with the Soviet Union. After the issuance of the Tripartite Statement, one British official emphasized that the British were no longer "even morally called upon to defend or support France vis-à-vis Spain." In late March

1946, after the closure of the Franco-Spanish border, the State Department sent a representative to meet with Spanish officials in order to emphasize the American sense that French actions were motivated primarily by Communist pressure, whereas the Americans praised the favorable "transformation" that was occurring in US-Spanish relations.[102] The "transformation" in the US position was even more apparent when it came to considering the fate of political prisoners. As noted, even after the border closure Hardion continued his policy of intervention in Spanish political trials. However, he no longer found support from his Anglo-American allies, despite requests from Paris that he seek to undertake joint interventions with his colleagues. Whereas he once could count on the British and American embassies joining him in pressing the Franco regime on particular cases, they now "refuse to protest, on principle, against the actions of a police that, while reprehensible or repugnant in its procedures, nonetheless, in their eyes, maintains order."[103]

France would maintain its policy of isolating Franco's Spain, through the closure of the Pyrenean border, for another two years. Bidault was fearful of challenging this policy, and he made it explicit that as long as such passions found political expression through the election of leftist candidates to the Assembly, he would not seek another confrontation.[104] In French relations toward Franco's Spain there was, if only briefly, a policy grounded in conceptions of democracy and morality consistent with the ideals of the Resistance experience. The basis of that influence was the ability of the Resistance, in all its manifestations (including within the Quai d'Orsay), to cast the Spanish question in light of issues that drew upon the power of France's own myth of resistance. The rhetoric of the period after fascism ended in France enabled many to cast the Spanish nation as one of resisters who had contributed so much to France's own liberation. Thus, France had an obligation to apply its influence to the Spanish republican cause using the lessons of justice and dignity, not power politics, as inspiration. This was especially true in the policy of intervention with the Spanish government when specific individuals became political prisoners. All of these themes, repeated in the French press, helped influence the direction of the French government's policy toward General Francisco Franco's Spanish regime. Franco, of course, did not pass from the scene until 1975, and French sanctions toward his regime ended early in 1948. However, for a moment in the early postwar period, the French Resistance succeeded in transforming French politics and policy and infusing it with a sense of the "new politics" it had promised its partisans.

Notes

[1] Georgette Elgey, *La République des Illusions, 1945-1951* (Paris: Fayard, 1966), 106.
[2] Jean-Pierre Rioux, *The Fourth Republic, 1944-1958* (Cambridge and New York: Cambridge University Press, 1989), 48.

[3] Henri Rousso, *The Vichy Syndrome: History and Memory in France since 1944,* trans. A, Goldhammer (Cambridge, MA: Harvard Univesity Press, 1991), 19; Rioux, 50–54.
[4] Rousso, 19.
[5] Alice Kaplan, *The Collaborator: The Trial and Execution of Robert Brasillach* (Chicago: University of Chicago Press, 2000), 228.
[6] In a similar vein, applied to the United States and the US hunt for Nazi war criminals in the 1980s, Norman Goda argues that even if far too late, the effort proved that the "lessons of the Nuremberg trials […] were ultimately internalized in official circles." Norman Goda, "Manhunts: The Official Search for Notorious Nazis," in *U.S. Intelligence and the Nazis,* ed. Richard Breitman, Norman Goda, Timothy Naftali, and Robert Wolfe (Washington: National Archives Trust Board for the Nazi War Crimes and the Japanese Imperial Government Interagency Working Group, 2004), 346.
[7] For a brief summary of the Axis-Spanish relationship during the war, see Christian Leitz, "Nazi Germany and Francoist Spain, 1939-1945," in *Spain and the Great Powers in the Twentieth Century,* ed. Sebastian Balfour and Paul Preston (London and New York: Routledge, 1999), 127–50.
[8] *Combat*, 7 September 1944.
[9] *La République du Sud Ouest*, 1 January 1946.
[10] "Procès-verbal de la Commission Mixte signé a Saint-Sebastien le 15 septembre 1945," *Archives du Ministère des Affaires Etrangères,* Paris (hereafter *AMAE*), Papiers d'Agents- Archives Privées Maurice Dejean, 62.
[11] *Le Populaire de Paris*, 8 January 1946.
[12] *Le Populaire de Paris*, 27 August 1944.
[13] Procès-verbaux, Commission des Affaires Etrangères, Assemblée Consultative Provisoire, 25 May 1945. *Archives Nationales de la France*, Paris (hereafter *AN*), Série C/15274.
[14] *Le Populaire de Paris*, 4 August 1945.
[15] Paul Preston, *A Concise History of the Spanish Civil War* (London: Fontana, 1996), 102–3, 113–4.
[16] *Combat*, 7 September 1944.
[17] *L'Espagne Républicaine*, December 29, 1945.
[18] Secundino Serrano, *Maquis: Historia de la guerrilla antifranquista* (Madrid: Temas de hoy, 2001), 123; Geneviève Dreyfus-Armand, *L'Exil des Républicains espagnols en France* (Paris: Albin-Michel, 1999), 53; Marie-Claude Rafaneau-Boj, *Odyssée pour la Liberté: Les Camps de prisonniers espagnols, 1939-1945* (Paris: Denoel, 1993), 12; Louis Stein, *Beyond Death and Exile: The Spanish Republicans in France, 1939-1955* (Cambridge, MA: Harvard University Press, 1979), 38. All estimate the figure at somewhere between 350,000 and 500,000.
[19] Rafaneau-Boj, 270.
[20] Dreyfus-Armand, 168–70.
[21] Serrano, 129.
[22] *La Voix du Midi*, 6 September 1944.
[23] *L'Espagne Républicaine*, 18 August 1945.
[24] Terreur Sur Espagne: Rapport du Congres National de l'Association France-Espagne, 8 June 1947. *Institut Francais d'Historie Sociale-Archives Nationales de la France*, Paris, Fonds Lamberet 14 AS 599 (38).
[25] *La Voix du Midi*, 15 September 1944.

[26] French Embassy, London to MAE Europe, 2 September 1944. *AMAE*, Série Z/Europe 1944-1949/Espagne, 34.
[27] Lt. Col. Richard, Commandement Militaire de la Frontière (Services Speciaux) to MAE Europe, 1 October 1944. *AMAE* Série Z/Europe 1944-1949/Espagne, 34.
[28] Sixto Agudo, "Participation des Espagnols à la Résistance dans le 4e région," 15 April 1976. Reproduced in Daniel Latapie, *L'Affaire du Val d'Aran: Témoignages et Documents* (Toulouse, 1984).
[29] Agudo in Latapie.
[30] For a detailed account of the Val d'Aran invasion and its political motivations, see Jean-Louis Dufour and Rolande Trempe, "La France, Base Arrière d'une Reconquete Républicaine de l'Espagne: L'Affaire du Val d'Aran" in *Les Français et la Guerre d'Espagne: Actes du Colloque de Perpignan,* ed. Jacques Sagnes and Sylvie Caucanas (Perpignan, 1990), 261–84. See also Pike, *Jours de Gloire, Jours de Honte: le parti communiste d'Espagne en France* (Paris: Société d'édition d'enseignement supérieur, 1984), 119–32 and Daniel Arasa, *Años 40: Los maquis y el PCE* (Barcelona: Argos Vergara, 1984), 121–241. For an account by one of the best friends of the Spanish guerrilleros, FFI commander and Commandement Militaire de la Frontière agent Daniel Latapie, see his self-published account, including a description of his own efforts to dissuade the UNE from action the night before the invasion. Latapie, *L'Affaire du Val d'Aran.*
[31] *Combat*, 21 November 1944.
[32] See comments by Madeleine Braun (PCF), 25 May 1945 and Gilbert de Chambrun, 19 December 1945, both in the National Assembly's Foreign Affairs Commission. *AN* Série C/15274, 15286; *L'Espagne Républicaine*, 18 August 1945.
[33] Note General, "Rélations France-Espagne," 1 December 1945. *AMAE*, Série Z/Europe 1944-1949/Espagne, 82.
[34] Note Generale, 1 December 1945. *AMAE* Série Z/Europe 1944-1949/Espagne, 82.
[35] Ministère des Affaires Etrangères to United States Embassy, Paris and British Embassy, Paris, 12 December 1945. *MAE* Série Z/Europe 1944-1949/Espagne, 66. State Department translation can be found in *Foreign Relations of the United States 1945*, V (Washington: US Government Printing Office, 1965) (hereafter *FRUS*), 698–9.
[36] Procès-verbaux of the Foreign Affairs Commission, 12 December 1945. *AN* Série C/15286.
[37] Note for Bidault, 3 December 1945. *AMAE* Série Z/Europe 1944-1949/Espagne, 66.
[38] Andre Mattei, Consl at San Sebastian, to Jacques Trulle, French Minister to Madrid, 18 April 1945. *AMAE* Serie Z/Europe 1944-1949/Espagne, 35.
[39] Michael Richards, *A Time of Silence: Civil War and the Culture of Repression in Franco's Spain, 1939-1945* (Cambridge and New York: Cambridge University Press, 1998), 1.
[40] Richards, 30–1.
[41] Cited in French Embassy Madrid to Bidault, 14 October 1944. *AMAE* Serie z/Europe 1944-1949/Espagne, 34.
[42] Commissioner of the Republic, Bordeaux, to Ministries of Interior, Foreign Affairs, War, 18 January 1945. *AMAE* Serie Z/Europe 1944-1949/Espagne, 34.
[43] *La République du Sud Ouest*, 8 December 1944.
[44] "Terreur Sur L'Espagne: Rapport du Congrès National de l'Assocation France-Espagne, 8 June 1947," *Institut Francais d'Historie Sociale-Archives Nationales de la France* Fonds Lamberet 14 AS 599 (38).

[45] For the text of the resolution, see *La Victoire,* 10 April 1945 and *Le Voix du Midi,* 6 April 1945.
[46] *Le Voix du Midi*, 27 April 1945.
[47] MAE-Direction Politique to Truelle, 29 April 1945. *AMAE* Serie Z/Europe 1944-1949/Espagne, 35.
[48] *Le Populaire de Paris*, 15 September 1945.
[49] Spanish Embassy in Paris to MAE, 12 October 1945. *AMAE* Sèrie Z/Europe 1944-1949/Espagne, 36.
[50] Cabinet du Ministre to MAE Europe, 28 November 1945. *AMAE* Sèrie Z/Europe 1944-1949/Espagne, 36.
[51] Ibid.
[52] Letter to Ministry of Foreign Affairs, December 1946; Raoul Calad, Deputy for Herault, to Bidault, 10 February 1947; Madelain Braun, Gilbert de Chambrun, Maurice Schumann, etc. to Bidault, 5 February 1947. *AMAE* Cabinet du Ministre/Bidault (1944-48), 18.
[53] Hardion to Coiffard, 5 November 1945. *AMAE* Sèrie Z/Europe 1944-1949/Espagne, 36.
[54] Coiffard to Hardion, 29 June 1945. *AMAE* Sèrie Z/Europe 1944-1949/Espagne, 35.
[55] Hardion to Paris, 9 January 1946. *AMAE* Série Z/Europe 1944-1949/Espagne, 36.
[56] Hardion to Paris, 4 January 1946. *AMAE* Sèrie Z/Europe 1944-1949/Espagne, 37.
[57] Hardion to Paris, 28 February 1946 and 18 March 1946. *AMAE* Sèrie Z/Europe 1944-1949/Espagne, 37, 38.
[58] Coiffard to Paris, 17 April 1946 and 29 April 1946. *AMAE* Sèrie Z/Europe 1944-1949/Espagne, 38.
[59] Hardion to Paris, 9 January 1946. *AMAE* Série Z/Europe 1944-1949/Espagne, 36.
[60] See David A. Messenger, "Our Spanish Brothers or As at Plombières? France and the anti-Franco Opposition in Spain 1945-1948," *French History* 19 (2005): 4.
[61] See, for example, head of the European Department Francois Coulet to Hardion concerning methodology of Francoist trials, 21 March 1946. *AMAE* Sèrie Z/Europe 1944-1949/Espagne, 38.
[62] Hardion to Paris, 8 October 1946. *AMAE* Sèrie Z/Europe 1944-1949/Espagne, 40.
[63] See, for example, Frederico Minana, Left Republican Party, and Jean Montala, Socialist Unified Party of Catalonia, to Georges Bidault, 15 May and 19 May 1946. *AMAE* Sèrie Z/Europe 1944-1949/Espagne, 38.
[64] Carmen de Pedro Zoroa to Maitre de Moro Giafferri, 28 November 1946. Copied in *AMAE* Cabinet du minister/Bidault (1944-48), 18.
[65] Hardion to Paris, 4 January 1946. *AMAE* Sèrie Z/Europe 1944-1949/Espagne, 37.
[66] Hardion to Paris, 9 January 1946. *AMAE* Série Z/Europe 1944-1949/Espagne, 36.
[67] Bidault testimony to Consituant Assembly's Foreign Affairs Commission, 12 December 1945. *AN* Série C/15286.
[68] Procès-verbaux of Foreign Affairs Commission, 19 December 1945. *AN* Série C/15286 and *France. Journal Official de la République française,* 17 January 1946.
[69] Publication of the three party accord in all newspapers examined. See, for example, the party organs, *L'Aube* (MRP), *Le Populaire de Paris* (SFIO) and *L'Humanité* (PCF), 25 January 1946. See also Jacques Dalloz, *Georges Bidault: Biographie Politique* (Paris: L'Harmattan, 1992), 129.
[70] John Young, *France, the Cold War and the Western Alliance, 1944-1949* (Leicester, 1990), 78.

[71] Dreyfus-Armand, 166, 200.
[72] Cabinet du Ministre to MAE Europe, 26 November 1945; Hardion to MAE, 9 January 1946; Coulet to Hardion, 7 February 1946. *AMAE* Série Z/Europe 1944-1949/Espagne, 36, 37.
[73] *L'Humanité*, 2 February 1946.
[74] See, for example, *L'Humanité*, 3/4, 7, 8, 10/11, and 16 February 1946.
[75] Cabinet du Ministre to MAE Europe,26 November 1945. *AMAE* Série Z/Europe 1944-1949/Espagne, 36.
[76] "Terreur sur l'Espagne: Congres de l'Association France-Espagne, Paris, 8 juin 1947," *Institut Francais d'Histoire Sociale-Archives Nationales de la France*, Fonds Lamberet 14 AS 599 (38).
[77] Ministry of Interior to Bidault, 8 May 1946. *AMAE* Série Z/Europe 1944-1949/Espagne, 38.
[78] Coulet to Hardion, 7 February 1946. *AMAE* Série Z/Europe 1944-1949/Espagne, 37; for Gouin statement, see *Le Populaire de Paris* and *L'Humanité*, 17 February 1946.
[79] *Le Populaire de Paris* and *L'Humanité*, 17 February 1946.
[80] *Le Populaire de Paris*, 23 February 1946.
[81] *La Voix du Midi*, 23 February 1946.
[82] *Franc-Tireur*, 26 February 1946.
[83] Ibid.
[84] *France. Journal Official de la République française,* February 22, 1946.
[85] *New York Times*, 24 and 26 February 1946.
[86] Note, "Consequences d'une rupture unilaterale de nos relations diplomatiques avec le Gouvernement Franco," 21 February 1946. *AMAE* Serie Z/Europe 1944-1949/Espagne, 67.
[87] Butterworth to State Department, February 27, 1946. *United States National Archives and Record Administration* College Park, MD (hereafter *NARA*), RG 59, State Department Central Files, 751.52/2-2746; Caffrey to State Department, 1 March 1946. *NARA* RG 59, State Department Central Files, 751.52/3-146.
[88] Georges Bidault, *D'une Résistance à l'autre* (Paris, 1965), 137.
[89] See, for example, Hardion's report of 23 May 1946 suggesting that in the aftermath of García's execution, Franco's police were targeting clandestine Communists even more aggressively but that with regard to Socialists or others French interventions seemed to bring greater success than ever before. *AMAE* Série Z/Europe 1944-1949/Espagne, 38.
[90] Hardion to Paris, 22 November 1946. *AMAE* Sèrie Z/Europe 1944-1949/Espagne, 40.
[91] MAE Europe to Blum, 16 December 1945. *AMAE* Sèrie Z/Europe 1944-1949/Espagne, 40.
[92] Anne Dulphy, *La politique de la France à l'égard de l'Espagne de 1945 à 1955* (Paris: Direction des Archives et de la documentation, Ministère des affaires étrangère, 2002), 172–74.
[93] Hardion to Paris, 12 July 1946. *AMAE* Sèrie Z/Europe 1944-1949/Espagne, 39.
[94] Hardion to Paris, 16 November 1945. *AMAE* Série Z/Europe 1944-1949/Espagne, 36.
[95] Embassy of the United States, Paris to Washington, 4 February 1946. *NARA*, RG 59 State Department Central Files, 751.52/2-446.
[96] MAE Europe to Blum, 16 December 1946. *AMAE* Sèrie Z/Europe 1944-1949/Espagne, 40.
[97] Jill Edwards, *Anglo-American Relations and the Franco Question, 1945-1955* (Oxford: Clarendon / New York: Oxford University Press, 1999), 41-44.

[98] Bowker to Eden, 23 July 1945. *United Kingdom-The National Archive, Public Record Office*, Kew (hereafter *TNA-PRO*), FO 425-423/ 32642/Z9062; Memorandum by Norman Armour, 10 August 1945. FRUS 1945, V, 684-87.
[99] Armour to Secretary of State, 30 November 1945. *FRUS* 1945, V, 694.
[100] United Kingdom, Cabinet Minutes. *TNA-PRO*, CAB 128/ CM 18 (46), 26 February 1946.
[101] Ministère des Affaires Etrangères, Service de l'Information et de Presse to French Embassy, Madrid, 4 March 1946. *AMAE* Série Z/Europe 1944-1949/Espagne, 67.
[102] Notes of Meeting with Bond and Warner, 22 March 1946. *Archivo General de Ministerio de Asuntos Exteriores*, Madrid, Archivo Renovado R 1372/22.
[103] Hardion to Paris, 15 November 1946. *AMAE* Sèrie Z/Europe 1944-1949/Espagne, 40.
[104] "Note, Bevin-Bidault talks of 25 July," 26 July 1946. *TNA-PRO*, FO 371/60378.

II. Reflections on Third Reich Successor Societies

Excluding, Rehabilitating, and Re-Integrating Former Nazis in Vienna: A Social Democratic Dilemma, 1945-48

Matthew Paul Berg

European Recovery Program assistance, postwar reconstruction, (re-) establishment of democratic political culture, economic miracle, perhaps NATO membership: most western European societies experienced some combination of these developments between the late 1940s and the early 1960s. In those lands subjected to Nazi occupation or under the regime's influence, punishment and eventual reintegration of collaborators—whether committed indigenous fascists or opportunists—tended to take a familiar course. Western European governments pursued a course of punishment for those citizens who had engaged in egregious brutality or held high office in the Third Reich or puppet regimes. However, the vast majority claimed to be, and were recognized as, cowed victims of fascism or, perhaps, heroic resistors.[1]

The case of Austria is particularly interesting in this context, and several factors must be noted. They include: a strong sense of German identity evident in the political and cultural discourses of the interwar years; the success of an indigenous fascist movement that discovered its "Austrianness" at the eleventh hour; the emergence of a small, yet determined National Socialist movement during the 1930s; enthusiastic reception of *Anschluss* by so many Austrians; the high number of Austrian NSDAP members as a percentage of the population, as compared with figures within Germany's 1937 borders; and the gradual, tentative emergence of a sense of Austrian identity as the war turned against the Third Reich after Stalingrad.[2] Juxtaposed with this deeply rooted German-Austrian identification—regional loyalties notwithstanding—existed the possibility, introduced via the Allies' Moscow Declaration in 1943, that Austrians could understand themselves as the *first victims* of German aggression. It was the Moscow Declaration, scholars remind us, which proved the basis for Second Republic claims to legitimacy.[3]

Yet if Austrians were victims plain and simple, there is evidence that suggests alternative interpretations. For example, since the late 1940s, a number of high-ranking former SS men and other well-known former National Socialists assumed leading positions in Austria's postwar political parties—particularly, but not exclusively, in the *Verband der Unabhängigen* (Alliance of Independents, VdU) and its successor the *Freiheitliche Partei Österreich* ("Austrian Freedom Party," FPÖ). Many former National Socialists became cabinet ministers, or achieved leading positions in medicine, the legal profession, and academia. Many more Austrians felt proud of their military service under the Third Reich—even as they acknowledged that, as Austrians, they were "victims of Nazi aggression"—and some might well have agreed with Federal President Kurt Waldheim's insistence in 1986 that he had merely fulfilled his duty while associated with an intelligence unit linked to *Wehrmacht* atrocities in the Balkans.[4] Moreover, a persistent segment of the postwar generation—represented most notably through the FPÖ/BZÖ (*Bündnis Zukunft Österreich*, Alliance for Austria's Future) leadership at the federal, provincial, and local levels—have expressed ambivalence towards Austria's "official first victim of National Socialism" status and flirted openly with a revisionist, apologetic understanding of "German-Austrianness" and of the Nazi era. Indeed, the vast majority of Austrians does not romanticize the Nazi past and is committed to the Second Republic's democratic political culture. However, into the 1990s the process of coming to terms with this past (*Vergangenheitsbewältigung*) and its reception in society broadly considered occurred, as M. Rainer Lepsius has argued, in a rather hesitant fashion within Austria—when contrasted with the open and sometimes quite controversial process that has taken place in the Federal Republic of Germany. The victimization taboo allowed that the "preconditions, substance, and consequences of National Socialism could be *externalized*; they had only secondary relevance for Austria, they belonged to Germany's history, not to that of Austria."[5]

The Austrian social democratic experience presents a particularly interesting case in *Vergangenheitsbewältigung*. Until the 1980s, Austrian social democratic self-representation emphasized heroic resistance to fascism above all else—in fact, the official *Sozialistische Partei Österreichs* (Austrian Socialist Party, SPÖ) position referred proudly to the ill-fated February 1934 fighting as Europe's first instance of armed resistance against the radical right. As a corollary, Austrian socialist democrats were depicted as facing a choice between exile and resistance to the *Vaterländische Front* (Fatherland Front, VF), and the same options after the *Anschluss*. While these possibilities did exist, they by no means exhausted the range of choices. Other options included passive or active complicity in indigenous and "German" fascist regimes. Historians who addressed the social democratic tradition during the first several decades of the Second Republic tended to fall into two general groups when they reflected on this past. On the one hand, a group wrote celebratory institutional histories; on the other were those who explored continuity/discontinuity in theory and organization from the founding Hainfeld conference into the second half of the twentieth century. In both instances, the periods 1934-45 and the early postwar years received scant attention.[6] By the 1980s, a number of important scholarly studies began to address the relationship between Social Democrats and the VF or the Third Reich more directly[7]; until recently, one would have been hard-pressed to find critical examinations of postwar Austrian social democracy concerned with the fate of former Nazis either individually or collectively.[8]

This essay examines the evolving social democratic position vis-à-vis former National Socialists—many of whom had, in fact, formerly been social democratic party comrades—and who subsequently sought (re-)entry into the SPÖ during the second half of the 1940s. It examines deliberations of party officials at the local, Viennese province, and federal levels as they worked to identify former comrades who might contribute to re-formation of a vigorous social democratic organization after eleven years of fascism. At the same time, this study takes closely into account the experiences and everyday concerns of a range of ordinary Austrians, rather than merely a limited number of prominent Social Democrats who had become Nazis. A Vienna focus is compelling for two reasons: 1) it was in the capital that the highest concentration of social democratic party members and voters resided up to the events of February 1934, and 2) the largest aggregate number of registered Nazis resided in Vienna after 1945. NSDAP members and non-Nazis alike had good reason to seek affiliation with organized, sanctioned political parties upon the collapse of Nazi hegemony in Austria. Significant damage to housing stock and workplaces, economic disruption and hunger brought about by total war and utter defeat, and with four power occupation brought tremendous uncertainty. The extent to which individuals could situate themselves securely in postwar political, social and economic fields could mean surviving and thriving on the one hand or withering and dying on the other.[9] In the immediate postwar years, this thriving/withering dualism must be understood literally; at issue were physical strength, corporeal safety, the possibility of enjoying the security of an income, or the prestige of a position and the benefits it might have brought. Membership in one of the three "democratic" political parties recognized by the occupation authorities—the conservative *Österreichische Volkspartei* (Austrian People's Party, ÖVP), the *Kommunistische Partei Österreichs* (Austrian Communist Party, KPÖ), and the SPÖ—provided people with the best hope for survival and the most realistic chance to improve their life circumstances.

Between the creation of the First Republic in 1918 and absorption into the German *Reich* in 1938, Austria—not unlike some of its neighbors—experienced a parliamentary system in which differences were decided at the ballot box alongside a state of latent civil war in which paramilitary political forces engaged in occasional paroxysms of violence.[10] These forces were primarily Social Democrats and Christian Socials—the Austrian Nazis and Austrian Communists were insignificant into 1934, and the Nazis only gathered momentum with moral and some financial support from Germany from 1933/34 onward as an illegal movement.[11] By late 1933, the Christian Socials in alliance with regional paramilitary movements (the *Heimwehren*) had strived to create a *Ständestaat* (corporatist state) based on a Concordat, friendship with the fascist regime in Italy, and anti-democratic and anti-socialist support from the majority of rural Austrians and conservatives in towns and cities. Historian Steven Beller notes "By the end of 1933 [...] Austria had already become an authoritarian, corporatist state that brooked neither National Socialist nor Social Democratic opposition" and the VF government had found it convenient to establish a concentration camp for opponents of the new regime at Wöllersdorf.[12] Open civil war erupted in February 1934 when Austrian army units cracked down on social democratic strongholds in Linz and Vienna; a general strike in support of preserving the democratic republic never materialized, and isolated pockets of striking workers and *Schutzbund* (social democratic paramilitary defense league) members fought against numerically superior and better equipped federal soldiers and supporting *Heimwehr* units. After a short few days Social Democratic Party leaders, trade union organizers, and *Schutzbund* fighters fled the country, attempted to go underground, or were incarcerated by the regime (there were also several death sentences carried out).[13] An attempted coup by Austrian Nazis in July 1934 resulted in Chancellor Dollfuss's death and intensified repression against National Socialists, along with measures against social democratic activists who re-designated themselves Revolutionary Socialists (RS) and Communists. Given that the Nazis enjoyed support from Germany, they took the lead in acts of violence and terror against the VF regime.

Historian Helmut Konrad has shown that despite admonition from old-time social democratic leaders in exile or underground and even from some new RS leaders, a not inconsiderable number of Revolutionary Socialists were impressed with Nazi energy directed against the VF and engaged in joint actions with the small, but dynamic illegal brownshirts where opportunities presented themselves. Shared anticlericalism and hatred for the regime led to what at times was a kind of benevolent tolerance; in other cases, former Social Democrats joined the Nazis outright, seeing in their dynamism a better opportunity to work energetically against the VF than the Revolutionary Socialists or the Communists represented. Still, workers generally remained underrepresented among the illegal Austrian NSDAP's ranks up to 1938, which suggests that—apart for some regional variations, such as in parts of Styria or Upper Austria—Social Democrats did not go over to the Nazis wholesale.[14]

The *Anschluss* met with considerable enthusiasm from large sections of the population; former social democratic workers invariably shared in this sentiment, whether as a result of frustration with almost a decade of economic hardship, anticlericalism, antisemitism, hostility to the VF government, fatalism, an enthusiasm for the political unity of those who considered themselves ethnic Germans, or some complex combination of these factors. Timothy Kirk points out that integration into the Reich brought unexpected difficulties and disappointment—long-time unemployment had contributed to a "de-skilling" of the Austrian working class and the obsolescence of Austrian industrial infrastructure, so that skilled German workers and German capital had to be introduced into the Austrian economy (the "Prussian carpetbagger" phenomenon). The result, he concludes was disaffection and grumbling.[15] Other scholars, such as historian Evan Bukey, have argued that as long as the war was going well enough, there are no indications that the loyalty of Austrian workers could have seriously been called into question. While he acknowledges Kirk's point that "the Nazis were not more successful in overcoming class divisions in Austria than they were in Germany," he challenges the latter's claim that "Workers were contained by, rather than integrated into, the new political order"[16] arguing instead that documentary evidence suggests Kirk "underrates the material and psychological benefits of Nazi social policy, especially in the provinces" after years of economic stagnation and that he does not appreciate "the enormous emotional appeal of Hitler's anticlerical campaign."[17] On the whole Austrian workers' attitudes towards National Socialism remained complex. Even if their overall numbers in party membership rolls were less significant than the representation of other social groups, after the *Anschluss* many former Social Democrats joined the NSDAP with some sense of conviction, others out of opportunism. Undoubtedly many hoped that their lot would improve without having to make a political commitment; still others rejected Nazism altogether.

Allied denazification measures, expressed in the Prohibition Law (*Verbotsgesetz*) of 8 May 1945, required all people who had maintained their primary residence or had extended stays in Austria between 1 July 1933 and 27 April 1945 and who had become members of or applicants for NSDAP membership or one of its paramilitary formations to register with the occupation authorities. Some 536,000 individuals were affected by this decree. For special cases, long-term prison sentences of ten to twenty years remained a possibility—despite a range of punishments and sanctions prescribed in the 1945 legislation (revised in 1947), it was not always quite clear what would happen to these people—as did the death penalty for those deemed to have been particularly dangerous.[18] However, the process distinguished between "ordinary Nazis" required to register and face certain limitations on their political and economic rights, and so-called *Illegalen* who had joined the NSDAP after it was outlawed in July 1933—and thus could be accused of high treason.[19] By June 1945, denazification proceeded on the basis of careful review of individual cases undertaken by politically reliable Austrian officials. An important provision in the law permitted granting of amnesties on a highly selective basis; the provisional government was empowered to strike people from the list of registered Nazis if such individuals were considered vital to reconstruction efforts—provided the occupation authorities did not object. These amnesties could enter into effect only after reexamining the nature and length of NSDAP affiliation for those in question, discerning whether they held any party decorations, and reviewing whether they exercised positions of responsibility within the party or its paramilitary organizations.[20]

Adjudicating Rehabilitation Requests

While individual Social Democrats may have succumbed to some form of violent, intolerant, and anti-democratic agenda, the social democratic party organization itself did not do so—something that could not be stated so unequivocally of its Communist or Catholic-Conservative counterparts. Rehabilitation requests allow us to explore social democratic gate-keeping as an additional, specifically inner-party, corrective to the provisional government's denazification measures during the six months leading up to the elections of November 1945, and even into early 1946. The interplay of applicants' petitions and party review boards' evaluations, set with in a context of a broad antifascist discourse framed by the SPÖ *Zentralsekretariat* (central secretariat) stimulated a renewal of the social democratic habitus in the early postwar years.[21]

Just several weeks after the creation of the provisional government, the SPÖ central secretariat issued a statement for party officials detailing the formal position on rehabilitation requests from former party comrades who had gone over to the Nazis. As a rule, this category of people would not be admitted; nonetheless, distinct procedures would allow party authorities to determine the worthiness of individual requests.[22] Petitioners were required to submit written justification for their NSDAP affiliation, witness statements appended, to the relevant *Bezirksprüfungsausschuss* or BPA (district review board). This local level body was entrusted with discussing the merits of the request and recommending acceptance or rejection of rehabilitation. It passed its judgment up to the *Landesprüfungsausschuss* or LPA (provincial review board), whose members examined recommendations forwarded by the district organizations under their jurisdiction and issued their own judgment before passing the case to the body entrusted with definitive adjudication, a *zentraler Prüfungsausschuss* or ZPA (central review board) whose members were selected by the SPÖ central secretariat.[23]

By mid June 1945, a significant number of rehabilitation requests had been received from those eager to escape the stigma of their Nazi connections. This influx of requests prompted the central secretariat to remind its party officials throughout Austria that the SPÖ's own party-specific rehabilitation did not supersede those carried out by the Allies—and later by Austrian federal authorities. If individuals wished to have their names removed from the list of registered Nazis, the inner-SP process would have no effect unless proper denazification steps had been followed and petitioners had been cleared (i.e., officially rehabilitated).[24] Confusion on the part of applicants became evident within the first few weeks of the inner-party review system's operation. SPÖ officials in the provisional government complained initially that they received improper requests from applicants who, in their eagerness to clear themselves, had found sympathetic functionaries in the district organizations willing to submit requests directly to top governmental officials. Such requests to affect simultaneous party-specific *and* official rehabilitation met with stern disapproval from high-ranking social democratic office holders.[25]

The overwhelming majority of those who submitted rehabilitation requests did so after they had been officially cleared in denazification proceedings, however. Some 160 files, complete with recommendations from all three levels of party review are located in the Verein für die Geschichte der Arbeiterbewegung/Neues Politisches Archiv (VGA/NPA) in Vienna. Additionally, approximately one dozen incomplete files are included in this collection; recommendations and decisions are missing, or applicants had not submitted denazification questionnaires and the review process ceased abruptly. Since all rehabilitation requests had to be passed up the chain of authority to the ZPA, it is quite likely that many more rehabilitation dossiers had been submitted. The small number of complete files suggests that the majority were lost or destroyed between their creation in 1945/46 and relocation of this material from SPÖ party main offices in Vienna's Löwelstraße to the VGA in the late 1980s. This quite representative collection of rehabilitation requests affords the historian ample material for qualitative study, however. From this body of documentation, we can arrive at important conclusions regarding the justifications people offered for having sought affiliation with the Nazi Party, the language they employed when describing their social democratic backgrounds, and the factors involved in the decisions taken within the Viennese review board hierarchy. The existing cases involve women and men, workers and white-collar employees, mostly former Social Democrats who had become Nazis, and almost exclusively Viennese residents.

Motives for NSDAP Membership or Member-Candidate Status

Requests for rehabilitation began in almost every instance with a recitation of one's social democratic credentials. Some applicants stressed their roots in established social democratic working-class families ("I was always organized as a Social Democrat, as was my father"; "I come from a working-class family"; "my father was a well-known social democratic employee").[26] Virtually every applicant detailed length of membership in the Social Democratic Workers' Party and either in its affiliated trade unions or in related party associations. Most dated their association from the formation of the First Republic in 1918/19 until 1934, when the authoritarian, Catholic-conservative *Vaterländische Front* (VF) regime—also known as the "Austrofascist" regime—suspended parliamentary government (March 1933) outlawed the social democratic party (February 1934). A small sample even dated their early party membership prior to the First World War. A significant minority claimed to have taken part in Revolutionary Socialist activity between 1934 and 1938, and had been subjected to imprisonment and other hardships as a result. Others noted that the Gestapo at some point had arrested them after 1938 because of their well-known social democratic activism (e.g., distribution of outlawed political material; participation in illegal Revolutionary Socialist trade unions and resistance cells; collecting donations for *Rote Hilfe*, the aid organization for victims of the February 1934 fighting or VF persecution, or their surviving family members).[27] In the overwhelming majority of cases, applicants took special care to emphasize that they had held true to their social democratic ideals after they entered into association with the NSDAP. Individuals who could not establish social democratic roots had almost no initial chance to secure permission to rejoin the SPÖ—an indication that the party placed a premium on solidifying its former member base in the initial postwar months, rather than accept people whose political pasts remained uncertain.

Once the vast majority of petitioners had underscored the legitimacy of their previous political credentials, they faced the delicate business of reconciling their commitment to democratic socialist principles with their turn to the NSDAP. A variety of explanations manifests themselves in the archival record, and fall into four categories. They are: *economic considerations* (either severe economic duress or opportunism); *fear* (i.e., harassment and threats issued by Nazi officials in the workplace or apartment block); those who claim to have been *misled by the Third Reich's ideology*; behavior designated as *antifascist activity* by review boards, such as desertion, sabotage, providing intelligence to anti-Nazi activists, or protecting those designated enemies of the state. Each of these factors will be addressed, in turn, below.

1. Economic Considerations

The collapse of the Habsburg monarchy precipitated severe economic challenges for the First Republic. Internal markets were destroyed, and sources of raw materials and foodstuffs disrupted. Severe unemployment plagued the republic during its democratic and authoritarian periods, and pensions were generally insufficient to cover living costs for the disabled and the retired.[28] For some Austrians these conditions became gravely exacerbated if the VF government or the Nazi regime decided to punish individuals designated as opponents of their systems—particularly those who championed socialist principles. These points figure prominently in many applications for rehabilitation.

Julius D. had managed to retain to his job as a social democratic member of the hotel workers' trade union branch during the trying years between 1918 and 1934, but found himself unemployed and "suffering severely" once the VF regime came to power. In order to overcome his precarious position as an older man with few options, he joined the NSDAP and secured a job. Apart from employment, he claimed never to have profited from his party membership. The BPA in his home district of Wien-Innere Stadt approved his request for rehabilitation; while its members agreed that he should have shown greater steadfastness and looked for work without seeking Nazis patronage, they understood that four years of unemployment could erode one's powers of resistance. The Viennese LPA overruled this finding, claiming D. had not demonstrated sufficiently compelling grounds for having joined the Nazi Party. In this instance, the ZPA modified the Viennese comrades' decision. D. would not be permitted to rejoin the party immediately, but on the strength of character witness' statements, he would be allowed to apply for admission in connection with a broad amnesty anticipated for March 1946 based on the revised *Verbotsgesetz* draft developed in January.[29] In the case of D. and others permitted to reapply after this expected amnesty, the Allied Council's rejection of the Austrian government draft put off the possibility of application for (re)admission until as late as 1948.

In another representative case of economic duress, Rudolf G. claimed that paralysis in his left hand and left foot left him seventy-five percent disabled, and that his pension provided insufficient support. His entry into the Nazi camp allegedly came about due to pressure from co-workers. G. served as a volunteer for the National Socialist public assistance association in the first two years after the *Anschluss*, became a *Blockwalter* in May 1940, and applied for membership in January 1942 to secure whatever benefits NSDAP patronage might bring. His application met with rejection at all three levels; each review board found that he had not provided compelling reason for having sought Nazi Party membership.[30]

Even erstwhile militant Social Democrats found themselves seeking Nazi affiliation to alleviate the stress of unemployment. Ludwig H., a *Schutzbund* fighter in February 1934 and proud member of a working-class family, was unemployed between 1934 and 1938. In 1936, an old childhood friend who had become an underground SA *Sturmführer* promised he would secure him a job if only H. would join the storm troopers. After the *Anschluss*, H.'s friend secured him a position as a security guard with Vienna's municipal park service. In the absence of what the LPA and ZPA found compelling reasons to have sought Nazi affiliation and no evidence of any positive antifascist activity, H. was denied rehabilitation. Quite apart from these important shortcomings, H.'s application lacked any trace of evidence that might have supported his case—e.g., signed witness statements or at the very least the signatures of witnesses on his own statement.[31] In such instances, applications met with immediate rejection. Applicants such as G. and H. did not make strong cases for the preservation of their social democratic principles, and SPÖ reviewers at each level were not sympathetic to the precariousness of these applicants' economic situations. Nonetheless, in other cases, as noted below, economic duress *was* cited as a mitigating factor, provided a given applicant could demonstrate activity that SPÖ officials recognized as sufficiently antifascist.

In a limited number of cases where rehabilitation was ultimately not forthcoming, party review board members could still appreciate the pathos of applicants' situations. For example, long-time Social Democrat Leopold S. lost his position as a typesetter in 1938 when the Nazis closed the paper for which he had worked. Unemployment left his morale broken and his financial situation in shambles, he asserted, and his turn to the Nazis for work came only after several months' inner turmoil. Upon joining the NSDAP, S. received a civil service position, which he held from late 1938 until the end of the war. Particularly interesting is his acknowledgement that his behavior was "morally spineless," but that he had remained a social democrat in his heart. Several witness statements, including one from a Jewish "U-Boot" whom Schuster and his wife knew, and whom they treated well in several encounters in a local air raid shelter, lent some credence that S. did not sympathize with Nazi principles. The BPA chair in Wien-Alsergrund wrote in his report:

> I have checked over this case, the confirmations of S.'s statements are correct, but do not speak to the actual behavior of this man during the Nazi period. I have the impression that there existed neither compulsion nor necessity to seek party membership; rather, that tremendous fear was the reason for it. The man came to me several times and his moral collapse seems to have been genuine. His regret is unmistakable. It remains to be determined if genuine necessity existed for his party membership, and if it can be reconciled with the character of a long-standing functionary who sank into a situation beneath his level of tolerance.[32]

Both the LPA and ZPA judged that S. had neither demonstrated pressing reasons for having joined the NSDAP, nor had engaged in any demonstrable antifascist activity. His rehabilitation was refused.

A particularly glaring example of an applicant unsuitable for rehabilitation is that of Johann S. a former Viennese police officer. Prior to his association with the Nazi Party, S. had actually joined the VF in late 1933—*prior* to the Social Democratic Party's February 1934 liquidation—simply to maintain his position. He claimed that his well-known political sentiments led to trouble with fellow officers, before and particularly after the *Anschluss*. Nazi colleagues made life difficult for him because of alleged brutality against illegal Nazis prior to March 1938. Thus, he was not allowed to join the NSDAP until autumn 1939. S. explained that he jumped ship in order to keep his job—a second damning example of opportunism. While he claimed never to have abused people as a function of his Nazi Party membership, he added, without any trace of self-awareness or appreciation of context, that he never abused Jews: "on the contrary," he explained, "[I] sought to ensure that they were not mistreated on transports."[33] This hardly qualified as positive antifascist engagement, and his application met with rejection at all levels. A lack of political insight and blatant opportunism sealed his fate. Officials concluded that such a person could not be considered vital for the reconstruction of the SPÖ or of Austrian society during the first months of the new republic.

A final case from the category "economic duress" demonstrates a representative example of suitability for rehabilitation. Leopold S. had served as a social democratic functionary from 1915, when he was demobilized as a war invalid, to

1934. From 1920 until 1934, he held a civil service position with the *Gemeinde* Liesing. Although arrested on 13 February 1934 and dismissed by the VF, intervention on the part of Liesing's chief civil servant led to his reinstatement. After the Nazi seizure of power, S. learned that there was no place for him in the *Gemeinde* administration; he was not a Nazi Party comrade (*Parteigenosse*, or Pg). The new Nazi chief civil servant dismissed his contract as a mere scrap of paper, and noted that he had been observed openly engaged in friendly conversation with Jews on the street. S.'s unemployment brought considerable financial hardship; he barely managed to scrape by on a fifty percent disability pension from the National Socialist war victims' association, which he secured only after an exhausting run-around. An old social democratic friend urged him to apply for NSDAP membership; S. had just moved to Vienna's 12th district, and no one there knew about his red past. He became a member candidate in March 1939, but still had to wait until August 1940 before gaining employment in Vienna's *Landesernährungsamt*, where he examined the records of companies involved in food processing and food delivery. From this point until the end of the war, S. detailed activities, confirmed by witness statements, that demonstrated his opposition to the Third Reich. First, he helped a half-Jewish Viennese businessperson who suffered persecution and economic collapse to acquire a permit allowing him to engage in his trade. Second, in early 1943 S. intervened on behalf of the director and chief assistant of the *Wiener Fleischbänke Gesellschaft*, both of them half-Jewish, after a dismissed Nazi employee brought difficulties to bear on them through citations and political pressure. In perhaps the deciding example in his favor, S. had been assigned to investigate a Dutch firm charged by Nazi authorities with delivering incomplete, unauthorized, or otherwise questionable foodstuff orders. When it became clear that the Dutch employees were all underground Social Democrats, and that these food items—all of which required ration cards—were secretly directed towards Jews and others persecuted by the Nazis, S. revealed his own social democratic roots and was delighted to provide protection for his Dutch comrades. The position of the various review boards on this case is quite interesting. While the BPA Wien-Josefstadt recommended rehabilitation, the LPA maintained that the justification for S.'s NSDAP membership was questionable, that no positive antifascist achievements were evident, and that even his claim to have opposed the Nazis was dubious. The LPA offered no explanation as to why it did not find his activities sufficient to warrant antifascist recognition, however. The ZPA resolved the matter by siding with the district board, noting in a letter to S.: "You joined NSDAP under economic duress, and you sabotaged Nazi decrees and laws during NS hegemony by supporting racially-persecuted people."[34]

2. Fear

Concern for one's own physical safety in the face of harassment or threats, or for that of loved ones, formed the second most frequently cited justification for having sought Nazi affiliation. This pressure could even come from family members, as was the case with Henriette D. In 1927, she established a modest clothing repair and laundry cleaning business in Vienna. After the Nazi seizure of power, well-connected competitors took advantage of aryanization laws to expand their operations. D.'s business began to suffer, and her domineering first husband browbeat her into joining the NSDAP in order to secure protection for the business. D. appealed to prevailing gender stereotypes when she noted "as a woman" she "didn't know a thing about politics." Nonetheless, her social and political consciousness appeared progressive enough for her to continue to employ several Jewish women—despite threats from local Nazi authorities that her shop would be closed—until these women were dismissed by the Nazi officials in September 1938. The ten women who continued to work for her were steadfast anti-Nazis; she claimed to have protected them through her party membership, which she characterized as "entirely passive" in nature. Accompanying affidavits corroborated this point, as well as the kindness she extended to her Jewish employees. After D.'s divorce some time in the early 1940s, she married an old-time Social Democrat who had remained true to his political convictions.[35] While there is no indication that she had ever been affiliated with the social democratic camp herself, her "proven resistance to National Socialism" earned her support from each of the three review boards. It is very likely that her second husband's long and heartfelt social democratic affiliation, and his participation in a joint communist-social democratic resistance cell in Horn, Lower Austria helped her case.

Threats from Nazi authorities weighed heavily in fear-driven NSDAP membership, as a compelling case from Upper Austria demonstrates. Ignatz B.'s active participation in the social democratic *Schutzbund* in Linz had led to his arrest by VF authorities in 1934 and to forced exile in Czechoslovakia by May 1937. Interestingly, B. opted to return to Linz directly after the *Anschluss*, but circumstances did not become any easier for him under the new regime; his well-known democratic and antifascist tendencies brought down upon him threats and surveillance by the NS *Blockleiter* in his apartment building. After the seizure of the Sudetenland in May 1938, the Gestapo briefly took B. into custody; subsequently, harassment from the *Blockleiter* increased. Finally, when the war began in September 1939, B. claimed to have faced a choice between membership in the NSDAP and slow death in a concentration camp. Fearing for his wife's future if he were to die, B. joined the party, but still encountered suspicion. His file provided evidence that Nazi functionaries accused him of sabotaging the "Hitler greeting" and of showing friendship towards foreigners. In fact, without the Gestapo's knowledge, B. had maintained contact with social democratic friends in an underground cell, and passed information to them that he gained as a party member. This rehabilitation request found approval at all three levels, but the Upper Austrian LPA stipulated that B. could not exercise a functionary position.[36]

The Henriette D. and Ignatz B. cases are examples of a far larger number of instances in which justifiable fear led to rehabilitation—provided an applicant's file contained well-documented corroborating statements and there existed no evidence that the applicant had opportunistically accrued advantages. Active antifascist activity virtually guaranteed rehabilitation, provided the applicant's character was unimpeachable in other key respects. Finally, even if one could not demonstrate proof of antifascist activity, extraordinary circumstances could bring leniency. The case of Theodor K. is instructive in this regard. This longtime Social Democrat lost his job as a bank official after the *Anschluss*, and his wife urged him to seek NSDAP membership to protect his daughter and her baptized Jewish husband from abuse. On *Kristallnacht* hoodlums robbed the young couple of jewelry, their savings book, and apartment keys. K.'s daughter, as a so-called Aryan, went to the local NSDAP office to demand return of these items—they represented the couple's only possessions of value, which they depended upon for survival. Although she received the looted items back, she was bullied and insulted viciously in the process. Just days later, K.'s son-in-law and daughter were forced to sell their apartment for a pittance, and his grandsons departed for the safety of Sweden. When K.'s daughter became pregnant with the couple's third child in April 1940 and Nazi officials drove them out of yet another apartment, K. felt driven to seek party membership in order to protect his family. The LPA criticized K.'s conduct, claiming that there had been no compelling reason for him to seek NSDAP membership. The ZPA overruled this decision, and while it did not permit him to rejoin the party immediately—there had been no proof of antifascist activity to which K. could refer—he was invited to resubmit his request for membership after the anticipated March 1946 amnesty.[37]

3. False Understanding of National Socialism

When considering which former party colleagues were vital for the reconstruction of the social democratic habitus, the only political sin at least as egregious as opportunism or morally objectionable behavior was the claim to have misunderstood Nazi doctrine. A number of these excuses appear in rehabilitation requests. For instance, one petitioner claimed that Nazi clients persuaded him to apply for membership directly after the *Anschluss* in part to attain concrete financial advantages, but also because they had convinced him that the "political compatibility between the Social Democratic Party and the NSDAP" meant that he would not have to abandon his convictions. He was not rehabilitated, but the ZPA permitted him to reapply after March 1946, despite BPA Wien-Penzing and LPA disapproval. This individual had not exercised any Nazi Party functions, and statements in support of his character from Social Democrats and Communists in his Viennese neighborhood, as well as from "Aryans" married to Jews.[38] Because the BPA knew the applicants or their witnesses better than did members of the LPA or ZPA, in other cases, they recommended rehabilitation, only to be overruled at one or both of the higher levels. For instance, a married couple, both long-time Social Democrats, claimed outright that they had joined the NSDAP in opposition to the VF, yet after the annexation of the Czech lands overt Nazi imperialism left them disillusioned—even though Hitler and other leading Nazis had never made a secret of their expansionist ambitions for "Greater Germany."[39] While they were not invited to join the SPÖ immediately, positive affidavits resulted in permission to reapply after the anticipated amnesty. In yet another case, an applicant claimed that he had become "increasingly disappointed with the ways in which political and economic developments deviated from Nazi principles and promises." Despite support from the BPA Wien-Rudolfsheim/Fünfhaus, the LPA and ZPA rejected him on the grounds of a lack of political constancy and a glaring misunderstanding of Nazi doctrine.[40]

4. Antifascist Activity

As we have seen, review boards at each level expected applicants for rehabilitation to have not merely harbored antifascist attitudes, but to have manifested them in some form of active oppositional behavior towards the Nazi regime. Some sought to demonstrate that such engagement outweighed any of the factors that had led them to seek Nazi affiliation in the first place. Still other applicants justified their NSDAP membership as a way to undermine the regime or as a way to strike back at the hated VF (included among the latter were some who also fall into the category designated as "False Understanding of National Socialism"). In the latter case, historians Helmut Konrad and Hans Schafranek provide us with a number of compelling insights into the ways in which Austrian Nazis and Social Democrats not merely coexisted, but frequently cooperated against a common enemy under indigenous fascism. Konrad reminds us that the success of National Socialism in Germany in 1933 and the destruction of Austria's first constitutionally-guaranteed democracy in late 1933, then the ill-fated social democratic uprising in February 1934 led to an expansion of the outlawed Austrian Nazi movement and a corresponding reduction of social democratic activity to a few underground organizational nodes. Does this mean that Social Democrats began to shift their allegiances to an Austrian Nazi movement that, with covert assistance from Germany, was better situated to wage an underground struggle against the Dollfuss-Schuschnigg regime? Konrad calculates that some 20,000 *Schutzbund* members had stood ready to defend the Social Democratic Party and the Austrian Republic up to 12 February 1934. After the February 1934 defeat, some 1,000 Social Democrats sought safety abroad, and perhaps 200 of them—the most well-known figure being Upper Austrian *Schutzbund* leader Richard Bernaschek—found sanctuary and hospitality within the territory of the Third Reich. Another 1,000 were arrested alongside their social democratic trade union and party colleagues. According to Konrad's estimate, ca. 6,000 of the remaining social democratic paramilitary members resigned themselves to political defeat (some of them would later become Nazis). "The rest of the roughly 12,000 had four political options," he concludes. They could "a) work with the illegal 'Revolutionary Socialists' [a number did so, as we shall see below], b) attempt to sustain the *Schutzbund* as an autonomous paramilitary organization [few regarded this as realistic], c) switch to the Communists [an indeterminate, but quite small number embraced this option], d) turn to the National Socialists."[41]

It is difficult to determine precisely how many *Schutzbündler* and other Social Democrats opted to work with the Revolutionary Socialists. Initially, at least, the majority of those who remained actively opposed to the VF moved in this direction, rather than towards the Communists or Nazis.[42] Konrad does not speculate on the precise number of Social Democrats who actually joined the Nazis as pre-1938 *Illegale*, but points out that "the underground NSDAP's activism vis-à-vis representatives of the Catholic *Ständestaat* pleased [...] the militant adherents of outlawed social democracy."[43] It seems to have been the case that, apart from a degree of shared political and social sentiments—e.g., an undercurrent of "vulgar antisemitism" discernible in some rank-and-file Social Democrats[44]—a segment of Revolutionary Socialist Youth activists had become enamored of the Nazis' fighting spirit and frustrated with the perceived passivity on the part of erstwhile social democratic leaders. Moreover, a number of those former politicians and theoreticians were Jews. Hans Schafranek notes the Austrian police observed, "While social democratic leaders take pains to save what is left to be saved [of their organizational structure and operational autonomy], *younger* adherents run into the brown camp."[45] Between 1934 and 1938, far fewer seem to have joined the NSDAP outright, while the majority of those seeking a *modus vivendi* with militant illegal Nazis shared intelligence, and both Nazis and Social Democrats supported one another in underground activities—for instance, occasionally coordinating the distribution of leaflets for both organizations and affixing posters for one another.[46]

Rehabilitation requests directed to the SPÖ during the second half of 1945 reflect the aforementioned factors. In the end, the extent to which the social democratic authorities were willing to forgive political transgressions depended on three factors. First, an applicant's claims had to be credible and verifiable. Second, the gravity of the personal risk undertaken in opposition to the Third Reich had to be consequential. Third, authorities at the BPA, LPA, or ZPA levels linked many an applicant's rehabilitation to how essential her/his work would be to reestablishing the party and serving the social democratic cause in Austrian reconstruction efforts.

While one would expect that refusal to fight for an abhorrent cause might have represented sufficient grounds for rehabilitation, military desertion cases met with particular scrutiny, and review boards considered such antifascist activity only under certain circumstances—for example, justification for entering the Nazi camp in the first place, and behavior patterns prior to desertion. For example, Anton G. verified that he had deserted from the *Volkssturm* on 5 April 1945 during the initial Soviet assault on Vienna. This action was not without risk; deserters from the ranks of either the *Wehrmacht* or *Volkssturm* could reckon with execution if caught by SS troops, and even at the hands of zealous *Wehrmacht* officers or non-commissioned officers. G. could also point to written testimonies that he had never profited from his party membership or mistreated anyone, that he threw away Nazi propaganda literature he was entrusted with distributing, and that he listened to prohibited foreign radio broadcasts. Any chance that he could have been rehabilitated at once, or even after the forecasted amnesty, was dashed by the fact that he admitted freely to leveraging his membership in the German Labor Front to obtain a more desirable apartment, and that he applied for a Nazi Party card to improve his credit rating.[47] Opportunism overshadowed any benefit of the doubt he may have drawn from fleeing the *Volkssturm*, or from some other expression of anti-Nazi sentiment. A representative contrasting case is that of Karl K. Economic duress had prompted K. to apply for Nazi Party membership shortly after the *Anschluss*. He had been unemployed for much of the period 1934-38, and his father lost his job after VF police officials arrested him as a social democratic activist. Drafted in 1939, just in time to take part in the invasion of Poland, K. told his family not to pay his party dues. He became active in an Austrian resistance cell within his *Wehrmacht* unit in late 1944. Just days before the German capitulation in Vienna, a military court found K. guilty on charges of planning to desert and inciting defeatism, along with twenty-three other NCOs and officers. The impending approach of Allied forces interrupted the implementation of death sentences, and K. joined several colleagues in an escape over the Upper Austrian border into Czechoslovakia. In the waning hours of the war they were arrested anew on desertion charges—this time by Nazi criminal police officials—but managed to escape with the assistance of communist underground resistance fighters. Several witness statements confirmed K.'s account, and affidavits from Social Democrats and Communists in the underground Austrian *Freiheitsbewegung* (independence movement) and from his neighborhood in Wien-Landstraße attested that K. was a decent man and a firm anti-Nazi, and that his desertion proved his opposition to the regime. Supported by the BPA, K. encountered opposition at the LPA level because he presented no evidence of resistance activity prior to April 1945. Unlike the G. case, however, the ZPA ruled that because he had suffered arrest and a death sentence, K had manifested his opposition to the regime, and was thus entitled to reenter the social democratic camp.[48] Support from SPÖ and KPÖ officials in the *Freiheitsbewegung*, as well as social democratic and communist functionaries in the applicant's home district, weighed heavily in his favor. While the LPA may have been correct that K. had not demonstrated active antifascist engagement prior to his desertion—e.g., he merely asserted he was an opponent of National Socialism—he had not compromised his previous social democratic credentials by seeking advantage through his Nazi party affiliation.

Resistance cases embraced a broad spectrum of activity; desertion represented only one possibility. The grounds upon which non-desertion cases were adjudicated appear less ambiguous, however. For example, Franz L. had been affiliated with the social democratic movement since 1918, and from 1934 until his 1943 induction into the *Wehrmacht* he had been an underground Revolutionary Socialist trade unionist and co-founder of an illegal cell through his workplace at the Wien Westbahnhof post office. In 1940, local Nazi officials ordered him to become a German Labor Front functionary, which required an application for NSDAP membership. L. accepted, at the urging of his Revolutionary Socialist colleagues, in order to provide the cell with intelligence reports—a point confirmed in a statement signed by ten of his comrades. At each level of review he was deemed an underground social democratic activist and welcomed to rejoin the party.[49]

Otto T., together with his brother Leo, had been well-known underground Revolutionary Socialist activists even before the *Anschluss*. T. submitted a rehabilitation request on behalf of his wife Philomena, who had not been an underground activist prior to 1938, but joined the National Socialist women's organization allegedly in order to both provide the T. brothers' cell with better and more consistent insider information and to try to protect Jewish friends. High-ranking social democratic official Alois Piperger and communist activist Alexandra Jakl, both widely respected left-wing antifascists, confirmed the services Philomena rendered. By 1940, Philomena was advanced to a leadership position and enrolled as a party member applicant. It was at this point that the Gestapo cracked down on the T. brothers' illegal cell, for which Leo later paid with his life; Otto then urged his wife to withdraw from Nazi women's organization activities. While the BPA in Wien-Hietzing urged that Philomena be rehabilitated, the LPA demurred, arguing that awareness of her husband's and brother-in-law's underground activities was not sufficient to counterbalance the fact that she herself assumed a leadership role in a Nazi organization *without* proof of having provided useful information (despite the Piperger and Jakl testimonies). A ZPA intervention resolved the matter in Philomena's favor, deciding that her activities had been undertaken to cover her husband's illegal political work and provide information to his cell.[50] In the case of Franziska T., the LPA seemed to argue inconsistently when it stated that, as a naive country girl, she allowed Nazi party membership to be forced upon her without understanding the consequences. T. regretted her decision in short order, and marshaled letters of support from several established Revolutionary Socialists who held leading party positions in her home district of Wien-Penzing. In this instance, the LPA supported BPA calls for rehabilitation, noting that "as a waitress [she] maintained a supportive relationship with several comrades in the district and passed along important news to them." The ZPA supported rehabilitation in this case also.[51]

Along with using Nazi party membership to pass intelligence to illegal Revolutionary Socialist cells, applicants cited protection of individuals targeted by Nazi authorities for harassment and destruction as evidence of their antifascist sentiments. Heinrich H. knew that illegal communist meetings were being held in his Wien-Penzing apartment building and that a *Wehrmacht* deserter had taken sanctuary there. Nineteen character witnesses signed a letter attesting that H. was widely known as a virulent antifascist, and had never used his Nazi party membership to derive advantages. The LPA recommended rejection, but the ZPA supported H.'s rehabilitation.[52] In another case, Rudolf L., a member of the NSDAP since 1940 who continued to lead the illegal Revolutionary Socialist cell in his firm, was placed on trial in a broad crackdown against suspected leftists. His testimony both cleared his name and persuaded the *Volksgericht* to commute the sentences of four known illegal communist activists from high treason and the death penalty to long prison terms. Several trusted Social Democrats and Communists verified his actions and confirmed his deeply rooted socialist convictions. L. enjoyed support at all three levels of review.[53] Finally, according to eyewitness testimonies Alfred H. frequently assisted a Jewish man and his "Aryan" wife, chauffeuring them about to facilitate completion of their errands rather than allow them to face harassment and abuse on the streets of Vienna. Employees in his shoe varnishing business were never subjected to German Labor Front or other forms of Nazi propaganda, and H. took care that the foreign forced laborers and the half dozen Soviet POWs assigned to his factory received decent treatment and adequate nourishment. In the latter instance, H. supplemented their meager rations at his own personal expense. Citing irreproachable antifascist behavior, the LPA and ZPA supported the recommendation for H.'s rehabilitation advanced by the BPA in Wien-Ottakring.[54]

Such cases reveal the difficulties in ascertaining a consistent standard in the adjudication of rehabilitation applications. In most instances, review board officials considered it insufficient if applicants had merely avoided sullying themselves with morally troublesome or outright Nazi behavior. Because the BPA officials would have been familiar with most applicants, they would have been in a better position than the *Land* or federal boards to detect dissimulation and to assess the reliability of witness statements. Moreover, the BPA held face-to-face interviews with applicants, whereas the LPA and ZPA merely examined the dossiers that applicants had submitted and the commentaries from lower-level review board officials accompanying the files. Thus, both the LPA and ZPA did not consistently recognize the insights of district review board members. Although there are examples of the ZPA siding with the BPA against LPA objections, the ZPA more frequently tempered or overruled BPA decisions, and modified shared BPA and LPA judgments in other instances. Decisions in ambiguous cases seem to have been taken based on intuition, or whether a candidate had support from well established social democratic—or even communist—figures whose antifascist credentials were beyond reproach.

The examples cited above suggest that entrance into the Nazi fold due to unemployment woes or political harassment did not guarantee rehabilitation, even when witnesses confirmed an applicant's antifascist credentials. Rather, the testimony of powerful friends carried more weight than that of average Social Democrats who had managed to maintain their decency. Nonetheless, individuals who had previously enjoyed good social democratic connections did not always enjoy rehabilitation, nor did all who lacked powerful friends find the review boards unsympathetic to their petitions. In the end, the archival evidence clearly suggests that those who had *not* blemished their reputations by keeping questionable company, by engaging in amoral behavior, or by accumulating Nazi offices faced a far greater likelihood for rehabilitation if they had support from officials at the district, provincial, or federal party levels. Such individuals were women and men upon whom the party could rely to fill the ranks of qualified, dedicated functionaries. While they might not have remained faultless politically, party elites did not regard their transgressions as mortal sins against social democratic values, against their fellow Austrians, or against those who designated "undesirable" by the Nazis. Their efforts would be elemental to the renewal of social democratic principles, organizational practices, and policy implementation—in short, to the reestablishment and reproduction of a social democratic habitus in the wake of fascism.

Concluding Thoughts

Once the *Nationalsozialistengesetz* entered into force on 17 February 1947, the SPÖ central secretariat and party executive sent a highly confidential note to the provincial party executive committees that indicated, "it will be in the best interests of the party to settle exemption requests according to §27 [of the National Socialist Law]."[55] The provincial party executives were to establish special commissions to review these requests, and pass along recommendations on cases they considered particularly promising to the central secretariat in Vienna. Upon approval, these dossiers would be forwarded to Interior Minister Oskar Helmer, and ultimately to the Federal President Renner for final adjudication. Since both were SPÖ comrades, the central secretariat could feel confident that its recommendations would be viewed favorably—unless previously unknown, unfavorable information on applicants surfaced unexpectedly. The memo stressed that the applicants' cases had to meet the following conditions, consistent with §27: an applicant had never abused membership in the NSDAP or its ancillary organizations; an applicant evinced a positive orientation towards the Second Republic; a convincing case could be made that it was in the public interest to decide favorably on a petition (for example, the applicant had been a member of the Austrian resistance or had special talents or experience vital to reconstruction).[56]

Those former Nazis upon whose behalf SPÖ officials were prepared to argue were both women and men, had been adults as well as youths during the Third Reich, had been Social Democrats or in a few cases had no previous affiliation with the social democratic camp at all.[57] The vast majority had been civil servants with administrative or technical expertise (e.g., within the context of the municipal construction office, police service, or federal railways), business executives, teachers, or physicians. Surviving evidence reveals that workers—whether in the public or private sector—were distinctly underrepresented among those who requested exemption; with 19,757 blue-collar workers in public service or private firms out of a total of 108,405 registered Nazis employed in Vienna in 1947,[58] one would expect to find the number of working-class exemption requests roughly commensurate with this ratio. Perhaps individuals employed in white-collar positions placed greater emphasis upon clearing their names from the list of registered Nazis for professional or personal reasons, but in the absence of compelling evidence, this possibility must remain in the realm of speculation.

Party executive members understood it as their responsibility to preserve the SPÖ's position within public administration, institutions of state, the economy, and society from the influence of politically suspect individuals or those morally compromised through their flirtation with fascism. However, since white-collar workers in these areas possessed valuable expertise, failure to support approval of reasonable exemption requests would have ceded influence to the People's Party—viewed cautiously at best and with hostility at worst as the heirs to the "Austrofascist" tradition by Social Democrats—and those whom the People's Party could win over from the brown camp. Some twenty-five percent of *Minderbelasteten* remained excluded from employment with the federal or Viennese provincial governments, thirty-five percent from the courts and other branches of the justice ministry, eighty percent from the legal profession, and fifty percent from public finance authorities Austria-wide.[59] SPÖ leaders perceived it in the party's best interest to compete for a share of these experts. Any lingering reservations about the fascist background of such individuals were sacrificed to political expediency.

Tactical (re-)integration of erstwhile Nazis into Austrian society through the social democratic camp became the party executive's preferred approach to the "Nazi Question" after the 1945 elections. This served, then, to shore up the social democratic presence in the Social Partnership and in the federal, provincial, and municipal governments. Prior to the 1949 elections, the integration of former Nazis through amnesties could demonstrate to *Minderbelastete* soon to regain voting rights that the SPÖ was not more hostile to this population than were its political rivals. After 1949, the "Nazi Question" essentially ceased to be *the* salient political issue, except among the SPÖ left and among Communists. Other matters vied for the attention of politicians, among them efforts to secure the State Treaty, debates over wage-price agreements, and Marshall Plan-supported reconstruction projects. SPÖ parliamentary deputy Alfred Migsch, a man actively involved in denazification efforts, revealed the evolution of his party's position after 1945 when he declared "the old law from 1947 hindered the development of inner peace in our country."[60] Once the 1957 amnesty reintegrated large numbers of heavily implicated ex-Nazis,[61] a decade of efforts to balance reconstructing political life against denazification measures found legislative resolution. Post-fascist Austria had welcomed the great majority of former Nazis into the community of "first victims of German aggression"—among them social democrats, members of a political party that prided itself after 1945 as the only Austrians to reject fascism and dictatorship in every form. This achieved a significant measure of social peace, but it deferred meaningful efforts towards *Vergangenheitsbewältigung* to subsequent generations.

Notes

An extended version of this essay appeared as, "Die SPÖ und die Praxis der Entnazifizierung" in *Entnazifizierung zwischen politischem Anspruch, Parteienkonkurrenz und Kaltem Krieg*, ed. Maria Mesner (Vienna and Munich: Oldenbourg Verlag, 2005), 145-85. The revised version printed here with permission of Oldenbourg Verlag.

[1] See, for example, Klaus Dietmar-Henke and Hans Woller ed., *Politische Säuberung in Europa: die Abrechnung mit Faschismus und Kollaboration nach dem zweiten Weltkrieg* (Munich: Deutscher Taschenbuch Verlag, 1991).

[2] Evan Burr Bukey, *Hitler's Austria: Popular Sentiment in the Nazi Era, 1938-1945* (Chapel Hill and London: University of North Carolina Press, 2000); Peter Thaler, "'Germans' and 'Austrians' in World War II: Military History and National Identity," Working Papers, Center for Austrian Studies 99-1 (Minneapolis, September 1999); Emmerich Tálos, Ernst Hanisch, and Wolfgang Neugebauer ed., *NS-Herrschaft in Österreich 1938-1945* (Vienna: Verlag für Gesellschaftskritik, 1988); Stanley Suval, *The Anschluss Question in the Weimar Era: A Study of Nationalism in Germany and Austria, 1918-1932* (Baltimore: Johns Hopkins University Press, 1974).

[3] Gerhard Botz, "Geschichte und kollektives Gedächtnis in der Zweiten Republik: 'Opferthese', 'Lebenslüge' und Geschichtstabu in der Zeitgeschichtsschreibung" in *Inventur 45/55: Österreich im ersten Jahrzehnt der Zweiten Republik*, ed. Wolfgang Kos and Georg Rigele (Vienna: Sonderzahl Verlagsgesellschaft, 1996), 51-85. On the Moscow Declaration and the notion of victimization, see also Botz, "Österreich und die NS-Vergangenheit: Verdrängung, Pflichterfüllung, Geschichtsklitterung" in *Ist der Nationalsozialismus Geschichte? Zu Historisierung und Historikerstreit*, ed. Dan Diner

(Frankfurt a.M.: Fischer Taschenbuch Verlag, 1987), 141-52; Robert Keyserlingk, *Austria in World War II: An Anglo-American Dilemma* (Kingston, Ontario: McGill-Queen's University Press, 1988); Günter Bischof, "Die Instrumentaliserung der Moskauer Erklärung nach dem zweiten Weltkrieg," *Zeitgeschichte* 20 (1993): 345-66; Thomas Albrich, "'Es gibt keine jüdische Frage': Zur Aufrechterhaltung des österreichischen Mythos" in *Der Umgang mit dem Holocaust: Europa—USA—Israel*, ed. Rolf Steininger (Vienna: Böhlau, 1994), 147f; Hermann Langbein, "Darf man vergessen?" in *Das grosse Tabu. Österreichs Umgang mit seiner Vergangenheit*, ed. Anton Pelinka and Erika Weinzierl (Vienna: Verlag Österreich, 1997), 8-20.

4 On the tension between fulfillment of duty and victimization among Austrian veterans of the Second World War see Matthew Paul Berg, "Challenging Political Culture in Postwar Austria: Veterans' Associations, Identity, and the Problem of Contemporary History," *Central European History* 30 (1997): 513-44; on the Waldheim Affair, see Richard Mitten, *The Politics of Antisemitic Prejudice: The Waldheim Phenomenon in Austria* (Boulder, Colorado: Westview, 1992).

5 M. Rainer Lepsius, "Das Erbe des Nationalsozialismus und die politische Kultur der Nachfolgestaaten des 'Großdeutschen Reiches'," in idem, *Demokratie in Deutschland: Soziologisch-historische Konstellationsanalysen. Ausgewählte Aufsätze* (Göttingen: Vandenhoeck & Ruprecht, 1993), 232 and 245.

6 Examples of the celebratory variety include Walter Pollak, *Sozialismus in Österreich: Von der Donaumonarchie bis zur Ära Kreiskys* (Vienna and Düsseldorf: Econ, 1979). Among examples of studies concerned with continuity and transition, consider Kurt Shell, *The Transformation of Austrian Socialism* (New York: SUNY Press, 1962); Fritz Kaufmann, *Sozialdemokratie in Österreich. Idee und Geschichte einer Partei von 1889 bis zur Gegenwart* (Vienna and Munich: Amalthea, 1978); Melanie Sully, *Continuity and Change in Austrian Socialism* (Boulder and New York: East European Monographs/Columbia University Press, 1982); Peter Pelinka and Gerhard Steger ed., *Auf dem Weg zur Staatspartei. Zur Geschichte und Politik der SPÖ seit 1945* (Vienna: Verlag für Gesellschaftskritik, 1988); Wolfgang Maderthaner ed., *Die Organisation der österreichischen Sozialdemokratie 1889-1995* (Vienna: Löcker Verlag, 1996); Erich Fröschl, Maria Mesner, and Helge Zoitl ed., *Die Bewegung. Hundert Jahre Sozialdemokratie in Österreich* (Vienna: Passagen Verlag, 1990), esp. 462-597; and Fritz Weber ed., *Nichts als Pragmatismus? Österreich zwischen Rekonstruktion und Restauration 1945-1966* (Vienna: Löcker Verlag, 2000). Exceptions here include Fritz Weber, *Der kalte Krieg in der SPÖ. Koalitionswächter, Pragmatiker und Revolutionäre Sozialisten 1945-1950* (Vienna: Verlag für Gesellschaftskritik, 1986) and Erika Thurner, *"Nach '45 war man als 'Rote/Roter' auch ein Mensch." Der Wiederaufbau der Salzburger Sozialdemokratie nach 1945* (Vienna and Zurich: Europaverlag, 1990).

7 The subject of Social Democrats in the Nazi milieu between 1934 and 1945 has begun to receive more intensive scholarly attention in recent years, and several important studies have contributed to our understanding of several important themes. These themes include illegal social democratic resistance to the Dollfuss-Schuschnigg regime; Social Democrats who made common cause with Austrian Nazis (or joined their ranks outright) to combat indigenous Austrian fascism; social democratic and broader Austrian voting patterns vis-à-vis the NSDAP; and working-class and other expressions of Austrian support for National Socialism after the *Anschluss*. See, for example, Rudolf G. Ardelt and Hans Hautmann ed., *Arbeiterschaft und Nationalsozialismus in Österreich*; Robert Schwarz, "Nazi Wooing of Austrian Social Democracy between *Anschluss* and

War" in *Conquering the Past: Austrian Nazism Yesterday and Today*, ed. F. Parkinson (Detroit: Wayne State University Press, 1989), 125-36; Everhard Holtmann, *Zwischen Unterdrückung und Befreiung. Sozialistische Arbeiterbewegung und autoritäres Regime in Österreich 1933-1938* (Munich: Oldenbourg, 1978); Manfred Marschalek ed., *Untergrund und Exil. Österreichs Sozialisten 1934-1945* (Vienna: Löcker Verlag, 1990); Dirk Hänisch, *Die österreichischen NSDAP-Wähler. Eine empirische Analyse ihrer politischen Herkunft und ihres Sozialprofils* (Vienna - Cologne - Weimar: Böhlau, 1998); Timothy Kirk, *Nazism and the Working Class in Austria: Industrial Unrest and Political Dissent in the National Community* (Cambridge and New York: Cambridge University Press, 1996); and Bukey, *Hitler's Austria.* For a wide-ranging treatment of Austria under the Third Reich, see Tálos, Hanisch, and Neugebauer ed., *NS-Herrschaft in Österreich.*

[8] See, for example, Wolfgang Neugebauer and Peter Schwarz, *Der Wille zum aufrechten Gang. Offenlegung der Rolle des BSA bei der gesellschaftlichen Reintegration ehemaliger Nationalsozialisten* (Vienna: Czernin Verlag, 2005) and Maria Mesner ed., *Entnazifizierung zwischen politischem Anspruch, Parteienkonkurrenz und Kaltem Krieg: Das Beispiel der SPÖ* (Vienna: Oldenbourg, 2005); Andrei S. Markovits and Anson Rabinbach, "Die dunkle Seite der österreichischen Sozialdemokratie," http://www.blaetter.de/kommenta/mark1000.htm, 14 July 2004; Oliver Rathkolb, "'Braune Flecken' in der SPÖ (2000-1945-1938-1933/34)," German language manuscript of "La sozialdemocrazia che non ricorda e le sue, macche brune'"in *Limes: Revista italiana di geopolitica* 3 (2000): 81-91.

On denazification and the social democratic position concerning it, see, for example, Dieter Stiefel, *Entnazifizierung in Österreich* (Vienna: Europaverlag, 1981); Sebastian Meissl, Klaus-Dieter Mulley, and Oliver Rathkolb ed., *Verdrängte Schuld, verfehlte Sühne: Entnazifizierung in Österreich 1945-1955* (Bad Vöslau: Verlag für Gesellschaftskritik, 1986); Winfried R. Garscha and Claudia Kuretsidis-Haider, *Die Nachkriegsjustiz als nicht-bürokratische Form der Entnazifizierung: österreichische Justizakten im europäischen Vergleich* (Vienna: Dokumentationsarchiv des österreichischen Widerstandes, 1995); Walter Manoschek, "Verschmähte Erbschaft. Österreichs Umgang mit dem Nationalsozialismus 1945 bis 1955" in *Österreich 1945-1955: Gesellschaft—Politik—Kultur*, ed. Reinhard Sieder, Heinz Steinert and Emmerich Tálos (Vienna: Verlag für Gesellschaftskritik, 1995), 94-106; and Richard Mitten, "'Die Sühne . . . möglichst milde zu gestalten'. Die sozialdemokratische 'Bearbeitung' des Nationalsozialismus und des Antisemitismus in Österreich" in *Schwieriges Erbe. Der Umgang mit Nationalsozialismus und Antisemitismus in Österreich, der DDR und der Bundesrepublik Deutschland*, ed. Werner Bergmann, Rainer Erb, and Albert Lichtblau (Frankfurt a.M. and New York: Campus Verlag, 1995), 102-119.

[9] "Field" in this sense can be understood in terms of what sociologist Richard Jenkins has described in his treatment of Pierre Bourdieu's work as "a structured system of social positions—occupied either by individuals or institutions—the nature of which defines the situation for their occupants." Richard Jenkins, *Pierre Bourdieu* (London and New York: Routledge, 1992), 85.

[10] On paramilitary violence in Austria, see Gerhard Botz, *Krisenzonen einer Demokratie. Gewalt, Streik und Konfliktunterdrückung in Österreich seit 1918* (Frankfurt a.M. and New York: Campus Verlag, 1987) and *Gewalt in der Politik. Attentate, Zusammenstöße, Putschversuche, Unruhen in Österreich 1918 bis 1938* (Munich: W. Fink, 1983).

[11] On Austrian National Socialism prior to the *Anschluss*, see Hanisch, *Die österreichischen NSDAP-Wähler* and Bruce F. Pauley, *From Prejudice to Persecution: A History of Austrian Anti-Semitism* (Chapel Hill and London: University of North Carolina Press, 1992).
[12] Steven Beller, *A Concise History of Austria* (Cambridge and New York: Cambridge University Press, 2006), 223.
[13] It is impossible to do justice to the vast literature on Austrian social democracy, organized labor, and indigenous fascism during this period. However, interested readers would profit from consulting Jill Lewis, *Fascism and the Working Class in Austria, 1918-1934: The Failure of Labour in the First Republic* (Oxford and New York: Berg, 1991); Charlie Jeffery, *Social Democracy in the Austrian Provinces, 1918-1934: Beyond Red Vienna* (London: Leicester University Press, 1995); Anson Rabinbach, *The Crisis of Austrian Socialism: From Red Vienna to Civil War* (Chicago and London: University of Chicago Press, 1983); and Emmerich Tálos and Wolfgang Neugebauer ed., *"Austrofaschismus": Beiträge über Politik Ökonomie und Kultur 1934-1938*, 4. Ergänzte Auflage (Vienna: Verlag für Gesellschaftskritik, 1988), to cite a few titles.
[14] Helmut Konrad, "Das Werben der NSDAP um die Sozialdemokraten 1933-1938" in *Arbeiterschaft und Nationalsozialismus in Österreich*, ed. Rudolf G. Ardelt and Hans Hautmann (Vienna and Zurich: Europaverlag, 1990), 82-85; see also Timothy Kirk, *Nazism and the Working Class in Austria*, 45-47.
[15] Kirk, 57.
[16] Ibid., 111.
[17] Bukey, *Hitler's Austria*, 91.
[18] "Artikel I: Verbot der NSDAP" and "Artikel II: Registrierung der Nationalsozialisten," "Verfassungsgesetz vom 8. Mai 1945 über das Verbot der NSDAP (Verbotsgesetz), StGBl. Nr. 13, in der Fassung der 2. Verbotsgesetznovelle vom 16. November 1945" in *Das Nationalsozialistengesetz. Bundesverfassungsgesetz vom 6.II.1947, BGBl. Nr. 25*, ed. Egon Praunegger and Christian Friedrich Hain (Graz, 1947), 59.
[19] In contrast to the Austrian distinction between two categories, "[West] German denazification legislation divided former National Socialists into five categories: 'Hauptschuldige,' 'Belastete,' 'Minderbelastete,' 'Mitläufer,' and 'Entlastete'." Garscha and Kuretsidis-Haider, 29 and 34.
[20] Artikel VI: Ausnahmebestimmungen, §27 (1) and (2), "Verfassungsgesetz vom 8. Mai 1945 über das Verbot der NSDAP," 63-4.
[21] I have borrowed sociologist Pierre Bourdieu's concept of *habitus* as "system of durable, transposable dispositions, structured structures predisposed to function as structuring structures, that is, as principles which generate and organize practices and representations that can be objectively adapted to their outcomes without presupposing a conscious aiming at ends or an express mastery of the operations necessary in order to attain them [...] The practical world that is constituted in relation with the *habitus*, acting as a system of cognitive and motivating structures, is a world of already realized ends—procedures to follow, paths to take. [...]" Pierre Bourdieu, *The Logic of Practice*, translated by Richard Nice (Stanford: Stanford University Press, 1990), 53. "The *habitus*," Bourdieu continues, "a product of history, produces individual and collective practices—more history—in accordance with the schemes generated by history. It ensures the active presence of past experiences, which, deposited in each organism in the form of schemes of perceptions, thought and action, tend to guarantee the 'correctness' of

practices and their constancy over time more reliably than all formal rules and explicit norms" (54).
Bourdieu himself states that "[T]hrough systematic 'choices' it makes among the places, events, and people that might be frequented, the *habitus* tends to protect itself from crises and critical challenges by providing itself with a milieu *to which it is as pre-adapted as possible*, that is, a relatively constant universe of situations tending to reinforce its dispositions [. . .]" (61, emphasis added). I am not convinced that subjective behavior never manifests itself within the realm of *habitus*, particularly when one examines historical contexts marked by unprecedented challenges, where the systematic choices do not provide security against the radically unfamiliar newness of a situation. One might consider, for example, choices between accommodation and resistance (active or subtle) that people find themselves making under circumstances of violent, repressive dictatorships.

[22] The central secretariat circulated a working directive on rehabilitation procedures for district and provincial party directorates in response to queries from former Social Democrats who had become "Parteianwärter, bzw. auch Mitglieder der NSDAP" and sought to join the SPÖ. VGA/NPA—Zentralsekretariat, Diverse Rundschreiben: Ref.Presse u. Propaganda, Mundfunk, Betriebsrat u.a. ab 1945, "Informationsdienst der Sozialistischen Partei Österreich Nr. 2 vom 29.Mai 1945 betr. Rehabilitierungsverfahren."

[23] VGA/NPA—Zentralsekretariat, Diverse Rundschreiben: Ref.Presse u. Propaganda, Mundfunk, Betriebsrat u.a. ab 1945, "Informationsdienst der Sozialistischen Partei Österreichs Nr. 2 vom 29.Mai 1945."

[24] VGA/NPA—Zentralsekretariat, Allg. Korrespondenzen: NS Rehabilitierungsansuchen, Bd. A - J. "Rehabilitierungsverfahren, 14 Juni 1945."

[25] For example, Johann Böhm, state secretary in the social affairs ministry, wrote to the SPÖ central secretariat to express his frustrations "that individual comrades are passing on to me requests from National Socialists with the unreasonable demand that I approve them. I maintain that this is not only nonsense, but also an absolute abuse [perpetrated by] party functionaries. [...] I would welcome if it were brought to the attention of district offices, that intervention for National Socialists is not reconcilable with the position of a party functionary, and must answered with a disciplinary hearing by a party review board. [...] Toleration of special actions by some functionaries can quickly lead to further abuses, and cannot be nipped in the bud quickly enough." VGA/NPA—Zentralsekretariat, Allg. Korrespondenzen, 1945, "Staatssekretär J. Böhm an dem VGA/NPA—Zentralsekretariat, Allg. Korrespondenzen, 1945, "Staatssekretär J. Böhm an das Parteisekretariat Wien I., 20. Juni 1945."

[26] See VGA/NPA—Zentralsekretariat, Allg. Korrespondenzen: NS Rehabilitierungsansuchen Bd. A - J: G. Peter (submitted 26 June 1945); Bd. R-Z: Hilde R. [date not available]; Ludwig H. (submitted without date prior to 19 July 1945), respectively.

[27] See VGA/NPA—Zentralsekretariat, Allg. Korrespondenzen: NS Rehabilitierungsansuchen Bd. A - J: Ignatz B., submitted 23 July 1945. B., a Linz *Schutzbund* member, took an active role in the 12 February 1934 fighting and later spent eighteen months in prison in connection with Revolutionary Socialist (RS) activities. He was arrested by the Gestapo in May 1938, and in September 1939 briefly incarcerated in an unnamed concentration camp. Konrad G. (submitted 12.6.1945) pointed to his engagement in a range of RS tasks from 1934/38 and was dogged by Nazis after *Anschluss* because of his democratic sentiments and previous underground activism. Bd. R - Z: Johann W.

(submitted 10 August 1945) had been a *Schutzbund* member in Vienna and fought on 12 February 1934, had to join VF to maintain his job with the municipal civil service, but was expelled for critical statements about regime; he became active in illegal RS cell distributing outlawed *Arbeiter-Zeitung* and flyers.

[28] These themes are elaborated upon in Hans Kernbauer and Fritz Weber, "Von der Inflation zur Depression: Österreichs Wirtschaft 1914-1938" and Siegfried Mattl, "Die Finanzdiktatur: Wirtschaftspolitik in Österreich 1933-1938" in *"Austrofaschismus"*, ed. Emmerich Tálos and Wolfgang Neugebauer, 1-30 and 133-59, respectively; Dieter Stiefel, *Arbeitslosigkeit. Soziale, politische und wirtschaftliche Auswirkungen am Beispiel Österreich 1918-1939* (Berlin: Dunker & Humblot, 1979); and Hans Kernbauer, Eduard März, and Fritz Weber, "Die wirtschaftliche Entwicklung" in *Österreich 1918-1938*, ed. Erika Weinzierl and Kurt Skalnik (Graz - Vienna - Cologne: Styria Verlag, 1983), I: 343-79.

[29] VGA/NPA—Zentralsekretariat, Allg. Korrespondenzen: NS Rehabilitierungsansuchen Bd. A - J: Julius D., submitted 24 May 1945; Wien I. *Bezirksprüfungsausschuss* [hereafter BPA] decision 11 June 1945, *Landesprüfungsausschuss* and *zentraler Prüfungsausschuss* [hereafter LPA and ZPA, respectively] rendered in late June (no precise date present). An amnesty did not actually enter into effect in March 1946, for the Allied Council rejected the draft version of the new National Socialist Law forwarded by the parliamentary representatives of the three Austrian political parties. Instead, a version of the new National Socialist Law satisfactory to the occupation powers entered into effect in early February 1947, and amnesties for youth and the less-implicated entered into effect in 1948.

[30] VGA/NPA—Zentralsekretariat, Allg. Korrespondenzen: NS Rehabilitierungsansuchen Bd. A - J: Rudolf G., submitted 11 June 1945.

[31] VGA/NPA—Zentralsekretariat, Allg. Korrespondenzen: NS Rehabilitierungsansuchen Bd. A - J: Ludwig H., submitted without date, but sometime before 19 July 1945.

[32] VGA/NPA—Zentralsekretariat, Allg. Korrespondenzen: NS Rehabilitierungsansuchen Bd. R - Z: Leopold S., submitted 7 June 1945.

[33] VGA/NPA—Zentralsekretariat, Allg. Korrespondenzen: NS Rehabilitierungsansuchen Bd. R - Z: Johann Sch., submitted 17 June 1945.

[34] VGA/NPA—Zentralsekretariat, Allg. Korrespondenzen: NS Rehabilitierungsansuchen Bd. R - Z: Leopold Sch., submitted 20 May 1945 (nine days before formal announcement of party-specific rehabilitation procedures).

[35] VGA/NPA—Zentralsekretariat, Allg. Korrespondenzen: NS Rehabilitierungsansuchen Bd. A - J: Henriette D., submitted 21 June 1945.

[36] VGA/NPA—Zentralsekretariat, Allg. Korrespondenzen: NS Rehabilitierungsansuchen Bd. A - J: Ignatz B., submitted 17 July 1945.

[37] VGA/NPA—Zentralsekretariat, Allg. Korrespondenzen: NS Rehabilitierungsansuchen Bd. A - J: Theodor K., submitted 5 July 1945.

[38] VGA/NPA—Zentralsekretariat, Allg. Korrespondenzen: NS Rehabilitierungsansuchen Bd. A - J: Peter G., submitted 26 June 1945.

[39] VGA/NPA—Zentralsekretariat, Allg. Korrespondenzen: NS Rehabilitierungsansuchen Bd. K - Q: Hertha and Alfred M., submitted 18 June 1945. In contrast, consider the case of Johann K., whose application met with BPA support but LPA and ZPA rejection. A Viennese social democrat since 1923, K. jumped on the Nazi bandwagon in 1938 and gained party membership in 1939. Although he became a *Blockleiter* ("under

pressure"), K.'s smoldering anger seems to have been directed much more clearly against former VF personalities than against the Nazis—and much of this may have stemmed from his inability to understand that Nazi and social democratic principles were incompatible. Witness statements confirm that he was arrested and condemned to twenty years' imprisonment for his role as a *Schutzbund* company commander in the February 12th events, an understandable reason that he would detest the indigenous fascist system. K. provided affidavits that he never behaved like a Nazi or drew any advantage from his party membership, and stated that his thoughts and actions were always consistent with social democratic principles. As evidence for the latter assertion, K. included with his rehabilitation request a letter to his NSDAP *Ortsgruppe* from 26 April 1940, in which he denounced two former *Heimwehr* men—but "with Heil Hitler" as his closing salutation. The BPA urged that K. be rehabilitated; the LPA and ZPA refused on the grounds of absence of both compelling reasons for having joined the NSDAP and proof of antifascist activity. VGA/NPA—Zentralsekretariat, Allg. Korrespondenzen. NS Rehabilitierungsansuchen Bd. K - Q: Hans K., submitted 13 July 1945.

[40] VGA/NPA—Zentralsekretariat, Allg. Korrespondenzen: NS Rehabilitierungsansuchen Bd. K - Q: Rudolf K., submitted 12 June 1945.

[41] Helmut Konrad, "Das Werben der NSDAP um die Sozialdemokraten 1933-1938" in *Arbeiterschaft in Nationalsozialismus in Deutschland*, 81. See also Wolfgang Neugebauer, "Die Folgen des Februar 1934: die österreichische Arbeiterbewegung in der Illegalität," in *Februar 1934. Ursachen—Fakten—Folgen*, 369ff.

[42] On the Revolutionary Socialists under the VF regime, see Peter Pelinka, *Erbe und Neubeginn. Die Revolutionäre Sozialisten in Österreich 1934-1938* (Vienna: Europaverlag, 1981) and Marschalek, *Untergrund und Exil.* On the dynamics of the clerical-authoritarian regime, consult Emmerich Tálos and Wolfgang Neugebauer ed., *"Austrofaschismus": Beiträge über Politik, Ökonomie nd Kultur 1934-1938, 4., ergänzte Auflage* (Vienna: Verlag für Gesellschaftskritik, 1988) and Ulrich Kluge, *Der österreichische Ständestaat, 1934-1938: Entstehung und Scheitern* (Vienna: Verlag für Geschichte und Politik, 1984).

[43] Konrad, 85.

[44] On antisemitism among the Austrian proletariat and throughout much of Austrian society, see Peter Pulzer, *The Rise of Political Anti-Semitism in Germany and Austria* (Cambridge, MA: Harvard University Press, 1988); Pauley, *From Prejudice to Persecution*; John Bunzl and Bernd Marin, *Antisemitismus in Österreich. Sozialhistorische und soziologische Studien* (Innsbruck: Inn-Verlag, 1982); and Gerhard Botz, Ivar Oxaal, and Michael Pollak ed., *Jews, Anti-Semitism and Culture in Vienna* (London and New York: Routledge & Kegan Paul, 1987). See also Bruno Kreisky's description of antisemitism, even during the crisis of February 1934 in Matthew Paul Berg et al. ed., *The Struggle for a Democratic Austria: Bruno Kreisky on Peace and Social Justice* (New York and Oxford: Berghahn Books, 2000), 110.

[45] Hans Schafranek, "NSDAP und Sozialisten nach dem Februar 1934" in *Arbeiterschaft und Nationalsozialismus in Österreich*, 93. Emphasis added. A similar observation might be made for young revolutionary socialists who turned to the communist camp, but this point does not concern us here. For more on this theme, see Franz West, *Die Linke im Ständestaat Österreich. Revolutionäre Sozialisten und Kommunisten 1934-1938* (Vienna: Europa Verlag, 1978).

[46] Schafranek, 108-113.

[47] VGA/NPA—Zentralsekretariat, Allg. Korrespondenzen: NS Rehabilitierungsansuchen Bd. K - Q: Anton G., submitted 20 June 1945.

[48] VGA/NPA—Zentralsekretariat, Allg. Korrespondenzen: NS Rehabilitierungsansuchen Bd. K - Q: Karl K., submitted 30 May 1945.

[49] VGA/NPA—Zentralsekretariat, Allg. Korrespondenzen: NS Rehabilitierungsansuchen Bd. K - Q: Franz L., submitted 18 October 1945.

[50] VGA/NPA—Zentralsekretariat, Allg. Korrespondenzen: NS Rehabilitierungsansuchen Bd. R - Z: Otto T., submitted 19 May 1945, ca. one week before the SPÖ announcement concerning procedures to handle rehabilitation requests.

[51] VGA/NPA—Zentralsekretariat, Allg. Korrespondenzen: NS Rehabilitierungsansuchen Bd. R - Z: Franziska T., submitted 10 June 1945.

[52] VGA/NPA—Zentralsekretariat, Allg. Korrespondenzen: NS Rehabilitierungsansuchen Bd. A - J: Heinrich H., submitted 13 June 1945.

[53] VGA/NPA—Zentralsekretariat, Allg. Korrespondenzen: NS Rehabilitierungsansuchen Bd. K - Q: Richard L., submitted 14 June 1945.

[54] VGA/NPA—Zentralsekretariat, Allg. Korrespondenzen: NS Rehabilitierungsansuchen Bd. A - J: Alfred H., submitted 20 May 1945.

[55] VGA/NPA—Ansuchen um Nachsicht der Sühnefolgen April 1947-April 1948, "Rundschreiben an alle Landesparteivorstände"(undated, probably late February/early March 1947). See also *Verbotsgesetz 1947 StF StGBl. Nr. 13/1945 idF.: BGBl. Nr. 148/1992*, www.dagegenhalten.at/files/Verbotsgesetz/pdf.

[56] VGA/NPA—Ansuchen um Nachsicht der Sühnefolgen April 1947-April 1948, "Rundschreiben an alle Landesparteivorstände". Emphasis in the original.

[57] It stands to reason that the ÖVP and KPÖ were also involved in reviewing and processing exemption requests, yet analysis of how these two parties proceeded falls outside the scope of this study.

[58] Stiefel, Table "Übersicht der 1947 registrierten Nationalsozialisten nach Beruf," 220.

[59] Ibid., Table "Prozentsatz der Minderbelasteten im öffentlichen Dienst nach Dienststellen, " 140.

[60] Sten.Prot.NR, 97. *Sitzung*, 18 July 1952, 3885. Migsch also referred to the 1947 *Nationalsozialistengesetz* as an "Allied law" in reference to the occupation powers' opposition to the 1946 modification of the *Verbotsgesetz* agreed upon by the three Austrian political parties.

[61] BGBl. 82/57, 24. Stück. "Bundesverfassungsgesetz vom 14. März 1957 womit Bestimmungen des Nationalsozialistengesetzes, BGBl. Nr. 25/1947, abgeändert oder aufgehoben werden (NS-Amnestie 1957)."

Fighting Antisemitism—Democratizing Society? Reflections on Germany's Rocky Path Towards a Civil Society After the Second World War

Christoph Jahr

In his famous essay "The Jews and Europe," Max Horkheimer made the assumption that whoever prefers not to talk about capitalism should also remain silent on fascism. This essay contends that whoever talks of re-democratization after the fall of a fascist regime cannot remain silent on the struggle against antisemitism.[1] That was the case for every country in Europe after 1945, but all the more so in Germany. Xenophobia, racism, and discrimination against minorities have been features of all fascist regimes, yet annihilatory antisemitism remained a hallmark of National Socialism alone.[2] For this reason, the western Allies considered the future attitude of the Germans towards the Jews and their stance on antisemitism to be the true "touchstone of democracy"[3]. Since antisemitism was *the* key element of Nazi ideology, its renunciation was an obvious objective for the re-democratization of Germany. Therefore, any form of public antisemitism was to be banned politically, ideologically, culturally, and *legally*—despite the fact that an undercurrent of anti-Jewish bias could be found within the societies of each victorious power.

Changing legal statutes might be straightforward enough, but enforcing anti-discriminatory legislation and changing popular attitudes is a process likely to take years, if not decades. This essay examines the relationship between politics and law from the immediate postwar period to approximately 1960 in order to assess the evolution of legal norms counter to antisemitism and their implications for the creation of a democratic German political culture. Recent historical research has emphasized the significance of the 1960s as an incubation phase for that far-reaching liberalization of West German society commonly associated with "1968."[4] This process reached the judicial system too, its built-in conservatism notwithstanding[5]; thus, this essay also aims to contribute to a greater understanding of the immediate pre-history to changes initiated by the events of 1968, particularly the role of the Cold War. Although I focus on the western occupied zones and the Federal Republic, I will also briefly touch on the debate regarding anti-discrimination articles in the constitution and in the legislation of the Soviet zone of occupation.

Learning from Defeat . . . or Debating the Lessons of Weimar

"Democratization" is a complex, multifaceted, sometimes linear, haphazard, and tenuous process that is potentially reversible and sometimes contradictory. While the debate within the realm of political science literature is rich and diverse, historical research on this issue has lagged considerably. The paradigm of modernization, characterized by unavoidable teleological implications, tends to persist as the dominant model for understanding historical development. The same must be said about the nation-state as frame of reference. A careful comparative European perspective might provide fresh insights and would allow for identifying similarities, common features and parallel developments as well as fragmentation, discontinuity and historical specificity.[6] At first glance, the emergence of democracy in Europe since the beginning of the nineteenth century, in theory and in practice, has led many historians to posit the hypothesis of a halting but nevertheless inexorable process.[7] Yet after the German military successes of 1938–40 and the defeat or intimidation of most remaining democracies, this form of government no longer appeared to have a future in continental Europe. Therefore, it would be wishful thinking to present the post-1945 regimes as the culmination of progressive democratization; indeed, Martin Conway convincingly concludes that postwar democracy in Europe "seems to have been a product more of a rupture than of a gradual evolution."[8] At the same time, the process of democratization in the late 1940s and 1950s was, to a large extent, introduced externally by the United States. This fact is most obvious in the case of Germany (and, to a lesser extent, Austria) but even there this evolution built upon democratic traditions and the remnants of civil society that had survived fascism.

From this perspective developments in Germany did not diverge as significantly from those in other western European countries as one might have expected. The lack of a culture of active and participatory citizenship, the absence of effective purges directed against those tainted by a fascist or collaborationist past, or the state-enforced marginalization of Communist political activity could be identified as common western European features during the first two postwar decades.

Hitler's rise to power initiated intense deliberations among scholars, politicians, and journalists about the political and constitutional causes of the Weimar Republic's collapse. It was a widely held view that the lack of determination to defend democracy against its left- and right-wing enemies contributed decisively to the catastrophe of 1933.[9] Although the impact of exile discourse should not be overestimated; however, one might recall that the model of "militant democracy" (*wehrhafte Demokratie*)—considered the answer to the "totalitarian challenge"—had been conceptualized by German immigrants to Great Britain and the United States. As early as 1937, legal scholar Karl Loewenstein had published his article "Militant Democracy and Fundamental Rights" in the influential *American Political Science Review*. He voiced confidence that democracy's "legalistic self-complacency and suicidal lethargy" had given way "to a better grasp of realities." [10] One of these realities was the fact that the fascist challenge had to be understood as a "virtual state of siege" against European democracies. "If democracy believes in the superiority of its absolute values over the opportunistic platitudes of fascism," Loewenstein continued, "every possible effort must be made to rescue it, even at the risk and cost of violating fundamental principles."[11] In a public lecture in Oxford four years later, sociologist Karl Mannheim blamed "laissez-faire liberalism" for mistaking "neutrality for tolerance." Instead, he insisted, supporters of democracy should not refrain from taking a stand in support of what they held as their highest principles. "Our democracy has to become militant if it is to survive," Mannheim concluded, but "only in the defense of the agreed right procedure of social change and those basic virtues and values [...] which are acceptable to everybody who shares the tradition of Western civilization."[12]

While it would be naive to designate the Second World War as a "crusade for democracy," the establishment of regimes compatible with the values and interests of the United Kingdom and the USA was nevertheless one of the Western Allies' war aims enshrined in the Atlantic Charter. This was discussed in programs for re-democratizing Germany and for briefing British and American officers for their future tasks as occupation authorities. However, it was only after victory had been achieved that a systematic focus on re-democratization crystallized in the form of the "Long-Range Policy Statement on German Reeducation" drafted in summer 1945. This document, which included "primary principles of justice" and emphatically stated "toleration between diverse cultural and racial groups is the basis of national and international tranquillity," served as a kind of blueprint for West Germany's Basic Law in 1949.[13] Moreover, despite the segregationist practice in the United States, the repression of Nazi racism loomed large in the plans for re-education; even comic strips like "There are no Master Races" by Ruth Benedict and Gene Weltfish from Columbia University in 1944 were used for this purpose.[14]

From Theory to Practice: The Western Zones of Occupation and the Early Federal Republic

The Nazi regime lost the war in 1945, but National Socialists—and Jewish survivors of the Third Reich's genocidal policies—remained, and the shock caused by the confrontation with the Nazi atrocities following the liberation of the concentration camps did not last long.[15] Reproaches against antisemitic prejudices and pleas such as Gustav Radbruch's 1947 demand for a "return to humanity"—which took place under the most varied conditions in eastern and western occupation zones— was part of a slow process, full of inconsistencies.[16] Antisemitism reasserted itself—most vigorously in Bavaria where a temporary exceptional concentration of Jews attracted the attention of agitators.[17] For example, rumours of an alleged "ritual murder" case spread through the northeastern Bavaria town of Weiden in April 1947; in 1948 a wave of desecrations of Jewish cemeteries spread through Franconia and various other parts of Germany.[18] It was less the tiny remnant of indigenous Jews than the predominantly eastern European "Displaced Persons" (DPs), against whom antisemites directed their sentiment. Agitators could point out that the Jewish population in some parts of Germany was far more numerous in 1946 than it had been when the Nazis seized power—up to 230,000 Jewish DPs resided in Germany, about 100,000 of them in makeshift camps in Munich and the surrounding countryside.[19] Consistent with ancient and more recent anti-Jewish stereotypes, these people were demonized as "racketeers," "black market hyenas," and "sources of infection"; occasionally incidents of antisemitic violence surfaced too.[20] Such sentiments were not confined to either Bavaria or western Germany, however. In the Soviet occupation zone, rumours and semi-official newspaper reports created an atmosphere in which anti-Jewish sentiments could and often did flourish, especially after Stalin's anti-Zionistic about-face.[21]

Sensational incidents such as those described above, while far from pervasive when compared with the Nazi era, nonetheless suggested a more widespread ambivalence towards Jews. Indeed, surveys carried out by the American Military Government revealed that even after the horrors of the Holocaust, forty percent of Germans harbored strong antisemitic sentiments.[22] In fact, as early as 1946 an American observer had noticed a new form of antisemitism alongside the persistence of older forms: "The Jews now in Germany [...] are the *corpus delicti* [...]. As long as the Germans lack the moral courage to accept the consequences of the Nazi crimes against the Jews, they will seek to banish the accuser and they will denounce him as a disturber of their peace."[23] This "secondary" antisemitism distinguished itself from other forms insofar as it responded to genocide with denial of guilt; it has since emerged in many countries even without the actual presence of a considerable number of Jews, is no longer asserted primarily on the basis of "racial theories," and—since the foundation of the state of Israel—frequently assumes the mask of anti-Zionism.[24]

Under these circumstances the eradication of antisemitism was not at an easy task. On the one hand, we have explored the persistence of antisemitic stereotypes; on the other hand, the Allied Control Council sought to establish "anti-antisemitic" norms through the annulment or alteration of Nazi legislation.[25] At the Potsdam Conference, "all Nazi laws which provided the basis of the Hitler regime or established discriminations on grounds of race, creed, or political opinion" were abolished. Furthermore, the judicial system was to be "reorganized in accordance with the principles of democracy, of justice under law, and of equal rights for all citizens without distinction of race, nationality or religion."[26] Historian Frank Stern has argued that Allied policy towards Jewish DPs and measures to contain antisemitism amounted to what some Germans perceived as an "ordained philosemitism"—which, in turn, served to further arouse those inclined towards antisemitism.[27] Yet the efficacy of the principles agreed upon at the Potsdam Conference required enforcement at the regional level if they were to be effective; initiatives in the Western zones turned out be somewhat more far-reaching, at least on paper. For example, Baden, Bavaria, and Rhineland-Palatinate each contained articles in their constitutions that expressly forbade "incitement to racial hatred" and made doing so a punishable offence.[28] The provisional constitution of Greater Berlin from August 1946 did not include such an article, but the SPD draft constitution of September 1947 explicitly denied the right to free expression of opinion to all those who "pursue National Socialist or militaristic aims"[29]; Social Democrats justified this position with the argument that enemies of democracy should not be able to exploit basic rights in order to "undermine democracy again. These rights must be denied to all reactionary, military and anti-democratic forces."[30] The constitution of September 1950, which was valid only for the western sectors of Berlin, designated "incitement to racial hatred" as a contradiction of "the spirit of the constitution," as well as the "expression of national or religious hatred," as punishable offences.[31]

Bavaria occupied a special position due to "Law Number 14 against Racial Fanaticism and Hatred of Other Peoples" (*Gesetz Nr. 14 gegen Rassenwahn und Völkerhaß*) of 13 March 1946, which was enacted to prosecute antisemitic comments. This law had been in effect some nine months before the Bavarian constitution's ratification. Efforts to pass a "Law for the Protection of Democratic Freedom" (*Gesetz zum Schutz der demokratischen Freiheit*) in Hessen—which would have incriminated violent assaults or public insults directed against communities defined by race, creed, or political affiliation—ultimately failed.[32] The West German Basic Law later guaranteed equality before the law regardless of gender, descent, race, or religion (Article 3.3) but did not explicitly incriminate "incitement to racial hatred".[33] The Basic Law also made provisions for safeguarding the democratic order against any form of political radicalism. Carlo Schmid, a leading SPD-participant of the Herrenchiemsee Constitutional Convention (*Verfassungskonvent*) characterized these arrangements as lessons drawn from the fate of the Weimar Republic. "It is not constitutive for the idea of democracy", he insisted, "that it caters for its abolition."[34] The extent to which such deliberations concerning the shortcomings of the first German democracy match with reality is open to question, however; none of the alleged "lessons of Weimar" have ever been applied seriously in the history of the Federal Republic.[35]

The political parties also included passages in their programs, in which the fight against the dissemination of "racial hatred" was proclaimed. Nonetheless, they often refrained from making any explicit reference to antisemitism. That was clearly illustrated in the case of the conservative Bavarian Christian Social Union (*Christlich Soziale Union*, CSU). In October 1946 a draft of the party platform was proposed that included a paragraph proclaiming the CSU's determination to "reject forcefully every form of racial hatred, and especially antisemitism, as a disgraceful relapse into a bygone age of barbarism." But this unambiguous declaration went too far for the party hierarchy. In the end, any explicit reference to antisemitism was omitted, and the clause adopted was phrased in more general language—i.e., a rejection of "every form of racial hatred." A CSU pamphlet that detailed the party's "thirty point program" returned to the original phrase and included a section which condemned antisemitism as "directed against the origins and essence of Christianity."[36]

The Social Democrats were more outspoken on the matter of antisemitism, however. For example, party leader Kurt Schumacher declared at the Nuremberg Party Conference in summer 1947 that it was the task of the SPD not only to support the indemnification and reimbursement of the Jews, but also a ban on all antisemitic propaganda.[37] The above-mentioned motion in the Hessen assembly for a "Law for the Protection of Democratic Freedom" and later in the *Bundestag* for a "Law Against the Enemies of Democracy" were also drafted and advanced by the SPD.

The German Basic Law mandates that political parties observe democratic principles. Parties unwilling to play by these rules risk a ban. Contrary to the common perception of fecklessness, the Weimar Republic prohibited political parties in almost 200 cases. Based on the "Law for the Protection of the Republic" (*Gesetz zum Schutz der Republik*), responsibility for this procedure resided with the respective States. During the course of the interwar republic, Prussia banned twenty-nine, mainly right-wing, parties and associations; Bavaria refrained from taking such action.[38] By contrast, the Federal Republic can ban political parties through the Federal Constitutional Court. This was done for the first time in October 1952 in the case of the radical right-wing and antisemitic Socialist Reich Party (*Sozialistische Reichspartei*, SRP)."[39] This Supreme Court ruling conceptualized the idea of a "liberal-democratic constitutional order" (*freiheitlich demokratische Grundordnung*), not established in the Basic Law itself. In 1956 the Federal Constitutional Court outlawed the Communist Party of Germany (*Kommunistische Partei Deutschlands*, KPD). Although bans on political parties were taken into consideration in subsequent years, they were no longer proposed on the federal level—that is, until the request for proceedings against the NPD initiated by the federal government on 30 January 2001 and which failed in March 2003.[40] The fact that bans on extremist political parties in the 1950s targeted both far left and far right wing reveals that the government's concern was not merely a question of addressing potential dangers to the democratic order, but also a case of demonstrating and symbolically consolidating an official anti-totalitarian consensus and translating the model of "militant" or "well-fortified democracy" into judicially manageable forms.

The overarching significance of the Cold War in general—and the rivalry between East and West Germany in particular—introduced a significant new level of complexity into efforts to legislatively create and judicially ensure a reliable democratic consensus. The following, representative cases richly illustrate the point. Instigated by a scandal surrounding the right-wing *Bundestag* deputy Wolfgang Hedler, the SPD submitted a draft "Law Against Enemies of Democracy" (*Gesetz gegen die Feinde der Demokratie*) to the *Bundestag* in February 1950. According to §9.1, assaults on communities shaped by "race, creed, or world view" or on any of their members "by violating their human dignity"[41] were made punishable offences. Although all parties (except one on the far right) signalled their agreement *in principle* to defend the democratic order, the idea that penal law could be an appropriate means to that end met with determined opposition from the government coalition. One deputy from the "Bavarian Party" (*Bayernpartei*) even went so far as to denounce the bill as "being in line with the 'Malicious Practices Law'" of 1934.[42] The law was ultimately rejected in the *Bundestag*; however, Chancellor Konrad Adenauer's conservative coalition government soon proposed amendments to the penal code that incorporated substantial parts of the SPD draft. The government bill included an intensification of §130 concerning incitement to class hatred. By substituting "a class of society" (*Klasse der Bevölkerung*) with "section of society (*Bevölkerungsgruppe*) constituted by common descent, religion, or world view," the criminalization of antisemitic agitation would have been accomplished swiftly.[43] This time it was the SPD who rejected the idea that "liberty should be sacrificed in order to secure it" and KPD deputy Hugo Paul warned of the unpleasant memories of the "Malicious Practices Law."[44]

Discussion of alteration to §130 virtually vanished from the political agenda for an entire decade with outbreak of hostilities on the Korean peninsula and a new surge of anti-communist sentiment in West Germany that accompanied it.[45] Perceived threats from the Soviet Union and its Eastern European satellite states elicited far more attention than the activities of unrepentant Nazis or new radical rightists. West German politicians tended to attribute the persistence of antisemitism manifestations during the 1950s as communist agitation, and placed particular blame on the East German government for manipulating such incidents in order to damage the Federal Republic's reputation abroad. In 1959, for example, Wilhelm Probst, *Bundestag* deputy of the conservative "German Party" (*Deutsche Partei*, DP) shifted the responsibility for antisemitic incidents on to obstinate outsiders or to "agents provocateurs employed by instigators in the bolshevist Zone of occupation."[46] Chancellor Adenauer equally made it clear that "whatever happens there is conducted by Communists in order to spread the rumor worldwide that the Germans are still Nazis."[47] The same conclusions were drawn vis-à-vis a wave of desecrations of synagogues and Jewish cemeteries originating in Cologne during 1959/60, although the government never succeeded in providing compelling evidence to sustain these assumptions.[48]

On the whole, the Cold War had contradictory influences on West Germany during the 1950s. On the one hand it boosted an anti-totalitarian consensus and helped to stabilize the new political order; on the other it promoted a process of democratization that was still centered around the State[49] and made relatively little reference to Germany's antisemitic past or its lingering presence in the

Federal Republic. This contradiction allowed for a particular form of criticism of West Germany's political culture, namely that semi-authoritarian structures had been restored, but were acceptably presented as a form of "militant democracy"—a price most West Germans willingly paid for political stability.[50] Indeed, certain personnel and institutional continuities in the administration of justice between the Adenauer government and the Nazi era played successfully into the hands of East German propaganda.[51] The Federal Republic as a "refuge for old Nazis" was an oft-repeated reference in East German efforts to discredit West Germany; it also contributed to rationalization for ignoring the German Democratic Republic's own not entirely vigilant attitude towards the Nazi legacy. Although not all GDR criticisms proved accurate, some resonated significantly enough to serve as a source of irritation or embarrassment; there were too many examples of influential ex-Nazis, not all of them as prominent as individuals such as Hans Globke and Theodor Oberländer, in federal or state administrations whose successful political careers—unconstrained by dubious conduct during the Nazi regime—cast a shadow on the West German government's determination to fight antisemitism[52] "As long as notorious Nazis like Globke and Oberländer remain as ministers in Adenauer's cabinet," an American Zionist newspaper stated, "the Chancellor's cries of horror at burgeoning neo-Nazism must be taken with several grains of salt."[53]

In addition to constitutional safeguards, several other mechanisms were established to protect the new democratic order during the Federal Republic's early years, not least of which was the creation of a federal intelligence service. The Federal Agency for the Protection of the Constitution (*Bundesamt für Verfassungsschutz*) was established officially in 1950, but its origins can be traced to 1947 and linked to concerns about the reorganization of radical right-wing groups in the British zone and the re-animation of antisemitism.[54] The Agency's responsibility is to monitor the activities of associations and political parties both on the right and the left fringes whose activities are directed against a free and democratic order. Over the following years, West German authorities established other institutions to contain malicious agitation, such as the Federal Investigative Office for Publications Endangering Youth (*Bundesprüfstelle für jugendgefährdende Schriften*) established in 1954. This institution worked on the basis of legislation that established standards for print material judged to be "indecent, brutalizing, likely to incite violence, criminal acts or racial hatred, as well as writings glorifying war."[55] It is worth noting that neo-Nazi and antisemitic writings were rarely forbidden in the 1950s, as the Federal Investigative Office placed a premium on heightened vigilance directed against "sexually obscene and offensive literature" and comic books.[56] A complimentary agency working in the area of film supervision, the Voluntary Self-Regulation of Film Industry (*Freiwillige Selbstkontrolle der Filmwirtschaft*, FSK), had already been established in 1949, and saw its task as combating productions that exhibited traces of "anti-democratic (National Socialistic, Bolshevik etc.), militarist, imperialist, nationalist, or racial baiting" sentiment.[57]

Scandalizing Antisemitism

The good intentions of judicial or constitutional considerations or the establishment of new agencies of censorship, education and enlightenment notwithstanding, it was the embarrassment of antisemitic scandals that played perhaps the most significant role in the reinforcement of new democratic norms.[58] One of the earliest examples was the scandal that emerged when the liberal *Süddeutsche Zeitung* published an antisemitic letter to the editor with the pseudonym "Adolf Bleibtreu" in August 1949.[59] Referring to the above-noted "Law against Racial Fanaticism and Hatred of other Peoples" the Bavarian Association of the Federal Jewish Religious Community Association lodged a complaint against the two responsible editors. However, the State Prosecutor pushed for acquittal in this case because he saw no evidence of pro-Nazi propaganda.

Positions that still shape the contours of debate concerning the handling of publicly expressions of antisemitism were already apparent in this case. On the one side stood those in favor of suppressing such remarks; they based their argument on references to the negative consequences for West German foreign relations and the temperamental nature of the population on the basis of their uncertain democratic and anti-Nazi views. Werner Friedmann, publisher of the *Süddeutsche Zeitung* made it clear that he was not happy with his editors' decision. Such an "inhumane document" like the Bleibtreu letter should not have been published, he argued, since "we Germans are in a glass house, surveyed by an outside world that is not friendly towards us."[60] The editors responsible for publication of the letter emphasized the importance of a new climate in West Germany, rather than continuity with National Socialist sentiments, one in which Germans should be able to endure antisemitic remarks without accepting them. This new, free and democratic order ran the risk of undermining itself for prosecuting people on the basis of their convictions rather than their actions; thus, instead of stifling the expression of antisemitism, persuasive debate its proponents would unmask the primitiveness and absurdity of their thinking and provide an important public-pedagogic opportunity. Consequently, the *SZ* editors justified the uncensored publication of the Bleibtreu letter, arguing that the newspaper did not want to "falsify the reactions of the public" towards antisemitic expression, for "a tactic of hushing up or calming [reality] can never be the right way to fight antisemitism."[61]

But the astounding success story of the Federal Republic—which despite manifold continuities with the Third Reich became a stable democracy where extreme right-wing and openly antisemitic parties had no lasting success—cannot be explained sufficiently by merely focusing on legislative changes. The fact that antisemitic incidents after 1945 elicited shock, particularly when compared to the Weimar Republic, appears to be of no small importance. Let us consider the legal proceedings surrounding the Nazi propaganda filmmaker Veit Harlan, director of the infamous "Jud Süß" lauded by Goebbels as "an antisemitic film exactly as we could wish for."[62] Harlan was charged with "crimes against humanity" under Allied Control Council Law No. 10 in 1948/49, but acquitted by a West German jury and finally by an appeals court in 1950. The Harlan case reveals a broader trend in which court judgements can generally be characterized as ignorant or indifferent to the targets/victims of antisemitic agitation (rather similar to traditions of the Reich Court during the Weimar Republic). On the other hand, small but increasingly vocal and incrementally larger segments of the population mobilized for public protests against such judgments. For example, in 1949 the above-mentioned Wolfgang Hedler, a *Bundestag* deputy for the *Deutsche Partei* delivered an antisemitic speech at a party convention. He was charged with libel and instigation to hatred but acquitted in February 1950.[63] The decision drew some 10,000 protesters to rally in Kiel.[64] Two years later students represented themselves prominently at protest rallies directed against Veit Harlan.[65] Incidents such as these suggest that long before 1968 West Germans were beginning to establish the foundations for a more wide-ranging dispute about the Nazi past that a) put an end to the practice of "communicative silencing,"[66] and b) also paved the way for the emergence of a civil society with a greater sense of ownership and responsibility in a democratic process that had previously been considered primarily a concern of the State. All the same, we must recognize that this process was certainly not linear. While the Federal Republic's history has included occasional, intense debates on the Nazi past in general and antisemitism in particular, the years from 1949/50 to 1958 must be characterized as a time of stagnation, perhaps even retrogression—the above-mentioned examples of civic protests against antisemitic scandals notwithstanding. The results of public opinion polls can illustrate this fact quite clearly. In 1949 a mere forty-one percent of the Germans were in favor of harsh punishment for antisemitic remarks; in 1958 this figure had risen to just fifty percent, while it skyrocketed to eighty-two percent by 1960 and has remained this high ever since.[67]

One final judicial development also deserves attention in this respect, a court ruling dealing with the Nazi past that turned out to be an important milestone in the emergence of the Federal Republic's *Verfassungsgerichtsbarkeit* (Supreme Court Ruling). The so-called "Lüth-Urteil" ruled by the Federal Constitutional Court (*Bundesverfassungsgericht*) in 1959, in a case once again connected with film director Veit Harlan paved the way for antidiscrimination legislation.[68]

The Supreme Court acknowledged that the principles of a liberal-democratic society enshrined in the constitution are binding not only in the relationship between state and citizens, but also for the mutual interaction of the citizens ("horizontal effect of fundamental rights," or *Drittwirkung der Grundrechte*). This kind of legislation would have been unthinkable in the decades before and not merely promoted, but placed a premium on the state's ability to enforce equality of rights granted in the Basic Law a decade earlier. But it is not only in this respect that the years around 1960 appear to be a turning point in the history of (West) Germany's attitude towards democracy and antisemitism. It took a decade or so before the idea gained ground that antisemitism is not just an assault on a minority but a blow against democracy itself, an assault on the very basis of a pluralistic society. When rationalizing the proposed amendment to Section 130 of the penal code, Federal Minister of Justice Fritz Schäffer stated that it was the task of the penal law "to establish highly visible signs of value (*weithin sichtbare Werttafeln*)." At the same time he acknowledged pluralism to be a "usually very healthy and welcome reality"[69]. SPD *Bundestag* deputy Karl Wittrock justified his "no" to the amendment by saying that "the state cannot achieve through a law what society itself ought to do. [...] he who infringes upon the principles of society must be disqualified morally."[70] A 1960 commentary on the alteration made to Section 130 in a legal journal also manifested this change of mentality insofar as it stated that antisemitic propaganda is "directed against the Federal Republic's liberal-democratic constitutional order."[71]

Same People, Different Path: The Soviet Occupation Zone

The halting developments toward a greater appreciation for democracy and rejection of antisemitism we have explored in West Germany were denied to those living in the Soviet-occupied zone. Nonetheless, discussion of anti-discrimination laws did take place in 1947/48 and the articles of the constitution provided protection against "racial hatred." In various East German state constitutions, bans on "incitement to racial hatred" were firmly established. For example, in 1947, the state parliament in Saxony-Anhalt passed a "Law for Safeguarding Democracy". In Article IV, slander or damaging of body or health of human beings on the basis of their "membership of a particular religious community, race, nation or [...] because of their status as a victim of fascism"[72] was instituted. At a state conference in March 1948, the "German Central Administration for Justice" (*Deutsche Zentralverwaltung für Justiz*, DJV—the precursor of the GDR's Ministry of Justice) nevertheless indicated that it was not in favor of the state laws for the protection of democracy—not least because this "state particularism" was an obstacle to the claim of the DJV to central regulation.[73] The DJV foiled further state laws, although in the first eight months of 1949, 132 different legal proceedings leading to 112 convictions were instituted in Saxony-Anhalt alone.[74]

Still, the question of legal measures against radical right-wing propaganda as part of the larger debate over central authority vs. states' legal authority remained a bitter one. In June 1948, the Saxon Minister of Justice, Johannes Dieckmann, sent the first draft of a "Law Against the Expression of National, Religious, and Racial Hatred" (*Gesetz gegen die Bekundung von Völker-, Glaubens- und Rassenhaß*) to the DJV; this draft was followed in mid-July by a slightly revised document, which was presented to the DJV as the basis for a regulation which would be uniform in all zones.[75] In this Saxon draft law, the explicit linkage of an anti-discrimination rule to an article of the constitution—i.e., the implicitly held view that concrete legal instructions that are binding on the legislature follow from constitutional regulations—was new. Reactions to this Saxon draft differed considerable after the DJV circulated it to the justice ministries of other East German regions for commentary. Whereas the state of Mecklenburg signalled its agreement,[76] the Thuringian Ministry of Justice warned of "unpleasant memories of earlier practices" during National Socialism and of the danger of a criminal law that prosecutes convictions rather than actions. Max Fechner, the new Chief of the DJV following the resignation of Eugen Schiffer, balanced out the comments of the state governments to the effect that "some day a law must be created through which the protection extended by criminal law in both the new democratic institutions and democratic values is guaranteed," although he didn't think the right moment had yet come. Although almost all comments from the states had criticized the general, preventative character of the Saxon draft, Fechner wanted to go even further on this very point: one should "not be content with the comparatively narrowly defined facts of the case, as taken as a basis for the Saxon draft," but "regulate the entire matter of the protection of democracy in a self-contained law [...]. However, such a law requires a thorough preliminary examination, not only with respect to legal considerations, but also to the political."[77] Fechner had clearly stated thereby that for him the political aspects of law as decided by the Socialist Unity Party (*Sozialistische Einheitspartei Deutschlands*, SED), took precedence over all other considerations. The DJV stuck to its dilatory approach, so that a special law against the dissemination of racial hatred in the Soviet occupied zone ultimately did not come about.[78]

The fact that the balance sheet for the Soviet occupied zone turned out so negatively may not be a surprise. It is nevertheless worth mentioning that until 1948, judicial and constitutional measures against antisemitic agitation could be discussed rather openly. Only in 1948/49 was the judiciary in the Soviet occupied zone subordinated to the dictatorial claims of the SED leadership and "Sovietized"; this put an end to all federal *Sonderwege*.[79] At no time, however, were the representatives of the Jewish community involved in deliberations on legal and constitutional protection against antisemitism. Only after an inquiry from the Dresden community did they receive substantial information about the Saxon draft by Justice Minister Dieckmann in December 1948. The Association of Jewish Communities in the Russian Zone of Occupation (*Landesverband der jüdischen Gemeinden in der Russischen Okkupationszone*) had voiced its appreciation of a uniform law based on the Saxon draft, because "this would be the most efficient and most radical way to eradicate antisemitism." The DJV, however, did not consider this petition seriously.[80]

Conclusion

When we consider legal/judicial debates in both West and East Germany, it is striking that the very people affected by antisemitism were, for the most part, not involved in the discussions. This is revealed in the examples introduced earlier, and manifested most plainly in two notions: first, that combating antisemitism was a utilitarian, political considerations that had very little, if anything at all, to do with empathy for the victims; second, the further one goes down the road of prevention, the closer one comes to a criminal law that prosecutes convictions rather than actions—an approach incompatible with the principles of liberal-democratic societies. Considering the history and intensity of antisemitism in Germany it may not be surprising that it took such a long time before appreciable parts of the German population grew willing to make the connection between liberal democratic values and the fight against antisemitism.[81] The perception of "Germans" and "Jews" as two separate communities remains a legacy of both antisemitic agitation and the self-victimization that has characterized the German debate on "coming to terms with the past."

Many of the problems which had been characteristic of the prosecution of antisemitic agitation since the founding of the German Empire existed unchanged after 1945 and continue to define the debate up to the present, despite the experience of the Holocaust. The model of a collective learning process brought about by public debate over antisemitic agitation, which Werner Bergmann has described in detail, has recently been criticized.[82] It is certainly correct that this learning process was neither direct and linear, nor complete. For some time now, it has been commonplace in the Sunday speeches of the politicians to say that democracy must not be a state of affairs that is reached once and for all, but is the result of an ongoing process that helps retain stability in times of crisis. In short, the old adage holds true when one examines the Germany case: democracy requires democrats. Although public discourses on the importance of defense against various forms of racism and xenophobia may still be more closely centered on the State in Germany than in other western countries, it seems that German society has finally learned the lesson that a social movement like antisemitism cannot be suppressed by legal means alone. As early as 1937, Karl

Loewenstein warned his readers "democracy should be on its guard against too much optimism. To overestimate the ultimate efficiency of legislative provisions against fascist emotional technique would be a dangerous self-deception. The statute book is only a subsidiary expedient of the militant will for self-preservation."[83] There is much evidence to support the notion that this statement remains one of enduring value.

Notes

[1] I wish to thank Alex J. Kay for his translation of the original conference paper and his thorough proofreading of this substantially augmented essay. The thoughts presented here derive from my forthcoming study on the legal defense against antisemitism in Germany between 1879 and 1960.

[2] See Thomas Schlemmer and Hans Woller, "Der italienische Faschismus und die Juden 1922 bis 1945," *Vierteljahrshefte für Zeitgeschichte* 53 (2005). The authors question the common interpretation that racism and antisemitism are major distinguishing factors between Italian fascism and National Socialism; nevertheless, they concede that the anti-Jewish policy pursued by the Mussolini regime never came close to the murderous dynamism of its German counterpart.

[3] John McCloy, American High Commissioner to Germany, 1949, quoted in Frank Stern, *Im Anfang war Auschwitz. Antisemitismus und Philosemitismus im deutschen Nachkrieg* (Gerlingen: Bleicher, 1991), 264.

[4] See Ulrich Herbert ed., *Wandlungsprozesse in Westdeutschland: Belastung, Integration, Liberalisierung 1945-1980* (Göttingen: Wallstein, 2002).

[5] See Jörg Requate, "Standespolitik als Gesellschaftspolitik. Zur Debatte um den Reformbedarf der Justiz in den 60er Jahren" in *Dynamische Zeiten. Die 60er Jahre in den beiden deutschen Gesellschaften*, ed. Axel Schildt et. al. (Hamburg: Christians, 2000), 424-43.

[6] These processes were subject of the Anglo-German conference "Europeanisation & History: Concepts, Conflicts, Cohesion" held 29-31 May 2005 in Berlin and jointly organized by Henning Grunwald, Kiran Klaus Patel, and the author. For a conference report see http://hsozkult.geschichte.hu-berlin.de/tagungsberichte/id=803.

[7] Dirk Berg-Schlosser, ed., *Democratization: The State of the Art* (Wiesbaden: VS – Verlag für Sozialwissenschaften, 2004), 16, Figure 1. For the critique of Samuel Huntington's "wave theory," see Jean Grugel, *Democratization: A Critical Introduction* (Basingstoke and New York: Palgrave, 2002), 34-37.

[8] Martin Conway, "Democracy in Postwar Western Europe: The Triumph of a Political Model," *European History Quarterly* 32 (2002): 63 and 63-67.

[9] The fight against antisemitism was insufficient, too. See Christoph Jahr, "Policing Anti-Semitic Crime in Weimar Germany" in *Conflict and Legality: Policing Mid-Twentieth Century Europe* ed. Gerard Oram (London: Francis Boutle Publishers, 2003).

[10] Karl Loewenstein, "Militant Democracy and Fundamental Rights (Part I)," *American Political Science Review* 31 (1937): 431. See also Alfons Söllner, "Jüdische Emigranten in den USA: Ihr Einfluß auf die amerikanische Deutschlandpolitik 1933-1949" in *Gegen alle Vergeblichkeit. Jüdischer Widerstand gegen den Nationalsozialismus*, ed. Hans Erler, Arnold Paucker and Ernst Ludwig Ehrlich (Frankfurt/Main and New York:

Campus, 2003); Matthias Stoffregen, *Kämpfen für ein demokratisches Deutschland. Emigranten zwischen Politik und Politikwissenschaft* (Opladen: Leske & Budrich, 2002), 132-43.

[11] Loewenstein, 432.

[12] Karl Mannheim, *Diagnosis of Our Time. Wartime Essays of a Sociologist* (Westport, Connecticut: Greenwood Press, 1986), 7.

[13] Quoted in Uta Gerhardt, "Das Reeducation-Programm der USA" in *Gegen alle Vergeblichkeit. Jüdischer Widerstand gegen den Nationalsozialismus*, ed. Hans Erler, Arnold Paucker and Ernst Ludwig Ehrlich (Frankfurt/Main and New York: Campus, 2003), 426 footnote 20.

[14] See Felicitas Hentschke, *Demokratisierung als Ziel der amerikanischen Besatzungspolitik in Deutschland und Japan, 1943-1947* (Münster: LIT-Verlag, 2001), 147-49.

[15] For an overview, see Michael Brenner, *Nach dem Holocaust. Juden in Deutschland 1945-1950* (Munich: Beck 1995) and Jay Howard Geller, *Jews in Post-Holocaust Germany, 1945-1953* (Cambridge and New York: Cambridge University Press, 2005).

[16] Konrad H. Jarausch, *Die Umkehr. Deutsche Wandlungen 1945-1995* (Munich: Beck, 2004), 10.

[17] See Julia Schulze Wessel, "Neue Formen des Antisemitismus in der deutschen Nachkriegsgesellschaft. Eine Analyse deutscher Polizeiakten der Jahre 1945-1948," *Jahrbuch für Antisemitismusforschung* 8 (1999); Julia Schulze Wessel and Susanne Dietrich, *Zwischen Selbstorganisation und Stigmatisierung. Die Lebenswirklichkeit jüdischer Displaced Persons und die neue Gestalt des Antisemitismus in der deutschen Nachkriegsgesellschaft* (Stuttgart: Klett-Cotta, 1998); Michael Brenner, "East European and German Jews in Postwar Germany, 1945-50" in *Jews, Germans, Memory. Reconstructions of Jewish Life in Germany,* ed. Michal Y. Bodemann (Ann Arbor: The University of Michigan Press, 1996).

[18] See Stern, *Im Anfang war Auschwitz*, 149. See also Juliane Wetzel, *Jüdisches Leben in München 1945-1951. Durchgangsstation oder Wiederaufbau?* (Munich: Buchendorfer Verlag, 1987), 53-62. On the desecration of cemeteries see Constantin Goschler, "The Attitude towards Jews in Bavaria after the Second World War," *Leo Baeck Institute Year Book* 36 (1991): 451-53.

[19] See Frank Stern, "The Historic Triangle: Occupiers, Germans and Jews in Postwar Germany," *Tel Aviver Jahrbuch für Deutsche Geschichte* 19 (1990): 61; Juliane Wetzel, "'Mir szeinen doh'. München und Umgebung als Zuflucht von Überlebenden des Holocaust 1945-1948" in *Von Stalingrad zur Währungsreform. Zur Sozialgeschichte des Umbruchs in Deutschland*, ed. Martin Broszat, Klaus-Dietmar Henke and Hans Woller (Munich: Oldenbourg, 1988).

[20] See Anthony Kauders, "Catholics, the Jews and Democratization in Postwar Germany, Munich 1945-65," *German History* 18 (2000): 477.

[21] See Klaus Schulte, "'Was ist denn das überhaupt, ein Jude?' Anna Seghers' Einspruch anlässlich der antisemitischen Hetze gegen die Insassen der Berliner Transitlager für 'displaced persons' in der Presse der Vier-Sektoren-Stadt im Jahre 1948: Rekonstruktion, Lektüre, Kommentar," *Jahrbuch für Kommunikationsgeschichte* 4 (2002). On the antisemitism of the left see Thomas Haury, *Antisemitismus von links. Kommunistische Ideologie, Nationalismus und Antizionismus in der frühen DDR* (Hamburg: Hamburger Edition, 2002) and Nora Goldenbogen, "Zum Zusammenhang zwischen Antisemitismus und spätstalinistischen Säuberungswellen in Sachsen zwischen 1949

und 1953" in *Antisemitismus in Sachsen im 19. und 20. Jahrhundert*, ed. Solvejg Höppner (Dresden: Goldenbogen, 2004).

[22] See Wolfgang Benz, "Antisemitismus nach Hitler. Beobachtungen der amerikanischen Militärregierung aus dem Jahre 1947," *Jahrbuch für Antisemitismusforschung* 6 (1997): 351-59. See also Stern, *Im Anfang war Auschwitz*, 115-33 and Goschler, 443-45.

[23] Moses Moskowitz, "The Germans and the Jews: Postwar Report. The Enigma of German Irresponsibility," *Commentary* vol. II, No. 1 (July 1946): 13.

[24] See Werner Bergmann, "Auschwitz zum Trotz. Formen und Funktionen des Antisemitismus nach 1945" in *"Das 'bewegliche' Vorurteil". Aspekte des internationalen Antisemitismus*, ed. Christina v. Braun and Eva-Maria Ziege (Würzburg: Königshausen & Neumann, 2004), 117.

[25] See Matthias Etzel, *Die Aufhebung von nationalsozialistischen Gesetzen durch den Alliierten Kontrollrat 1945-1948* (Tübingen: Mohr, 1992), 223-34.

[26] Quoted in Michael Balfour, "Four-Power Control in Germany 1945-1945" in *Survey of International Affairs 1939-1946, vol. 6: Four-Power Control in Germany and Austria 1945-1945*, ed. Arnold Toynbee (London, New York, and Toronto: Oxford University Press, 1956), 80-81.

[27] Frank Stern, "Entstehung, Bedeutung und Funktion des Philosemitismus in Westdeutschland nach 1945" in *Antisemitismus in der politischen Kultur nach 1945*, ed. Werner Bergmann and Rainer Erb (Opladen: Westdeutscher Verlag, 1990), 183 and 193. For a sharp critique of Stern's approach see Kauders, 473-4, footnote 48.

[28] See Bernhard Diestelkamp, "Verfassungsgebung in den Westzonen nach 1945 – Länderverfassungen und Grundgesetz," *Zeitschrift für Neuere Rechtsgeschichte* 11 (1989), as well as Wilhelm Wegener, *Die neuen deutschen Verfassungen* (Essen: West-Verlag, 1947).

[29] Quoted in Werner Breunig, *Verfassungsgebung in Berlin 1945-1950* (Berlin: Duncker & Humblot, 1990), 256.

[30] The SPD city councillor Friedrich-Wilhelm Luchts cited in Breunig, 261.

[31] Quoted in Breunig, 453.

[32] See Reinhard Schiffers, *Zwischen Bürgerfreiheit und Staatsschutz. Wiederherstellung und Neufassung des politischen Strafrechts in der Bundesrepublik Deutschland 1949-1951* (Düsseldorf: Droste, 1989), 39-46.

[33] See Frank R. Pfetsch, *Ursprünge der Zweiten Republik. Prozesse der Verfassungsgebung* (Opladen: Westdeutscher Verlag, 1990) and, particularly, Gregor Paul Boventer, *Grenzen politischer Freiheit im demokratischen Staat. Das Konzept der streitbaren Demokratie in einem internationalen Vergleich* (Berlin: Duncker & Humblot, 1985), who emphasizes the similarities of western democracies. More critical in this respect is Dietrich Schindler, "Über die Notwendigkeit gemeinsamer Grundüberzeugungen in der Demokratie und die Versuche, sie rechtlich zu verankern" in *Kritik und Vertrauen. Festschrift für Peter Schneider zum 70. Geburtstag*, ed. Erhard Denninger et. al. (Frankfurt/Main: Hain, 1990).

[34] Quoted in Sebastian Ullrich, "Im Schatten einer gescheiterten Demokratie. Die Weimarer Republik und der demokratische Neubeginn in den Westzonen 1945-1949" in, *Griff nach der Deutungsmacht. Zur Geschichte der Geschichtspolitik in Deutschland*, ed. Heinrich August Winkler (Göttingen: Wallstein, 2004), 201. See also Kathrin Groh, "Zwischen Skylla und Charybdis: Die streitbare Demokratie" in *Weimars lange Schat-*

ten – "Weimar" als Argument nach 1945, ed. Christoph Gusy (Baden-Baden: Nomos, 2003).

[35] See Dieter Grimm, "Mißglückt oder glücklos? Die Weimarer Reichsverfassung im Widerstreit der Meinungen" in Heinrich August Winkler (ed.), *Weimar im Widerstreit. Deutungen der ersten deutschen Republik im geteilten Deutschland* (Munich: Oldenbourg, 2002).

[36] See Kauders, 475.

[37] Shlomo Shafir, "Die SPD und die Wiedergutmachung gegenüber Israel" in *Wiedergutmachung in der Bundesrepublik Deutschland*, ed. Ludolf Herbst and Constantin Goschler (Munich: Oldenbourg 1989), 193.

[38] See Gotthard Jasper, *Der Schutz der Republik. Studien zur staatlichen Sicherung der Demokratie in der Weimarer Republik 1922-1930* (Tübingen: Mohr 1963), 316-20.

[39] Supreme Court Ruling 23 October 1952, in: *Entscheidungen des Bundesverfassungsgerichts*, vol. 2 (Tübingen: Mohr, 1952): 68.

[40] See Sebastian Lovens, "Parteiverbote in der Bundesrepublik Deutschland. Zur verfassungsrechtlichen Ausgangslage der Anträge gegen die NPD," *Zeitschrift für Parlamentsfragen* 32 (2001); Horst Meier and Claus Leggewie ed., *Verbot der NPD oder Mit Rechtsradikalen leben?* (Frankfurt/Main: Suhrkamp, 2002); Hans-Heinz Lynen von Berg and Jochen Tschiche ed., *NPD – Herausforderung für die Demokratie?* (Berlin: Metropol, 2002).

[41] *Verhandlungen des Deutschen Bundestages. Stenographische Berichte*, Attachments, vol. 2, 15 February 1950, Printed Matter No. 563.

[42] *Verhandlungen des Deutschen Bundestages*, vol. 2, 16 March 1950: 1,607.

[43] *Verhandlungen des Deutschen Bundestages*, Attachments, vol. 6, Printed Matter No. 1,307, 4 September 1950: 13.

[44] Adolf Arndt, SPD, *Verhandlungen des Deutschen Bundestages*, vol. 5, 12 September 1950: 3,117, as well as Hugo Paul, KPD, in ibid.

[45] See, for example, Joachim Jahn, *Strafrechtliche Mittel gegen Rechtsextremismus. Die Änderungen der §§ 130 und 86a StGB als Reaktion auf fremdenfeindliche Gewalt im Lichte der Geschichte des politischen Strafrechts in Deutschland* (Frankfurt/Main: Lang, 1998); Markus Wehinger, *Kollektivbeleidigung – Volksverhetzung. Der strafrechtliche Schutz von Bevölkerungsgruppen durch die §§ 185ff. und § 130 StGB* (Baden-Baden: Nomos, 1994); Peter Paepcke, *Antisemitismus und Strafrecht* (Freiburg: Jur. Diss., 1962).

[46] *Verhandlungen des Deutschen Bundestages*, vol. 43, 8 April 1959: 3,623-4.

[47] Cited in Ulrich Brochhagen, *Nach Nürnberg. Vergangenheitsbewältigung und Westintegration in der Ära Adenauer* (Hamburg: Junius, 1994), 280. Adenauer made this statement during an informal meeting with journalists, March 1959.

[48] See, for example, the speech of Federal Interior Minister Gerhard Schröder in *Verhandlungen des Deutschen Bundestages*, vol 35, 18 February 1960: 5,575.

[49] See Anselm Doering-Manteuffel, "Freiheitliche demokratische Grundordnung und Gewaltdiskurs. Überlegungen zur 'streitbaren Demokratie' in der politischen Kultur der Bundesrepublik" in *Politische Gewalt in der Moderne. Festschrift für Hans-Ulrich Thamer*, ed. Frank Becker et. al. (Münster: Aschendorff, 2003), 275-6.

[50] See Johannes Lameyer, *Streitbare Demokratie. Eine verfassungshermeneutische Untersuchung* (Berlin: Duncker & Humblot, 1978), 207. Lameyer concludes that the idea of "militant democracy" helped promote the call for intensified state intervention at the expense of constitutional rights.

[51] See Hans-Eckhard Niermann, "Zwischen Unbehagen und Verdrängung. Die Reaktion von Richterschaft und Justizverwaltung des Oberlandesgerichtsbezirks Hamm auf die 'Braunbuch-Kampagne' der DDR 1957 bis 1968" in *Recht und Justiz im gesellschaftlichen Aufbruch (1960-1975). Bundesrepublik Deutschland, Italien und Frankreich*, ed. Jörg Requate (Baden-Baden: Nomos, 2003), 103-129.
[52] See Erik Lommatzsch, "Hans Globke und der Nationalsozialismus. Eine Skizze," *Historisch-Politische Mitteilungen* 10 (2003) and Philipp-Christian Wachs, *Der Fall Theodor Oberländer (1905-1998). Ein Lehrstück deutscher Geschichte* (Frankfurt/Main and New York: Campus, 2000).
[53] "Editorial Comment: Swastikas – Foreign and Domestic," *Jewish Frontier* 27, No. 2 (February 1960): 3, cited in Jay Howard Geller, "Das Bild Konrad Adenauers vom Judentum und seine Beziehungen zu Vertretern jüdischer Organisationen" in *Adenauer, Israel und das Judentum*, ed. Hanns Jürgen Küsters (Bonn: Bouvier, 2004), 152, footnote 48. Globke was not a federal minister but served as state secretary in the federal chancellery.
[54] See Wolfgang Buschfort, *Geheime Hüter der Verfassung. Von der Düsseldorfer Informationsstelle zum ersten Verfassungsschutz der Bundesrepublik (1947-1961)* (Paderborn: Schöningh, 2004).
[55] Quoted in Michael Kohlstruck, *Rechtsextreme Jugendkultur und Gewalt. Eine Herausforderung für die pädagogische Praxis* (Berlin: Metropol, 2002), 139.
[56] See Dieter Bertz, *Die Bundesprüfstelle für jugendgefährdende Schriften. Zum Problem der politisch-staatlichen Zensur* (Diplomarbeit, Freie Universität Berlin, 1991).
[57] "Grundsätze der FSK," 2 April 1949, quoted in Werner Wohland, *Informationsfreiheit und politische Filmkontrolle. Ein Beitrag zur Konkretisierung von Art. 5 Grundgesetz* (Berlin: Duncker & Humblot, 1968), 194. See also Heinz-Dietrich Fischer, "Renaissance der 'äußeren' und Etappen zur Realisierung von 'innerer' Kommunikationsfreiheit (1949-1980)" in *Deutsche Kommunikationskontrolle des 15. bis 20. Jahrhunderts*, ed. Heinz-Dietrich Fischer (Munich: Saur, 1982) and Helmut Cron, "Die Organisation der Selbstkontrolle" in *Selbstkontrolle von Presse, Funk und Film*, ed. Martin Löffler (Munich and Berlin: Beck, 1960).
[58] Scandals and sensational trials always played an important role in the history of modern antisemitism. See Christoph Jahr, "Ahlwardt on Trial: Reactions to the Antisemitic Agitation of the 1890s in Germany," *Leo Baeck-Institute Year Book* 48 (2003).
[59] This letter is reproduced in Wetzel, *Jüdisches Leben in München 1945-1951*, Appendix 13. See also Werner Bergmann, *Antisemitismus in öffentlichen Konflikten. Kollektives Lernen in der politischen Kultur der Bundesrepublik 1949-1989* (Frankfurt/Main and New York: Campus, 1997), 73-86.
[60] Article in the *Süddeutsche Zeitung*, 16 August 1949, cited in Werner Bergmann, "Medienöffentlichkeit und extremistisches Meinungsspektrum. Die *Süddeutsche Zeitung* und der Fall 'Adolf Bleibtreu'," *Jahrbuch für Antisemitismusforschung* 3 (1994): 59.
[61] Article in the *Süddeutsche Zeitung*, 11 August 1949, cited in Bergmann, 55.
[62] Quoted in Wolfgang Benz, "Postwar Society and National Socialism: Remembrance, Amnesia, Rejection," *Tel Aviver Jahrbuch für Deutsche Geschichte* 19 (1990): 4.
[63] See Detlef Korte, "Der Hedler-Skandal 1949-53. Ein rechtsradikales MdB aus Rendsburg und eine Schlägerei im Bundestag," *Demokratische Geschichte. Jahrbuch zur Arbeiterbewegung und Demokratie in Schleswig-Holstein* 9 (1995); Norbert Frei, *Vergangenheitspolitik. Die Anfänge der Bundesrepublik und die NS-Vergangenheit*

(Munich: Beck, 1996), 311-25; Bergmann, *Antisemitismus in öffentlichen Konflikten*, 117-45; and Heiko Buschke, *Deutsche Presse, Rechtsextremismus und nationalsozialistische Vergangenheit in der Ära Adenauer* (Frankfurt/Main and New York: Campus, 2003), 115-46.

[64] See Korte, 282-3.

[65] See Wolfgang Kraushaar, "Der Kampf gegen den 'Jud-Süß'-Regisseur Veit Harlan. Ein Meilenstein in der Grundrechtssprechung des Bundesverfassungsgerichts," *Mittelweg* 36, No. 6 (1995): 18-30.

[66] See Peter Dudek, *"Der Rückblick auf die Vergangenheit wird sich nicht vermeiden lassen". Zur pädagogischen Verarbeitung des Nationalsozialismus in Deutschland (1945-1990)* (Opladen: Westdeutscher Verlag, 1995), 265.

[67] See Bergmann, *Antisemitismus in öffentlichen Konflikten*, 270, table 4.

[68] See Thomas Henne and Arne Riedlinger ed., *Das Lüth-Urteil in (rechts-)historischer Sicht. Die Konflikte um Veit Harlan und die Grundrechtsjudikatur des Bundesverfassungsgerichts* (Berlin: Berliner Wissenschafts-Verlag, 2005).

[69] *Verhandlungen des Deutschen Bundestages*, vol. 44, 3 December 1959: 5,081.

[70] Ibid., 5,083.

[71] Klaus Louven, "Die Strafbarkeit antisemitischer Ausschreitungen," *Deutsche Richter-Zeitung* 38 (1960): 213.

[72] All citations in Karl Wilhelm Fricke, *Politik und Justiz in der DDR. Zur Geschichte der politischen Verfolgung 1945-1968. Bericht und Dokumentation* Second Imprint (Cologne: Verlag Wissenschaft und Politik, 1990), 48-9.

[73] Bundesarchiv Berlin (BA-B), DP 1 VA No. 131, fol. 27.

[74] Ibid., fol. 31.

[75] BA-B, DP 1 VA Nr. 119, fol. 21 and 23.

[76] BA-B, DP 1 VA No. 119, fol. 37.

[77] Ibid., fol. 54.

[78] Ibid., fol. 56, 60, and 64.

[79] See Hermann Wentker, *Justiz in der SBZ/DDR 1945-1953. Transformation und Rolle ihrer zentralen Institutionen* (Munich: Oldenbourg, 2001).

[80] See BA-B, DP 1 VA Nr. 119, fol. 55, 61 and 64r, quote: 55.

[81] This point is emphasized in Kauders, 479.

[82] See Lars Rensmann, *Demokratie und Judenbild. Antisemitismus in der politischen Kultur der Bundesrepublik Deutschland* (Wiesbaden: VS – Verlag für Sozialwissenschaften, 2004), 501.

[83] Loewenstein, 657.

The Politics of Punishment: War Criminals and the Struggle for German Reintegration with the West, 1948-1958

Valerie Hébert

"How to win friends for the States? Open the Landsberg Prison gates!"[1]

Reeling from the devastating losses of the war and confronting the unprecedented scope and scale of Nazi crimes, when peace finally came to Europe the Allies groped and struggled to articulate a response. Certainly, conducting one or more war crimes trials was not the obvious or unanimous policy choice. The British, still smarting from their disastrous attempt at war crimes prosecutions after World War One initially preferred simply to execute a dozen or so arch perpetrators. The Soviets would have added a few thousand more. Even within the ranks of the American government, there were calls for summary execution to be followed by a vindictive peace settlement. However, other voices in Washington argued passionately for trials. These individuals believed that retribution by judicial decision would not only punish the guilty, but would also serve an educative and redemptive function: reconciling the German people to their past, performing a kind of national catharsis, and leading the country back into the community of democratic nations. Further, recording and publicizing the crimes of the Third Reich and modeling the basic democratic principles of due process and human rights would, in their view, more likely secure a lasting peace and ensure the abandonment of fascist perspectives.[2] As one of the earliest advocates for trials noted, if these proceedings were not carried out:

> Germany will simply have lost another war. The German people will not *know* the barbarians they have supported, nor will they have any *understanding* of the criminal character of their conduct and the world's judgment upon it.[3]

Therefore, from the earliest planning stages, the war crimes trials had three goals: justice, education, and the democratization of West Germany. Through an analysis of the German response to one of the American-led trials, the 1948 High Command Case, this article will assess the effectiveness of the judicial exercise for the rehabilitation of fascist Germany.

The United States participated in three sets of war crimes trials. The International Military Tribunal at Nuremberg (IMT) was prosecuted jointly with the British, Soviets, and French and targeted the highest level Nazis and military leaders. American military authorities conducted 486 trials on the grounds of the former concentration camp at Dachau, in which the defendants were mainly lower-ranking perpetrators accused of crimes against American nationals and crimes committed in concentration camps liberated by American forces.[4] The US also carried out twelve "Subsequent Nuremberg Proceedings" (SNP) against high-level representatives of all branches of the Nazi State, including the judiciary, medical officials, SS and Gestapo, industry, government ministries, the Nazi party, and the military. The last of these trials was called the High Command Case. Over nine months in 1948, fourteen *Wehrmacht* (German Armed Forces) field marshals and generals faced the bar on charges of crimes against peace, war crimes, crimes against humanity, and the common plan or conspiracy to commit these crimes.[5] The indictment included, among other offenses: the deliberate abuse and liquidation of millions of Soviet prisoners of war, the murder of Western Allied soldiers and airmen, the extermination of Polish and Soviet civilians (particularly Jews, the intelligentsia, and political leadership), retaliation killings of civilian hostages, reprisals against "partisans" and "partisan-suspects," and participation in the regime's slave labor program.[6] Criminal responsibility was proven both by showing the formulation and communication of illegal orders or policies from the highest echelons of military leadership, and by the countless ground level reports from areas under the defendants' command that demonstrated their implementation. Eleven of the defendants were found guilty and sentenced to prison terms spanning from time already served to life. They came under the jurisdiction of the office of the US High Commissioner for Germany (HICOG) and were imprisoned at Landsberg prison in Bavaria.[7]

Beginning with the International Military Tribunal and continuing through the conclusion of the Subsequent Nuremberg Proceedings, these trials in general and the High Command Case in particular were dogged by persistent criticism in Germany that they were no more than an application of retroactive law and an exercise in double-standard victors' justice. A constantly recurring theme in public responses to the High Command Case was that all parties to the war, but especially the Soviets, had committed similar abuses and that, in the end, it was a soldier's duty to serve his nation and obey orders. Moreover, the prevailing political and social circumstances proved inhospitable ground in which to root the lessons of the trial. Hardening Cold War battle lines weakened the Americans' capacity to convince the German people of *Wehrmacht* participation in Nazi crimes. Having recently sentenced German soldiers for wartime atrocities against largely Soviet nationals, the Allies would soon be making overtures to the Federal Republic to join in the defense of the West against the same Communist superpower. Further, the convicted generals interned at Landsberg still enjoyed the respect and loyalty of men who were now asked to don uniforms in league with their comrades' captors.

The release of imprisoned soldiers became a major bargaining chip in the negotiations over West German integration in Western defense plans. It should be noted, however, that since the Americans had conducted the greatest number of trials and possessed the largest population of convicted war criminals (three times that of the British and French), the debate was mainly a German-American one.[8] For the West German leaders who entered into this dialogue, the necessary prerequisite for any contribution to Western defense centered on the restoration of German military honor. This required a return of all POWs still in Allied custody, and, significantly, the release of all military men convicted of war crimes serving terms in occupation authorities' prisons. The incremental transformation of West Germany from occupied territory to sovereign state gave it the political leverage required to press its demands ever more forcefully. Indeed, shortly after the establishment of the Federal Republic in May 1949, the Adenauer government announced its goal to "pardon … offenses … arising from the bygone period of distress and transition" and its intention to request a general amnesty for individuals sentenced by military government courts.[9] The West German press and veterans quickly joined their government in this demand. Although articulated differently at different times, the intention to secure amnesty for convicted war criminals occupied a central place in all discussions between the Federal Republic and the Western Allies, and did not abate until the release of the last Landsberg inmate in 1958.[10]

The law devised for the Subsequent Nuremberg Proceedings stipulated that judgments were final. Consequently, American authorities established no formal appeals process in which the convicted could challenge the verdicts passed against them. Prior to the Federal Republic's demand for amnesty, reviews had taken place on an ad hoc basis. This caused widespread apprehension over the equitability of the sentences and the rights of the convicts. Given the US desire to preserve political stability in Germany and its loyalty to the West, occupation officials wished to appear responsive to prisoners' rights. Accordingly, in December 1949, the recently installed US High Commissioner for Germany John J. McCloy instituted a system wherein convicts were granted remission of one third of their sentence for good behavior.[11] Although the "good time" credit drastically reduced the amount of time yet to be served by all convicts other than those facing life terms or execution, the implicit insistence on the validity of the trials' conclusions irritated German groups intent on securing sweeping pardons, and their appeals persisted. In response, McCloy created the "Advisory Board on Clemency for War Criminals" in spring 1950 which had a mandate to consider petitions and recommend further sentence modification based on the convict's health, family conditions, or other mitigating factors.[12] Because these revisions concerned themselves only with extenuating circumstances applicable to the sentences, technically they had no bearing on the original guilty verdicts.[13]

During the summer of the Clemency Board's work, the eruption of the Korean War heightened East-West tensions and highlighted the obvious need for a West German military force.[14] Only five years since Germany had been told it must never again possess weapons, Cold War considerations prompted the abandonment of this policy. The dilemma was how to make West Germany simultaneously strong enough to help deter the Soviets, while not so strong as to pose a threat to the West. The French, understandably the most apprehensive of Germany's neighbors, devised a plan that would both rearm and contain West Germany. Brainchild of the French Prime Minister André Pleven, the European Defense Community, or EDC, envisioned a West European army in which the military forces of various states would be integrated under an amalgamated command structure—i.e., no single state would be able to deploy troops independently. The EDC met with broad approval. From Adenauer's point of view, rearmament under any guise meant increased national sovereignty. From the American perspective, the EDC more closely unified Western Europe and created a military force whose strength and resources no single state would have been able to muster.[15] Although formal negotiations over the EDC were still some months away, intensified concern with the rearmament question created an entrée for individuals seeking leverage in the matter of imprisoned soldiers.

Not surprisingly, during the Clemency Board's deliberations and prior to McCloy's final decisions, the High Commissioner received hundreds of letters on behalf of the military men in prison. The prisoners themselves, their counsel, their relatives and friends, clergy, church and school groups, public officials, and notably, former soldiers, submitted petitions. Many of these communications began by reminding McCloy of the West's need for a German contribution to defense plans. They stated plainly that no German soldier could be expected to join such a force after "six years of defamation."[16] General Heinz Guderian explained:

> The former German soldiers cannot understand that the United States of America emphatically demand a German contribution to the defense of Western Europe, while at the same time many of their comrades are languishing in prisons.... [I]f the United States are interested in preparing the Germans for a contribution to the defense of Western Europe, I, in concurrence with all my comrades, consider it an urgent necessity that first the so-called "war criminals' question" be settled.[17]

The enormous number of petitions from former officers and ordinary citizens alike convinced McCloy that the German people did not understand what the trials had been about or what the defendants had done.[18] Having carefully studied the trial records and being particularly interested personally in the cases involving soldiers, the High Commissioner was at pains to communicate the truth of the situation to the men and women who appealed to him. To retired Admiral Gottfried Hansen he wrote:

> No one aware of the facts can possibly say that these men observed either the ethics of their profession or the fundamental principles of humanity and law.... I cannot believe that allowance should be made for a profes-

> sional soldier who either connived or participated in … [the] slaughter of Jews because they were Jews, communists, parachutists, aviators, commandos, and other "undesirables." Such connivance and participation took place and there can be no doubt of it.[19]

During a meeting with a Bundestag delegation in which they requested "that the excesses of the Nazis … be cancelled by a great gesture of clemency," McCloy expressed his indignation at the Germans' "tendency to put things under the carpet and refus[al] to acknowledge what actually happened."[20]

At the end of January 1951, upon the Clemency Board's recommendations, McCloy commuted the executions of ten of the fifteen prisoners under sentence of death and further reduced the sentences of sixty-seven of the seventy-three convicts serving jail terms. Almost one third were granted immediate release. He attributed his decisions to several factors: the attempt to equalize sentences for comparable crimes, the relative subordinate authority of the convict, new evidence not available to the tribunals, and in exceptional cases, the prisoner's acute illness or other special circumstances. Interestingly, he shortened the sentences of only three of the seven High Command Case convicts still at Landsberg.[21] In the written précis of his rulings, entitled "Landsberg: A Documentary Report," which was distributed widely among German political, religious, and institutional leaders and interested members of the public, McCloy made a special point of explaining his position vis-à-vis the military men in his custody.[22] Contrary to the common impression that the sentences against former soldiers maligned the German military profession as a whole, McCloy insisted that the judgments rendered at Nuremberg were based on charges of excess far surpassing anything that could be considered militarily necessary. He declared that he understood the bitter realities of partisan warfare and that when "the heat of battle" or "true military considerations" could be convincingly argued, he moderated the sentences. Regarding the High Command Case convicts, he concluded that there remained "an area of real guilt which … a professional soldier … cannot countenance."[23] In a letter of thanks to the Clemency Board, McCloy admitted that the battle for German public opinion had not yet been won, but concluded hopefully: "it looks as if we have gotten a good start toward writing a successful end to the chapter."[24] McCloy's optimism was misplaced.

West German criticism of the Landsberg action was widespread and settled largely on the confirmation of soldiers' sentences. The Federal Government's military advisers publicly condemned the decisions regarding their former colleagues and a veterans' association issued a statement declaring that the Landsberg rulings "prove that the discrimination of the victors against the vanquished continues to exist." Another report opined that the cases of the generals remained "a serious psychological burden for the German rearmament problem."[25] Perhaps the most telling piece appeared in an editorial in the *Frankfurter Allgemeine Zeitung* entitled: "Landsberg—not the last chapter." The author reproached the High Commissioner's decisions on soldiers as misunderstanding contemporary realities: "It seems that the main argument for the approval of the hard sentences imposed on German generals is out of place in modern wars.... The case of soldiers shows clearly that Mr. McCloy's action of January 31 cannot mean the last word. It is Landsberg's last chapter but one, not the last."[26]

German opponents were unmoved by the Landsberg revisions. Analyzing over 1,000 letters written to McCloy in response to the clemency action, HICOG officials noted that over 95 percent favored further sentence reductions, and half of these advocated their total abrogation. Pastors writing on behalf of their congregations and local chapters of political organizations made appeals. Particularly striking were the letters from primary to university level school groups that emphasized that the outcome of the Landsberg cases would have a decisive effect on their attitude toward cooperating in Western defense.[27] These letters represented all genders, ages, and institutions, although 60 percent were from former soldiers or family members of soldiers. The fact that this correspondence contained, on the whole, a few standard arguments and at times even identical phrasing suggested that it was part of a well-organized campaign.[28]

Meanwhile, West German officials had begun working with the Allied High Commissions (i.e., the American, British, and French) on an agreement to end occupation law and formalize the terms of West Germany's contribution to the anticipated European Defense Community. The 1952 negotiations in Bonn over the "Convention on the Settlement of Matters Arising out of the War and Occupation Treaty," included discussion of the war criminals question. Exploiting the former Allies' desire to secure West German commitment to the EDC, Chancellor Adenauer, with the backing of almost the entire *Bundestag*, demanded the general release of prisoners convicted of war crimes.[29] Erich Mende, the Chairman of the Foreign Policy Committee of the Free Democratic Party (part of Adenauer's coalition) had written to McCloy in November 1951: "[I]f our common purpose of keeping Germany in the Western orbit... is to be achieved, it is essential to make further visible progress toward getting rid of the *rankling complex* of Landsberg."[30] During talks the Allies offered to transfer jurisdiction over the war criminals to the Federal Republic provided that it promise to enforce the sentences.[31] Alternatively the Allies proposed establishing a Mixed Board (including Allied and German members) to consider appeals and advise on clemency. Ultimately, since the German government refused to acknowledge the legitimacy of the trial judgments, when the western occupation powers and Germany signed the Bonn Settlement Convention on 26 May 1952, they dropped the proposal for the transference of custody, but retained the plan for the institution of a Mixed Board.

While recognized by a few individuals as progress on the issue, many more from the *Bundestag*, veterans' associations and the press were displeased. They saw the proposed Board not as a solution to the war criminals problem but rather as an institutionalization of it. That is, as the Foreign Ministry noted (shamelessly!), this was no one-time total "*Endlösung*" ("Final Solution") of the war criminals problem; rather, it entailed a procedure whereby convicts would only be dealt with individually via a process that affirmed the propriety of the original judgments and sentences.[32] Irrespective of immediate German opinion on the proposed plan, however, the Mixed Board could not begin its work until the parliamentary ratification of the Convention. Fifteen months of energetic campaigns for the securing of a general amnesty followed.

It should be noted that by May 1952, only thirty-five men out of an original 142 convicted by the Subsequent Nuremberg Proceedings remained at Landsberg.[33] The rhetoric employed by groups lobbying for their release obscured the fact that even fewer were actually soldiers. Indeed, all incarcerated war criminals were referred to as soldiers, even though many had had no connection to the *Wehrmacht* at all. Further, lobbyists conflated the category of "war criminals" with prisoners of war, identifying them with the POWs still held in foreign (particularly Soviet) territory. In general, the term "war criminals" appeared only in quotation marks or preceded by the qualifier "so-called." Discussion within the *Bundestag* perpetuated the view that the trials were simply acts of political retribution without valid legal foundation. In each of the debates on the subject of war criminals, "speakers from every German political party except the communists attacked the theory of the trials—or the continued imprisonment of convicts—or both" and called for a single, sweeping amnesty.[34]

Writing as chairman of the League of German Soldiers and the Union of Career Soldiers (altogether representing, he claimed, two million veterans—the Americans estimated 80,000[35]) and backed by another ten POW and veterans' associations, retired Admiral Gottfried Hansen forwarded a resolution to the American High Commission declaring: "no German can be expected to don a military uniform again until the question of 'war criminals' has been satisfactorily settled." The resolution rejected the remedy proposed by the Bonn Convention and urged the speedy granting of a general amnesty.[36] Through its journal *Der Heimkehrer* (The Returnee) another veterans' group organized a write-in campaign that elicited 40,000 postcards from German citizens demanding amnesty.[37]

The German press echoed and encouraged these sentiments and demands. HICOG officials noted the almost daily appearance of articles campaigning for the release of war criminals, focusing particular attention on former soldiers. Their arguments tended to fall along the following lines: 1) there were no war crimes and therefore no basis for trials; 2) the Allies had applied victors' justice and ex post facto law and 3) soldiers had only followed orders. Moreover, the newspapers rarely referenced facts, and because they lumped all prisoners into the category of soldiers and all common crimes into the now dubious category of "war crimes," American analysts concluded that they had been able to "thoroughly mislead and confuse the German public."[38] Indeed, a 1952 poll revealed that 63 percent of respondents did not believe that German generals held as war criminals were actually guilty and that only 10 percent supported the war crimes program as a whole.[39]

Initially McCloy held firm, stating plainly that an indiscriminate release of prisoners was simply too high a price to pay for confirmation of the Bonn Treaty. In a *Neue Zeitung* article entitled "A Necessary Clarification," occupation officials warned Germans not to make the war criminals question a political issue and declared: "during World War II things took place in the German *Wehrmacht* that until then had been absent from the armies of all civilized countries." They announced that neither the US nor any other future partner of Germany in the EDC was prepared to purchase Germany's military commitment with political concessions on the issue of war criminals.[40] However, US authorities realized privately that the continued incarceration of ten *Wehrmacht* generals (five of whom had been convicted in the High Command Case) ensured the persistence of "a war criminals problem."[41]

Interestingly, American authorities were willing to accept a share of the responsibility for the failure of the German press, politicians, and general public to understand the reasons for and findings of their war crimes trials. A July 1952 memorandum prepared for Eli Whitney Debevoise, deputy general counsel with the US High Commission, lamented that a lack of available trial records had prevented the war criminals issue from having been more satisfactorily resolved. The memo's author, Frederick Hulse, reminded Debevoise that the original purpose of the trials "was to document the Nazi period and bring before the world generally and the Germans particularly a working knowledge of the Nazi state…." Hulse stated pointedly that had American authorities honored their goal of education by ensuring the timely availability of the trial materials, then the present "scandalous deterioration" in the German public's understanding of war criminals and their crimes might have been avoided.[42] Debevoise communicated these sentiments to Assistant High Commissioner Samuel Reber, pointing out that at that time there were fewer than ten sets of the trial records available in German in all of Germany. (In fact, there were only seven, none of which were complete.[43]) "As the German public is not informed," Debevoise explained, "unfriendly newspapers, unfriendly members of the legislature, and unfriendly officials are able to focus attention on the prisoners without revealing any facts as we have not made the facts available…. [We] are and will continue to be at a disadvantage for many years to come."[44]

What explains this "scandalous" state of affairs? From the start, the Americans believed that they could control the situation. As the Subsequent Proceedings drew to a close, Chief Prosecutor Telford Taylor admonished his superiors against lapsing in their educational efforts. Recommending that significant excerpts of the trials be published in English and German, he reasoned:

> The United States Government has made a heavy moral investment in these trials, and this investment will not show a favorable rate of return if the records are left in the dust on the top shelf out of reach.... The Nuernberg record is a good one. We must not provide an excuse for ill-informed discussion of the Nuernberg trials by making access to the truth difficult.[45]

At first, Taylor's advice was followed, but from the outset the English edition of trial materials was privileged over the German in terms of staff, budget, and page spread. The army controlled the purse strings. Although a minimally sufficient budget was granted for the preparation of the German manuscripts, no funds were promised for the actual printing of these volumes.[46] At various times Taylor and his assistants all wrote to appeal for more generous support. They struggled to keep the preparation of the manuscripts underway, despite unending difficulties in obtaining and retaining qualified staff for the organizing and editing of the German volumes, and in full awareness that these editions "[might] never see the light of day."[47] To the army they forwarded correspondence from German scholars and citizens alike who had requested access to trial records to demonstrate the level of interest in Germany for these documents.[48] They argued that compared to the costs incurred by the proceedings, the publication project was insignificant, and yet bore such important implications:

> [F]ailure to publish these proceedings in German will be regarded, especially by the Germans, as a sign of timidity and uncertainty in our occupation policy. Nuernberg has been too large a project, and its announced objectives too important and too closely associated with the occupation of Germany, to justify its deactivation without its activities being made a matter of record in the German language.[49]

Answering the critique that the proceedings should not be published because they constituted a "sore spot" in German-American relations and the advice that they should simply be permitted to "sink into oblivion," Taylor argued that these records constituted the necessary ammunition to end the dispute over war criminals and rebuild a democratic German society.[50] Thomas Carson, who was in charge of the project's budget, was unmoved by Taylor's plea, and expressed his doubt that the publication of the trial records "would reach the German masses and leave an imprint on the German mind."[51] In June 1949, his office made clear that from its point of view "the printing of completed German manuscripts cannot be assured."[52]

In the conclusion to his August 1949 "Final Report," Taylor expressed his profound disappointment with the American authorities' disposition of the trial materials and again tried to impress upon his superiors the crucial importance of this issue:

> It seems to me that there has been an unfortunate lack of planned effort to utilize the documents and other evidence disclosed at the trials so as to advance the purposes of the occupation of Germany.... The least we can do is to insure that the documents which expose the true nature of the Third Reich are circulated throughout Germany. The Nuernberg documents must be used to the full... if the Germans of today are to grasp the truth about the past.[53]

Taylor's arguments and warnings fell on deaf ears. In late October 1949, Secretary of the Army Gordon Gray revealed that the military regarded the trial reports "of insufficient value ... to warrant their publication," and had suspended work on both editions. Although under pressure from the State Department and with funds granted by Congress efforts did resume on the English version, the German edition was never resuscitated.[54]

As matters stood in mid-1952, the only document in German on the trials issued by the American occupation authorities was the "Landsberg" report, which explained McCloy's 1951 clemency decisions. A mere eight pages of this publication were dedicated to summarizing all twelve Subsequent Proceedings. Described as "only a good newspaper article," it had undeservedly become the "authoritative" German record of the trials.[55] Soon after this document was released, and in view of the fact that occupation headquarters continued to be bombarded by criticisms and appeals, there was some discussion whether there would be any benefit in disseminating additional material. But even at this point certain officials advised against such a strategy. One HICOG advisor told McCloy that releasing justifications "had the tendency to keep issues alive and to invite further counter-blasts to the point where it became a form of scab-picking" and that he would do well to let the matter "die down."[56] Although this advisor was aware of the strong reasons for keeping the matter alive, he concluded that publication of trial material would have the opposite effect intended: "[T]he more we ourselves publish or release the more rebuttal material we invite.... We have been through this mill enough times so that we may fairly know what to expect."[57]

However, withholding trial documents had not allowed the matter to die down. Rather, as Debevoise and Hulse noted, it was the absence of court records from both the Germans and American occupation authorities that had, they believed, unnecessarily complicated negotiations over the end to occupation and future military cooperation and had, moreover, disadvantaged the US position.[58]

Hulse wrote: "It is now apparent that had the records been published and *even if bound records had been available to us,* the grief experienced with the clemency decisions of January 1951 … and the contract flap of 1952 would have been more easily, satisfactorily and convincingly dealt with by referring to them."[59] It was all the more frustrating given that, as Debevoise explained, it had been his and other HICOG officials' experience that individual Germans' attitudes changed once they found out what the Subsequent Proceedings actually involved.[60]

By the end of 1952, belief in the possibility of winning over German public opinion vis-à-vis war criminals had so diminished that the HICOG Office of Political Affairs undertook to devise a solution that would leave the verdicts untouched but would solve the problem from a practical point of view. Noting that both the Protestant and Catholic churches and virtually all political parties had not relaxed their campaigns for release, analysts believed that if German public opinion on this issue did not change soon, then the EDC, the Bonn Convention and even the Adenauer government were in danger of failing.[61] A telegram to the State Department reported:

> It is clear that Ger[man] agitation for release of war criminals has gained considerable momentum and it can be predicted that the increase will continue over the coming months. Problem will undoubtedly cause Chancellor difficulty in ratification process and may cut his majority by enough coalition votes to cast doubt on validity and finality of ratification vote. But the problem will not end with ratification. On the contrary, it will affect both the wholeheartedness of the Ger[man] defense effort and the Chancellor's chances of success at the polls in early summer 1953 unless problem has been both rapidly and finally solved after EDC comes into effect.[62]

Indeed opposition to the continued imprisonment of soldiers showed no signs of relenting. West German Ministry of Defense officials informed occupation authorities that it had been receiving a "flood of letters" from former colleagues and veterans' associations stating that they would "never volunteer for service until the war criminals problem had been solved."[63] The idea that military men were guilty of war crimes had simply not penetrated public consciousness and careful explanation was by now seen to be pointless. As one HICOG commentator explained:

> With regard to … those convicted of shooting hostages and partisans, there is real disagreement as to their guilt…. Even when every argument has been met, as we have attempted to do through a study of all case records available to this office, and the protest dies down from want of further fuel, it has been found that within a week the same protest will be

> made again by the same person, who apparently feels that he was argued down but not proved wrong.[64]

With regret, the High Commission concluded that US authorities now found themselves in two inescapable, yet fundamentally contradictory roles: "occupier and executor of occupation justice" and "Germany's ally and friend." Added to this realization was the belief that there was no time left to coax the Germans around to seeing the validity of the trials' conclusions. With the Bonn Convention's ratification and a federal election looming large, American authorities noted that the crucial time for the resolution of the war criminals issue was now, and could not wait for the planned Mixed Board to come into existence, let alone for prisoners' sentences to expire.[65] Disappointed by their own failings, worn down by the uncertainty of their military security and by relentless pressure from the West German public, and worn out by what was now the eighth year of occupation, the Americans opted for the disposition of the war criminals problem via a joint American-German administered process which would implement "a more lenient system of sentence reduction and parole."[66]

The HICOG Office of Political Affairs advised that the US should first release those prisoners "whose retention will continue to occasion major outcry." At the top of their list were the High Command generals.[67] At the same time, the authors of this plan did not regard it as a betrayal of the war crimes trial program's original goals since it would "leave untouched both the sentences and their legal basis." Further, parole would involve close supervision and a prohibition against political activity and public statements or writing by the parolees.[68] When the Interim Mixed Parole and Clemency Board (as it was called) began its work in October 1953, there were still 307 prisoners at Landsberg or on medical parole. All told, the Board released 250 prisoners on parole and reduced two convicts' sentences to time served.[69] By September 1954, the last five remaining High Command Case generals had been returned to their homes, their families, their communities and their pensions, and lived out their days in peace.[70]

In October 1954, the *Bundestag* ratified the Bonn Convention. Notably, that same year the EDC failed ratification in France. However, because West Germany was later invited to join NATO, the main elements of the debate linking the release of war criminals with German integration in Western defense plans did not change significantly, and pressure to free imprisoned war criminals did not relax. When the occupation of West Germany formally ended in May 1955, the Mixed Parole and Clemency Board (the body envisioned during the 1952 Bonn Convention negotiations) was established and it assumed responsibility for reviewing the remaining war criminals cases. In the interest of "bind[ing] Germany to the West," the American Embassy (which assumed jurisdiction over the Landsbergers after HICOG was dissolved) assured the US State Department that their member of the Mixed Board would be "as lenient as is appropriate" in dealing with the remaining US cases.[71] Indeed, the last inmates of Landsberg were released in May 1958.[72]

In one respect the American war crimes trial of representatives of the German High Command was a success: prosecutors meticulously catalogued and proved the criminal activities of the *Wehrmacht* during the war. But considering that even the most conservative estimates of the Third Reich military's total victims numbered in the millions, the sentences imposed on the guilty field marshals and generals seemed more a symbolic gesture than genuine justice. Unfortunately, those political authorities who were entrusted with the trial record and the responsibility to honor its conclusions by publicizing its truths and enforcing even the meager sentences failed in their task. By not having communicated the substance of the proceedings in a timely and effective fashion, American authorities squandered whatever opportunity they might have possessed to convince the German people under their administration of the legitimacy of the trials' judgments and reconcile them to their recent traumatic past. Particularly in the case of imprisoned soldiers, this omission was deliberately exploited by the press and veterans' associations—who, with little grounding in the facts, mounted and sustained a campaign to empty Landsberg of its inmates. The West German government strengthened the offensive by using its increasing political weight and military indispensability to pry convicted war criminals loose from American custody. The "resolution" of the war criminals "problem" raises pressing questions about the limitations on the court's power to make its work relevant to public understanding and memory. Although organized and prosecuted with a view to their educational function, the American Subsequent Proceedings at Nuremberg required strong political commitments to carry their lessons beyond the bench. In the context of the nascent Cold War, commitments to education were, albeit regretfully, politically inopportune.

Measuring the significance of the war crimes trials for Germany's transition from fascism to democracy is, moreover, complicated by paradox. Despite the premature release of convicted war criminals, West Germany did not re-Nazify. Rather, it emerged as a strong and stabilizing democratic force on the European continent. How do we explain this? Certainly, the trials' goals of justice and education were a failure. However, the same cannot be said with equal assurance of the trials' third objective: democratization. For the most part, West Germans approached the war criminals issue in a "democratic" way: they did not storm the walls of Landsberg, they did not attack occupation forces, and they only rarely threatened violence. Rather, as individuals and as members of organizations, they wrote letters, submitted petitions, debated in the *Bundestag* and in newspapers. An official with the US High Commission noted the irony of the situation when he remarked that although it would have been preferable for the Germans to focus their attention on more "important" matters than the fate of convicted war criminals, "that [they] are taking advantage of the *democ-*

ratic privilege of expressing their views on controversial issues is commendable."[73] Indeed, the undoing of the war crimes trial program was very much a negotiated process, with concessions ceded by both sides. The Germans wanted amnesty, they obtained early release; the Americans let the war criminals go, but their criminal records were not erased. Although morally unsatisfying, American responsiveness to German criticism of their trial program may actually have furthered the goal of democratization. Reflecting on the US occupation authorities' early revisions of the war crimes cases, General Lucius Clay, McCloy's predecessor as Military Governor of the American zone, remarked:

> [T]he obvious interest of the American people in justice and fair play rather impressed the German population. At least they learned that an official representing the United States must exercise his responsibilities in the bright light of public discussion. This was another and valuable lesson in democracy.[74]

Notes

This article was made possible in part by funds granted to the author through a Charles H. Revson Foundation Fellowship at the Center for Advanced Holocaust Studies, United States Holocaust Memorial Museum. The statements made and views expressed, however, are solely the responsibility of the author.

[1] August Fischer, mayor of the town of Kempten and president of the "Association of Returnees, POWs and Family Members of Missing Germans," letter to all US Congressmen and Senators, 10 November 1953, Bundesarchiv Koblenz (hereafter BAK), B305/55: Tätigkeit des Gemischten Ausschußes, insb. für die Landsberger Häftlinge.

[2] Henry Stimson to Franklin Roosevelt, 9 September 1944, in *The American Road to Nuremberg: The Documentary Record 1944-1945*, ed. Bradley Smith (Stanford: Hoover Institution Press, 1982), 30-31. On the goals for the American war crimes trial program, see also Lawrence Douglas, *The Memory of Judgment: Making Law and History in the Trials of the Holocaust* (New Haven: Yale University Press, 2001), Arieh Kochavi, *Prelude to Nuremberg: Allied War Crimes Policy and the Question of Punishment* (Chapel Hill: University of North Carolina Press, 1998), Stephan Landsman, *Crimes of the Holocaust: The Law Confronts Hard Cases* (Philadelphia: University of Pennsylvania Press, 2005), and Telford Taylor, *The Anatomy of the Nuremberg Trials: A Personal Memoir* (New York: Knopf, 1992).

[3] Murray Bernays, "Memorandum on Trial of European War Criminals, 15 September 1944," in *The American Road to Nuremberg*, 36.

[4] The most commonly held figure for the Dachau trials is 489 cases involving 1,672 defendants. Recent research has revealed that there were in fact 486 cases with 1,676 defendants. See Lisa Yavnai, "Military Justice: The U.S. Army War Crimes Trials in Germany, 1944-1947" (PhD diss., London School of Economics and Political Science, 2007). The US played vital roles in two other sets of trials: the 1946-1948 International Military Tribunal for the Far East which prosecuted twenty-eight former Japanese officers for war crimes, and the vast 1945-1948 denazification program, which was de-

signed to root out all traces of Nazism from German society by subjecting all individuals in positions of leadership to a thorough examination of past political sympathies and activities.

[5] The High Command Case defendants were: Gen. Johannes Blaskowitz, Gen. Karl Hollidt; Gen. Hermann Hoth, Lt.-Gen. Rudolf Lehmann, Lt.-Gen. Hermann Reinecke, Gen. Hans Reinhardt, Adm. Otto Schniewind, Field Marshal Hugo Sperrle, Field Marshal Georg von Kuechler, Field Marshal Wilhelm von Leeb, Lt.-Gen. Karl von Roques, Gen. Hans von Salmuth, Lt.-Gen. Walter Warlimont, Lt.-Gen. Otto Woehler. Blaskowitz committed suicide during the trial, and Sperrle and Schniewind were found not guilty. All of the remaining defendants were found guilty of war crimes and crimes against humanity. Two other of the Subsequent Proceedings concerned military men, but neither were as comprehensive in their examinations of *Wehrmacht* participation in the broad spectrum of crimes as the High Command Case. The Milch trial focused on *Luftwaffe* exploitation of slave labor and the Southeast Generals' case focused on the army's hostage reprisal policy in the Balkans. For more on these trials, see Germany (Territory under Allied Occupation, 1945-1955: U.S. Zone), Military Tribunals, *Trials of War Criminals before the Nuernberg Military Tribunals under Control Council Law No. 10; Nuernberg, October 1946-April 1949.* 15 vols. (Buffalo: William S. Hein & Co., Inc., 1997), Cases II and VII.

[6] The most egregious of these crimes were based on orders originating with or communicated through the offices or headquarters of the men on trial (who represented both staff and field officers) and included the now infamous Commissar Order, Barbarossa Jurisdiction Order, the Commando Order, the Reichenau Order, and support for and cooperation with the *Einsatzgruppen* in the mass murder of racial and ideological "enemies" of the state and with the Reich Economic Office in the enslavement of civilian populations. The terms "partisan" and "partisan-suspect" were applied to anyone presumed to be acting against German forces. In practice, *Wehrmacht* officers executed Jews and even unarmed women and children believed to be sympathizing with or offering aid to partisans.

[7] Defendants convicted at Dachau were incarcerated in Landsberg alongside the Subsequent Nuremberg Proceedings convicts, however the army retained jurisdiction over them.

[7] HICOG Office of Political Affairs Memorandum, Subject: "The War Criminals Question," 22 December 1942, National Archives and Records Administration Record Group 466: *Records of the US High Command for Germany (HICOG) Office of the US High Commissioner for Germany, Bonn* (Hereafter NARA RG 466), Entry 10A: Security-Segregated Records, 1949-1952 (later: 1953-1955, Box 28, Folder: 321.6 German War Criminals – General.

[8] Ibid.

[9] German Federal Government, letter to the High Commissioners, undated, BAK, B305/141: Auswärtiges Amt, Deutsche Kriegsverurteilte in Landsberg 1949-1952.

[10] Dr. Gebhard Müller, Staatspräsident, Land Württemberg-Hohenzollern, letter to Chancellor Adenauer re. Decree of an Amnesty for Germans who were sentenced by Allied military courts, 21 October 1949, BAK, B305/141: Auswärtiges Amt, Deutsche Kriegsverurteilte in Landsberg, 1949-1952, and Rudolf Aschenauer, letter to Bundesjustizminister Dr. Thomas Dehler, 10 November 1949, BAK, B305/132: Deutsche Kriegsverurteilte in Landsberg: Allgemeines und Einzelfälle: 1949 – 1952. On the Adenauer government's policy of integration of former Nazis and convicted war criminals into

West German society, see especially: Ulrich Brochhagen, *Nach Nürnberg: Vergangenheitsbewältigung und Westintegration in der Ära Adenauer* (Hamburg: Junius Verlag, 1994), Frank Buscher, *The U.S. War Crimes Trial Program in Germany, 1946-1955* (New York: Greenwood Press, 1989), Norbert Frei, *Adenauer's Germany and the Nazi Past: The Politics of Amnesty and Integration* (New York: Columbia University Press, 2002), Jörg Freidrich, *Die kalte Amnestie: NS-Täter in der Bundersrepublik* (Frankfurt: Fischer Taschenbuch Verlag, 1984), and Jeffrey Herf, *Divided Memory: The Nazi Past in the Two Germanys* (Cambridge: Harvard University Press, 1997).

[11] This is the same formula that applied in US prisons. HICOG, Letter to Colonel Damon Gunn, JAG, 22 May 1950, and Robert Bowie, HICOG General Counsel, Memorandum for John J. McCloy, 3 August 1950, National Archives and Records Administration Record Group 238 *National Archives Collection of World War II War Crimes Records Advisory Board on Clemency for War Criminals Office of the High Commissioner for Germany 1947-1950, Miscellaneous Correspondence* (Hereafter NARA RG 238), Entry 213: Correspondence and other Records, 1950, Box 2, Folder: Clemency Committee, General File. On John McCloy's tenure as High Commissioner see Kai Bird, *The Chairman: John J. McCloy – The Making of the American Establishment* (New York: Simon & Schuster, 1992), Thomas Alan Schwarz, *America's Germany: John J. McCloy and the Federal Republic of Germany* (Cambridge: Harvard University Press, 1991), and Charles Thayer, *The Unquiet Germans* (New York: Harper, 1957).

[12] John McCloy, letter to Mr. C. M. Bolds, Office of the Land Commissioner for Bavaria, March 1950, and HICOG Staff Announcement No. 117: "Establishment of Advisory Board on Clemency for War Criminals," 18 July 1950, NARA RG 238, Entry 213: Correspondence and other Records, 1950, Box 2, Folder: Clemency Committee, General File, and Major Joseph Haefele, Headquarters, European Command, Office of the Judge Advocate (JAG), memo on war crimes for Colonel Stanley Jones, Acting Judge Advocate General, 3 August 1950, NARA RG 549 *Records of US Army Europe Judge Advocate Division War Crimes Branch,* Entry 2237: Records Relating to Post Trial Activities 1945-1947, Clemency Files 1947-1950, Box 2, Folder: Clemency Files 1949-1950 General Administration.

[13] HICOG, letter to Colonel Damon Gunn, 22 May 1950, NARA RG 238, Entry 213: Correspondence and other Records, 1950, Box 2, Folder: Clemency Committee, General File.

[14] Dennis Bark and David Gress, *A History of West Germany,* vol. 1, *From Shadow to Substance 1945-1963* (Oxford: Blackwell, 1989), 280.

[15] Schwartz, *America's Germany*, 231. On the European Defense Community, see: Edward Fursdon, *The European Defense Community: A History* (New York: St. Martin's Press, 1980).

[16] Admiral (Ret.) Gottfried Hansen, Letter to John J. McCloy, 31 December 1950, NARA RG 466, Entry 1: Classified General Records, 1949-1952, 1951 #1-134, Box 24, Folder: January 1951 – D(51) 126 War Crimes.

[17] General Heinz Guderian, Letter to John J. McCloy, 1 January 1951, NARA RG 466, Entry 1: Classified General Records, 1949-1952, 1951 #1-134, Box 24, Folder: January 1951 – D(51)1 – D(51)30.

[18] Draft Memorandum, Subject: "Meeting Between Mr. McCloy and Delegation from Bundestag, 9 January 1951," NARA RG 466, Entry 1: Classified General Records, 1949-1952, 1951 #1-134, Box 24, Folder: January 1951 – D(51)1 – D(51)30.

[19] John J. McCloy, Letter to Gottfried Hansen, 22 January 1951, NARA RG 466, Entry 1: Classified General Records, 1949-1952, 1951 #1-134, Box 24, Folder: January 1951 – D(51)126 War Crimes.
[20] Draft Memorandum, “Meeting Between Mr. McCloy and Delegation from Bundestag, 9 January 1951,” NARA RG 466, Entry 1: Classified General Records, 1949-1952, 1951 #1-134, Box 24, Folder: January 1951 – D(51)1 – D(51)30.
[21] McCloy also released one prisoner on medical parole. McCloy’s decisions applied to eighty-eight cases. Convicts in the IG Farben and Flick cases were not concerned as they had either already been released or were scheduled for release during the time of the Clemency Board’s reviews. The three High Command Case reductions were to shorter prison terms, none were to “time served” as in many other cases. The remaining death sentences were carried out amidst great protest in June 1951. Office of the US High Commissioner for Germany, “Landsberg: A Documentary Report,” 31 January 1951, NARA RG 466, Entry 17: Publications Relating to the US’ Occupation of Germany, 1945-1953, Displaced Populations thru The Special Projects Program, Box 3, Folder: Landsberg, A Documentary Report 31 January 1951.
[22] John J. McCloy, Secret Outgoing Telegram to Kellermann, Subject: McCloy’s final decisions on Landsberg war criminals, 30 January 1951, NARA RG 466, Entry 1: Classified General Records, 1949-1952, 1951 #1-134, Box 24, Folder: Jan 1951 D(51)94 - D(51)134.
[23] Office of the US High Commissioner for Germany, “Landsberg: A Documentary Report,” 31 January 1951, NARA RG 466, Entry 17: Publications Relating to the US’ Occupation of Germany, 1945-1953, Displaced Populations thru The Special Projects Program, Box 3, Folder: Landsberg, A Documentary Report 31 January 1951.
[24] John J. McCloy, Letter to David Peck, Presiding Justice, Supreme Court Appellate Division, 5 February 1951, NARA RG 466, Entry 1: Classified General Records, 1949-1952, 1951 #1-134, Box 24, Folder: January 1951 – D(51)1 – D(51)126 War Crimes.
[25] Office of the US High Commissioner for Germany Public Affairs Division, “Review of German and Foreign Press Reaction to the Clemency Decisions on Landsberg War Crimes Cases,” 10 February 1951, NARA RG 466, Entry 1: Classified General Records, 1949-1952, 1951 #1-134, Box 24, Folder: January 1951 – D(51)1 – D(51)126 War Crimes.
[26] Ibid.
[27] Ibid., and B. R. Shute, Director, Office of Intelligence, HICOG, Confidential Memorandum, Subject: “Analysis of letters on the Landsberg decisions,” 19 March 1951, NARA RG 466, Entry 10A: Security-Segregated Records, 1949-1952 (later: 1953-1955, Box 28, Folder: 321.6 German War Criminals - General.
[28] Ibid., and B.R. Shute, Director, Office of Intelligence, HICOG, Confidential Office Memorandum, Office of the US High Commissioner for Germany for John J McCloy, Subject: “Analysis of Letters on Landsberg Decisions,” 9 March 1951, NARA RG 466, Entry 1: Classified General Records, 1949-1952, Box 24, Folder: Jan 1951 – D(51) 126 War Crimes.
[29] Charles Thayer, Chief, Reports Division, Office of Political Affairs, HICOG, Report: “Some German Comments on the Continued Allied Imprisonment of German Generals,” 12 March 1952, NARA RG 466, Entry 10A: Security-Segregated Records, 1949-1952 (later: 1953-1955), Box 28, Folder: 321.6 German War Criminals - General.

[30] Erich Mende, Free Democratic Party, Letter to John J. McCloy, 27 November 1951, BAK, B305/131: Deutsche Kriegsverurteilte in Landsberg, Allgemeines und Einzelfälle 1949-1952. Emphasis added.
[31] Frei, *Adenauer's Germany and the Nazi Past*, 190.
[32] Ibid., 195.
[33] Eli Whitney Debevoise, HICOG General Counsel, Report, Subject: "Summary Background War Criminal Information," 6 September 1952, NARA RG 466, Entry 10A: Security-Segregated Records, 1949-1952 (later: 1953-1955), Box 28, Folder: 321.6 German War Criminals - General.
[34] Ibid., and Foreign Service of the United States of America Classified Telegram summarizing *Bundestag* debate, 7 September 1952, NARA RG 466, Entry 10A: Security-Segregated Records, 1949-1952 (later: 1953-1955), 321.4 – 321.6, Box 28, Folder: 321.6 German War Criminals – General and Dr. Erich Mende, Letter to Konrad Adenauer, 19 July 1952, NARA RG 466, Entry 10A: Security-Segregated Records, 1949-1952 (later: 1953-1955), 321.4 – 321.6, Box 28, Folder: 321.6 German War Criminals – General.
[35] Eli Whitney Debevoise, HICOG General Counsel, Report, Subject: "Summary Background War Criminal Information," 6 September 1952, NARA RG 466, Entry 10A: Security-Segregated Records, 1949-1952 (later: 1953-1955), Box 28, Folder: 321.6 German War Criminals - General.
[36] Admiral (ret.) Gottfried Hansen, letter to General Ridgway, Commander in Chief, Atlantic Pact Forces, Paris, 10 August 1952, NARA RG 466, Entry 10A: Security-Segregated Records, 1949-1952 (later: 1953-1955), 321.4 – 321.6, Box 28, Folder: 321.6 German War Criminals – General. Copies of both the letter and the resolution were sent to HICOG as well. *Verband Deutscher Soldaten* and *Bund der Berufssoldaten,* "Resolution," 14 July 1952, NARA RG 466, Entry 56: War Crimes Case File and Related Records, War Crimes Prisoner Data, Box 1, Folder: War Crimes (Material from Mr. Hulse). On the strength and significance of German veterans' associations in shaping postwar politics, particularly their involvement in the rearmament debate, see especially: James Diehl, *The Thanks of the Fatherland: German Veterans after the Second World* War (Chapel Hill: The University of North Carolina Press, 1993), David Clay Large, *Germans to the Front: West German Rearmament in the Adenauer Era* (Chapel Hill: The University of North Carolina Press, 1996), Jay Lockenour, *Soldiers as Citizens: Former Wehrmacht Officers in the Federal Republic of Germany, 1945-1955* (Lincoln: University of Nebraska Press, 2001), Robert Moeller, *War Stories: The Search for a Usable Past in the Federal Republic of Germany* (Berkeley: University of California Press, 2001), and Alaric Searle, *Wehrmacht Generals, West German Society, and the Debate on Rearmament, 1949-1959* (Westport: Praeger, 2003).
[37] Buscher, *The US War Crimes Trial Program in Germany,* 107.
[38] Eli Whitney Debevoise, Report, Subject: "Summary Background War Criminal Information," 6 September 1952, and HICOG translation of an editorial by Adelbert Weinstein, "A Mortgage of a Special Kind," *Frankfurter Allgemeine Zeitung,* 18 August 1952, NARA RG 466, Entry 10A: Security-Segregated Records, 1949-1952 (later: 1953-1955) 321.4 – 321.6, Box 28, Folder: 321.6 German War Criminals – General.
[39] "Confidential-Security Political Brief Number 5, Subject: "Political Aspects of the War Criminals Question," undated but likely January 1953, NARA RG 466, Entry 48: Security Segregated Records of the Prisons Division, Box 10, Folder: War Crimes Trial

– War Crimes - 118. This brief cites the results of an October 1952 HICOG public opinion survey, mentioned above; Buscher, *The US War Crimes Program Trial in Germany,* 91.
[40] *Die Neue Zeitung*, 9-10 August 1952, quoted in Frei, *Adenauer's Germany and the Nazi Past,* 211.
[41] Eli Whitney Debevoise, Report, Subject: "Summary Background War Criminal Information," 6 September 1952, NARA RG 466, Entry 10A: Security-Segregated Records, 1949-1952 (later: 1953-1955) 321.4 – 321.6, Box 28, Folder: 321.6 German War Criminals – General, and "Confidential-Security Political Brief Number 5, Subject: "Political Aspects of the War Criminals Question," undated but likely January 1953, NARA RG 466, Entry 48: Security Segregated Records of the Prisons Division, Box 10, Folder: War Crimes Trial – War Crimes - 118. In the time since the Landsberg decisions, one of the High Command Generals (Reinhardt) was released on compassionate parole, and another (Woehler) was released in accordance with his good conduct time credit.
[42] F. G. Hulse, HICOG Office Memorandum for Eli Whitney Debevoise, Subject: "Publication of the Records and Justments [sic] Made and Given in the Trials Conducted at Nuremberg under Control Council Law 10," 22 July 1952, NARA RG 466, Entry 48: Security Segregated Records of the Prisons Division, Box 6, Folder: Control Council Law No. 10 (Exchange of information re. persons transferred pursuant to Control Council Law No. 10 1952).
[43] Eli Whitney Debevoise, Report, Subject: "Summary Background War Criminal Information," 6 September 1952, NARA RG 466, Entry 10A: Security-Segregated Records, 1949-1952 (later: 1953-1955) 321.4 – 321.6, Box 28, Folder: 321.6 German War Criminals – General.
[44] Eli Whitney Debevoise, HICOG Office Memorandum for Assistant High Commissioner Reber, Subject: "Publication of the Records and Judgments Made and Given in the Trials conducted at Nuremberg under Control Council Law 10," undated but after 22 July 1952, NARA RG 466, Entry 48: Security Segregated Records of the Prisons Division, Box 6, Folder: Control Council Law No. 10 (Exchange of information re. persons transferred pursuant to Control Council Law No. 10 1952).
[45] Telford Taylor, *Final Report to the Secretary of the Army on Nuernberg War Crimes Trials under Control Council Law no. 10* (Washington DC: US Government Printing Office), 100.
[46] Telford Taylor, Memorandum for US Military Governor for Germany, Subject: "Publication of the Nurnberg Trial Proceedings under Law No. 10 in the German Language," 15 April 1949, and Paul Gantt, Memorandum, Subject: "Telephone Conversation with Mr. Thomas Carson on 18 May 1949," 18 May 1949, NARA RG 238, Entry 196: Correspondence, Reports and Other Records, 1948-1949, Correspondence, Memos, Bulletins, Box 1, Folder: Volume XV Publications (A) English (B) German Paul H. Gantt.
[47] Drexel Sprecher, Memorandum for Telford Taylor, Subject: "Weekly Report," 29 December 1948, NARA RG 238, Entry 196: Correspondence, Reports and Other Records, 1948-1949, Correspondence, Memos, Bulletins, Box 1, Folder: Volume IX Publication Paul H. Gantt.
[48] Drexel Sprecher, Memorandum for Colonel Edward H. Young, Subject: "Requests by Germans for copies of German and English edition of the official publication on the subsequent proceedings," 18 March 1949, NARA RG 238, Entry 196: Correspondence, Reports and Other Records, 1948-1949, Correspondence, Memos, Bulletins, Box 1,

Folder: Volume XV Publications (A) English (B) German Paul H Gantt, and Drexel Sprecher, Letter to Dr. P. Barandon, 16 December 1948, in: NARA RG 238, Entry 196: Correspondence, Reports and Other Records, 1948-1949, Correspondence, Memos, Bulletins, Box 1, Folder: Volume IX Publication Paul H. Gantt.

[49] Telford Taylor, Memorandum for US Military Governor for Germany, Subject: "Publication of the Nurnberg Trial Proceedings under Law No. 10 in the German Language," 15 April 1949, NARA RG 238, Entry 196: Correspondence, Reports and Other Records, 1948-1949, Correspondence, Memos, Bulletins, Box 1, Folder: Volume XV Publications (A) English (B) German Paul H. Gantt.

[50] Ibid.

[51] Paul Gantt, Memorandum, Subject: "Telephone Conversation with Mr. Thomas Carson on 18 May 1949," 18 May 1949, NARA RG 238, Entry 196: Correspondence, Reports and Other Records, 1948-1949, Correspondence, Memos, Bulletins, Box 1, Folder: Volume XV Publications (A) English (B) German Paul H. Gantt.

[52] Fred Niebergall, Memorandum for Paul Gantt, Subject: "Telephone conversation with Mr. T. Carson in Berlin," 9 June 1949 NARA RG 238, Entry 196: Correspondence, Reports and Other Records, 1948-1949, Correspondence, Memos, Bulletins, Box 1, Folder: Volume XV Publications (A) English (B) German Paul H. Gantt, and Hays (OMGUS), Cable to Department of the Army and Office of Chief of Counsel for War Crimes, 17 June 1949, NARA RG 238, Entry 196: Correspondence, Reports and Other Records, 1948-1949, Correspondence, Memos, Bulletins, Box 1, Folder: Volume IX Publication Paul H. Gantt.

[53] Taylor, *Final Report,* 106.

[54] Gordon Gray, letter to Emanuel Celler, House of Representatives, 31 October 1949, NARA RG 466, Entry 56: War Criminal Case Files, Box 1, Folder: Publication – German Text – Major Nuremberg Trials, and Major Abraham S. Hyman, Acting Adviser on Jewish Affairs, Headquarters, European Command, Letter to John J. McCloy, Subject: "Publication in German of records of major Nurnberg War Crimes trials," 19 December 1949, NARA RG 466, Entry 56: War Criminal Case Files and Related Records, Box 1, Folder: Publication - German Text - Major Nurnberg Trials. The English fifteen volume edition, called *Trials of War Criminals before the Nuernberg Military Tribunals under Control Council Law no. 10, Nuernberg 1946 – April 1949* was published in installments by the Washington US Government Printing Office between 1949 and 1953. It is commonly referred to as the "Green Series" because of the books' green covers. A private Buffalo, New York publisher re-issued the series in 1997. No equivalent in German exists.

[55] Frederick G. Hulse, HICOG Office Memorandum for Eli Whitney Debevoise, Subject: "Publication of the Records and Justments [sic] Made and Given in the Trials Conducted at Nuremberg under Control Council Law 10," 22 July 1952, NARA RG 466, Entry 48: Security Segregated Records of the Prisons Division, Box 6, Folder: Control Council Law No. 10 (Exchange of information re. persons transferred pursuant to Control Council Law No. 10 1952). A little over one page of the Landsberg Report was dedicated to the High Command Case that could in no way do justice to the mass of incriminating evidence and nuances of the lengthy judgment. The High Command Case comprised over 10 300 pages of transcript, 1778 prosecution and 2121 defense evidence exhibits (which ranged from one to several hundred pages each), plus several thousand pages of prosecution and defense briefs and memoranda.

[56] Jonathan Rintels, Letter to Sheperd Stone, 27 February 1951, NARA RG 466, Entry 56: War Criminal Case Files and Related Records, Box 1, Folder: War Crimes (materials from Mr. Hulse).
[57] Ibid.
[58] Eli Whitney Debevoise, Office Memorandum, for Assistant High Commissioner Reber, Subject: "Publication of the Records and Judgments Made and Given in the Trials conducted at Nuremberg under Control Council Law 10," undated but after 22 July 1952, NARA RG 466, Entry 48: Security Segregated Records of the Prisons Division, Box 6, Folder: Control Council Law No. 10 (Exchange of information re. persons transferred pursuant to Control Council Law No. 10 1952).
[59] Frederick G. Hulse, HICOG Office Memorandum for Eli Whitney Debevoise, Subject: "Publication of the Records and Justments [sic] Made and Given in the Trials Conducted at Nuremberg under Control Council Law 10," 22 July 1952, NARA RG 466, Entry 48: Security Segregated Records of the Prisons Division, Box 6, Folder: Control Council Law No. 10 (Exchange of information re. persons transferred pursuant to Control Council Law No. 10 1952). Emphasis in the original text.
[60] Eli Whitney Debevoise, Office Memorandum for Assistant High Commissioner Reber, Subject: "Publication of the Records and Judgments Made and Given in the Trials conducted at Nuremberg under Control Council Law 10," undated but after 22 July 1952, NARA RG 466, Entry 48: Security Segregated Records of the Prisons Division, Box 6, Folder: Control Council Law No. 10 (Exchange of information re. persons transferred pursuant to Control Council Law No. 10 1952).
[61] HICOG Office of Political Affairs, Memorandum for the Department of State, Subject: "The War Criminals Question," 22 December 1952, NARA RG 466, Entry 10A: Security-Segregated Records, 1949-1952 (later: 1953-1955), 321.4 – 321.6, Box 28, Folder: 321.6 German War Criminals – General.
[62] Classified Telegram to Secretary of State, 12 September 1952, NARA RG 466, Entry 10A: Security-Segregated Records, 1949-1952 (later: 1953-1955), 321.4 – 321.6, Box 28, Folder: 321.6 German War Criminals – General.
[63] HICOG Office of Political Affairs, Memorandum for the Department of State, Subject: "The War Criminals Question," 22 December 1952, NARA RG 466, Entry 10A: Security-Segregated Records, 1949-1952 (later: 1953-1955), 321.4 – 321.6, Box 28, Folder: 321.6 German War Criminals – General.
[64] The Foreign Service of the United States of America, Classified Telegram to Harben, HICOG, 19 January 1953, NARA RG 466, Entry 10A: Security-Segregated Records, 1953-1955, 321.4 - 321.6, Box 164, Folder: 321.6 War Criminals - General 1953-55.
[65] HICOG Office of Political Affairs, Memorandum for the Department of State, Subject: "The War Criminals Question," 22 December 1952, NARA RG 466, Entry 10A: Security-Segregated Records, 1949-1952 (later: 1953-1955), 321.4 – 321.6, Box 28, Folder: 321.6 German War Criminals – General.
[66] Ibid.
[67] Ibid.
[68] HICOG Office of Political Affairs, Memorandum for the Department of State, Subject: "The War Criminals Question," 22 December 1952, NARA RG 466, Entry 10A: Security-Segregated Records, 1949-1952 (later: 1953-1955) 321.4 – 321.6, Box 28, Folder: 321.6 German War Criminals – General.
[69] Edwin A. Plitt, American Embassy, Bonn, Foreign Service Dispatch to Department of State, Washington: "History of the Interim Mixed Parole and Clemency Board, with

Comments for the Guidance of Future Bodies of Similar Assignment," 15 September 1955, NARA RG 466, Entry 10A: Security Segregated Records 1953-55, 321.4 – 321.6, Box 164, Folder: 321.6 War Criminals – Mixed Board 1953-55.

[70] Interim Mixed Parole and Clemency Board, Report for US High Commissioner James Conant, 22 October 1954, NARA RG 466, Entry 9: General Records, 1953-55, 321.6 – 321.6B, Box 48, Folder: 321.6 War Criminals – General 1953-55.

[71] American Embassy, Bonn, Classified Foreign Service Despatch to the Department of State, Subject: "War Criminals," 3 August 1955, NARA RG 466, Entry 10A: Security Segregated Records 1953-55, 321.4 – 321.6, Box 164, Folder: 321.6 War Criminals – General.

[72] Henri Eschbach, Gottfried Kuhnt, Emil Lersch, A. Michelson, Spencer Phenix and Hellmuth Weber, "To the Signatories of the Convention on the settlement of matters arising out of the war and the occupation signed at Bonn on 26 May 1952": Final Report of the Mixed Board, 21 October 1958, BAK, B305/56: Zentrale Rechtsschutzstelle, Tätigkeit des Gemischten Ausschusses, insb. (Nr. 55 und 56) für die Landsberger Häftlinge.

[73] Roger Dow, Chief, Reports and Analysis Division, HICOG, report: "West German Reactions to the Landsberg Decisions," 19 March 1951, NARA RG 466, Entry 10A: Security Segregated Records 1953-55, 321.4 – 321.6, Box 164, Folder: 321.6 War Criminals – Mixed Board 1953-55. Emphasis added.

[74] Lucius Clay, *Decision in Germany* (Garden City: Doubleday & Co., 1950), 254-5.

The Dorotheum as a Case Study of Austria after Fascism: Narratives of *Opfermythos* and *Wiederaufbau* after 1945.

Sonja Niederacher and Stefan August Lütgenau

The Dorotheum in Vienna is the largest auction house in continental Europe today. Founded in 1707, it is also the second oldest auction house on the Continent; only the *Auktionsverket*, established in Stockholm in 1687, is older. Until the twentieth century, the Dorotheum functioned mainly as a pawn brokerage and as an organizer of estate sales, but also an auction house in the world of the arts. Since 1900 it proved able to strengthen its position in the art market considerably, in addition to developing a banking branch. The Dorotheum was owned by the Austrian state until 2001, at which point the government sold the auction house to private investors, yet the statute of 1923 had long since freed it from direct governmental supervision of its commercial activities, and in 1979 the Dorotheum was transformed into a limited liability corporation. The 1923 legal structure forced the Dorotheum and its management to act more or less as a profit-oriented private enterprise despite being owned, controlled, and to some extend restricted in its business activities by the State and the Dorotheum statutes. [1] The Dorotheum auction house, pawn brokerage, and bank were established as a hybrid structure combining "benevolent" pawn activities with market-oriented auction and bank activities. This structure developed over the centuries of its existence and remained more or less unchanged during the Nazi period. Attempts to restructure the Dorotheum following the model of much smaller municipal pawn brokerages in Germany were abandoned by the National Socialist administration in Vienna and in the so-called "Ostmark" in 1939.

During the Nazi regime, various authorities in charge of confiscation of Jewish assets sold everything from household items to furniture to personal valuables through the Dorotheum. Moreover, the Dorotheum took over a major competitor in the Viennese pawn brokerage business in 1940.[2] Thanks to Nazi policies it could maintain and even significantly expand its position on the market. Indeed, an institution such as the Dorotheum provides an interesting case study on Europe after fascism given that in the late 1990s it had to confront serious allegations concerning its collaboration with the Nazi regime. The following section explains the historical context in which this theme is situated, namely the recent work of historical commissions in Austria that investigated Nazi era assets. This starting point provides the focus for investigation into the Dorotheum's self-perception vis-à-vis the Austrofascist period (1934-38) and Nazi era (1938-45) during the postwar decades prior to the process of coming to terms with the past (*Vergangenheitsbewältigung*) intensified in the 1990s. Indeed, with respect to its self-perception with regard to the Nazi past, the Dorotheum may deservedly be considered as a "micro-model" for broader trends in Austrian society and economy.

Our examination is thus twofold in nature, on the one hand we focus on the Dorotheum's own historiography, on the other we consider its economic positioning during the Second Republic with regard to the National Socialist legacy and the exigencies of reconstruction. In the process, we explore the way in which the Dorotheum constructed its postwar corporate identity, recast the narrative of its history and role during the fascist years, and represented itself in the post-fascist era as an active participant in reconstruction through corporate unity, hard work, and heroic reconfiguration. While we deconstruct the Dorotheum's own victim narrative and are critical of the postwar myth of a "Stunde Null" that suggests total destruction and a heroic rebuilding from absolutely nothing after the Nazi defeat, there is compelling evidence that the Dorotheum's economic reconstruction and the re-launch of business was achieved in the face of hardships caused by a devastated postwar economic system. Nevertheless we will show that economic activity and key personnel continuities from the pre- to post -1945 eras, represent striking contradiction to the Dorotheum's self-perception and official narrative. One of the features of this narrative that makes it so significant for historians (and lends the Dorotheum micro-model status for the Austrian context) is that it links accounts of economic reconstruction after two fascist regimes and war that characterized broader postwar Austrian historical meta-narrative—including the postulate that National Socialism was alien to Austria, and that Austrians had fallen victim to it.

The Dorotheum's Own Historiography after 1945 in Light of Recent Restitution Debates

Debate over stolen artwork and other objects looted during the Nazi era directed media scrutiny and widespread criticism towards the Dorotheum in recent years. These discussions forced the Dorotheum to take action that included permitting historians to examine the history of its business transactions during the years 1938-45. Art historians and restitution experts considered the Dorotheum report that emerged from investigative research as one of the most important missing links contributing to a deeper understanding of the Nazi system of art theft. Indeed, the previous absence of information concerning the Dorotheum raised suspicions that the institution might have been hiding dreadful facts[3]; during the process of investigation into the Dorotheum's past dealings, speculation had been rife in the media and the Dorotheum faced criticized for its reluctance to confront its own past.[4] The Dorotheum's key position in fencing Nazi looted valuables notwithstanding, we must remember that it was only one part (albeit a very significant one) of a highly effective deprivation network that extended into the political, economic, and social spheres.[5] Examination of the Dorotheum's past must be considered within the context of a global negotiation of the past that began during the 1990s and opened up new avenues for understanding and facing up to the National Socialist legacy. National and local governments, corporations, and museums found themselves confronted with their Nazi past.[6] Because of claims in the United States and elsewhere against the Austrian State and Austrian companies engaged in business during the National Socialist era, in 1998 the Austrian Republic found itself obliged to appoint a committee of historians commissioned with engaging in a comprehensive reappraisal of the expropriation of property that had belonged to Jewish citizens from 1938 onwards, and of other areas such as the exploitation of forced labor. Taken together, these investigations have reopened the previously closed chapter of compensation for victims of Nazi persecution. The commission's 2003 final report illustrates Austria's half-hearted approach towards the restitution of confiscated and aryanized Jewish assets and emphasizes the lack of legal support for victims who sought to reclaim their belongings during the decades following the war.[7]

This process of adjudication and restitution that has been characterized by historian Elazar Barkan as one of "amending historical injustices in international morality."[8] The international emergence of reconciliation and restitution after the end of the Cold War, he argues, has corresponded with an empowerment of victim status as an identity marker and political factor.[9] Indeed, the definition of victim has expanded to new groups who had not previously been considered as such.[10] Barkan identifies the political acknowledgment of guilt as the basis of this process.[11] Sixty years after the collapse of National Socialism, victims of the regime's policies can now expect Austrian society to take their demands for restitution seriously. The official acknowledgement of responsibility and regret is an essential part of the reconciliation process, in addition to legally mandated material compensation.[12] Austria has had a long way to go in this area, particularly compared with steps taken by the Federal Republic of Germany. In the case of the Dorotheum, many critics do not merely blame the auction house for its activities in the Nazi era, but even more so for its behavior towards victims in recent years. The myth of Austria-as-victim of National Socialism dominated collective memory and was stubbornly resistant to critical scrutiny until the mid 1980s, when for the first time historians aroused public interest by casting doubt on this interpretation.[13] The myth had served as a basic pillar in reconstructing Austrian national identity after the fall of the Third Reich. Since the "Anschluss" was considered an occupation of the country that contravened international law, no blame for the crimes of National Socialism was accepted; the separation from Germany also constituted an attempt to detach Austria from guilt associated with the Nazi regime. This article focuses on a period before the Dorotheum came under pressure to deal with its past, insofar as we focus on the institution's own historical treatment of its past at two distinct moments during the 1950s and the 1980s, well before *Vergangenheitsbewältigung* had become a significant issue for Austrian society. We will explore the ways in which the auction house perceived its position during the Nazi period and how it managed to integrate this perception into the official postwar narrative.

The Dorotheum is proud of its long tradition, as evident in the company sign's reference to its founding in 1707. Several anniversaries or other celebrations occasioned the management to commission either trained historians or interested employees to write up the Dorotheum's history. The oldest historical account, written by Albert Starzer, dates to 1901 and provides a profound overview of the history of pawn brokerage in the Habsburg Monarchy.[14] Later works relied primarily on this study, such as the short survey by Theodor Mayer from 1920.[15] Starzer also inspired Marcel Ségur-Cabanac's commemorative brochure in 1957 published by the Dorotheum,[16] as well as the work by Felix Czeike marking the 275th anniversary in 1982.[17] The latter remains the most comprehensive work on the history of the auction house published to date that includes the twentieth century.

We have selected Marcel Ségur-Cabanac's 1957 brochure and Felix Czeike's 1982 volume as case studies in the Dorotheum's narratives of self-perception, its experience of political ruptures, and of war-related destruction and postwar reconstruction. It must be stressed that the Dorotheum did not intend to sponsor critical retrospectives from the standpoint of past economic activity or moral/ethical behavior. In general, institutional memoirs like these present an affirmative picture of the company in order to cultivate a positive public image. They develop their stories as positively as possible, minimizing or omitting disturbing facts, attributing good intentions to management and attributing negatives to external factors. Such factors may be the product of international economic developments or the result of governmental policy. As we have alluded to above, and will explore in further detail below, the overall picture promoted in these works correlates closely with the then-dominant Austrian interpretation of history. In their description of the twentieth century, official Dorotheum historians never left the path of standardized national narratives. Many patterns of the Austrian postwar narrative that was based on the myth of Austrian victim status (*Opfermythos*) find their parallel in the historical self-portrayal of the auction house. Like any text, the two versions of Dorotheum history on which we focus here reveal more about the period in which they were produced than about the period they actually address.[18]

Marcel Ségur-Cabanac, author of the 24-paged brochure commemorating the 250th anniversary, was a member of the Dorotheum's management not a historian by profession. He had been one of twelve employees dismissed for political reasons right after the "Anschluss" on the initiative of former illegal Nazis working at the Dorotheum. This suggests that Ségur-Cabanac had been friendly to the Austrofascist staff organization. After World War II he returned to work for his former employer, and he eventually attained the position of general secretary. His brochure was the first to present the Dorotheum's history during the

1930s-1940s, and advanced perspectives that would emerge again in Felix Czeike's comprehensive work marking the 275th anniversary, right down to instances of identical phrasing.

Felix Czeike is a renowned Austrian historian with a particular research focus on the history of the city of Vienna. This might explain why there are portions of the text in which the Dorotheum appears to tell a Viennese history rather than a company history. The author provides historical details related to each building owned by the Dorotheum and describes in depth the environment of Vienna's First District in the eighteenth and nineteenth century. Unfortunately, he does not provide references for any of the archival sources he consulted. Although both texts were published to mark an anniversary, Czeike's work was intended for a broader audience than Ségur-Cabanac's brochure, insofar as the latter was intended for the Dorotheum itself; nonetheless, we can safely conclude that both texts were commissioned by the Dorotheum. To highlight their "official" character, Interior Minister Oskar Helmer wrote the foreword to the 1957 brochure and Federal President Rudolf Kirchschläger penned the 1982 foreword. Given Ségur-Cabanac's personal experience of the events taking place in the Dorotheum during the 1930s-1940s vs. Czeike's status as an academically trained historian without Ségur-Cabanac's close affiliation with the institution, it is noteworthy that their versions resembled each other so closely. Moreover, the reader would not notice the twenty-five year gap between publication of these texts, so similar seem their points of view toward the Nazi era. This illustrates the rather stable attitude vis-à-vis the Nazi past during the Second Republic until the Waldheim affair rocked both society and challenged established scholarly interpretation. In contrast to the dominant perspective at the beginning of the twenty-first century that place the Dorotheum's profits from Nazi looting front and center, Felix Czeike expressed concern about potential clients lost through Nazi persecution, which made it necessary for the Dorotheum to reestablish a new clientele after 1945.[19]

Austrofascism and National Socialism

To better understand National Socialism in Austria it is necessary to consider the Austrofascist period that preceded it. This is particularly the case for the Dorotheum, since the takeover of the institution by Nazi employees began in the early 1930s; 1938 marked the culmination of this process. There has been lively historiographic debate as to whether the Dollfuß-Schuschnigg regime can be considered fascist or merely authoritarian. For example, the elimination of parliamentary governance, was consistent with developments in Italy, Spain, and Germany, but the rejection of Nazi anti-clericalism marked a significant difference from the German model (one, in fact, designed to appeal to Austrians and take the edge of any enthusiasm that Austrians might muster for National

Socialism). Following historian Jill Lewis , we favor the term “Austrofascism,”, to demarcate the Austrian case from other examples. Not unlike the National Socialists, the Austrofascist regime also sought to ensure that the public—and private—sector met the regime’s requirements.[20] Social Democrats and National Socialists were declared illegal and became the main target of political cleansing in the public sector. When the Nazis assumed power in 1938, they settled old scores and tried to kick those employees out of the Dorotheum who had denounced them in 1934. In the main, both Ségur-Cabanac and Czeike minimalized the years under authoritarian and dictatorial regimes; rather they content themselves with generic statements. Even Ségur-Cabanac, an eyewitness who could have relied on first-hand experience with National Socialist harassment and loss of employment did not devote any attention to the Nazi authorities’ replacement of the entire Dorotheum management in 1938 and dismissal of employees according to ideological criteria—including Ségur-Cabanac himself. It is inconceivable that in 1957 parts of the staff would not have known this based on their own experiences. Not only did he not address this, his audience likely did not expect him to do so. The first decades of the Second Republic were characterized by tacit agreement between the Catholic-conservative Austrian People’s Party (*Österreichische Volkspartei*, ÖVP) and the Social Democrats (*Sozialistische Partei Österreichs*, SPÖ) not to bring up the Austrofascist period, since interpretations of the origins of the 1934 civil war and the antidemocratic nature for the indigenous fascist Fatherland Front (*Vaterländische Front*, VF) remained a sore spot for their grand coalition government.[21] Nothing in the short paragraph Ségur-Cabanac devoted to the subject leads the reader to conclude that National Socialism had been not only an outside menace, but an internal consideration in Austrian politics since the early 1930s.[22] Who else but the author would have known that the activities of National Socialist employees of the Dorotheum had more impact on the auction house than any outside bureaucracy? Twenty-five years later Felix Czeike cast at least a brief glance at the Austrofascist period. For instance, he attributes the belated opening of a subsidiary to the difficult economic situation and the political tensions between the Austrofascist regime, the illegal Social Democrats, and the increasingly menacing National Socialists.

The Dorotheum as an Opponent of National Socialism?

Both authors advance the same central argument on the National Socialist era, namely that the institution had been in danger of being closed by the Nazis and only the early collapse of the Third Reich had prevented such action. In short, Dorotheum historiography placed itself squarely within the *Opfermythos* and characterized Nazism as a decidedly German phenomenon. Ségur-Cabanac’s text asserts that Nazi authorities were eager to shut down the Dorotheum because they regarded it as a welfare institution. "Shortly after the take over of power," he concludes, "it became evident that the National Socialists' intentions towards the institute were not at all friendly."[23] Czeike employs exactly the same words as Ségur-Cabanac; moreover, he spices up the story with an unverified anecdote of a Nazi official visiting the Dorotheum who he reports to have proclaimed, "I could imagine the Dorotheum to be closed."[24] Consultation of archival records reveals a different process at work, however. NS administration files confirm that Nazi authorities indeed thought of reorganizing the complexly structured institution. In the course of adapting the Austrian civil service to the German system, authorities considered separating the banking sector from the auction house and integrating the latter into the range of Viennese communal responsibilities.[25] However, this plan was abandoned in 1940 due to various economic considerations. This was very much to the satisfaction of the Dorotheum employees who had worried about their jobs and had started to intervene in this matter, writing petitions to government officials and even to Adolf Hitler. It seems that the rumors spreading through the house had survived the war and had reemerged in the official self-description.

Ségur-Cabanac and Czeike each assert unequivocally that the auction house was inescapably at the mercy of larger political machinations. However, instead of finding itself in a position to struggle for its survival—or, on the other hand, in order to survive, perhaps—the Dorotheum rose to become a favorite business partner of Nazi authorities, through its role in auctioning off looted Jewish possessions. The graphs in the appendix of the 1957 brochure indicate a considerable increase in sales for the late 1930s but the author neither comments on the fact nor raises the matter of business with looted Jewish property; aryanization was not a theme widely discussed in Second Republic society at the time. Instead, Ségur-Cabanac draws the reader's attention to the devastating consequences of the last weeks of the war. In March 1945 Allied bombers hit the main building in the Dorotheergasse as well as nine branch offices and residential buildings in different Viennese districts. Between 1957 and 1982 the Dorotheum historiography persistently states that the Dorotheum suffered extremely under the war, that both National Socialism and the war had been disastrous for business, and that in 1945 the Dorotheum had to restart its operations from virtually nothing. Thus, the Dorotheum again came across as a victim, not only of Nazism but of the war, too. "At the end of World War II the Dorotheum was left with nothing."[26] The official Dorotheum narrative had its own "Stunde Null" and could effectively disassociate itself with the taint of association with the NS regime. In particular, devastating Allied air raids served as a catharsis preceding the leap into a new period under different circumstances. Despite this sleight of hand, references to the past were fundamental for identity building in the Dorotheum; both Dorotheum accounts refer repeatedly to the founding year 1707 and focus on essential economical decisions from the eighteenth through the nineteenth centuries and conveniently side-step honest introspection.

Reconstruction

Eleven years of dictatorship and six years of war (including two years of air raids) devastated Austrian society and the Viennese cityscape. Reconstruction (*Wiederaufbau*) absorbed the attention of the city's administration and its residents in order to ward off long-term economic impoverishment and short-term threats to survival. Postwar society set to work transforming the end of the war into a new beginning, one generally characterized by optimism and a strong orientation towards the future. Retrospective narratives generally underline the positive aspects of *Wiederaufbau*, which also served as a psychological distraction from traumatic events. Personal testimonies reveal that this mentality influenced great parts of society.[27]

The Dorotheum narrative starts with reconstruction at precisely this point of devastation. "That which remained of the Dorotheum was, at first glance, only its trunk," wrote Ségur-Cabanac.[28] His brochure and Czeike's book suggest that aerial bombardment had destroyed everything that had been the Dorotheum; in fact, the main building had only been damaged and could reopen business within a short period of time. In this context, the buildings symbolize the embodiment of the Dorotheum, rather than simply real estate as part of the enterprise. The metaphor of the company *as the building* corresponds to the postwar image of reconstructing the republic by showing men at work building the new Austrian democracy as if it were a physical object. For example, in 1947 the Viennese City government organized an exhibition entitled "Wien baut auf. Zwei Jahre Wiederaufbau der Stadt Wien" ("Vienna Rebuilds: Two Years' Reconstruction of the City of Vienna"). The poster announcing the 1947 exhibition shows a man carrying a wooden beam. In the background, a woman plays what looks like "ring around the roses" with three children silhouetted against Vienna's city hall and the construction site of an apartment building. The man symbolizes the *Held der Arbeit* ("hero of labor"), whose contribution to reconstruction ensures a safe future for his family.[29]

"Wien baut auf"
Österreichische Nationalbibliothek, Call Number: OeNB M1097/06

The poster supports traditional gender roles by showing men at work and women with family. It also encodes *Wiederaufbau* as a male effort, while women seem mostly as the beneficiates of male activity. This image of *Wiederaufbau* was quite common at the time, as also indicated by other visual sources, for example posters by the Social Democratic Party. The motto surrounding the exhibition was "After death and destruction with planning and construction to peace and wealth." The municipal government used the impressive figures of 122 bridges reconstructed, and sixteen percent of living space reestablished within only two years to highlight its effectiveness. The self-representation makes the municipality appear as the most reliable force for reconstruction. Austrian works of art and a historical survey of political development rounded out the exhibition. At the same time reconstruction is presented as a common effort shared by those working in the social, cultural, and economic realms. Half of the exhibition catalogue consists of advertisements for approximately 500 Viennese firms and shops. This section bears the title "cultural, economical, and technical reconstruction." Reconstruction made people appear equal in their needs and hopes and helped to establish a community spirit. Furthermore, it provided the basis for a new national identity in the Second Republic.

Within this framework of the importance of community to reconstruction work, the dynamic individual assumed a key role in ensuring the success of *Wiederaufbau.* Dorotheum employees, as presented in the brochure, were ready to make sacrifices and were willing to reconstruct the building and reestablish the institution in the figurative sense. Furthermore, Ségur-Cabanac explained the upsurge of the postwar years as a product of sacrifices taken on in the reestablishment of the Dorotheum.

> The Dorotheum's situation seemed hopeless. The damage was extensive; still the will of the Dorotheum's personnel to reconstruct what had been destroyed was stronger still. Everybody—man and woman, young and old—helped, there was no distinction between classes, everyone worked according to his physical capacity, digging, sweeping, determined to do everything to let business reopen again as soon as possible.[30]

No passage in the brochure plays on the emotional register quite like this one. This was also the place to officially celebrate the particular contributions of distinct individuals. This is the first and only time that historical accounts featured ordinary staff members. A trace of democracy is evident in the lines when readers confronted the text and image of the bombed house being rebuilt through the exertion of Dorotheum staff members. This implication became even stronger through the symbolic reduction of the reconstruction of the main building and the complex workings of the firm to a simple image of the physical structure. This metaphor enhanced the reader's identification with the fate of the Dorotheum.

Coming to Terms with the Nazi Past: The Economic Dimension

As we have seen, between 1938 and 1945 the Dorotheum can be understood as a business unit amalgamated with the National Socialist regime, executing its policy of selling off expropriated Jewish property under the watchful eye of Nazi authorities. While in 1945 the newly re-established Austrian democratic government eliminated changes the Nazis had introduced into the Dorotheum's organizational structure, the institution's basic structure, aim, organization, and element of public control were left unchanged. Public ownership and control contributed to the Dorotheum management's pattern of closely aligning itself with the political system in power, whether dictatorial or democratic. When the management tried to expand the business activities of the Dorotheum—e.g., to act as a dealer of art, confiscated jewellery and real estate that had belonged to Jews—it faced unequivocal resistance from the Reich presidium, which argued that acting as trading or real estate agency would be action beyond the scope of the Dorotheum's competency. While in some cases (for example, art trade and trade in jewellery confiscated from Jews) the management was able to accomplish its aims despite concerns on the political level, it did not succeed in its attempt to establish the Dorotheum as the only authorized broker for aryanized real estate—if fact, at the end the Dorotheum did not deal with aryanized real estate at all.

Just as Austrian state and society had to adjust to a quite different economic environment following the collapse of the NS regime, the Dorotheum had to remodel its business strategy and adjust to new political, legal and economic circumstances as defined by the Allied occupation authorities. Not surprisingly, the macro economic environment the Dorotheum faced had changed dramatically. Due to the shortage of everyday consumer goods, people attempted to purchase used items of all kinds at auctions, even as the sources of goods to be auctioned withered away. Between 1942 and the first part of 1944 the shortages of everyday goods were at least partly compensated for by auctioning clothes, home furnishings, and household items confiscated from expelled or deported Jewish people. On the other hand, luxury goods were also sold through the Dorotheum, particularly pieces of art that had been bought by the Dorotheum in occupied western European countries (France, Belgium, and the Netherlands) and were auctioned or sold in Vienna. This was a significant source of income; for instance, a single purchase of jewellery from the Gestapo in Prague and sale to customers in Bohemia, Croatia, and Hungary contributed to more than twenty-two percent of 1943 revenues. The NS regime's criminal practice of basing its social policy on a system of looting occupied Europe (and particularly European Jews) and exploiting forced labor contributed to the Dorotheum's micro-level concerns both directly and indirectly: directly in terms of providing vast amounts of stolen goods and valuables to be sold or auctioned; indirectly insofar as between 1942 and 1944, art purchased in occupied western European countries at favorable currency exchange rates could be auctioned in an economic environment that would not otherwise have been ideal for auction houses under ordinary conditions, or in accordance with the rule of the law. [31]

Reviving Business and "Stunde Null"

With the defeat of National Socialism in April 1945, the Dorotheum was subject to changes on the board level as well as on the personnel level. The Dorotheum was reorganized along the lines of the statutes of 1923; members of the board of directors were suspended, one second-level manager was promoted to co-director status; a former long-serving manager who had fallen victim to political persecution in 1938 was reappointed in 1945 and promoted to the position of director. The re-established controlling body, the board of trusties (*Kuratorium*), was filled with reliable civil servants and former members of parliament free of association with National Socialism.

In terms of its economic operations, the Dorotheum had to adjust to the new situation. Enthusiasm associated with reconstruction notwithstanding, the economic situation in postwar Austria was characterized by what economic historian Hans Seidel has called the "three bottlenecks": shortages of food and goods, shortages in transportation, and shortages of energy and fuel.[32] These circumstances, a combination of a host of factors including the impact of occupation zones and new legal arrangements, cut the Dorotheum off from its previous supply of goods for auction. The Dorotheum's 1945 financial statement made evident these new challenges. Due to the extraordinary situation connected with the final stage of the war in the first quarter and the uncertainties connected to the end of war in the second quarter, the Dorotheum was only able to present a tentative balance total of 63.8 million Austrian Schillings for 1945. This total may appear solid at first glance.[33] The company had unusually high liquidity, with cash deposits at the Nationalbank and the Postsparkasse of 17.16 million Schillings and deposits of 23.33 million Schillings in bank accounts at the Zentralsparkasse, Creditanstalt, and Länderbank. At the same time the Dorotheum held fixed-interest bonds of the German Reich amounting to 9.37 million Schillings. As a result of the experience of World War I—i.e., the collapse of the German monetary system in 1918/19 and the distrust the general public had towards war bonds—the NS regime followed a strategy of hiding the high costs of war from the public.[34] Due to its policy of silently financing the war, the German government did not sell war bonds to individuals but forced intermediaries (banks, insurance companies, manufacturing concerns) to invest parts of their profits in war bonds. This can be understood as another form of war taxation. The Reich skimmed the at times significant profits made by private enterprises for its war. Germany would have been unable to pay back its bonds or even service them without the economic benefits of a "final victory" and further plundering of occupied Europe.[35] In April 1945 these bonds, just like the war loans from the First World War, could only be regarded as dead securities. Liquidity and German bonds (dead securities) amounted to a total of nearly 33 million Schillings, or forty-seven percent of the Dorotheum's annual balance.

The high liquidity resulted from several factors. On the one hand, the Dorotheum was able to constantly increase its revenues between 1941 and 1944 under conditions of the wartime economy. Due to its statutes the companies was limited in the extent to which it could apply its profits. Next to investment, profits could only be used to feed the Dorotheum's three funds: the pension fund, the reserve fund regularly amounting to half of the total loan on pawn given out by the company; and the fund to assist poor pawn debtors. Although the Dorotheum paid into these funds, a substantial part of its profits between 1939 and 1944 was ploughed back with the consent of the controlling institution in the Reich presidium. Throughout this period Dorotheum management awaited in vain a decision from its controlling political bodies to lift the strict regulations on using and investing profits.

The liquidity accounted for in the 1945 balance was devalued by both the hidden inflation that emerged during the war and postwar inflation.[36] Moreover, this apparently high liquidity evaporated under the effects of the Second Republic's monetary reform through the Schillinggesetz 1945[37] and the Währungsschutzgesetz.[38] The Schillinggesetz reintroduced the Austrian Schilling as the only currency in Austria, replacing the Reichsmark (RM) and the Militärschilling issued by the Allied Commission. The exchange rate of the old Reichsmark to the new Schilling was fixed 1:1. Individuals received a cash payment of up to 150 Schillings, while sums exceeding these amounts were deposited into frozen accounts. Corporate bodies received credit notes for RM in cash; while sixty percent of their money deposited in accounts was frozen, forty percent were available with certain restrictions.

The Währungsschutzgesetz of 19 November 1947 fought inflation by simply erasing liquidity, in effect by transforming blocked cash accounts into claims against the republic (*Bundesschuldverschreibungen*). As Hans Seidel has shown, the government tried to cover Austrian banks and insurance companies, which were more or less insolvent, and allowed them to issue tentative balances as a temporary solution until they could regain their financial health. In 1955 the economy had stabilized and developed significantly, and private consumption had recovered and closed the gap caused by circumstances prevailing during the war and the early postwar period.[39] Historian Oliver Rathkolb has called these mechanisms for restructuring the Austrian monetary system nothing less than "controlled state insolvency" (*geregelter Staatskonkurs*)[40]—a term that applied to most of the financial sector in the Austrian economy, including the Dorotheum.

Another important element of economic reconstruction policy alongside currency reform involved back taxation or profits. In the case of the Dorotheum, tax officials issued a supplementary tax claim resulting from a tax inspection started in 1943/44, allowing the needy republic to draw on the Dorotheum's untaxed profits from 1938-1944; during the second half of 1945, the company paid nearly nine million Schillings for taxes due during the period 1942-1944.

As a result of the Austrian postwar monetary reform, the monetary reconstruction measures, and tax auditing, the Dorotheum's liquidity shrank to 785,000 Schillings by 1947, 4.5% of the 1945 total. Like the nascent Republic itself, the company was capital-poor and close to insolvency—a problem common to all Austrian banks and financial institutions.[41] Half of the assets (*Aktiva*) of the Austrian banks were claims vis-á-vis Germany (German bonds) or locked in blocked bank accounts while forty percent of the liabilities (*Passiva*) were liabilities with the Austrian state due as per regulations stipulated by monetary reconstruction. The Dorotheum's liquidity rose to 21.75 million Schillings with liabilities of 9.5 million Schillings by 1948; liabilities with respect to the federal state resulting from Währungsschutzgesetz regulations still amounted to 24.29 million Schillings. Since restructuring measures focused closely on capital, the economic basis of the enterprise was severely shaken.[42] The war effects on the Dorotheum were limited. Some of the real estate was struck by allied air raids, while the impact of the immediate fighting's in Austria and plundering by the occupying Soviet forces was—despite the Dorotheum's narrative—minor. Most of these damages were written off in 1945, turning a net annual profit into a net loss of nearly 355,000 Schillings.

During the initial postwar years the Dorotheum's financial condition remained quite weak. While war damages (*Kriegssachschäden*) could be written off in 1945, the Dorotheum— like other financials enterprises—was allowed to allocate dead securities (*Reichsanleihen*) to liabilities vis-à-vis the federal state, thereby reducing them to ca.13.59 million Schillings.[43] This allowed the Dorotheum to share the direct, negative wartime effects with the Austrian taxpayer to a significant degree. Nonetheless, the company's overall development remained weak, as indicated in figures for net profit/loss for the period 1945-1949:

Fiscal Year	Net profit in 1,000 Schillings
1945	*-355*
1946	3,000
1947	5,449
1948	*-1,082*
1949	46

Table 1: Dorotheum's Net Profits/Losses 1945-1949[44]

Even though the Dorotheum was allowed to hand a part of the costs related to the war and war-related destruction to the taxpayer, the firm took over a significant social burden with respect to its employees. In 1945, the fact that ca. 100,000 Austrian men were held as POWs and thus were unable to support their families contributed to additional social hardship. In order to assist at least some of these families, the Dorotheum kept employees who had been drafted into the German military and were still held as POW in 1945 on the payroll; indeed, no less than twenty-nine percent (266) of the company's staff were still on the payroll although they were held as military prisoners. Most of the men returned during the course of 1945 but between 1946 and 1948, 6.6% and 1.5%, respectively, of staff members held in POW camps remained on the payroll.

When the war ended and for some months afterward there was little interest in purchasing goods for cash, and the pawn brokerage business suffered accordingly. However, with the stabilization of the Austrian currency system, the pawn brokerage business recovered quickly, and the Dorotheum benefited from this development. While the company disbursed 4,663 Schillings for pawned items in 1945, the amount rose by 386% to 22.67 million Schillings in 1946.[45] This jump could only be explained by the extreme need for all kinds of goods and services and the restrictive policies set up under the conditions of monetary reform. In 1947 the pawn loan total sank by twenty-seven percent, only to jump by 248% in 1948. Earnings from the pawn business grew from 1.51 millions Schillings in 1945 to 7.27 million in 1948 and just under 12 million in 1949. The auction business expanded much more slowly, with growth rates of 11% (1946), 91% (1947) and -33% (1948). The direct negative effects of the reconstruction of the monetary system were at least partly balanced by the positive effects of resurgent pawn and auction activity in 1946. Nonetheless, the Dorotheum was able to offset at least some of the decline in business during the second half of 1945 by taking advantage of a practice introduced by the NS regime. As we have emphasized, the initial period of reconstruction was characterized by as extreme shortage of goods of virtually every sort. However, the Dorotheum had stockpiled everyday goods from so-called *Tauschbörsen*—exchange markets opened and managed by the Dorotheum in response to requests by National Socialist officials who, as early as 1943/44, sought to offset the destruction wrought by aerial bombardment. Through these *Tauschbörsen*, victims of Allied air raids had an opportunity to satisfy their basic needs for clothing, furnishing, and housewares. These goods, often of very low quality, met the extraordinary demand of the Viennese population and became a central element of restarting business once the war ended. This, state ordered partial regression from a monetised economy to a barter economy is a very significant proof for the hidden devaluation of the Reichsmark already 1943/44.

Trafficking in Looted Valuables

Beginning in 1942 the Dorotheum bought art from dealers in France, Belgium, and Netherlands and turned continually increasing profits. Various pieces art and other valuables purchased in Western Europe that had not been sold during the war could be auctioned off after 1945. For example, several hundred diamonds as well as more than one hundred strings of pearls from the 1943 Prague Gestapo office jewellery purchase referred to above were not sold until after the war; these sales contributed significantly to the overall 1945 balance.[46] We have noted that much of this merchandise were confiscated Jewish assets, and those who survived Nazi rule or had escaped the Continent faced considerable difficulties in trying to reclaim jewellery and other categories of valuables. On the other hand, Dorotheum acquisition and sale of works of art were scaled back significantly when the Western Allies ordered the Dorotheum to return paintings and a collection of precious coins, purchased in France during 1943/44, to the French art recovery and restitution authorities. The Dorotheum resisted meeting French restitution claims as long as it could, for the firm's officials regarded all acquisitions during the Nazi period as just and legal. Postwar director Heribert Katzele complained that the company faced a loss of 500,000 Schillings for the restitution of French goods.[47] While the Dorotheum was generally cooperative with Allied art recovery unit inquiries into the whereabouts of pieces sold 1942-45, French demands for restitution of any works bought on the open market at market prices under German occupation was considered unjust violation of the right of possession by a superior power.

The Dorotheum's overall business model remained unchanged throughout the first half of the century. Except for the extraordinary transactions in art and jewellery between 1942 and 1944, [48] the main submitters of items for auction had been—apart from art dealers or public authorities such as tax and customs officials—district courts with their garnishment (execution) departments. Policies surrounding submission of items for auction were never called into questioned by the Dorotheum's management. In 1945/46, a small number of items that had been confiscated under the Nazi regime were still up for auction. Due to the legal construction of the auction business, the owner of these questionable assets was the institution sending the item in for auction. Tax authorities, district courts, and/or custom institutions controlled by the Federal Ministry of Finance did not recall the items, and never investigated whether they had been confiscated by Nazi authorities. The Dorotheum could conclude that it had no right and obviously no reason to refuse auctioning off these goods. Indeed, as a publicly-owned body controlled by the Ministry of Interior and the Ministry of Finance,[49] the Dorotheum was very closely bound into the overall restitution policy of the Austrian federal state, its provincial governments, and municipal authorities. In congruence with the policy of the Austrian Republic the Dorotheum "regarded any liability for actions taken by the Nazi Regime as a non-issue."[50] However, according to regulations concerning looted assets detailed in the 1946 *Vermögensentziehungs-Anmeldungsverordnung* (VEAV) owners had to declare any property that might have been looted from Jewish owners. [51] Under this decree, the jewellery bought in Prague would have to have been declared by the Dorotheum, insofar as the items had not been sold before the decree came into force. The Dorotheum met this obligation only reluctantly and in small measure. Again, this was in line with the general policy and attitude in Austria towards the VEAV, even by publicly-owned institutions. Even federal and municipal museums, which had bought looted Jewish art extensively, did not declare their acquisitions. Notably, it was the lax response to the VEAV on the part of institutions or individuals who had acquired questionable property that the decree was amended to give victims the possibility of making claims on looted assets. More than forty years after fascism, the Austrian Republic has initiated several additional attempts to come to terms with its National Socialist past in the area of settlement of claims from looted Jewish property, namely through the Nationalfonds (1995), the Mauerbachfonds (1996), the Kunstrückgabegesetz (1998), and the Versöhnungsfonds (2001).[52]

Reconstruction of Management and Staff

After National Socialist control in Austria was broken, the new governmental authorities were keen to maintain continuity at the level of management. While Dorotheum directors Jennewein (a leading Viennese Nazi) and Hofbauer were fired in April 1945, Theodor Körner, governor of the province of Vienna, appointed two members of the second tier management as new directors, Heribert Katzele on 17 April and Viktor Imhof on 30 May 1945. Katzele was politically indifferent and had maintained no affiliation with National Socialism or its organizations, but made his career under Jennewein leadership. On the whole, the Dorotheum's new managing body was more or less a reconstruction of the pre-1938 team, including some who had fallen victim to anti-Jewish discrimination in 1938/39. Former leading managers who had suffered in this way were installed in top management positions as executive director (Imhoff), as vice-director general (Friedrich Siebert), and as general secretary (Tauber), or found their way into other managerial posts. Reconstruction of the staff generally followed the pragmatic lines described with respect to management: denazification and reintegration of those who had been expelled under National Socialism. Some 200 staff members were dismissed in accordance with federal denazification measures; 140 were regarded as "lesser offenders" (*Minderbelastete*), of whom 100 were later rehired and the other forty pensioned off. Some thirty fell under the classification of "offenders" (Belastete).[53] In cases where employees were laid off due to their involvement in National Socialism, the company paid financial assistance to "support innocent family members." Finally, Nazi fellow travellers were generally reintegrated, as were quite a number of staff members who had been victimized by the racist laws and regulations in 1938/39. In the latter instance, it proved vital to be present in Austria; controlling bodies ordered the rejection of reinstatement claims from former staff members who had been able to flee the country in 1938/39.

Conclusion

In terms of visible war damage to infrastructure, political uncertainties, the need to reconstruct basic infrastructure, and prevailing financial conditions, one might conclude that something of a "Stunde Null" existed for the Dorotheum during the second half of 1945. However, this conclusion would be inconsistent with respect to continued business relations with the public authorities, the seamless reorganization of the firm's statutes, continuity in the Dorotheum's business model, and the kinds of items sold in 1945/46. The often overestimated "Stunde Null" was of only limited relevance to the Dorotheum's business, yet substantial to its self-perception. As we have seen, the new corporate identity represented the Dorotheum as 1) a truly Austrian institution and opponent of the Nazi regime; 2) a target of National Socialist meddling and reorganization; 3) an institution with a high social awareness; 4) a victim of wartime economy; 5) a victim of Allied air raids and plundering by Soviet troops.

The formal legal status of the company and the post-1945 management and staff were mostly a reconstruction of the pre-1938 period with selective elimination of Austrofascist influences. The new corporate identity and its social composition covered most of the group of offenders and lesser offenders, the vast majority of staff members from the pre-1945 period, as well as employees held as POWs. Victims of racial discrimination faced the more difficult problems of reintegration into the company or receiving the social services the company offered, particularly when they lived abroad. Within the Dorotheum's own historiography these implications are left aside. As we have seen, the myth of *Wiederaufbau* tended to portray all employees as equal, which can be interpreted as an acknowledgement of their endeavours during the bombings and clearance of rubble afterwards.

All this can be read along the lines of Austria's national self-perception and presentation as the first victim of Nazi German aggression in Europe. The Dorotheum could employ this *Opfermythos* in its efforts to rebuild business and its corporate identity, while reducing its culpability in the Nazi system to a minimum. As was the case with Austrian society in general, the Dorotheum covered its Nazi past under a layer of both repression and self-victimization. Today the Opfermythos can be considered obsolete, while the process of finding a critical and unadorned approach to the past is still ongoing. Austria is still to finding its way between nationalism, self-accusation, and a new interaction between perpetrators and victims that might be considered acceptable by all sides.[54]

Notes

[1] The controlling body was the *Österreichische Landesregierung*, *Reichsstatthalter*, initially Josef Bürckel, the "Reichskommissar für die Wiedervereinigung Österreichs mit dem Deutschen Reich" (Reich Commissioner for the Reunification of Austria with the German Reich), from 1940 Reichsstatthalter Baldur von Schirach.

[2] This was the case with the Gerhold-Anstalten, also a Viennese pawn brokerage, over which the Dorotheum took control in 1941. See "Das erweiterte Wiener Dorotheum. Nach der Übernahme der Gerhold-Betriebe – 12,9 Mill. Rm Eigenmittel, 16 Mill. Rm Spareinlagen," *Neues Wiener Tagblatt*, 1 February 1941; for the postwar perspective see Dorotheum House Archive (hereafter: HAD), Kuratoriumsprotokolle 1946, box 77—Generaldirektor Heribert Katzele's report to the board of trustees from 23 July 1946.

[3] Gabriele Anderl and Alexandra Caruso, "Einleitung" in *NS-Kunstraub in Österreich und die Folgen*, ed. Gabriele Anderl and Alexandra Caruso (Innsbruck-Vienna-Bozen: Studienverlag, 2005), 11–25.

[4] See, for instance, Stephan Templ, "Das Ende der Gutgläubigkeit. Das Wiener Dorotheum und seine Geschichte," *Neue Zürcher Zeitung*, 11 February 2003 and Dorit Bader Whiteman, "Was bedeutet 'Entschädigung'? Oder 'Die Maus, die brüllte'. – Ein Kommentar der anderen," *Der Standard*, 23 September 2005.

[5] During the Third Reich, Vienna held the reputation as a model city for looting and persecution of its Jewish population. See Hans Safrian, "Beschleunigung der Beraubung und Vertreibung. Zur Bedeutung des 'Wiener Modells' für die antijüdische Politik des 'Dritten Reiches' im Jahr 1938," in *"Arisierung" und Restitution. Die Rückerstattung jüdischen Eigentums in Deutschland und Österreich nach 1945 und 1989*, ed. Constantin Goschler and Jürgen Lillteicher (Göttingen: Wallstein Verlag, 2002), 61–89.

[6] Oliver Rathkolb ed., *Revisting the National Socialist Legacy. Coming to Terms with Forced Labor, Expropriation, Compensation, and Restitution* (Innsbruck-Vienna-Munich-Bozen: Studienverlag, 2002).

[7] Clemens Jabloner et al., eds., *Schlussbericht der Historikerkommission der Republik Österreich: Vermögensentzug während der NS-Zeit sowie Rückstellungen und Entschädigungen seit 1945* (Vienna: Oldenbourg, 2003).

[8] Elazar Barkan, *The Guilt of Nations. Restitution and Negotiating Historical Injustices* (New York: W. W. Norton & Co, 2000), XV.

[9] For the development of Jewish victimhood after the Holocaust see Peter Novick, *The Holocaust in American Life* (Boston and New York: Mariner, 1999) and Jean-Michel Chaumont, *La concurrence des victimes. Génocide, identité, reconnaissance* (Paris: Edition La Découverte, 1997).

[10] In Austria, victims of forced sterilization and euthanasia, those persecuted because they were classified as "asocial," and homosexuals were not eligible for any form of financial compensation. Only when the National Fund was established in 1995 did these victims come into consideration. See Sonja Niederacher, "The Myth of Austria as Victim of Nazism, the Emigres and the Discipline of Exile Studies," *Austrian Studies 12* (2003): 22.

[11] Barkan, XV.

[12] Oliver Rathkolb, "Is Historical Truth Impossible? A Look at Restitution Efforts Concerning Nazi Looted Artworks and the Altmann Case," *Contemporary Austrian Studies* 13 (2005): 193–95.

[13] See for example Heidemarie Uhl, "Das 'erste Opfer'. Der österreichische Opfermythos und seine Transformationen in der Zweiten Republik," *Österreichische Zeitschrift für Politikwissenschaft* 30/i (2001).
[14] Albert Starzer, *Das K. K. Versatzamt in Wien von 1707 bis 1900*, ed. Direction des K. K. Versatzamtes von Wien (Vienna: Jasper, 1901).
[15] Theodor Mayer, *Das Wiener Versatzamt (Dorotheum)* (Vienna: publisher unknown, 1920).
[16] Marcel Ségur-Cabanac, *250 Jahre Dorotheum* (Vienna: Eigenverlag Dorotheum, 1957).
[17] Felix Czeike, *Das Dorotheum. Vom Versatz- und Fragamt zum modernen Auktionshaus* (Vienna and Munich: Jugend und Volk, 1982).
[18] Going a step further, Hayden White maintains one can say that narratives generally apply to certain rules of storytelling that consequently determine the structure of historical events and how they are presented: "The events must be not only registered within the chronological framework of their original occurrence but narrated as well, that is to say, revealed as possessing a structure, an order of meaning, that they do not possess as mere sequence", Hayden White, *The Content of the Form. Narrative Discourse and Historical Representation* (Baltimore: John Hopkins University Press, 1990), 5.
[19] Czeike, 134.
[20] For discussion of whether the Dollfuß-Schuschnigg regime as fascist or authoritarian, see Emmerich Tálos and Wolfgang Neugebauer eds., *"Austrofaschismus": Beiträge über Politik, Ökonomie und Kultur 1934-1938*, (Vienna: Verlag f. Gesellschaftskritik, 1985). Jill Lewis, "Conservatives and Fasists in Austria, 1918-34" in *Fascists and Conservatives*, ed. Martin Blinkhorn (London: Unwin Hyman, 1990), 98-117, 104.
[21] See Elisabeth Klamper, "'Ein einig Volk von Brüdern'. Vergessen und Erinnern im Zeichen des Burgfriedens," *Zeitgeschichte* 5-6 (1997): 170–85; Sonja Niederacher, "Die öffentliche Rede über Entnazifizierung 1945-1949," in *Entnazifizierung zwischen politischem Anspruch, Parteienkonkurrenz und Kaltem Krieg. Das Beispiel der SPÖ*, ed. Maria Mesner (Vienna and Munich: Oldenbourg, 2005), 51–2.
[22] Ségur-Cabanac, 11.
[23] Czeike, 131. All translations the authors' unless noted otherwise.
[24] Czeike, 131.
[25] ÖStA/AdR 04, Bürckel-Materie, Gesetz über die Übernahme des Versatz-, Verwahrungs- und Versteigerungsamtes "Dorotheum" in Wien durch die Stadt Wien, 1757/9/2.
[26] Czeike, 134.
[27] Gabriele Rosenthal, "Das soziale Schweigegebot zu den Nazi-Verbrechen. Bedingungen der Institutionalisierung einer Abwehrhaltung," in *Wiederaufbau Weiblich. Dokumentation der Tagung "Frauen in der österreichischen und deutschen Nachkriegszeit"*, ed. Irene Bandhauer-Schöffmann and Ela Hornung (Vienna and Salzburg: Geyer Edition, 1992), 63–5.
[28] Ségur-Cabanac, 11.
[29] Siegfried Mattl, "'Aufbau' – eine männliche Chiffre der Nachkriegszeit," in *Wiederaufbau Weiblich*, 15-23.
[30] Ségur-Cabanac, 12.
[31] For an analysis of the inhumane and illegal constituent elements of Nazi "Sozialpolitik," see Götz Aly, *Hitlers Volksstaat. Raub, Rassenkrieg und nationaler Sozialismus* (Frankfurt/Main: Fischer, 2005);

Pierre Ayçoberry, *The Social History of the Third Reich, 1933-1945* (New York: The New Press, 1999); and Marie-Luise Recker, *Nationalsozialistische Sozialpolitik im Zweiten Weltkrieg* (Munich: Oldenbourg, 1985).
For an analysis of the upsurge associated with the Nazi war economy, see Christoph Buchheim, "Zur Natur des Wirtschaftsaufschwungs in der NS-Zeit," in *Zerrissene Zwischenkriegszeit. Wirtschaftshistorische Beiträge*, ed. Christoph Buchheim, Michael Hutter and Harold James (Baden-Baden: Nomos, 1994).

[32] Hans Seidel, *Österreichs Wirtschaft und Wirtschaftspolitik nach dem Zweiten Weltkrieg* (Vienna: Manz, 2005).

[33] Due to special regulation for the banking business, like other financial institutions the Dorotheum presented tentative balances until the "Schillingseröffnungsbilanz" of 1958.

[34] For German war financing in World War I, see Walther Lotz, *Die deutsche Staatsfinanzwirtschaft im Kriege* (Stuttgart-Berlin-Leipzig; Deutsche Verlags-Anstalt/Wirtschafts und Sozialgeschichte des Weltkrieges, Deutsche Serie, 1927).

[35] See Aly, *Hitlers Volksstaat.*

[36] For hidden inflation and postwar inflation in Austria see: Seidel, 108 and 224.

[37] "Gesetz über die Maßnahmen auf dem Gebiete der Währung, Schillinggesetz," StGBl. Nr. 231/1945.

[38] "Währungsschutzgesetz," WSchG, BGBl. Nr. 250/47.

[39] Seidel, 377.

[40] Oliver Rathkolb, *Die paradoxe Republik* (Vienna: Zsolnay, 2005), 125.

[41] On the reconstruction of Austrian banks see Bruno Tichy, "Der Wiederaufbau des österreichischen Bankwesens" (PhD diss., Hochschule für Welthandel, Vienna 1957); Seidel, 549; and Rathkolb, 125.

[42] War damages (damages from aerial bombardment and plundering) amounted to nearly four million Schillings in 1945. HAD box 13—"Vorbericht über die durchgeführte Überprüfung der provisorischen Jahresabschlüsse zum 31. Dezember 1945, 1946, 1947, 1948 und 1949 des Versatz-, Verwahrungs- und Versteigerungsamtes ‚Dorotheum'" Wien, Gesellschaft für Revision und Treuhändige Verwaltung, Wien, 1950.

[43] HAD, box 18—Schillingeröffnungsbilanz, 1956.

[44] HAD box 13—Vorbericht über die durchgeführte Überprüfung der provisorischen Jahresabschlüsse zum 31. Dezember 1945, 1946, 1947, 1948 und 1949 des Versatz-, Verwahrungs- und Versteigerungsamtes "Dorotheum", Wien, Gesellschaft für Revision und Treuhändige Verwaltung, Wien, 1950.

[45] Ibid.

[46] Ibid.

[47] HAD, Kuratoriumsprotokolle 1946, box 77—Katzele report to the Board of Trustees, 23 July 1946.

[48] The Dorotheum as well as the controlling bodies referred to the transactions always as "Sondergeschäfte".

[49] 1945-mid 1946, the Dorotheum's superior body was the Ministry of Interior, from than on the Ministry of Finance.

[50] HAD, box 59—Circular letter (Dienstrundschreiben) Nr. 51, 21 January 1946.

[51] BGBl 1946/166, September 15, 1946.

[52] For an overview on Austrian restitution and compensation debate, see Oliver Rathkolb ed., *Revisiting the National Socialist Legacy: Coming to Terms with Forced Labor, Expropriation, Compensation, and Restitution* (Summerst, NJ: Transaction Publisher, 2004). For the foreign policy dimensions, see Michael Gehler, *Von der alliierten Besat-*

zung zur Europäischen Gemeinschaft: Österreichs Außenpolitik von 1945 bis zur Gegenwart, (Innsbruck: Studienverlag, 2005), 941.

[53] Following the "Nationalsozialistengesetz", BGBl. Nr. 25/1947: Bundesverfassungsgesetz vom 6. Februar 1947 über die Behandlung der Nationalsozialisten the classification of National Socialists consisted of five categories: 1. Major offenders 2., 3. Lesser offenders, 4. Followers, 5. Exonerated persons.

[54] Ernst Hanisch, "Die Präsenz des Dritten Reiches in der Zweiten Republik," in *Inventur 45/55. Österreich im ersten Jahrzehnt der Zweiten Republik*, ed. Wolfgang Kos (Vienna: Sonderzahl, 1996), 33–38.

"Einmal im Leben:" Rooting the "Little Man" to Conservative Values in Postwar West Germany

Alexandra Staub

Against the backdrop of early postwar uncertainties, in the 1950s German legislators turned to homeownership and the single-family house as keys to social stability, producing two major pieces of legislation that clearly defined how they wished the population to live. "*Man baut nur einmal im Leben,*"[1] the saying goes, and expresses the once-in-a-lifetime dream of one's own house with a garden that was to now be made available to all. Although legislation facilitating homeownership typically benefits the upper classes, it was the working and lower middle classes, their left-wing politics spawned in the crowded urban living conditions they had customarily inhabited, who now found themselves included in this effort to create a new, postwar social order. Aided by the general conservative mood of the Adenauer era, a caste that had traditionally been more involved with labor movements than lawn mowers was encouraged to settle into a new, bourgeois German existence. How new were these policies really? How successful were they ultimately? This following article explores some of the forces that helped foster the idea of homeownership, and ultimately helped root the "man on the street" to a new postwar order.

This chapter examines three distinct phenomena and their interrelationship: 1) a legislative debate, 2) a series of popular films that acted as a cultural translator,[2] and 3) the resulting rise and formation of prefabricated homes as housing that "the masses" could afford. Examining these phenomena requires a transdisciplinary methodological approach that is typical of discussions on architecture. The first section, which deals with the postwar parliamentary debate on housing, employs straightforward archival research. The next section, which treats the representation of house spaces in films and new, prefabricated houses, uses methodologies that have been established in architecture and film studies within the framework of cultural studies. Here the discussion shifts to spatial analysis as an interpretive instrument for understanding cultural, political, and gender implications of our built world.[3] Using these two methods as analytical tools, this article investigates the following thesis: In the 1950s there was a largely unsuccessful legislative push for the single-family house in West Germany. At the same time, popular culture in the form of films gave the working class visual access to single-family homes, a form of dwelling with which many would have been unfamiliar. By the 1960s an affordable form of the single-family house became ever more popular and had the same sorts of stereotyped spaces that had been modeled in films. These spaces and the overall move to the owner-occupied single-family house had cultural implications that are a focus of the text. Taken together, the three distinct phenomena frame a more comprehensive understanding of German housing than is possible when they are examined separately.

The idea of using homeownership to instill conservative values in and tame the population runs through German history from the eighteenth century onwards. Early efforts to reform working-class urban housing concentrated on the separation of nuclear families and the establishment of patriarchal family structures, as exemplified by the writings of Berlin reformer Carl Hoffmann, here from 1847:

> If one wishes to bind the worker to his wife and children after his daily toil, to keep him from the inn, so the best method is to give him a flat deserving of that name, a room of which he is the master.[4]

According to this equation, promoting the bourgeois patriarchal family ideal among the working class would keep the men from fraternizing—and politicizing themselves—in bars. In an era of severely overcrowded living conditions, separation of households and an emphasis on family life were key to hindering working class unrest and fostering moral values more typical of the bourgeoisie. Separation of households from one another, according to Hoffmann, would guarantee that "no one may have cause for complaint, and no one is privy to the affairs of another."[5] Although Hoffmann's text referred to the separation of families into individual apartments, the conditions he described seemed closer to the reality of the single-family house—a housing form that, at the time, was hardly feasible for the working class.

By the 1920s this had changed, however, as both conservative and leftist politicians supported a variety of single-family housing possibilities, such as the vast social housing programs in cities such as Frankfurt and Berlin. Intended for the working class, the rents for such projects were often beyond their means, yet the effort demonstrates the perceived importance of single-family housing for all classes. Built on the edges of existing cities, the row houses mixed with low-rise apartment blocks were, in effect, an early form of German suburb.

The garden city, with its abundance of single-family housing, was also seen as a healthy alternative to urban living, although the small-town model such projects were based on contributed to a controversial turn in the larger discussion of the concept. Conservatives, such as architect Paul Schmitthenner, saw them as moral cleansers, and emphasized their positive influence on German "racial vigor." Schmitthenner called his 1928 garden city project in Staaken, "a model for propriety and love of one's fatherland as well as for physical health,"[6] clearly equating housing with social and political regulation.

Inspired by, and more widespread than the garden city projects, were the *Siedler* or *Heimstätten* (homestead) projects, suburban settlements consisting of a small house on a plot of land that was to be farmed to augment the family income. In the early part of the century such settlements had cropped up as unplanned shantytowns at the edge of larger cities. It was only after 1918 that they were built in greater numbers, as part of an official self-help program to aid poorer families get back onto their feet.[7] Under the program, war veterans and widows, as well as families with many children were the first to receive one of the small *Siedler* houses.[8] The movement received its impetus after 1931, when the worldwide depression led German politicians to implement the *Brüningsche Stadtrandsiedlungsprogramm* (Brüning Suburban Settlement Program). In its first stage from 1931-34, almost 18,000 houses in 233 communities were built.[9] The houses had a very traditional appearance, and were based on rural German models. The workers who received one of the *Siedler* homes were expected to help in its construction, with appropriate skills being one of the criteria for selection.[10] An extensive garden, which included areas for small livestock, such as chickens, rabbits, geese or ducks, goats, and in some cases even a pig, made the unemployed urban settlers into part-time farmers.[11] The goals of the *Siedler* legislation—strengthening the working class's economic base by making it possible for them to own property, strengthening the bond to the homeland as well as to nature and the soil upon which one lived, and strengthening the German family[12]—were similar to those that would be cited both by the Nazis and in postwar German housing debates.

The *Siedler* programs continued during the Third Reich, with the new government consolidating the various *Siedler* organizations. The *Heimstättenamt der Deutschen Arbeitsfront*, a central government office that controlled *Siedler* programs, was founded in 1934, and between 1937 and 1940 new federal legislation, the *Reichsheimstättengesetz*, replaced various state laws. In terms of housing, the National Socialist government's aim was to lead the population towards the acquisition of owner-occupied single-family houses, both through legislation and by invoking images of homeownership as the key to stability, security, and a patriarchal state supremacy.[13]

The houses built under the Nazi programs from 1933-1940,[14] although often called *Heimstätten* or *Siedler* houses, differed from *Siedler* houses of the Weimar Republic in several important ways. The programs of the Weimar Republic had largely benefited the unemployed, with the housing types showing a strong working class and rural influence. The working class *Wohnküche*—a combined living room/kitchen—was the norm, and houses with spaces for livestock under the same roof as the family were not uncommon. Houses built after 1933, on the other hand, more often followed middle-class ideals. Families who received one of the *Siedler* houses were usually employed, with many being members of, or sympathetic to, the Nazi party.[15] The *Wohnküche* had been replaced by a utilitarian *Kochküche*, a smaller space that was completely separated from the living room. The living room was a representative space, while the kitchen and its associated vapors (*Kochdünste*) became the housewife's realm. Properties had become much smaller, and there were no longer stables or other spaces for livestock. The yard was now seen as an area for recreation and growing flowers (*Ziergarten*), not as a space to grow vegetables and keep livestock (*Nutzgarten*). In their social and spatial organization, the *Siedler* houses had become close to what would later be a postwar suburban ideal.

Not everyone saw the move towards suburbanization and the single-family house as a destined or even desirable phenomenon. As early as 1930 Alexander Schwab assessed in his *Buch vom Bauen* how the desire for homeownership could be used by the upper classes as a means to control "the masses":

> It may be seen as a certainty that the greatest part of working class families in Germany would prefer to live in a little house [...]. It is equally certain that this tendency has not sprung uninfluenced from the soul of the working class. It is much rather the case that after the [Great] War and the revolution a planned manipulation took place, which saw as its aim to plant the ideal of one's "own" little house and garden in the hearts of the masses. [...] Every worker was to have as an ultimate aim to once again become a "free man on free soil," which is to say his existence as a miniature villa owner or a miniature feudal lord, who, incidentally and just for the fun of it, works a bit in a factory.[16]

The working class man, Schwab argues here, was led to aspire to a standard of luxury and freedom he could never really attain.

As Schwab's pre-World War II text shows, reformers' and government attempts to promote conservative values in the often Marxist-influenced working class were not without controversy even in the early part of the century, long before Germany's division into East and West, communist and capitalist, made the issue even more acute. When the Nazis assumed power, these tendencies were intensified, with homeownership used not only indirectly for social means, but also directly as a means to reward those who followed government agendas. As we shall see, in the rubble of 1945 the question of housing would quickly become an issue of highest priority with proponents of single-family homeownership again taking a prominent stand.

After World War II, Europe's political, social, and economic environment and Germany's unique position as a nation divided between two ideological spheres quickly forced the question of housing to the forefront. The Cold War and the fact that Germany was now divided between two systems led to understandable fears that the communist East could somehow gain control over the West, given the opportunity. Fear of a communist takeover, perhaps through infiltration of the historically leftist working class, greatly aided West German conservatives in continuing the propagation of the owner-occupied, single-family house as a way to root the "little man" to conservative political and social values and—as a postwar addition—to the new American-influenced ideal of material consumption.

The Adenauer government promoted homeownership legislatively through the First Housing Law of 1950 and, more importantly, the Second Housing Law of 1956. Subtler, but just as explicit, however, West Germany's burgeoning movie industry presented family homes and domestic scenes that advanced images of single-family housing that viewers could attempt to emulate and achieve. Movies were a popular form of entertainment in the 1950s.[17] With seventy percent of Germans preferring German films,[18] and so many films showing their protagonists in the context of their domestic environments,[19] the German film—no matter how unrealistic the story line—provided important visual information about the family home such as lawmakers endorsed.

The First Housing Law was conceived as financial legislation that would provide sources of capital for the large-scale housing construction necessary after the war, yet it also provided for the rationalization of the housing industry—two directions the Nazis themselves had followed between 1940 and 1945.[20] In the new legislation, three paths were followed: 1) research on construction methods, 2) standardization of building materials, and 3) development of a typology for buildings and their materials.[21] Because of the vast number of homeless, the First Housing Law pragmatically did not call for single-family housing. In fact, realistic considerations often spoke for multi-family units: Article 16 explicitly called for areas that had once contained multi-family housing to be reconstructed with the same type of buildings, since subterraneous infrastructure (sewage, gas and water mains) was often intact and could be reused.[22] Equally pragmatic were stipulations that the needs of single people, "namely, working women with children and the elderly" be considered, a tribute to the many single women and war widows after 1945.[23] In contrast to later legislation, the First Housing Law of 1950 focused on creating rental units for "broad segments of the population," and especially considered those Germans who had lost their homes—and most of their property—through border shifts or wartime destruction.[24] The law allowed the federal government to maintain control of the building process by distributing funds to the state governments, who were then to coordinate and implement specific construction schedules.[25] The law thus gave the central government the power of the purse, a factor that would become increasingly important as the housing debates intensified.

The First Housing Law underwent a revision in 1953, in which the number of housing units to be built by 1956 was increased from 1.8 to two million. More important were stipulations regarding the types of housing that were to be financed and built. Whereas the 1950 version of the law spoke of rental units, the reworked law called for, "the construction of owner-occupied houses, homesteads, developer housing [to be purchased] and privately owned apartments [...]."[26] In the case of multi-party housing, the financing of condominium apartments was to be favored over the construction of rental units,[27] showing the attempt to move away from rental housing. When rental housing was built, however, the maximum rent for subsidized housing was controlled. In this manner, builders received funds for the construction of new rental units, but rent limits did not allow them to charge what the market would bear. Only where rental units were constructed on sites that had contained housing before the war could maximum rents be exceeded by up to thirty percent.[28] Taken together, these stipulations were meant to discourage the construction of new rental units beyond what had existed before the war.

The second legislative period beginning in 1953 saw a renewed focus on the West German housing issue. In a State of the Union speech on 20 October, Konrad Adenauer made the owner-occupied single-family house the government's number one housing priority.[29] This housing form became known as the *Familienheim*—literally "family home"—a term that marked it as part of a larger, postwar government effort to actively promote the traditional nuclear family with several children, with a male breadwinner and a female homemaker creating a conservative "normalcy" that had largely disappeared during the war.[30]

On 14 January 1954, the ruling CDU/CSU (Christian Democratic Union/Christian Social Union) presented a draft for a new housing law that would advance homeownership, noting that despite the government's intention to encourage owner-occupied housing, over eighty percent of all subsidized units built in 1952 were rental housing.[31] The CDU/CSU could find no explanation for this, since, according to their statistics at least sixty-five percent of the population desired a single-family house with a garden,[32] and the First Housing Law had theoretically made it possible for condominium apartment buildings to be constructed in areas where single-family housing was not feasible, such as in inner cities.[33] The governing parties clearly considered rental housing as temporary accommodations for "those who do not have a permanent base yet [...] or especially for single people."[34] Owning property was seen not only as a mature housing form, but also as a "bulwark against Bolshevism,"[35]—the acute threat of which was represented in the "other Germany" right next door.

Support for owner-occupied, single-family housing was at least, in part, shared by the opposition SPD (Social Democratic Party).[36] Despite the fact that the SPD supported measures to, "allow broad segments of the population to purchase [homes],"[37] they did not believe that a vast majority of the population wished to live in a single-family house with a garden, and cited studies that supported their claim.[38] They saw the attempt to increase funding for the *Familienheim* at the expense of rental housing as discrimination against who could not afford even a subsidized home—which included much of the SPD's clientele.[39] To better accommodate the lower class and lower middle classes, the SPD attempted to introduce a clause that would favor the *Kleinsiedlung*—a house with arable land and a stable for small livestock, such had been built under the *Siedler* programs of the Weimar Republic—noting that any other form of subsidized single-family housing could only benefit the upper classes.[40] Here the SPD sought a compromise in the housing debate, seeing the *Kleinsiedlung* as a single-family housing form to which the lower classes historically had access. In response, the housing minister, Victor-Emanuel Preusker, answered that although the CDU also supported the *Kleinsiedlung*, the better availability of foodstuffs and above all, Germany's burgeoning employment rate, had made the work-intensive *Kleinsiedlung* less attractive to the lower classes.[41]

The debates over the virtues and drawbacks of financing the *Familienheim* at the expense of all other housing forms became contentious at times, with various agendas expounded in great detail. Thus, a member of the CDU/CSU fraction, Dr. Else Brökelschen, herself a professional woman, saw the promise of a family home as a way to lead the population towards abstinence from "gambling pleasures" and towards assuming responsibility, noting that a house with a garden keeps a woman busy in an era in which technological advances in the household have given her "too much free time."[42]

The housing debate continued until 1956, with the CDU/CSU stressing the need for the *Familienheim*, and the SPD stressing the importance of accommodating the needs of the working class and lower middle class who, they claimed, did not benefit from existing housing legislation.[43] Although they agreed to home-ownership in principle (among other things, to distance themselves from their own Marxist past) the brunt of their arguments revolved around rental housing the broad masses would be able to afford. To this end, they proposed a law that would create four categories of such housing, with controlled rents of eighty pfennigs to 1.10 deutschmarks for a subsidized apartment of forty-five to eighty square meters. In their system, a family of four could have a monthly income of 610 deutschmarks[44]—the lowest income category in the SPD proposal, but a rather high limit when one considers that the average monthly salary for a working class male was only about 400 marks at the time.[45] For the average worker, this subsidized housing would have been quite reasonable, with a sixty square meter apartment consuming twelve to seventeen percent of the family's gross income. The proposed income limits were later lowered to 400 deutschmarks a month, which was thirteen percent less than the average salary for a working class male.[46] In this spirit, the SPD also proposed rent subsidies for those with especially low incomes.[47]

Despite the SPD's concerns, the CDU/CSU-led government passed the Second Housing Law in 1956, specifically making the *Familienheim* the financially privileged form of housing. The text was close to the drafts the conservative coalition had introduced, with the new law calling for the "amassing of private property, especially in the form of family homes, in order to root the population to the soil."[48] Homes large enough to accommodate families with three or more children were also encouraged, a point the CDU/CSU had promoted for years.[49] Families building or buying a home could apply for subsidized loans, and the Second Housing Law provided a detailed hierarchy of which applications were to receive priority. Only after all applications for family homes had been processed could applications for "other housing" be considered.[50] Federal funds for housing subsidies were distributed to the states, which in turn were responsible for distributing them to applicants. Although the Second Housing Law stipulated that those with low incomes—less than 500 deutschmarks a month for a family of four—were to be accommodated at a bearable rent or monthly cost, the federal government put the responsibility for providing housing for lower income groups squarely on the shoulders of the state governments without suggesting how they were to accomplish this task.[51] At any rate, if the applications for the more expensive single-family houses were to receive clear funding priority, the additional requirement that states provide low-income housing put them into a bit of a bind.

As federal legislation clearly favored the *Familienheim*, visual media, especially films and still photographs of house interiors, became an important, albeit informal and much subtler form of information and influence.[52] German films from the 1950s through the mid 1960s were regularly set in a detached, single-family house, no matter if the family portrayed was wealthy or from the working class. For the family going to the movies, such films provided a ready source of information about how others lived—i.e., how house spaces could be arranged, furnished, and used—and gave a sense of cushy normality to *Familienheim* living. The type of information that was shown in films could later be found in advertisements showing prefabricated housing interiors, as we shall see below.

The prefabricated house played a special role in postwar German housing. Off the silver screen, it was often the most feasible form of single-family housing for the lower classes, due to its cost efficient construction methods and guaranteed price. The prefab was not a "starter home" (Germans tend to build only once in a lifetime) but often represented the best alternative for those seeking the most house for the money and unable or unwilling to do much of the construction work themselves. Consequently, prefab housing companies saw an increase in business. These companies often began as sawmills or other large wood industries that later turned to prefabricated houses; for example, the market giant Okal offered its first standardized prefabricated houses in 1959.[53] Although different companies used a variety of materials, such as steel, composite panels, and even brick, many prefab houses were made of standardized, modular wood panels and were relatively inexpensive. Not surprisingly, perhaps, the idea of prefab housing attracted wide public attention beginning in the early 1960s. The popular weekly *Stern* published a major report on prefabricated housing in 1963.[54] Large general catalog companies such as Quelle and

Neckermann[55] entered the prefab market in the early 1960s, adding to the sector's visibility, while in 1964 a specialized monthly magazine on prefab housing, *bauen + Fertighaus*, was launched as a consumer guide.[56]

Despite this publicity, the prefab encountered several problems in its early years. The first houses were often aesthetically crude, with the seams between the large wooden panels clearly visible in the façade. Buyers found it more difficult to obtain loans for a prefab in a system that was tailored towards financing the conventionally built (brick or stone) house.[57] Set against these hurdles, the prefab industry's growth during the early 1960s is noteworthy.

The prefab's (guaranteed) price remained one of its main selling points. In 1962, the average conventionally built single-family house cost roughly 72,500 deutschmarks[58]; by comparison, in 1965 the *Neckermann Standardhaus* (seventy square meters) retailed at 33,000 deutschmarks, while Okal's least expensive model (seventy-nine square meters) cost 40,000 marks,[59] or roughly four times the average male worker's gross annual salary.[60] The average house in the *Stern* exhibit had a higher price tag. The least expensive house, an Italian model named *Grazia*, had fifty square meters and cost 27,500 marks. A three bedroom house with basement (100 square meters total) by the firm Quelle retailed for 61,300 marks,[61] while a three bedroom, two story house with basement (*Hummel-Eigenheimbau Typ Wedel III*) with 102 square meters and a conventional appearance (stucco façade and steeply-pitched roof) sold for 85,044 marks.[62] Based on these prices, *Stern* predicted that only about twenty percent of all West German families would ever be able to have their own detached house with several hundred square meters of yard. Yet *Stern*'s pessimistic view was not without purpose. In a lengthy editorial, editor-in-chief Henri Nannen warned that the single-family house contributed to suburban sprawl, with a double-page, aerial photo of Los Angeles underscoring the warning.[63] This message at the end of a series that had so positively endorsed the prefabricated, single-family house was certainly unusual, and shows that even in popular journalism the *Familienheim* was not without its critics.

In 1968 Stern made amends, this time presenting a solid-looking three-bedroom prefab house with ninety-four square meters and a twenty-two square meter basement for 50,000 marks. Including property costs, the total price was valued at 75,000 marks. Stern calculated that the monthly mortgage would be 350 marks, a price comparable to renting an apartment of this size.[64] With this example, *Stern* demonstrated that the prefab had, indeed, become within reach of wide segments of the population.

Prefabs never became Germany's dominant housing form, yet in time the industry came to command a respectable part of the market. The total number of single-family houses in the Federal Republic rose sharply from 1950 throughout the late 1980s (Table 1) and within this market, the number of prefabs rose proportionately from 1971 (the first year such statistics were noted) onward. By 1980, over twenty percent of all detached single-family houses built were prefabs.[65]

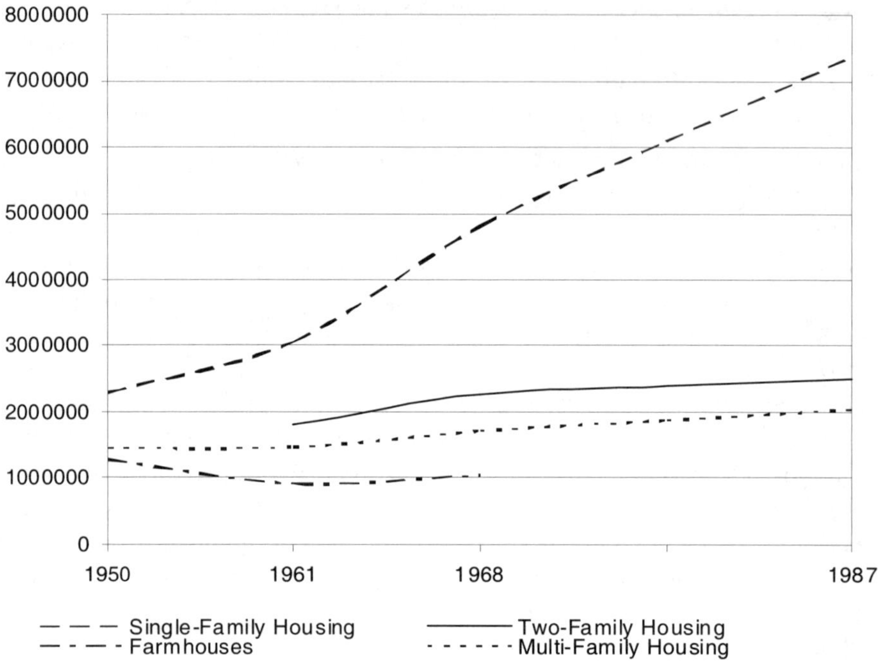

Table 1: Housing by Type in the Federal Republic of Germany 1950-87

In 1950, two-family houses were counted as multi-family houses. In the other years, the term was reserved for buildings with three or more units. Farmhouses remained a separate category until 1968. After this, they were counted according to the number of units they contained.

Statistisches Bundesamt, Gebäudezählungen von 1950, 1961, 1968, 1987

How did idealized images of the *Familienheim* in films compare to the products offered on the prefab market? The following section looks at several house spaces, comparing their film representation with the version for sale in the prefab catalogs.

The Diele

The *Diele* can be traced back to the thirteenth century. Historically, the interior of northern German houses consisted of a large space with high ceilings that was production room, storage space and shop all-in-one. The back part of this room contained a fireplace that was used for cooking. This room was a place of great activity, shared by the family, hired help, and guests. However, by the late nineteenth century the bourgeois *Diele* had become a large entrance hall in a villa (Illustration 1). It was a representative reception and living space. The *Diele* was a circulation hub from which more specialized living quarters led off, and allowed a hierarchy of spaces within the house, from public to private. The husband's office or study was next to the *Diele*, so that business visitors could quickly be shown in. As in the medieval *Diele*, the upper class *Diele* was a two-story space, but unlike its predecessor, it had an ornate staircase placed against a wall, leading to second floor rooms. A fireplace was considered essential. Seating was arranged to be intimate, with club chairs and groups around small tables underscoring the coziness and warmth of the space. This coziness and intimacy masked a deeper social role. Whereas the medieval *Diele* had been open and egalitarian, shared by the master and apprentices and family and visitors, the nineteenth century *Diele* had become a way to shield the family from public view, reinforcing the sanctity and seclusion of family life. In its function as ante-living room it protected the other spaces of the house, especially those occupied by women and children, from the intrusion of public life.

Illustration 1: 19th Century *Diele* in a large house

Issel, Hans. *Die Wohnungs-Baukunde (Bürgerliche Baukunde).* 3rd ed. Leipzig: Bernhard Friedrich Voigt Verlag, 1910. Facsimile reprint Augsburg: Weltbild Verlag, 1998, p.176

Postwar German films often showed houses with a large, furnished *Diele*. If the family was extremely wealthy, the *Diele* was a modeled on the feudal type, often located in a nineteenth century mansion. In such cases, the house contained additional, usually specialized, living rooms beyond the *Diele*. If the family was upper middle class, the *Diele* was a scaled-down version, with several of the same functions as in the upper class house. A small but dignified seating arrangement was placed so that the *Diele* could function as a receiving room. From this space it was only possible to advance to other areas of the house if a housekeeper or some other person "showed in" the guest. A representative example of this type of *Diele* is shown in Erich Engel's 1957 film *Witwer mit fünf Töchtern*. In this family consisting of a widowed father with five daughters, the *Diele* functions as a reception space that is far removed from private family life. Although the older girls' boyfriends are not allowed in the house, adult visitors may be let into the *Diele*, while the girls retreat to call their father or fetch what is needed. In one scene, the father has placed an ad for a new housekeeper. The women are let into the *Diele* and seated closely together as if in a waiting room, while the father interviews one after another in the adjacent study (Illustration 2).

Illustration 2: *Witwer mit fünf Töchtern*, women waiting in the *Diele*

In other films, the *Diele* functioned as the main living room, with only an entry vestibule separating it from the street. The staircase was a prominent element in this two-story space, although the fireplace was usually missing. This kind of *Diele* was closer in atmosphere to its nineteenth century predecessor, although without the range of further living rooms the latter contained. The house in Viktor Tourjansky's 1951 film *Mutter sein dagegen sehr* shows a living room type of *Diele*. Despite the house's traditional architectural language, the floor plan is quite modern, with open flowing spaces making up most of the first floor. Because the staircase is located here, the living room is of double height, further adding to the expansive flow of space (Illustration 3). A library containing a grand piano, a collection of fine porcelain, books, and a comfortable chair for reading is separated from the main living room through an iron grillwork panel, while a dining area is in another niche of the main living room. On the whole, however, these spaces flow into the main area of the living room, with its expressively curved staircase. Despite the openness of the floor plan, the living room in this film remains an adult space, with stainable surfaces and breakable objects. The family's three children spend time either in their room or outside, where they may move about more freely.

Illustration 3: *Mutter sein dagegen sehr*, living room type of *Diele*

Many prefabricated homes also had a space that the manufacturers called a *Diele*. Often, this was little more than a tiny entry hallway, with doors leading to the living room and kitchen, and a staircase leading to upstairs bedrooms. There was no room for a seating arrangement in such a space, so that the designation "*Diele*" functioned more as a marketing tool that would give the man on the street a sense of having a formal and upper class type of reception space (Illustration 4).

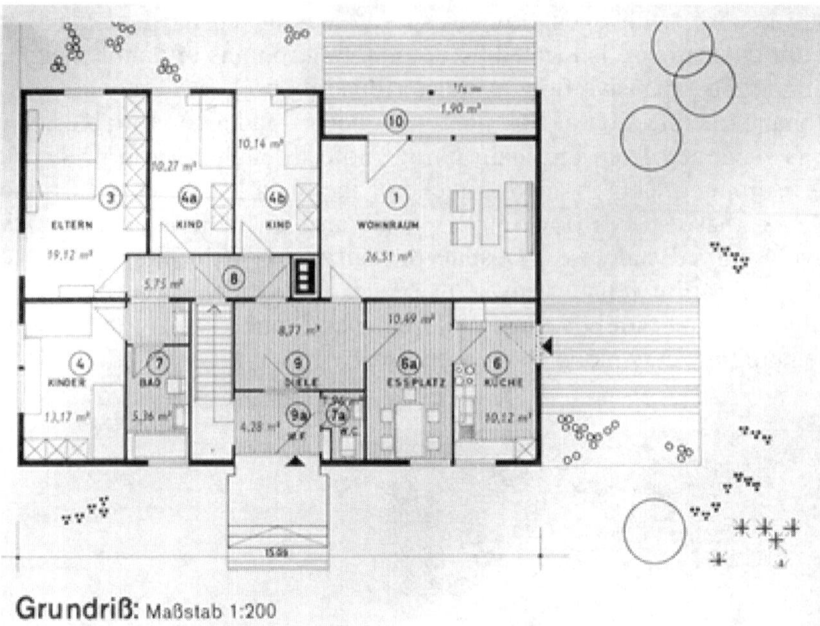

Illustration 4: *Neckermann Haus Avenue 56* (1965)

Strebel, Ottmar, ed. *Fertighaus-Katalog: das Sammel/ u. Nachschlagwerk vom Fertighaus- und Montagehaus-Angebot*. Schmiden: Fachschriftenverlag, 1965.

Some manufacturers went another route. Instead of using sparse square footage for actual living spaces, they chose to incorporate a large entry space that was decorated and furnished to serve as a representative reception area. Ornate staircases, rugs and paintings, side tables and wardrobes, storage chests and seating were not uncommon. Entry into the living room was through a door that was kept closed, or a double door that, in a prior era, could be thrown open before a visitor to let him gaze in awe at the splendor beyond.[66] This type of *Diele* allowed the lower middle class family at which the prefab market was aimed to adopt a representative reception space that would effectively serve as a buffer for the actual living room. It also created a space from which visitors had to be "shown in" to other rooms. As such, the lower class family was emulating the actions of the upper class family with its servants or housekeepers by creating a reception area from which visitors could not proceed without help.

Although the representative entry *Diele* was quite common in prefab houses, the *Diele* as the actual living room, an arrangement so frequently found in 1950s films, was not. When a house had two floors, the staircase was always located in an entry vestibule, never in the actual living room. A related arrangement consisted of a double-height living room with a staircase leading to a gallery (often a study or "studio"). This arrangement became quite common in conventionally-built houses from the 1970s onward, but it was rare in the prefab housing market, the one exception being the Huf company’s *Fachwerkhaus 2000*, offered beginning in the early 1970s (Illustration 5).

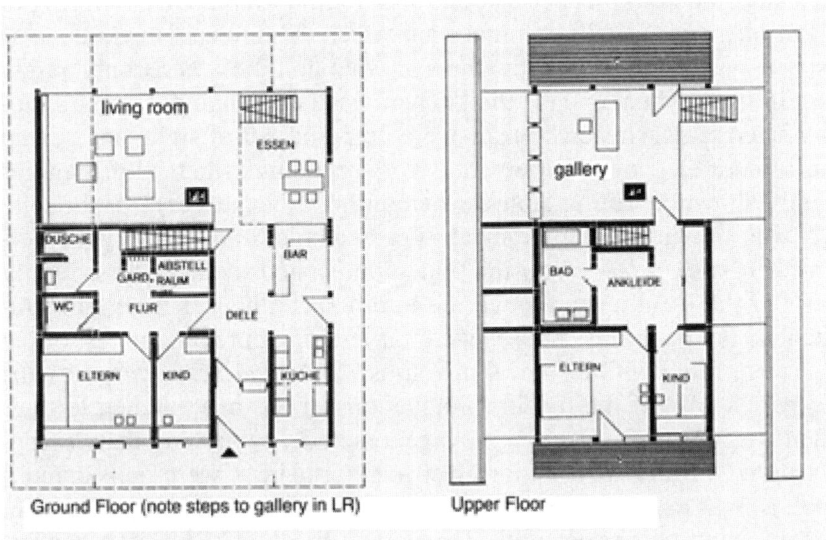

Illustration 5: *Huf Fachwerkhaus* 2000, developed in the early 1970s

Strebel, Ottmar. *Fertighaus-Katalog: das Sammel/ u. Nachschlagwerk vom Fertighaus- und Montagehaus-Angebot*. Fellbach: Fachschriftenverlag, 1980.

There were probably several reasons why the *Diele* as a living room never caught on. The prefab sector saw the house as a market-oriented product, and was careful to offer only features the buyers wanted. Although manufacturers were willing to sacrifice square footage for a representative entry hallway, they did not seem to feel the same about offering a house with a duplicate staircase or a double-height living room in an industry where price is calculated by the cubic foot. By the 1970s, the living room had advanced to being a family space no longer reserved for adults; yet putting the main staircase in the living room of a smaller house, thus effectively making the living room into a circulation space, would have hardly appealed to a customer wanting a place to relax after a hard day’s work. For this reason, the living room in the prefab house remained a space at the end of the line, and not a space that would encourage people to cross through it on their way to elsewhere, and the *Diele* remained a more or less representative entry vestibule with a stairwell.

The Kitchen

Kitchens in postwar German films were not frequently shown. Many were service spaces not generally occupied by the family; when they were depicted, it was often because the housekeeper had left and a family member was trying to cook a meal or clean up, usually to humorous effect. The role of the kitchen as a service space was underscored by the fact that families were only rarely shown eating in the kitchen, even if the kitchen was large enough to accommodate a dining-sized table. Instead, meals were prepared out of sight, and served and eaten in a more elegant environment. Not surprisingly then, film families were frequently shown at dining tables, where either a housekeeper or the wife of the family was shown serving the meal. For example, in the 1953 Paul Verhoeven film *Vergiss die Liebe nicht* the underappreciated mother of the family is shown serving the meal, even though the family has a housekeeper (Illustration 6). Kitchens in upper-class houses were far less opulent than the rest of the dwelling, yet were fitted with technical novelties. In *Mutter sein dagegen sehr*, the housekeepers show off the modern innovations of the new kitchen to their mistress when she returns from a long voyage, excitedly remarking that "everything's electrified." Major and minor electrical appliances were considered a status symbol, as was the more modern fitted kitchen. We should note that film kitchens (when shown) were generally larger than those of the prefab houses, yet were not open to or integrated into the rest of the house. Both spatially and atmospherically they were set apart, with the message apparent that such kitchens were not living spaces, but areas of service to be occupied by domestics.

Illustration 6: *Vergiss die Liebe nicht*, mother serving family

Being served, and maintaining an area of the house to contain domestic work, was clearly not a ritual of German working class or lower middle-class life. For the working class, the kitchen had been *the* main living space, and work performed there had been open and visible. Prewar housing programs often adopted this arrangement by offering a *Wohnküche*, a combined living room and kitchen. Only in the 1920s to late 1930s had the smaller *Arbeitsküche* gradually replaced the working class *Wohnküche*, thus putting "women's work" out of view of everyday family life. The working kitchen of the 1950s was touted as progressive and modern, a descendant from functionalist 1920s kitchens such as the minimalist Frankfurt Kitchen developed by Margarete Schütte-Lihotzky (Illustration 7). Postwar films reinforced the message that in a bourgeois household there were serving and served spaces, and the kitchen was to be kept out of view. Mention of new gadgets, such as electrical appliances, picked up on trends introduced in the 1920s, when rational kitchen design was seen as a way to make housework both more efficient and pleasant.

Illustration 7: *Frankfurter Küche*, developed in the 1920s

Victoria and Albert Museum, London http://www.vam.ac.uk/vastatic/ microsites/ 1331_ modernism/artist_94_330.html

Despite their working class and lower middle class clientele, German prefab manufacturers of the 1950s and 1960s retained the service-type *Arbeitsküche* with separate dining area. Only Swedish manufacturers offered larger eat-in kitchens, marketing them as part of a somewhat exotic "Scandinavian way of life." The working kitchens were an expression of the housewife's new role as supervisor in a world of technological advancements and her new, bourgeois status as housewife—a woman who did not work outside the home. With the proper kitchen, she was meant to feel like a professional. Fitted kitchens, also called "American kitchens," were a status symbol. Electric stoves (instead of gas), stainless steel sinks (instead of enamel) and built-in appliances and counters (instead of free-standing units) underscored their modernity. Tables served the individual, and were illustrated as workspaces (Illustration 8). That German prefab manufacturers offered the *Arbeitsküche* almost exclusively shows how the role of this room had changed for the working class and lower middle class. Instead of having the whole family spend most of their free time in an informal living room/kitchen, the two functions had become separate; the kitchen had become a service area, with the wife of the family taking on the role of housekeeper. When meal preparation was finished, the housewife would serve the waiting family at the dining table, much as servants or housekeepers did in films (Illustration 9). Thus, the real life family enjoyed the same type of service atmosphere as film families, with the exception that the service role now rested on the wife/mother. Her compensation for this role was a kitchen configured as a stylish and modern laboratory that she could proudly call her own.

Illustration 8: *Liebermann Typ L4-2* Kitchen (1975)

Strebel, Ottmar. *Fertighaus-Katalog: das Sammel/ u. Nachschlagwerk vom Fertighaus- und Montagehaus-Angebot*. Fellbach: Fachschriftenverlag, 1975.

Illustration 9: *Okal Typ E130* advertising (1975)

Strebel, Ottmar. *Fertighaus-Katalog: das Sammel/ u. Nachschlagwerk vom Fertighaus- und Montagehaus-Angebot*. Fellbach: Fachschriftenverlag, 1975.

The Master Bedroom

German films generally portrayed bedrooms as feminine spaces, sometimes going so far as to set up a duality between the living room—a more public space with restrained, "masculine" furnishings—and the pronounced frilliness of the bedroom. In doing so, films emphasized the need to keep women's spaces out of public view, especially when they were associated with ideas of her sexuality. Nowhere is this more clearly pronounced than in the 1955 Rolf Hansen film *Teufel in Seide*. In the open plan 1950s house, a large living room and the master bedroom are placed side by side in the plan, facing the rear garden. The living room is furnished with leather sofas, wood and glass tables, and modern paintings (Illustration 10), while the bedroom, furnished with a bed, a vanity and a small seating area, is a medley of floral prints, frilly textiles and mirrors (Illustration 11). The analogous position of the two rooms underscores the dual spatial system of the house. The wife uses the bedroom as her private retreat. She seems to spend much of her time here, although it is not quite clear what activities she pursues. During a dispute, the wife bars the husband access to the bedroom by blocking the doorway with her arms, using access to her space (and thus to her) as a power play within the relationship.

Illustration 10: *Teufel in Seide*, Living Room

Illustration 11: *Teufel in Seide*, Bedroom

The idea of the bedroom as a space the woman could define and control was also portrayed in prefab housing catalogs. Although placement of the master bedroom next to the living room was more common in conventionally built houses, whose plans tended to be more sprawling, some prefab manufacturers also offered an arrangement where the living room and master bedroom occupied analogous positions in the rear façade (Illustration 12). In advertising photos, living rooms tended to be more restrained, while bedrooms in the prefab house were often portrayed as feminine, with flowing and frilly textiles making them clearly *her* space. The vanity was a common piece of furniture, showing that women could use the privacy of the bedroom to preen themselves. In making the house's bedroom the wife's secluded place, the prefab manufacturers propagated typical gender roles: the woman as both a chaste being who must defend her virtue against a pursuing male mixed with images of seductive sensuality, as expressed through the tactile pleasures of plush and frill.

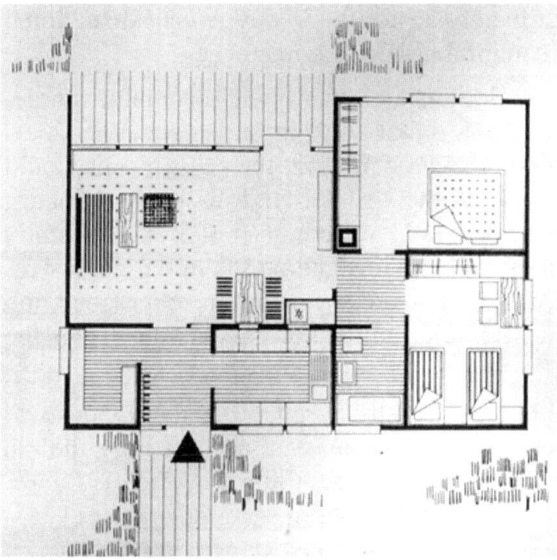

Illustration 12: *Barth Schwäbisches Fertighaus Typ Wildbad* (1969)

Strebel, Ottmar, ed. *Fertighaus-Katalog: das Sammel/ u. Nachschlagwerk vom Fertighaus- und Montagehaus-Angebot*. Schmiden: Fachschriftenverlag, 1969.

Conclusion

The perceived "fresh start" after World War II allowed West Germans to approach the housing question with new gusto. The conservative Adenauer government saw an opportunity not only to support a conservative family ideal, but also to capitalize on general anti-communist sentiments in order to push for the amassment of private property. Both themes were hardly new. Reform efforts from the nineteenth century onwards had concentrated on furthering the idea of isolating family life, with the *Heimstätten* programs of the Weimar Republic and the Nazi era offering the owner-occupied, single-family house as a means towards promoting political and social stability. Living in a house on a patch of one's own land was, by 1945, a seemingly tried-and-true recipe for happiness and prosperity.

The stumbling blocks the Adenauer government faced in implementing its wishes were also familiar. Put simply, the single-family house was generally beyond the reach of working class and lower-middle class consumers. This becomes evident in the legislative debate preceding the Second Housing Law of 1956, in which the most contentious issues were whether to finance only the owner-occupied *Familienheim*, or, as the SPD argued, whether to subsidize rental apartments that would more directly benefit the lower classes. That the

Second Housing Law of 1956 ultimately made the *Familienheim* a national priority speaks for the unbroken dream of a nation of homeowners.

Nonetheless, despite its legislative dominance, the owner-occupied single-family house faced stiff competition from rental housing in postwar West Germany. There were surely less *Familienheime* built than the government would have wished; in addition, projects such as the Grindel High Rises in Hamburg (1946-56) and Berlin's Interbau exhibit of 1957 were high-profile, multi-family housing projects that offered rental units. Notwithstanding the initial pervasiveness of apartment living, however, the seeds were sown for the suburbanization boom that led to a great increase in single-family housing taking off in the 1970s.

While the government encouraged homeownership through legislation, postwar German movies established images of social groups that an upwardly mobile population could aspire to and emulate. Although film families often led unrealistically wealthy lives (many, for example, had live-in servants or housekeepers), the spaces these families occupied were translated into rooms for sale in the prefab housing catalogs. The images presented by the prefab manufacturers allowed a lower middle class clientele to approximate the dream of a glamorous life—and helped cement conservative positions on such issues as gender roles and family life.

It is within this context that we can read the *Diele* as a formal receiving area that shielded the family from the outside world, and the service-type of kitchen as a reflection of conservative views of women as homemakers whose role was to assure her husband's comfort when he came home after a hard day at work. The bedroom, again a space kept from public view, was full of sensuality, in contrast to the more public and restrained living room. It was an idea of a house that was clearly designed from a male perspective.

Moving images of "ideal" houses and visual images of actual houses became powerful tools in furthering the concepts of "home" and home ownership in postwar West Germany. Both helped establish the conservative political and social climate of the Adenauer years, as well as anchoring the Federal Republic in the capitalist system of the West.

Notes

Publication of this text was in part made possible through the generous support of the College of Arts and Architecture of the Pennsylvania State University.

[1] English translation: "One only builds once in a lifetime." All translations of German text are by the author.

[2] The films portrayed are typical of the time and were selected according to pre-established criteria. I began this research by examining the entire West German film production for the 1950s and 1960s and viewing all available films that substantially

showed the interiors of single-family houses. All films considered also had a minimum box-office rating (as reported in trade journals) in order to guarantee that the film had a significant cultural impact at the time of its release. The films presented here are representative of the sample examined.

[3] Visual and spatial analysis as part of critical theory has been standard methodological fare in architecture since the 1960s, used for example in postmodernism (e.g., texts by Edward Soja) structuralism (e.g., essays by Diana Agrest and Mario Gandelsonas) or phenomenology (e.g., writings of Christian Norberg-Schulz or Kenneth Frampton).

[4] Cited in Eduard Führ and Daniel Stemmrich, *Nach gethaner Arbeit verbleibt im Kreise der Eurigen: Arbeiterwohnungen im 19. Jahrhundert* (Wuppertal: Peter Hammer Verlag, 1985), 89.

[5] Cited in Gerhard Fehl, "Der Kleinwohnungsbau, der Grundlage des Städtebaus? Von 'offenen Kleinwohnungen' in Berlin und vom unbeirrt seit 1847 verfolgten Reformprojekt der 'abgeschoossenen Kleinwohnung'," in *Die Kleinwohnungsfrage: Zu den Ursprungen des sozialen Wohnungsbaus in Europa*, ed. Juan Rodriguez-Lores and Gerhard Fehl (Hamburg: Christians Verlag, 1987), 95–134, 110.

[6] Paul Schmitthenner, *Die Gartenstadt Staaken* (Berlin: Verlag Erst Wasmuth, ca. 1929), 7.

[7] Hans Bechly, *Die Heimstätte des Angestellten: Eine Denkschrift über die Möglichkeit, die Wohnungsverhältnisse der Versichterten der Reichsversicherungs-Anstalt für Angestellte durch Erbauung von Kleinhäusern zu verbessern*, 2. ed. (Hamburg: Deutschnationale Verlags-Anstalt, 1918, first published 1917), 5.

[8] See Thomas Hafner, "Eigenheim und Kleinsiedlung,"in *Geschichte des Wohnens 1918-1945: Reform, Reaktion, Zerstörung,* ed. Gerd Kähler (Stuttgart: Deutsche Verlags-Anstalt, 1996), 557–98, here 562.

[9] Deutsche Bau und Bodenbank AG, *Denkschrift über die vorstädtische Kleinsiedlung, ihre bisherigen Erfahrungen und Entwicklungstendenzen* (Berlin: n.p., 1934), cited in Tilman Harlander, Katrin Hater, and Franz Meiers, *Siedeln in der Not. Umbruch von Wohnungspolitik und Siedlungsbau am Ende der Weimarer Republik* (Hamburg: Christians Verlag, 1988), 73.

[10] Hafner, 567.

[11] Harlander et al., 85.

[12] Hafner , 561.

[13] Ibid., 584ff.

[14] After 1940 and with the increasing destruction of German cities, the Nazis shifted their planning aims, developing "bomb-proof" urban housing as well as temporary shelters for families whose housing had been destroyed. See Hafner (1996), 592 ff, and Werner Durth, *Deutsche Architekten: Biographische Verflechtungen 1900-1970* (Munich: Deutscher Taschenbuch Verlag, 1992, first published 1986), 183–4. In addition, planners developed "social housing" ideals for a postwar era. See Anna Teut, *Architektur im Dritten Reich 1933-45* (Berlin: Ullstein, 1967), 250ff. Despite these planning activities, the wartime economy caused housing production to grind to a halt.

[15] Hafner, 585–6.

[16] Cited in Durth, 98–9.

[17] West Germans attending the cinema an average of 15.4 times in 1956—up from 6.5 times just ten years before. Götz von Pestalozza, ed., *Filmstatistisches Taschenbuch* (Wiesbaden: n.p., 1957), 25.

[18] Heide Fehrenbach, *Cinema in Democratizing Germany: Reconstructing National Identity after Hitler* (Chapel Hill and London: University of North Carolina Press, 1995), 163.
[19] Martin Osterland, *Gesellschaftsbilder in Filmen: Eine soziologische Untersuchung des Filmangebots der Jahre 1949-64* (Stuttgart: Enke, 1970), 116.
[20] See Teut.
[21] *Erstes Wohnungsbaugesetz vom 24. April 1950* (Bundesgesetzblatt Nr. 16, 83–8) (Munich: Beck, 1950), Art. 6: 1 and 2.
[22] *Erstes Wohnungsbaugesetz* (1950), Art. 16: 2.
[23] *Erstes Wohnungsbaugesetz*, (1950), Art. 16: 1.
[24] *Erstes Wohnungsbaugesetz* (1950), Art. 1.
[25] *Erstes Wohnungsbaugesetz* (1950), Art. 13 and 14.
[26] [die] Finanzierung des Baues von Eigenheimen, Kleinsiedlungen, Kaufeigenheimen, Wohnungen in der Rechtsform des Wohnungseigentums…," *Erstes Wohnungsbaugesetz in der Fassung vom 25. August 1953* (Bundesgesetzblatt Nr. 54: 1,047-59) (Bonn: Bundesanzeiger-Verlags-GmbH, 1953), Art. 19: 1.
[27] *Erstes Wohnungsbaugesetz* (1953), Art. 19: 3.
[28] The same rule applied to units that were especially luxurious. *Erstes Wohnungsbaugesetz* (1953) Art. 29: 3.
[29] *Verhandlungen des deutschen Bundestages. 2. Wahlperiode 1953. Stenografische Berichte*. Vol. 18, 20, 21 (Bonn: no publisher noted, 1954), cited in Verhandlungen des deutschen Bundestages. Stenografische Berichte (hereafter VdB) vol. 18 (1953/54): 246.
[30] For a discussion see Robert G. Moeller, *Protecting Motherhood: Women and the Family in the Politics of Postwar West Germany* (Berkeley: Univ. of California Press, 1993).
[31] VdB vol. 18 (1953/54): 246.
[32] Ibid., 248.
[33] Ibid., 247.
[34] Ibid., 248.
[35] Ibid.
[36] Ibid., 251.
[37] Ibid.
[38] Ibid., 253.
[39] Ibid., 254.
[40] VdB vol. 29 (1956): 7,431.
[41] Ibid.
[42] VdB vol. 18 (1953/54): 256.
[43] VdB vol. 21 (1953/54): 2,372; VdB vol. 29 (1956): 7,411.
[44] VdB vol. 21 (1953/54): 2,374.
[45] This group included workers and tradespeople occupied in the production sector. *Statistisches Bundesamt Deutschland 2005*, http://www.destatis.de/indicators/d/lrver04ad.htm (accessed 10 July 2005).
[46] VdB vol. 29 (1956): 7,449. The average male worker's salary was 460 deutschmarks in 1956 according to *Statistisches Bundesamt Deutschland 2005*, http://www.destatis.de/indicators/d/lrver04ad.htm (accessed 10 July 2005).
[47] VdB vol. 21 (1953/54): 2,375.

[48] "Die Förderung des Wohnungsbaus hat das Ziel, die Wohnungsnot, namentlich auch der Wohnungsuchenden mit geringem Einkommen, zu beseitigen und zugleich weite Kreise des Volkes durch Bildung von Einzeleigentum, besonders in der Form von Familienheimen, mit dem Grund und Boden zu verbinden. [...] In ausreichendem Maße sind solche Wohnungen zu fördern, die die Entfaltung eines gesunden Familienlebens, namentlich für kinderreiche Familien, gewährleisten." *Zweites Wohnungsbaugesetz vom 28. Juni 1956,* Bundesgesetzblatt Nr. 30: 523-58 (Wiesbaden: Gabler, 1956), Art. 1: 2.
[49] VdB vol. 20 (1954): 1,711.
[50] *Zweites Wohnungsbaugesetz,* Art. 30: 1.
[51] *Zweites Wohnungsbaugesetz,* Art. 27: 1.
[52] The attempt to change German culture through film had even been made more blatantly; during the mid- to late 1940s, American occupying powers systematically, but rather ineptly, tried to use Hollywood films as an instrument to teach Germans about the American concept of democracy. See Fehrenbach (1995), 54.
[53] Arno Vangerow-Kühn and Monika Vangarow-Kühn, *Die Fertighaus-Bauindustrie in der Bundesrepublik Deutschland als Modell für Rationalisierung durch Industrialisierung im Bauen*, Schriftenreihe des Bundesministers für Raumordnung, Bauwesen und Städtebau Heft Nr. 04.100 (1984), 12.
[54] The series began in the 14 July issue with the article, "Stern baut 40 Häuser in 80 Tagen," and continued until 20 October, with every other issue of the weekly presenting new houses. In two issues, the article was the cover story. *Stern*, vol. 16 (14 July 1963 – 20 October 1963).
[55] Both are comparable to catalog companies such as Sears in the United States.
[56] The magazine appears today under the title *b+F Das Hausbau Magazin.*
[57] Vangerow-Kuhn, 13.
[58] Ibid., 78, 83.
[59] Ottmar Strebel ed., *Fertighaus-Katalog: das Sammel- u. Nachschlagwerk vom Fertighaus- und Montagehaus-Angebot* (Schmiden: Fachschriftenverlag, 1965).
[60] *Statistisches Bundesamt Deutschland 2005*, http://www.destatis.de/indicators/d/lrver04ad.htm (accessed 10 July 2005).
[61] *Stern* (1963) vol. 16, no. 39: 62–64.
[62] Ibid., 38.
[63] *Stern* (1963) vol. 16, no. 39: 44–5.
[64] *Stern*, vol. 21 (14 January 1968), no. 2: 68–9.
[65] Vangerow-Kuhn, 81.
[66] Guido Harbers, *Das eigene Heim im Einzelgrundstück, in der Plansiedlung und in der Reihe* (Ravensburg: Otto Maier Verlag, 1951), 8.

Between Igniting and Sustaining Democracy: Staging Brandt and the No-Confidence Vote 1972 in Letters to the German Chancellor*

Sabine Manke

Willy Brandt's "Janus Face"?

Since its founding in 1950, the weekly newspaper *Bayernkurier*, party organ of the Bavarian Christian Social Union (CSU), had been appreciated by a conservative readership for an outspoken, belligerent handling of the party's political opponents. In the last September issue of 1972 though, it opened with an editorial titled *Das Doppelgesicht* ("The Double Face") that caused an intense debate among its otherwise approving readers.[1] The polemical article claimed to provide a psychograph of the chancellor of the Federal Republic, the Social Democrat Willy Brandt. One and a half months before the early elections would bring the Social Democratic Party (SPD) its best electoral results to date, Wolfgang Horlacher wrote in *Das Doppelgesicht* about the *Janus-Kopf* ("Janus face") of Brandt:

> Düster, von der Tragik angeblichen Missverständnisses umwittert [...]. Das ist das eine Gesicht des Willy Brandt. Es ist die angemaßte Rolle des Staatsmannes, der von seinem Volk nicht verstanden wird. Es ist die Rolle, die in der unseligsten Periode deutscher Geschichte ihren Ausdruck darin fand, daß das Volk deshalb zu Grunde zu gehen habe, weil es seinem bedeutendsten Führer nicht würdig sei.
>
> [...]
>
> Das Doppelgesicht des Nichts im rötlichen Dämmer; ein Gezeichneter; ein Erlöser; aber zugleich einer, der sich nicht scheut, die Straße zu mobilisieren, um auf dem Altar seiner eigenen Karriere die deutsche Demokratie notfalls zu opfern.
>
> Sullen, surrounded by the tragic of alleged misunderstanding [...]. This is only one face of Willy Brandt. It is the appropriated role of the statesman who is misunderstood by his people. It is the role that, in the most disastrous period of German history, found its expression in [the conviction] that the people had to perish because they were not deserving of their leader.
>
> [...]

> The double face of nothing in the reddish dusk; a branded one; a redeemer; but at the same time someone who is not afraid to mobilize the street in order to sacrifice German democracy on the altar of his own career, if necessary.

The nebulosity of many of Horlacher's expressions did not hinder the readers to come up with their own unambiguous interpretation: "Was it necessary to compare Chancellor Brandt to Hitler?" asked Hans Jörg Riebel.[2] A woman from Tiefenbach called the editorial the ultimate reason for giving up her CSU party membership.[3] Nevertheless, a lot of readers cheered Horlacher's portrait of Brandt oscillating between a tragic martyr for his people and a totalitarian demagogue ready to sacrifice "German democracy."

The fact that so many people responded to this polemic, either with outrage or enthusiasm, indicates that a sensitive spot had been touched. Horlacher's article and the reactions to it not only display the malice and animosity, but also the redemptive expectations associated with the figure of Willy Brandt. I am interested in the specific quality of these affects and the semantic field within which they are articulated—an area marked by the concepts and experiences of "fascism" and "democracy." The *Bayernkurier*'s malicious description, I contend, cannot be understood as a reasonable characterization of Willy Brandt, but as an account of a collective process that took place within the German public during the early 1970s. This process brought to life the image of a new German national collective by means of "enacting a scene" from the past.[4] At the core of that scene is the figure of Willy Brandt, emigrant and resistance fighter during the Nazi period, lord mayor of Berlin from 1957 to 1966, state secretary and vice chancellor from 1966 until 1969, and then chancellor of West Germany until 1974. The principal sources upon which I draw are letters written to Willy Brandt by the general public between 24 April and 2 May 1972.[5] In a short nine-day period, tens of thousands of letters, postcards, and telegrams reached the chancellor's office.[6] About two-thirds of these letters were written on one single day—27 April 1972.[7] On that day Willy Brandt faced a vote of no-confidence in the *Bundestag*, the result of intense controversies surrounding the 1970 treaties of Moscow and Warsaw. These so-called *Ostverträge* ("Eastern Treaties") aimed at détente between Germany and its former "enemies" and awaited *Bundestag* ratification in spring 1972. Each of these treaties included a mutual commitment to non-violent politics, as well as the acknowledgement of frontiers and especially the recognition of the German Democratic Republic (GDR). The deep division of opinion that ran through West German society regarding the treaties was manifested in the *Bundestag*. By April 1972, several delegates from the liberal FDP—the coalition partner of Willy Brandt's SPD—had surrendered their party membership books in protest, and thereby left the government in the unpleasant situation of losing its majority in the parliament.

On 24 April Rainer Barzel, leader of the CDU/CSU opposition and supported by the CSU politician Franz-Josef Strauß introduced a motion of no-confidence, which was to take place three days later.

That day nearly everyone in the Federal Republic was alert; children and adults followed parliamentary debate via television or radio. People had taken radios with them to work, teachers set up TV sets in class, and participants in innumerable rallies in support of the *Ostverträge*, both spontaneous and organized, listened to proceedings in the streets. Around 1:20 p.m. the results were announced by *Bundestag* President Kai von Hassel: the opposition-sponsored vote of no-confidence had failed by two votes. Only a few minutes after the announcement, the first telegram congratulating Willy Brandt was wired to the chancellor's office. Shortly before half past one thousands and thousands of people took up pens, sat down before their typewriters, or walked to a nearby post office in order to compose their congratulations to Chancellor Brandt. They produced poems, children created drawings, some made recordings, they sent flowers, they reported praying, they wept and embraced strangers in the streets, consumed copious amounts of alcohol.[8] What might otherwise have been a brief outpouring of public excitement in fact culminated in one of the most profound processes of democratization in the history of the Federal Republic. Not only did many people announce their intention to join a political party, examination of party membership registers reveal that they obviously acted upon this intention; the SPD, CDU, CSU, and FDP were flooded with an unprecedented number of new members.[9] With a turnout of 91.1 percent, early elections in autumn 1972 marked the highest participation in a West German election ever.[10]

The letters to Willy Brandt provide a framework for understanding this process of democratization in relation to a larger post-fascist historical context that I argue can be understood as a form of "enactment." First, I will illustrate the core dynamic of this scenic process by focusing on one particular letter written by a middle-aged couple from Bochum[11]; in a very condensed form it mirrors some key patterns of the collective imaginary surrounding Willy Brandt and sets up the above-mentioned historical context within which these letters can be interpreted. Second, I will address the motif "fire" as it is manifested in the collection of letters in order to explore the specific metaphoric space that Willy Brandt occupied. In the end, my analysis takes up the image of a reunified Germany—the ultimate endpoint of the trajectory suggested in a great number of the letters.

The sheer volume of communications presents a significant obstacle to in-depth understanding of the letters' relevancy. An approach that focuses on only small passages of text in order to develop a wide variety of messages to the chancellor is unable to convey the various ways in which the letters mediate between their writers on the one hand, and the sphere of politics or the seemingly elusive realm of history on the other. To focus on a letter solely as a piece of writing which can be cut up in bits and pieces ignores the fact that it is a three-dimensional conceptual object, the result of a complex physical act and a cultural gesture. With sensitivity to this point I will limit my attention to a representative few, but significant, submissions and include their non-textual aspects where appropriate. The documents presented here are taken from a larger study that offers a comprehensive analysis of a representative number of letters.[12] The particular sample allows for rich insight into the scenario created by the letters, postcards and telegrams as a whole.

In theoretical as well as methodical respect my approach follows the critical hermeneutical cultural analysis of Alfred Lorenzer. As a border crosser between cognitive science, psychoanalysis, and historic-materialistic approaches in sociology, Lorenzer inspired the German postwar discourse on hermeneutics. His works have been discussed alongside the writings of Jürgen Habermas, Paul Ricoeur, and Hans-Georg Gadamer.[13] Lorenzer's elaboration on the "sensual-symbolic" side of social interaction, in particular—in contrast to its discursive aspects—as well as his methodological reflections on "scenic understanding" have informed not only post-Freudian metapsychology, but also some sectors of the social sciences, cultural studies, literary criticism, ethnology, and pedagogy. The following interpretations of letters to Willy Brandt reflect Lorenzer's viewpoint, as presented here in a translation by Josef Bleicher, that

> only in the concept of the subject can the dialectic between individual and society be thought of concretely. The asubjectivity of structuralism underlies also its ahistoricality and removes the point at which the individual is concretely mediated with *this* society. With the destruction of the subject, the relationship with everyday activity, with reality here and now, is cut-off.

"It is only necessary to add", Bleicher explicates aptly, "that the 'subject' is here to be understood non-subjectivistically, i.e. as formed by socio-historical processes which he [or she], in turn, influences."[14]

Diverse approaches in the historical sciences (e.g. Hayden White, the French school of the *Annales*) as well as in social and political philosophy (e.g., Cornelius Castoriadis, Jean-Francois Lyotard, Pierre Bourdieu) or cultural studies (e.g., Christina von Braun) have suggested that the link between individual and society is grounded in narrative constructions. Consequently, for a complex understanding of sociopolitical processes, empirical perspectives have to be complemented by hermeneutical approaches. The following interpretations of letters are committed to such an analysis.

Mary on Crutches vs. Mary the Immaculate—A Story of Guilt and Redemption

The first letter under consideration, dated 27 April and sent by a couple from an industrial region, demonstrates the ways in which the approach I take is valuable. In this instance it is a non-textual element that first strikes the reader's eye: the letter came in an envelope secured at three different spots with drops of dark red sealing wax. In addition to the addresses of Willy Brandt and the sender, the envelope carried a special note, "*Persönliche Privatpost*" (personal private mail). By sealing the letter the writers furnished a particular stage on which meaningful action is transmitted and can take place. As visitors to this performative space we are looking at a precarious scene of broken seals, a possibly sinful and therefore conspiratorial alliance, as much as we are affected—perhaps even exhilarated—by the childlike naiveté this play with candle wax communicates. The letter itself reflects this dichotomy of guilt and innocence in various ways. This letter's text was written with a blue ballpoint on white ruled paper and begins with a congratulating phrase:

> Hoch verehrter Herr Bundes Kanzler!
>
> Zu Ihrem großen Sieg, im Deutschen Bundestag, den nicht nur Sie, sondern Alle Ihre Freunde, ob in Deutschland oder im Ausland, mit Ihnen feiern möchten wir Ihnen, von ganzem Herzen die aller herzlichsten Glückwünsche übermitteln.[15]
>
> Highly revered Mr. Chancellor!
>
> [Regarding your great victory in the German *Bundestag*, which not only you but all of your friends, whether in Germany or abroad, are celebrating together with you we would like to send you most sincere congratulations with all our heart.]

Without any break in the text, the introductory congratulations move into what we might designate the first episode of this letter. However, this optical levelling of contents in fact conceals a significant (self-)degradation. Only momentarily do we see two people eye-to-eye with a third person, whose hand they shake in order to express their gratitude on the rather level terrain of human sympathy and esteem (*möchten wir Ihnen, von ganzem Herzen die aller herzlichsten Glückwünsche über mitteln* / "we would like to send you the most heartfelt congratulations from all our heart"). Suddenly, without our awareness, the ground seem to open up and swallow the two congratulators, who now look up from the perspective of two unworthy, poor, sick invalids:

> Sind Sie hoch verehrter Herr Bundes Kanzler uns bitte nicht böse, das wir Ihnen dieses nur auf einem einfachen Briefbogen schreiben, aber Sie wissen ja, wir sind arme kranke Frührentner, und am 27. zwei Tage vor Maria Empfängniss, das heist [sic] vor Renten Zahlung geht die Marie auf Krücken.
>
> [Please, highly revered Mr. Chancellor don't be angry with us, that we're writing this to you only on a simple sheet of paper, but, as you know, we are poor, sick, disabled pensioners, and on the 27th two days before Mary's Conception, that means before payment of pensions Marie is walking on crutches.]

The manifest level of this passage may simply have an explanatory character: it serves as an introduction of the writers ("poor, sick, early pensioners") and marks them as members of the lower class. It is the extraordinary reference to the figure of Mary that lends much greater importance to this introductory passage. Through a linguistic play on the name Mary the writers address the issue of their present desperate financial situation. The reference point of this play is the word "Marie," a colloquial expression for money. Combined with the idiomatic phrase *auf Krücken* / "on crutches" it signifies the writers' financial problems. Behind "Mary on crutches" appears Mary the mother of Christ. *Maria Empfängnis*—the Feast of the Immaculate Conception—does not mean a particular religious holiday in this instance[16]; in this context it refers to the day when pension payments are issued: "Mary on crutches" in two days, 29 April, will be redeemed through "Mother Mary" the giver of life. The issue of a disability pension implicitly evokes a certain relationship between the couple writing and the letter's recipient. As representative of the State, Willy Brandt appears as the benefactor on whom the couple's subsistence relies. Poor, sick invalids committing the sin of addressing the Chancellor on a simple sheet of paper and now pleading for his forgiveness form a kind of triptych image: the couple writing present themselves as condemned, together with "Mary on Crutches," but redeemed at the side of the Virgin through the figure in the middle, Willy Brandt. Like a threefold altarpiece this arrangement tells us a story of guilt and innocence, condemnation and salvation—the benefactor acting on behalf of the State, Chancellor Brandt, is thus elevated even higher. It seems that in this scenario he is feared as the vengeful judge of the Old Testament, and yearned for as the liberating figure of Christ.

Not at all unlike the story of "Holy Mary, Fallen Mary," the narrative immediately following the first part, which I call "Suitcase Episode," begins with a spectacular shift in perspective: the former sinners now sit on the bench of the public prosecutor passing judgement on the abominable offence of high treason:

> Aber trotzdem für uns, gab es trotz Vaterland Verräter keine Sekunde Zweifel darüber, das Sie uns erhalten blieben, denn Recht, muß Recht

> bleiben; auch wenn es gestern Abend im Fernsehn von Strauß und seinen Unkraut hieß, Sie wären sicher schon am Koffer packen. Das haben Sie doch nicht nötig Sie haben doch noch ihren Koffer in Berlin, und den schaffen auch Bartzel, Strauß, und alles andere Gemüße nicht von Berlin weg. Dieses hat sich heute Mittag bewiesen. Wie gerne wären wir im Bundeshaus dabei gewesen.
>
> [But for us, nevertheless, despite the traitors to the fatherland there was not even a second of doubt that you would stay with us, because justice must remain justice; even if last evening on television we heard from Strauß and his nasty weeds that you were surely packing your suitcase already. You certainly don't have to stand for that, for you still have a suitcase in Berlin, and neither Bartzel nor Strauß, or any other vegetable can take that one away from Berlin. This was proved today at noon. How much would we have liked to been there in the *Bundeshaus*.]

The suitcase episode, recounted in a significant number of letters, refers to an incident in the course of *Bundestag* debate the day before the no-confidence vote. In the course of his speech, CSU representative Franz Josef Strauss had been interrupted by CDU representative Dr. Werner Marx; Marx wanted to know if Strauss could account for why Willy Brandt was absent throughout his whole speech. Without waiting for an answer he added that the only explanation he could come up with was that Willy Brandt was already packing his suitcase. Strauss replied that Brandt was probably preparing for the following day. Apart from rather general comments on the *Bundestag* debates or on the style and behavior of the speakers, this is the only concrete episode that found its way into a considerable number of letters. Its comparatively frequent appearance in the material, as well as the discrepancy between its unspectacular character and the almost hysterical reactions it elicited, raise questions about the hidden dynamic which made this story so volatile. This particular anecdote not only offers a key to understanding this specific letter; it also helps to understand what the imagined struggle waged by Willy Brandt and good Germans against the *Vaterlandsverräter* ("traitors to the fatherland") is really about. Together with the images of rebirth and redemption that so frequently come up in the letters to Brandt, it refers to unresolved past conflicts. As a mainly subconscious process it is a form of "enactment" and brings to life the image of a new German national collective which resembles a much older one.

In the political struggles of the late 1960s and early 1970s, the use of polemical language was commonplace. Why, then, should anyone have become so excited about a sharp-witted comment in the parliament? In this incident the highly ambivalent history of a piece of luggage —the *Koffer* (suitcase)—relates to Willy Brandt's own biography. The circumstances of the Second World War had not only literally filled thousands of suitcases with things people wanted to save; the suitcase reference was symbolically laden with associations of voluntary or forced emigration. After the Auschwitz trials (1963-65) the suitcase in postwar Germany came to signify something else: for example, photographs of empty suitcases piled up in the *Effektenkammern* of concentration camps acquired the status of icons for the mass murder of Jews and other targeted peoples during the Nazi period.[17]

The two delegates joking about the former emigrant and victim of persecution Willy Brandt packing his suitcase is indeed a low point in tastelessness. The highly emotional response to the suitcase episode in the *Bundestag* not only articulates the Bochum couple's support for Chancellor Brandt. On the level of imagery they stage an inversion of a former relationship: the "traitors" are identified with former persecutors and with the former victims. This time "good Germans" are fighting for the target of persecution.

This conceptualization of the present through past images—or, perhaps equally the re-visioning of the past through re-ordering of its images in the present—is an overarching theme in the collection of letters. Frequently the leading opposition politicians are called "Nazis" or "fascists" who again try to seize power in a coup d'état. A woman of unknown, but supposedly advanced age, from suburban Dortmund writes:

> Wir wollen keine *Dicktatur*. Wir müssen dagegen kämpfen, das die Faschisten nicht *an* der Regierung kommen. Sonst sind wir *verloren*.[18]
>
> [We do not want a *dictatorship*. We have to fight against the [possibility of the] fascists coming to power. Otherwise we are *lost*.]

Some people, who sent a message to the chancellor shortly *before* the vote in the Bundestag was taken, announced their future emigration in case the opposition triumphed:

> Wir bekunden unsere Solidarität mit Ihrer Regierungspolitik. Ein Bundeskanzler Barzel würde uns zum Auswandern veranlassen.[19]
>
> [We announce our solidarity with your governmental policies. A Chancellor Barzel would cause us to emigrate.]

What seems troublesome is that the simple reversal of the historic scene—even if one prefers it that way—means the reassembling or reconstruction of a damaged German identity by using the reverse side of the broken pieces. The writers' use of the word *Unkraut* (weeds) for human beings in the letters mentioned above makes quite clear that the one-time fascist image of the parasite was still used bluntly and without reflection. The enthusiastic proclamation of a national "rebirth" that frequently appear in the letters to Willy Brandt may be envisioned firmly within a democratic context. Nonetheless, this new (West) German collective is based on images and experiences of the Nazis' homogeneous masses, even if they were individually and collectively repressed, as well as the idea of an enemy within.[20] In this context the figure of Willy Brandt functions as a mask through which the old German collective wants to be recognized as something new.

The image of the mask is helpful as well as misleading. It correctly describes the formation of a "collective body"[21] in a key respect—the mask is the cast for otherwise incoherent and diverse features. This cast defines the limits as well as the potential of the body politic. The image of the mask-as-cast is less beneficial insofar as it suggests that this specific form is either arbitrary or easy to mould. With this assertion in mind, we can turn to the question of why Willy Brandt could provide the contours for this "new" German society. Since the beginning of the 1950s, coinciding with Brandt's career as a West Berlin Social Democrat and in the SPD at the federal level, an embittered polemic had arisen around his person and biography, mainly centered on his political work against Nazi-led Germany as an émigré, his return to Germany in a Norwegian uniform, and the fact that he had kept the alias "Willy Brandt" that he had assumed as a member of the Resistance.[22] At no point had Brandt enjoyed unambiguous consent from the German public—not when he knelt down in front of the Warsaw Ghetto memorial in 1970, nor when he was awarded the Nobel Peace Prize one year later. Even some of the most supportive letters he received in 1972 reveal a fundamental ambivalence towards him! For these reasons it is the complete setting, the whole symbolic landscape surrounding him, which made Brandt so important for German society. The suitcase episode above may be just one minor example showing the power of imagery, and yet it is paradigmatic for the situation in April 1972; none of its various aspects—an opposition politician mocking him, his emigration during the Nazi period, etc.—would have been able to trigger such a fierce response in their own right. Only when taken in combination do these elements create a symbolic space that not only becomes meaningful because of its absences (e.g., the history behind the image of the packed vs. empty suitcase), but which come to dominate perceived political realities.[23] Within this symbolic landscape Rainer Barzel's and Franz-Josef Strauss's specific personal and political value orientations and backgrounds contribute their share to the "public meaning" deduced from the situation. It is likely that the two main adversaries' wives were also of some importance in this symbolic setting: Willy Brandt's spouse had the biblical name Ruth whereas Barzel's wife was called Kriemhild. Both names perfectly reflected and nurture the imaginary struggle against the return of the Nazis ("Jewish Ruth" versus "Germanic-Wagnerian Kriemhild").[24] Surely the Federal Republic's formal recognition of the post-1945 German-Polish border in the *Ostverträge* carried the potential to revive among the German public repressed experiences related to the war. However, the letters to Willy Brandt constitute an "active reading" of the parliamentary discussion which transcends the political realm, incorporating elements from supposedly remote spheres of meaning connected by a scenic logic.

The following poem was written by a seventy-six year old man from southwest Germany right after the no-confidence vote.[25] It clearly illuminates the enormous metaphoric space Willy Brandt occupies in this scenic constellation. Moreover, it further shows that the Federal Republic's democratic institutions are a space prone to unresolved conflicts related to war experiences from a fascist past.

Brandt as the "Burning Giant"

Similar to the couple mentioned above, the poem's writer introduces himself as "physically" handicapped. He signs his twenty-one typewritten stanzas with not only his name and address, but also adds the apposition "Krüppeldichter (76) brandevakuiert" ("cripple poet, seventy-six years old, fire-evacuated"). As a form of "micro-biography" this self-designation represents the core information the writer wants to bring to the readers' attention.[26] Strikingly, the author chooses a specific time-bound experience from, in all likelihood, the Second World War to describe his current state. He is thus rendering a crucial experience a timeless condition of his present life. The fire to which he refers was extinguished several decades ago, but in effect he describes it as burning still in the sense that it brands the letter writer. The poem's title "*Zum Sieg*" ("To Victory") first and foremost draws a connection to the result of the no-confidence vote. However, by drawing on various images of fire in his poem, the writer establishes a much broader network of interrelated meanings: he connects war-related experiences and developments in the *Bundestag* with fantasies about the *Bundeskanzler* and the act of writing itself. His sentences, marked neatly with rhymes, may work on the surface; nevertheless, the attempt to build stable meaning fails consistently, the result of a current of counter-signification running underneath the stanzas. Thus, the letter tells two contrary stories simultaneously. The poem's title is one obvious example: while the phrase "To Victory" praises the winner of the vote, the verses that follow focus on Rainer Barzel—a hymn to the loser?[27]

Focusing on the narrative structure of the poem itself, we can divide the document into two parts. The first, shorter section provides a detailed, negative account of someone called "Rainer," while the second, much longer part discusses the consequences of his actions. This alter ego *Bundestag* opposition leader

Rainer Barzel is depicted as a Machiavellian figure whose machinations fall short of the hubristic assertiveness of his speeches:

Zum Sieg

stanza

1 Es war einmal ein Rainer/nicht ganz zwei Meter hoch.
Kann Schimpfen, wie sonst keiner/als Dauerredner noch.

2 Parlamentarierregeln/umfährt er längste Zeit,
Schnellstenografensegeln/hinkt nach `ne Ewigkeit.

3 Mit Ewigkeitsgedanken/beschäftigt ihn nicht viel.
Seine Zedern ranken/ins politische Asyl.

4 Von seiner Tagesarbeit/im reichen Wirtschaftsleben,
Ist ihm der größte Schneid/im Wortgefecht gegeben.

[To Victory

1 Once upon a time there was a Rainer/not quite two meters long.
Can scold, like no one else/as a perpetual orator.

2 Parliamentary rules/he circumvents most of the time,
Sailing with rapid stenographers/he lags behind endlessly.

3 Thoughts of eternity/do not engage him much.
His cedars climb/into political asylum.

4 In his daily work/in the rich world of economy,
the greatest moxie/is endowed to him in [the form of] crosstalk.]

Starting off with the fairy tale-like beginning "*Es war einmal*" ("Once upon a time"), the poem's first stanza abandons its protagonist in a landscape which seems to be out of control:

stanza

5 Es blitzt mit Donnerkrachen/es fällt dem Frühling Schnee
in sein schönes Blumenlachen/in bitter härtester Idee!

[It flashes with thunderclaps/it snows into the spring's
beautiful laughter of flowers/in a bitter, most callous manner!]

After introducing a solidly negative character during his first four stanzas, the author presents the no-confidence vote in the guise of a nature description. He thereby disassociates it from human responsibilities and influence. When we take into account that the author wrote his poem during a period of East-West tensions, his seasonal reference evokes the habitual use of a meteorological imagery to describe political conflicts or processes—for example "Cold War" or "Prague Spring." It is also possible that the images of thunderstorm and snowfall in spring refer to "April weather." When interpreted in light of subsequent verses, a further meaning of this stanza becomes apparent: the fundamental antagonism of fire and water.

stanza

6 Brandauslöscher nennt er sich/mit seinem Riesenschneid!
Gegen Riesenbrand ohnmächtiglich/ist der Rainer in alle Ewigkeit!

[He calls himself fire extinguisher /with his great moxie
Against the giant burning powerless/is Rainer in all eternity!"]

Modelled on the German word *Feuerlöscher* (fire extinguisher) the neologism "*Brandauslöscher*" refers to Willy Brandt's political opponent Rainer Barzel. It is based on a conscious "misreading" (one might just as well say a homonymic interpretation) of Brandt's name as "Brand" (*fire*). Thus, political conflict is depicted as a conflagration. The image shows a logic of extinction. In a modern society that invests considerable sums and effort to protect itself against fires, this image is outright ambivalent. The confusion about who actually is the hero of this "victory" deepens; can it really be the adversary of the "*Brandauslöscher*" ("fire extinguisher"), the "*Riesenbrand*" ("burning giant")? Ultimately, the latter image consists of two mutually exclusive ideas: the powerful, protective Chancellor Brandt on one side and a life-endangering conflagration on the other. The paradox sharpens in the following verses, as the author addresses necessary measures in fighting a fire—i.e., the poem turns into a manual for fire extinguishing:

stanza

7 Ja, das kommt allein davon/, bei einem Wunder muß man Glauben!
Bei einer Brandlöschaktion/muß man Leben retten, niemals rauben.

8 Nicht einmal dem schlimmsten Feind/, darf man die Lebenskraft ausblasen.
Ist Not am Mann mit aller Kraft vereint/muß man Rettgut fester fassen!

9 Im Rainerfall sah es so aus/nicht Rettung vom Verderben,
Da sollte ja mit Strauß und Maus/das Lebende ja sterben!

10 Rainerle, so geht das nicht/beim Brand muß man helfen einander!
Hab selbst erlebt, ein Bösewicht/lacht beim Brand? porzelt umeinan-

der! -

Fragte mich, war der besoffen?/der schürt mit Sauerstoff das Feuer!
11 Bin lahm, sonst hätte ihn getroffen/ein Schnelltorpedo, größtes Ungeheuer!

Mit 450 Wortsilbenminuten/nicht, nein, im Parlamentarierton,
12 zur schnellen Hilfrettung sputen!Löschhydranten benützen! kein Argwohn?

Im Brandfall muß man nicht das End/in festem Massivgebäude sehn.
13 Ein Bauwerk, das geschaffen starke Händ/bleibt auch weiterhin bestehn!

[Yes, that happens only because of it,/a miracle you need to believe
7 in!
When you are fighting a fire,/you have to save lives, never take them.

Not even the worst enemy/may you extinguish.
8 In case of emergency one/must hold firmer to implements of rescue with united forces!

9 In the case of Rainer it looked as if/no rescue from mischief,
there, with Strauß and mouse/the living was supposed to die!

Little Rainer, it does not work that way/in case of fire one has to help
10 one other!
Experienced it myself, a villain/laughing in a case of fire? Tumbles all around! -

Was asking myself, was he drunk?/stoking the fire with oxygen!
11 Am lame, otherwise it would have hit him/a fast torpedo, biggest monster!

Not with 450 word syllables per minute/no, in the tonal key of the
12 parliamentarians,
Hasten to the rescue action! Use portable hydrants! No distrust?

In case of fire you don't need to see an end of /firm, massive buildings
13 A building that was created by strong hands/continues to exist further!]

Rather than explore fully the poem's rich signifying space or point out single cultural allusions in this context—they are less relevant for my argument—I will focus instead on the different "fire scenarios" held together by the figure of the "*Riesenbrand(t)*." Water images are also relevant in this context.

The author's starting point was the no-confidence vote, described as a calamitous lightning stroke in the middle of a blossoming but obviously deceptive landscape (stanza 5).[28] Even the large amounts of water (in the form of snow) are obviously not able to contain the blaze. Then, the author's imagery shifts constantly from the threat of burning to the danger of drowning. While on the manifest level these two elements are posited as antagonistic qualities, their balancing potential is completely destroyed in the poem's subtext. In fact, both "fire" and "water" are caught up in a double bind: the author urges a choice between the two, but both of them simultaneously endanger and facilitate "*das Lebende*" ("the living") (stanza 9).

The water images range from the beneficial "*Löschhydrant*" ("hydrant") (stanza 12) to the disastrous shipwreck ("Ist Not am Mann mit aller Kraft vereint/muß man Rettgut fester fassen!"/"In case of emergency one must hold firmer to implements of rescue with united forces!"—stanza 8), which is intensified by a phrase modelled after a German sailor's idiom used mostly in the context of sinking vessels: "mit Mann und Maus"/"with man and mouse" (stanza 9). Another watery spectacle of nature introduces a second "giant" in this catastrophic landscape: the "Rainerfall" (stanza 9). This invented word approximates a natural phenomenon close to the writer's residence: the Rheinfall at Schaffhausen, a huge thundering waterfall, long a destination of tourists and a prominent point of regional identification in Baden schoolbooks. As seen in an earlier stanza, the logic of the image—here, admiration for a magnificent waterfall—destroys the logic of the manifest text which clearly condemns the figure of Rainer and his actions.

"Fire," on the other hand, represents the fragile "*Lebenslicht*" ("light of life") which can easily be snuffed out ("Nicht einmal dem schlimmsten Feind,/darf man die Lebenskraft ausblasen"/" Not even the worst enemy/may you extinguish"—stanza 8); it also connects the reader to the disastrous blast mentioned above. In that last image, the "*Riesenbrand*" is obviously responsible for a collapse of temporal structure. Within the same stanza the author jumps from directly addressing "Rainerle" ("little Rainer") to mentioning an unspecified "Bösewicht" ("villain"). The identity of this blackguard who laughs diabolically in the face of fire ("lacht beim Brand"—stanza 10) does not become clear, until the alter ego of the *Bundestag* opposition leader and the ominous villain, as well as their respective deeds, are fused in the following verse:

> Fragte mich, war der besoffen?/der schürt mit Sauerstoff das Feuer!
> Bin lahm, sonst hätte ihn getroffen/ein Schnelltorpedo, größtes Ungeheuer!
>
> [I asked myself, was he drunk?/stoking the fire with oxygen!
> I am lame, otherwise a fast torpedo would have hit him/the biggest monster!]

The same author who just warned us never to kill anyone ("not even the worst enemy!"—stanza 8) now threatens to use a torpedo (stanza 11) in order to destroy "little Rainer" (i.e., "the villain"). It is quite unlikely that the writer has simply forgotten his former statement; rather, he is talking about some extraordinary situation in which his dictum "never" is rendered irrelevant: the mentioning of a weapon and the author's physical disability ("I am lame") in the same line hint at his recollection of World War II.[29] Together with the microbiography discussed above ("cripple poet, age seventy-six, fire-evacuated") it provides an explanation for localizing the poetic version of the no-confidence vote in a catastrophic landscape of war.

The democratic political procedure in the *Bundestag* at whose center Brandt found himself appears as a setting in which repressed memories are unleashed. It is the Chancellor's personal experience as an émigré between 1933-45 and his internationally renowned engagement in East-West détente that makes him a welcome representative of the new democratic Germany on the one hand; on the other, the associative potential of his last name seems to invite something very different: fantasies of total power and destruction which are rooted in the Nazi period and the Second World War. The writer's plea for democracy and peace thus feels strangely influenced by idioms and images associated with the "Third Reich." I do not contend that the image elicited by Brandt's last name is a necessary prerequisite for this kind of "traumatic repetition"; perhaps the symbolic landscape established by the political issue in question, Brandt's own biography, and the nature of his opponents would have been evocative enough. Nonetheless: the fire fantasies inspired by the Chancellor's family name enable us to identify positively with a democratic Germany and consciously reject the ideology and practices of National Socialism without cutting off—and thereby "betraying" the inter-generational alliance with the perpetrators as well as family accounts of victimhood real and imagined. In this respect Willy Brandt, personifies purgatory (*Fegefeuer*) and redeemer. Along these lines, a woman from Bingen on the Rhein precedes her letter to the Chancellor with some excerpts from a religious song composed by Rudolf Alexander Schröder, who had been member of the *Bekennende Kirche*, with her own arrangement:

> Es mag sein, daß Trug und List
> eine Weile Meister ist.
> Doch nach jedem Unterliegen
> wirst du den Gerechten sehn
> lebend aus dem Feuer gehn,
> neue Kräfte kriegen.[30]
>
> [It may be, that fraud and deceit/are master for a while./But after every defeat/you will see the Just/step out of the fire alive,/acquiring new forces."]

Further the way she images her cooperation with Willy Brandt rests upon a religious gesture that she fuses with a modern metamorphosis of the fire image: she talks about her praying for Brandt as a current flow—a highly ambivalent image oscillating between the transmission of energy and an aggressive electric shock.[31] The shortest version of the multiple connective characteristics of Brandt's name is presented by a writer from the Netherlands:

> Mit Hitler in den Weltbrand,
> mit *Brandt* ein neuer Weltband.[32]
>
> [With Hitler into a worldwide conflagration/with Brandt a new world bond.]

Certainly Brandt is introduced as Hitler's opposite in this verse; still, the homonymic association of Brandt's last name with the word for fire establishes an associative bond between the two ("Weltbrand"—"Brandt"). Twice in this poem a single letter is decisive. It is the "t" that transforms the apocalyptic fire into the winner of the Nobel Peace Prize and a missing "r" has the "worldwide conflagration" undergo a redemptive metamorphosis into a "world bond"—a world in which opposites have come terrifyingly close.

An "Imagined Reunification"

While the notion of a world community was important to some, the majority of letters to Willy Brandt raise the prospect of a reunified Germany through a complex process that involves both splitting off and integrating at the same time, in offering German society a link between its (fascist) history and (democratic) present without having to really work through the underlying conflicts and ambivalences. The figure of Brandt allows for different imaginations of a national rebirth:

> Mit tiefen Gefühlen innerer Verbundenheit nahm ich im Herzen auf Ihre Worte. Sie sprachen sie am 27. April 1972 im Bundestag. Die deutsche Volksseele erwachte zu neuem Bewusstsein. Sie verehrter Herr Willi Brandt sind ihr Organ.
>
> In „vorurteilsvoller Anschauungskraft“ beginnt die Zweiheit Ost und West sich neu zusammen zu finden in einer Einheit, die ein immer bewussteres Werden in sich birgt.[33]

> [With deep feelings of inner connection I took your words to heart. You spoke them on 27 April 1972 in the *Bundestag*. The soul of the German people awakened to a new awareness. You, esteemed Mr Brandt, are its organ. With a 'particular view' the East/West has begun to find its way to one another anew in a unity which bears an ever greater conscious sense of becoming.]

The solemn statement of a woman from Berlin about the re-awakened "soul of the German people" and Willy Brandt serving as "its organ" not only illustrates the imaginary aim and ultimate end of the collective scenic process, but also demonstrates that what is repressed in its course inevitably shows through: the new Germany and its "organ" make a ghostly appearance. A revived corpse tells not only the story of victory over death, but also one of unredeemed misdoing. The feelings of pain, grief, and guilt—as well as an abiding fascination with the totalitarian—are simultaneously present, but successfully relegated to the letters' hidden imagery. Keeping their eyes fixed on the rising "phoenix" that is the German people manifested in the figure of Brandt, the author ignores the still-smouldering ashes underneath their numbed feet. This becomes very clear in the case of the poem discussed above. The 76-year-old writer with a vision of a peacefully united Germany ("deutsche Brüder und Schwestern sollen einig und zufrieden werden"/"German brothers and sisters shall be united and content"—stanza 20) escapes from the devastated land into a picturesque, airy mountain retreat. Indeed the image constructed loses its foundation, at least metaphorically, in the allegory of the "deutscher Adler"/"German eagle" (stanza 18):

stanza	
15	Wir haben schon zuviel erlebt/im zerstörenden Vernichtungsschlagen! Nur da, wo man im Frieden lebt/wird ein Bauwerk musterhaft vorangetragen.
16	Nicht mit Worten, in der Tat/das Erschaffene bejahen, nicht verneinen. Eine Schaffenskraft höchstem Grad/entwickeln, das deutsche Volk zu einen!
17	Wie der Schweizernachbar im Freiheitslied!/singt ein halb Jahrtausend lang Das Blümlein, das auf steilen Höhen blüht/heißt Edelweiß lieblichem Gesang
18	Kein Bruderkrieg, der Freiheitssieg!/schenkt Liebe dem schönen Alpenland!

Europäisch und Weltwirtschaftlich flieg/deutscher Adler im Vaterland

19 Nicht mehr zum Streit dem Untergehn/zum arbeitsreichen einfachen Leben!
Wir Deutsche wollen mit allen Menschen Eintracht sehn/das sei zum Glück gegeben!

20 Aus segensreicher Gotteshand/in Zufriedenheit auf Erden!
Als das schönste Friedensunterpfand/deutsche Brüder und Schwestern sollen einig und zufrieden werden!

21 In der neuen, überraschungsvollen Zeit,/ die so schwer ist zum ergründen,
im kurzen ereignisvollen Leben heut/Ordnung möge uns alle verbinden!

15 [We have indeed experienced too much/in the destructive, annihilatory beating!
Only there, where one lives in peace/a building will be brought into being in exemplary fashion.

16 Not with words, in action/affirming that which has been created, not negating it.
A creative force of the highest degree/shall develop, to unite the German people!

17 As the Swiss neighbor in the song of freedom!/has been sung for five hundred years
The little flower, blooming on steep heights/in mellifluous song is called edelweiss

18 No fratricidal war, the victory of freedom!/give love to the beautiful Alps!
Fly in the fashion of Europe and the world economy/German eagle in the fatherland!

19 No longer for [the sake of] struggle and doom [,]/[but for the sake] of the diligent, simple life!
We Germans want to see harmony with all human beings/this shall mercifully be given!

20 From God's benedictory hand/in satisfaction on earth!
As the most beautiful pledge of peace/German brothers and sisters shall be united and content!

In this new, astonishing time/, that is so hard to fathom,
21 in a short eventful life today/orderliness may unite us all!]

The shift from an apocalyptic landscape into the idyllic, yet conventional scenery of a nineteenth century oil painting, albeit interspersed with signifiers of the modern ("europäisch und weltwirtschaftlich"/ "European and world economic"—stanza 18) rests heavily on one particular allegory: that of solid craftsmanship:

stanza

Nein. Nun wird es neugeformt/schön ausgeschmückt in allen Teilen.
14 Was zum Guten rechten genormt/muß man ins Kleinste scharf ausfeilen.

[No. Now it is being newly formed/beautifully embellished in all parts.
What is standardized to the good and right/has to be polished sharply in the smallest (detail).]

This wording is not only a fragile imaginary link between the old, war-obsessed and the new, peaceful Germany but also serves as a self-description of the poet as a "*Verseschmied*" ("rhymer,"—or, literally, a "forger of verses"). The idea champions the manual laborer over the intellectual, creative force over the reflective. Not only does it evoke the image of a community—a whole, undivided Germany—as something physical that is in the process of being manufactured; it also contains a notion of continuity, in that the new is constructed out of the old ("neugeformt"/"newly-formed"—stanza 14). The double face of Willy Brandt appears as the Janus face of the Federal Republic in 1972.

Concluding Thoughts

A democratic ritual like the no-confidence vote in April 1972 obviously could not be that alone, as long as (West) German society was in desperate need of "expression."[34] Seen through the eyes of the letter writers it appears reminiscent of the Nazi seizure of power. In equating 1972 with 1933, the letters to Willy Brandt articulate what we might regard a yearning for dating something—which is usually the first thing one does when writing a letter. Embedded in the practice of dating is the idea that there is a point where something proceeds and goes *either right or wrong*, where the action of individuals in fact becomes relevant in a very immediate sense. This may, indeed, appear a tremendous simplification of something far more complex, but I think it speaks for more than just discomfort with the confusing responsibilities and diffuse relations in a modern democratic society. The image of 1933 in these letters may have *nothing* to do with a concrete historical event that had occurred almost 40 years earlier, but it does express vague emotions in themes, and the 1972 vote of no-confidence allowed people to see their own interior conflicts acted out in the arena of parliament; it lent a specific shape to repressed feelings of grief, guilt, and shame, which indeed were connected with the past, but could not—or would not—be attached to specific events in people's own life stories. The no-confidence vote of 1972 made it possible to live through the disastrous political and human failures of the Nazi period once again, this time on an imaginary level, and see one on the side of right.

The figure of Willy Brandt was absolutely central to this process. Placed in a scenic constellation which was not only charged by his own personality and biography, the immediate topic of the *Ostverträge* at stake, and the particular political and personal characteristics of the people surrounding him, his being offered German society a huge associative space. It was a space that, on the one hand, supported the revival of collectively repressed experiences and images, but on the other served equally to delineate them to remote spheres of consciousness. I have demonstrated this process in respect to the fantasies surrounding Brandt's last name, which to the letter writers proved to be an enormous inspiration.

At the utopian end of this scenic enactment, a German collective appears which is not only immaculate, but also whole and undivided. Considered from today's perspective, the letters to Willy Brandt not only seem to restage the past but to anticipate reunification in 1989/90 on an imaginary level. Importantly, the fulfilment of the letters' crucial fantasy—a Germany made whole again— has since produced innumerable debates on the course of German history. In that sense, the events of April 1972 can be seen as some kind of "primal scene" which entangled and preserved two conflicting objectives: coming to terms with a conflicting past and the building of a new German national identity at the same time. The highly ambivalent quality of such an undertaking seems to have been articulated by a young man from southern Germany, who concludes his congratulatory letter to Willy Brandt with the following remarks:

> Möge Sie der heutige Erfolg stärken, so weiter zu arbeiten wie bisher, damit unsere Demokratie kein leeres Gerippe sondern ein lebendiger Körper beseelt mit dem Geist Ihres Charakters ist.[35]
>
> [May today's success encourage you to continue your work unaltered, so that our democracy is not an empty skeleton, but is animated by the spirit of your character.]

Notes

I would like to thank Susanne Gerner, Petra Naumann and Bernd Stübing for their valuable comments and critique at various stages, as well as Deborah Levine for proofreading the piece.

[1] Wolfgang Horlacher, "Das Doppelgesicht," *Bayernkurier* 40 (1972): 1. The readers' responses were published one week later as "'Das Doppelgesicht' im Widerstreit," *Bayernkurier* 41 (1972): 19.

[2] Hans Jörg Riebel, "Leserbrief," *Bayernkurier* 41 (1972): 19.

[3] Erika Frowein, "Leserbrief," *Bayernkurier* 41 (1972): 19.

[4] On the concept of the term "scene" as well as to the phrases a "scenic logic" or "scenic constellation" which I return to frequently in this paper, see Alfred Lorenzer, "Tiefenhermeneutische Kulturanalyse," in *Kultur-Analysen,* ed. Hans-Dieter König et al., (Frankfurt/Main: Fischer, 1986), 11–98.

[5] The letters are part of the (so-called) "personal bequest" of Willy Brandt which is kept in the Willy-Brandt-Archiv (WBA) as part of the Friedrich-Ebert-Stiftung's "Archiv der sozialen Demokratie" (AdsD).

[6] The volume of mail concerning the no-confidence vote that came to the chancellor's office must remain in the realm of estimation. With some certainty though, it can be claimed that the approximately 9,000 letters, postcards, telegrams, etc. that survive constitute only a portion of those received.

[7] This result is based on a sample of 758 letters dated between 24 April and 2 May, of which 506 were dated 27 April.

[8] It should be stressed in this context that, judging from the writers' own testimonies, the majority of these letters did not come from that small group accustomed to writing letters to politicians. Nor is the collection of letters restricted to a certain social group. Convicts from jailhouses, guest workers of different nationalities, all kinds of workers, engineers, teachers, pastors, self-employed people, managers, pensioners as well as high-ranking dignitaries, artists, and intellectuals (for example, the philosopher Ernst Bloch) contributed to the volume of letters, cards, and telegrams. One could certainly find that representatives from certain social groups wrote more frequently than those of others. The same asymmetry could be claimed in respect to other social parameters, e.g. sex; women seem to be slightly underrepresented in the collection. On the whole there are no indications of a particular social, age, or sex-related profile of the writers that would render the collection an unrepresentative sample of West German society in 1972.

[9] See volumes 2 (CDU/CSU), 3 (FDP), and 4 (SPD) of the *Handbuch zur Statistik der Parlamente und Parteien in den westlichen Besatzungszonen und in der Bundesrepublik Deutschland* (Düsseldorf: Droste, 2005). Due to a rapid increase in party members in 1972 that led to the CDU decision to record new members as an extra statistical category (volume 2: 42) . The same rapid increase was true for the CSU (volume 2: 591) and the SPD as well (volume 4: 419). See also Oskar Niedermayer, *Bürger und Politik: Politische Orientierungen und Verhaltensweisen der Deutschen. Eine Einführung* (Wiesbaden: Westdeutscher Verlag: 2001), 187–89.

[10] Only the first free *Volkskammer* elections in the German Democratic Republic (1990) topped this result with a 93.4 % turnout; http://www.wahlrecht.de/ergebnisse/volkskammerwahl-1990.htm.

[11] Letter from a couple in Bochum, 27 April 1972, WBA, *Zuschriften aus der Bevölkerung/Misstrauensvotum*, Folder Nr. 190.
[12] See Sabine Manke, *Brandt anfeuern: Das Misstrauensvotum 1972 in Bürgerbriefen an den Bundeskanzler. Ein kulturwissenschaftlicher Beitrag zu modernen Resonanz- und Korrespondenzphänomenen* (Marburg: Tectum, July 2008).
[13] See Josef Bleicher (ed.), *Contemporary hemeneutics: Hermeneutics as method, philosophy and critique* (London and Boston: Routledge & Kegan Paul, 1980).
[14] Ibid., 169–70.
[15] The following translations are not meant to meet literary standards but to reflect the imagery and the sentence structure of the German original as closely as possible. Misspellings in the German originals are left uncorrected, if not pointed out otherwise.
[16] The feast of the Immaculate Conception is celebrated on 8 December.
[17] Apart from the image of heaps of corpses, these suitcases also symbolized the economic link between the victims of death and concentration camps and the habitants of Germany who had profited financially from "aryanization." This kind of "family property" accumulated during the Nazi period also established a bond between the generation of perpetrators and those who had come of age in the Federal Republic by 1972. For a history of photographic images of the Holocaust, see Cornelia Brink, *Ikonen der Vernichtung: öffentlicher Gebrauch von Fotografien aus nationalsozialistischen Konzentrationslagern nach 1945* (Berlin: Akademie-Verlag, 1998) and Habbo Knoch, *Die Tat als Bild: Fotografien des Holocaust in der deutschen Erinnerungskultur* (Hamburg: Hamburger Edition, 2001).
[18] Letter from a woman in Dortmund, 25 April 1972, WBA, *Zuschriften aus der Bevölkerung/Misstrauensvotum*, Folder Nr. 173–174 (Emphasis in the original.)
It is impossible to determine if the double negative in the sentence construction was the result of an imperfect command of the German language—other mistakes in the letter do indicate that—or rather the outcome of unconscious ambivalence. Perhaps both are true.
[19] Telegram from a couple in Augsburg, 25 April 1972, WBA, *Zuschriften aus der Bevölkerung/Misstrauensvotum*, Folder Nr. 186–187.
[20] I do not want to imply that all of the letters, or even the majority, exhibit such obvious continuities with the logic of extinction. Some do, others focus solely on celebrating Willy Brandt. What I try to show is that the enthusiastic identification with Brandt and the return of reactionary sentiments are fed by the same source and—in order to understand their meaning—both have to be viewed as part of the same collective scene.
[21] I employ the expression "collective body" in the sense it is used in Sylvia Sasse and Stefanie Wenner ed., *Kollektivkörper, Kunst und Politik von Verbindung* (Bielefeld: transcript Verlag, 2002), a volume that explores the multiple cultural and political techniques for the manufacture of a collective.
[22] Peter Merseburger points out in his biography of Willy Brandt that a long time before Brandt became the target of hate for the extreme right during the 1960s, detractions and accusations levelled against him came from rivals within his own party ranks. See Peter Merseburger, *Willy Brandt: 1913–1992, Visionar und Realist* (Stuttgart, München: Deutsche Verlags-Anstalt, 2002), 307ff.
[23] By referring to political "realities" I do not suggest that the realm of the imaginary or the symbolic is by any means "unreal"; in fact, I contend that this essay argues quite the contrary.

[24] The collection of letters suggests that Ruth Brandt indeed stirred the imagination of the German society. Quite a number of submissions that reached the chancellor's office were explicitly directed to the chancellor's wife, others addressed the Brandts as a couple.

[25] Letter from a man in Simonswald, 28 April 1972, WBA, *Zuschriften aus der Bevölkerung/Misstrauensvotum*, Folder Nr. 229.

[26] The plural form "readers" in this case receives its legitimacy not only from the assumption that the writer of a *poem*—perhaps more so than the writer of a *letter* which is sent to an unknown but specific person—probably imagines some sort of abstract audience in the act of creation, even if the poem is actually dedicated to one particular individual. Moreover, the sender himself included two other (obviously undelivered) carbon copies of the poem to be forwarded to Karl Schiller (SPD, secretary of finance and economy) and Walter Scheel (FDP, state secretary and vice chancellor) and therefore expanded his imagined readership by at least two more people.

[27] In general, I do not view these kind of "inconsistencies" as "mistakes" committed by the sender which would then have to be abstracted in my analysis in order to get at what the writer "actually meant." Instead, I see them as symptomatic ambivalences which have to be accounted for in an interpretation of the letter's text.

[28] I would argue that even passages of the poem, which do not explicitly make use of the great variety of fire images can be read as associated with quite a number of "fire places." I think that this is specifically true for the fairy tale beginning "Es war einmal"/"Once upon a time" which brings to mind cosy storytelling in front of the fireplace—an image frequently seen in illustrated fairy tale books. It also is valid, I think, for the motives of craftsmanship that describe the writer's vision of a stable civil society, but at the same time do apply to his task as a poet too: they evoke the skills and activities of a blacksmith (see stanza 14).

[29] It may be an idle task to think about the nature of these experiences, but the combination of diverse hints by the author—the parallel threat of burning and drowning, the maritime metaphors, as well as the mentioning of a torpedo—suggests that it could relate to his service as a soldier in the German submarine fleet. It is not important, if this is actually true; much more relevant in this context is that in facing the no-confidence vote the author came up with these particular images.

[30] Letter from a woman in Bingen, 27 April 1972, WBA, *Zuschriften aus der Bevölkerung/Misstrauensvotum*, Folder Nr. 178.

[31] Ibid. "Wenn man nun nicht gerade mitmarschieren wollte, wovon Sie ja auch selbst abrieten, so war man letztlich auf dieses eine Mittel des 'intensiven Gedankenstromes' angewiesen, – vergleichbar vielleicht mit einer elektrischen Stromleitung."
"If one did not exactly want to march with the crowds, what you yourself advised against, one was dependent on this one means of the 'intense current of thought,'—comparable perhaps to a power supply line."

[32] Letter from a person in Immenweg-Lunteren, The Netherlands, 30 April 1972, WBA, *Zuschriften aus der Bevölkerung/Misstrauensvotum*, Folder Nr. 197.

[33] Letter from a woman in Berlin, 2 May 1972, WBA, *Zuschriften aus der Bevölkerung/Misstrauensvotum*, Folder Nr. 197.

[34] The word "expression" is fitting here, for it is as much about something surfacing as it is about the impulse to get rid of that same thing.

[35] Letter from a young man in Villingen, 27 April 1972, WBA, *Zuschriften aus der Bevölkerung/Misstrauensvotum*, Folder Nr. 198.

III. Selected European Case Studies After Fascism

"An Essential Way of Life": Women's Citizenship and the Renewal of Politics in Italy

Molly Tambor

> "... above all the battle [is] to make women understand, even through the most banal and most simple initiatives, that politics is not intrigue and scheming, but an essential way of life."[1]

It was once remarked that Italy's Republican Constitution of 1948 was like "a middle-aged gentleman with grey hair with two mistresses, one young and one old: the former pulled out all his white hairs to make him look younger, and the latter pulled out all his black hairs to make him look older, so that in the end he was left completely bald."[2] Successive scholars often agreed, declaring the constitution a mirror of the great chasm in postwar Italy between the Communists and the Christian Democrats, incoherent, a grab-bag of compromises, with something for everybody. It promises a republic of the workers (Article 1) but preserves Mussolini's 1929 Lateran Pacts with the Catholic Church (Article 7), and in the same breath guarantees both total liberty and complete social justice (Article 2). It is true that the constitution reveals the tensions inherent in the attempt of Right and Left to work together in the service of antifascism, and to create a foundational law which both protects individual rights and "directs their exercise towards the benefit of the entire collective."[3] But that attempt was not a cynical one; the Constitution at its best is a measure of how Italians hoped to reconcile the desire for social solidarity and justice with the need for guarantees of citizenship and democracy in the wake of fascism and World War II. In fact, there was a fundamental outlook shared by the "two churches" of Italy, the Catholic and the Communist, centered on a spirit of solidarity, a distrust of unlimited capitalism and consumer culture, and the sense that the destinies of equal individuals and democracy were interdependent. It was this common ground that allowed the Constitutional Assembly to move forward in its work.

The key article in this interpretation is number three; it forbids discrimination against any citizen and explicitly names sex (along with race, language, religion, political opinions, and personal or social conditions) as an unacceptable distinction among citizens; it proceeds to make the State itself responsible for that goal: "It is the duty of the republic to remove all economic and social obstacles" to citizens' liberty, equality, and participation in the life of the nation. Article 3 illustrates the two core arguments of this chapter: first, that the constituents wanted the State to lead reform in Italy rather than reflect society as it was; and second, that they believed the constitution should be a strong tool for enforcing the destruction of fascism and the creation of democracy. This chapter highlights the ways that women's citizenship was key to both the compromises and successes of the constitution, and shows how women's rights are linked to the democratization of Italy after fascism.

Women were not only important to the constitution's principles of equal citizenship, they were the key authors and proponents of some of its strongest language, including that of Article 3. In June 1946 twenty-one women were elected to Italy's 586 member Constitutional Assembly, the result of the first free election since the Fascist seizure of power in 1922—an election which had also decided by referendum that Italy would be a republic rather than a monarchy. That election also marked the first time women had ever voted in Italy. Of the 24,345,678 voters in that historic election 12,998,131 were women, over fifty-two percent. Eighty-nine percent of eligible women voted, sending a strong signal that with women in the majority of voters, postwar politics could not return to the elite structure of the Liberal era.[4] The twenty-one delegates, the first women ever elected to an Italian parliament, comprised a motley group. Divided by ideology, class, and region, they were also separated by age, with almost a complete absence of women in their thirties or forties. Most were born at the turn of the century, and many had spent years in jail, in concentration camps, or in exile; a few were extremely young, having just reached the twenty-five year old age minimum for deputies, and came from the ranks of the so-called "Resistance recruits," (*leva della Resistenza*), those who had joined the partisan brigades as teenagers as the regime systematically sought to wipe out the leadership generation of antifascists through execution, prison, and exile.

At a reception celebrating their election, the women articulated their collective goals: the new constitution of the Republic would have to respect women's legal equality with men in every field, guarantee recognition of the right to work (including access to all schools, professions, and careers), the right to protective legislation that "permits a woman to fulfill her task as a mother," and equal treatment and equal compensation for equal work.[5] Although none of these women explicitly called themselves feminists, by achieving these constitutional guarantees the twenty-one sparked a new wave of the women's movement that lasted the next fifteen years and saw a surge of women in parliament and new legislation implementing the constitutional articles that was unique in Italian history.[6]

Their success was also due, however, to an acceptance of new roles for women that the war and Resistance had helped spread throughout Italian society and especially political culture. Those political parties which pursued a mass electorate as the key to democratization after fascism shared a sense, whose first enunciation in Italy is usually credited to the head of the Italian Communist Party, Palmiro Togliatti, that women's emancipation and the stability and longevity of a democratic republic were mutually dependent.[7] Three main parties tried to court the new woman voter by presenting numerous female candidates: the Christian Democrats (*Democrazia Cristiana*, DC) and the Italian Communist Party (*Partito Comunista Italiano*, PCI), each elected nine women; the Socialists (*Partito Socalista Italiano*, PSI) elected two.[8] The even split between women of the Left and Christian Democrats in the Constituent Assembly was reflected in their male counterparts' numbers; but, on key issues, these women cooperated across the Cold War chasm separating their parties during the writing of the 1948 Constitution and the elections to the first republican parliament, acting as a coalition whenever women's rights and citizenship were debated. Perhaps because of the newly positive reaction towards women's increased visibility in public as they successfully filled the necessary roles to sustain civil society during the war, their achievements in securing both their own positions and the guarantees of equal citizenship for all women in the constitution expressed the strongly gendered character of the powerful surge of antifascist sentiment between 1943 and 1947. Women's participation as full citizens via suffrage was seen across the spectrum of antifascist parties as an essential guarantee of the break with the Fascist regime, the extension of truly democratic practices, and the victory of antifascist values.

Italy offers a particularly important case for studying the impact and meaning of women's citizenship after fascism. During the late nineteenth and early twentieth centuries Italian women had been both intensely enmeshed in family structures due to the longtime and widespread rural nature of most lives and to the hegemony of the Church, and extremely politicized by their immersion in Italy's subcultures of total identity, the mass movements of Catholic Action and socialism.[9] In the twenty-plus years of the Fascist regime this particularity intensified; the State's innovation in providing new welfare services and social rights may have succeeded as a tool to build consensus and to navigate the problems of modernization, but it addressed all citizens as members of corporatist bodies rather than as individuals possessed of inalienable rights. Women found increased opportunities for public visibility and participation in as a result of the regime's attention to sports, rallies, and social organization and services, but these experiences were not structured in such a way that a woman might gain autonomy, political influence, or individual empowerment.[10] The Fascist regime demanded that women perform their patriotic duty by reproducing and nurturing its people from within family networks, first in a rhetorical sense and then in an ever more literal one as the state became less and less able to provide basic necessities in the face of a poor economy, the U.N. embargo after Italy's invasion of Ethiopia, and the war.

The specificity of women's experience under fascism found a corollary in their different experience of the Resistance. While men often felt they had no choice but to escape to the hills or be conscripted into the Fascist army or Nazi forced labor, women who joined the Resistance made a conscious choice to put themselves in danger. They usually spent less time "underground," so that they had to sustain their "normal" lives at the same time that they pursued political activism; moreover, they performed more varied roles, from armed action to courier duty to the creation and distribution of the clandestine press. During the years of war and resistance activity, women discovered and repeatedly confirmed the falsity of the division between private and public spheres in a woman's civic life. Family space and domestic tasks could be intensely political, while politics and resistance could consist of traditionally feminine tasks like cooking, carrying messages, nursing, and keeping communication and transport lines open. The danger they faced, the courage they found in themselves, and the significance of their actions for the very survival of both family and political ideals led many female partisans to speak of becoming "protagonists," a sense they said never left them. Catholic or communist, all twenty-one delegates had been forged as political activists in this historical moment. They were not only linked by the specific formation and inspiration of women's resistance; they had already worked together and created a women's network during that time. They knew each other well and some had even saved each other's lives.

After 1945, democracy could not be established in Italy merely by giving women the vote; family law, labor law, judicial practice, fiscal and welfare policies would all have to change, because they defined political actors as greater or lesser citizens long before they arrived at the voting booth. Catholic and leftist women's shared program was to unite political and social rights for women, since they were convinced that one wouldn't serve women very well without the other.[11] Entering government, staffing the bureaucratic institutions that distributed social benefits, performing social work in local and national networks, women used older models of activism learned in the late nineteenth century in the first wave of feminism. But in the context of constitutional implementation and the expansion of participatory democracy, such activity became a kind of "female path to democracy" which carried with it the potential to transform the liberal representative democracy that men's votes had created.[12]

Because of their shared formative experiences under fascism and through resistance, the women activists of the Italian postwar period all believed that women would be trained into their full citizenship by encouraging their mass participation in public life, be it politics, social work, or the institutions of civil society. That mass participation would in turn, they believed, cement the overall success of democracy in Italy, protecting it from any return of fascism and making the State a perpetual progressive force toward greater freedoms and opportunities for all citizens. Thus, their intention in the Constitutional Assembly was twofold: first, to establish a foundational law which superseded and abolished all previous legal codes from the Liberal or Fascist eras; and second, to guarantee women's equal citizenship in language as explicit as possible, shaping a citizenship for both sexes that would base politics not on party leadership or state institutions, but on their own constant democratic participation. Yet in the end, the constitution—though it guaranteed equality to women in labor rights, legal status, and political representation—did not abrogate Fascist laws that affirmed male prerogatives in marriage, the family, and civil status. These ambiguities and contradictions in women's rights are in fact part of a larger pattern of continuity and discontinuity with the Fascist regime in the new republic, and they illuminate the mixed legacy of these years of reconstruction for Italy's politics and institutions throughout the period of the so-called "First Republic" of 1948-1992.

Gender and Postwar Settlements

Women's own activism and autonomy during the war and especially in the Resistance helped make the moment of suffrage in 1945 seem obvious, as women were "given" the vote by a decree widely understood as a reward for their wartime service and sacrifice.[13] Especially for the so-called "Resistance recruits," the young men and women who had experienced the radically egalitarian life of the partisan brigades, it was taken for granted that women had not only demonstrated their capacity and patriotism for full citizenship but that they were already living in equality—which merely needed to be made official after the fact. The Constitutional Assembly did not reflect quite the same level of acceptance; the twenty-one women constituents quickly found themselves in passionate conflict over the wording of Article 3, which guarantees equal treatment to all citizens regardless of sex; Article 29, announcing the legal equality of spouses; Article 37's guarantee of women's right to work and their right to equal pay for equal work, as well as the right to special and adequate provisions for working mothers; and Article 51's declaration that women are eligible for all public offices and elected positions on equal terms with men. In the course of the constitutional debates and postwar reconstruction a troubling double standard returned to the open which condoned women's formal equalities, but refused to reexamine gender roles in daily life and the family.

Principles of Equality: Article 3

Of the twenty-one women constituents, four were elected by their colleagues to the "Committee of 75," a smaller group given the task of writing a constitutional draft for the entire Assembly to debate and vote upon. These four women were Nilde Iotti and Teresa Noce for the PCI, Lina Merlin (PSI), and Maria Federici (DC).[14] Noce remembered, "The Party decided to present women as candidates in almost every district. Naturally those chosen were the most popular, the ones who had worked most in the Resistance, who had sacrificed themselves."[15] These women had not necessarily been elected purely on political merit, as Nadia Spano (PCI) wryly commented:

> I entered the Constituent Assembly because I wore a skirt. If I think back to the Federal Committee of those days, to the direction of the Rome Federation, there were many male comrades of my level or better. [...]

> The party wanted a woman and so I passed in front of everyone. So in a certain sense not only did being a woman not hurt me, it helped me. There were relatively a lot of women in the Constituent [Assembly] and also in the first legislature, from the other parties as well. And they had great importance, which doesn't necessarily show through in the minutes enough. In the months during which there was no activity in the plenary assembly, for example, the women in the Committee of 75 became the representatives for all the women of their district and their region as well, an essential element of linkage between the voters and the parties and organizations. […] To have a deputy [in the Constitutional Assembly] was an element of strength, of prestige, a stimulus to other women, pride for the female comrades. The women considered you "their" deputy.[16]

Maria Federici and Lina Merlin cooperated to defend the articulation of women's rights over and over again. Merlin proposed that Article 3 include sex as one of the factors on the basis of which a citizen could not be discriminated against; Federici argued in favor of Merlin's proposal on 22 May 1947:

> I remind you, and it is by now a principle recognized by all constitutions, that sex must no longer be a discriminating factor for the enjoyment of civil and social rights. It is strange that women, who nevertheless pay taxes and support all the duties of social life, shouldn't also have the ability to follow their careers in conditions of equality with men. I hope this is the last time that a constitution has to mention women's rights in order to claim them,; the last time that women have to demand their rights from men.[17]

Despite their male colleagues' argument that both men and women were understood in the words "all citizens," Federici and Merlin insisted on making this explicit until, in the end, Article 3 stated:

> All citizens have equal social dignity and are equal before the law, without distinction of sex, race, language, religion, political opinions, or personal or social condition. It is the duty of the Republic to remove all social or economic obstacles which, limiting de facto the liberty and equality of citizens, impede the full development of the human being and the effective participation of all workers in the political, social, and economic organization of the country.

Federici argued that the women constituents understood their election by a predominantly female electorate (52.2 percent of the 1946 voters were women) as a mandate to guarantee women's interests: the affirmation of women's rights, the rights of women workers, and reform of family law. In addition to the recognition of "the legal freedoms," she said, women wanted to be able to affirm their social presence, their equal access to the workplace and marketplace, and their right to protection from exploitation of their work and their property.[18] This meant that the constitution had to affirm equal rights, not just of citizenship, but also of labor and of the family. It was crucial that social rights become as valid as political and civil rights.

Women's Work and Women's Labor: Article 37

It is one of the peculiarities of the Italian constitution that it emphasizes labor rights as indistinguishable from citizenship rights. This is clear from its opening line, which states "Italy is a democratic Republic, founded on labor." As the constituents saw it, labor rights give concrete reality to social citizenship just as political rights—the vote—give concrete reality, a voice, to political citizenship.[19] When Teresa Noce, Maria Federici, and Lina Merlin were named proponents for the formulation of the section dealing with economic and social guarantees for the family, Federici proposed that the rights of women workers, especially if heads of family, would be best respected by the following: "Female workers who are heads of family are assured the same rights as male heads of family, to be integrated with social services dedicated to the tutelage of maternity and infancy."[20] As a Catholic she argued for loans and insurance to protect marriage and for family salaries instead of, like Noce and Merlin, for more guarantees for working women's independence; all three defended the social value of women's unpaid work and of maternity as topics belonging in the constitution, however. They argued for state salaries and pensions for motherhood: "The old age of mothers must be guaranteed in conformity with the principle that the maternal mission and domestic work are not less important for the collective than any other possible productive activity." Federici went on to argue that the state should also pay for the health care costs of pregnancy and abortion for every woman, demonstrating her independence from official DC policy.[21] Despite this and other proposals on women workers by these three women, the male constituents declined to even debate such details. All were eventually subsumed into a proposal that there be a section of the article which simply read "Women workers have all the same rights in labor relations as recognized for male workers." This was ultimately approved.[22]

Menstruating Magistrates: Article 51

While not as extensive as they had hoped, Article 37 was a victory for the women's coalition in the assembly. Next came Article 51, another victory which ratified their own achievement as the first women to be both electors and elected. It declared: "All citizens of either sex may fill public offices and elective offices in equal conditions, according to the conditions established by the law." The article was hard fought, given the massive presence of lawyers and judges in the assembly and their reluctance to open the halls of justice to the alleged sentimentality, hysteria, and subjective decision-making of women. Giovanni Leone, a DC deputy who had been elected Secretary of the Committee of 75's subcommittee on the judiciary, and future president of the Republic (1971-1978), argued that although the women around him in the Assembly were doing a good job, they should be happy with that achievement and satisfied with limitations on their participation. Women might help make the constitution and the laws, but women could not be magistrates because menstruation and menopause prevented them from achieving the serenity necessary to a judge.[23]

Maria Maddalena Rossi and Teresa Mattei had proposed an amendment to clarify that "Women have access to all the orders and ranks of the magistracy," but after this kind of debate it was defeated, on 26 November by a vote of 153 to 120. Maria Federici had warned that precisely such a thing would happen when she argued against any qualifier in the article on 22 May 1947, saying "It is strange that women, who pay taxes and bear all the same burdens of society, shouldn't be able to advance their careers under[?] equal conditions with men." A woman ought to be able to choose how she pursued her career "according to her own spontaneous desires, guided by education and by other elements including those with spiritual value, rather than by reason of a profoundly insulting injustice."[24] Federici argued that the only qualifying language should concern merit and preparation; anything else would be clearly discriminatory against women. To those who argued that the phrase "according to the conditions established by law" would not concern the magistracy, only the police and military, she again answered that no limiting language should be necessary at all: while it might be difficult to find a woman capable of leading the armed forces, it had recently proven equally as difficult to find a man capable of doing it![25] Heedful of Maria Federici's prediction, the next day all the women constituents united to pass an order of business which affirmed the intent of Article 51 to guarantee women's right to enter the magistracy, but the qualifying phrase "according to the conditions established by law," once part of the constitutional text, was interpreted to mean that the 1919 law that excluded women from those professions which "imply jurisdictional power, the exercise of political rights, or any authority over the military," remained in force.[26] A year later, a record number of women were elected to the first parliament, but some remarked that although a woman could theoretically become prime minister, no woman was allowed to represent her country at even the most junior level of the diplomatic corps or even sit in a jury box.[27]

Marriage and Family: Article 29

Such compromises were common; Togliatti led the PCI in particular to be as flexible as possible on social and moral politics in order to counter the DC tactic of demonizing the communists as the party of free love and the destruction of the family. Hence the inclusion of Mussolini's Lateran Pacts with the Church as Article 7. One of the key moments of conflict that Togliatti did not successfully avoid, however, came over the issue of divorce. This article in particular created a conflict between women's freedoms and the State's interest in enforcing family stability. Article 29 reads, "The Republic recognizes the rights of the family as a natural society founded on matrimony. Matrimony is based on the moral and legal equality of spouses within the limits established by law to guarantee family unity."[28] This articulation represents a major compromise between the Catholic and leftist forces in the Assembly: the Catholics had forcefully demanded that the family must be defended as the natural and most basic unit of society. This unit, they argued, could function in equality but must, in the final instance, have a head, or representative; this head of household they assumed to be male.[29] Communist and Socialist men were inclined to agree. But, again, it was the women constituents who made it clear that women's equal citizenship and the guarantee of democracy were interdependent at all such key points.

During a committee meeting to discuss the formulation Article 29, Piero Calamandrei, an august figure of Italian politics and culture, a founding member of the Action Party, and one of the most influential legal experts in the framing of the constitution, was against the women's proposal to declare the equality of spouses and in favor of the DC's plan to affirm the indissolubility of marriage. After presenting religious and moral arguments in support of a patriarchal view of the family, he added that since the entire corpus of current law was against spousal parity, one would have to change that entire corpus to implement the constitution if it were to proclaim equality, and this could not be done. Maria Maddalena Rossi, a communist who had been a Resistance partisan and was then president of the Union of Italian Women (UDI), fired back, saying she was putting him on notice that in fact there was now someone in Italy with the intention to change the entire civil code, and that someone was precisely Italian women. The minutes do not record his reaction, but those of Rossi's female colleagues present in the committee must have wanted to stand up and cheer.[30] These women had already been complaining about their male colleagues' willingness to compromise by resorting to generic formulations with the proviso "according to the conditions established by law," rather than confronting the specifics of controversial women's rights questions. The women constituents, on the contrary, saw their work in the assembly as precisely what Calamandrei wanted to avoid: the formulation of articles that would require new laws to be written, the creation of a constitution which would abrogate those old discriminatory laws and found a new, antifascist and democratic state. To rely on established law was, in substance, an acceptance of the Fascist and Liberal regimes and specifically their sexist, but also authoritarian and antidemocratic tendencies; it was important not to consider the new Republic bound by extant law or legal tradition.[31]

In the end, despite Togliatti's instructions not to debate divorce, a few wayward members of the assembly, including a PCI man, Giovanni Grilli, did succeed in upholding the guarantee of spousal parity and keeping any declaration on the indissolubility of marriage out of Article 29.[32] But in each of these articles, when finally approved, inequality snuck in through the back door: 37 said the equality of rights at work had to conform to the necessities of "*l'essenziale funzione familiare della donna*" (the essential familial function of women), 51 offered "conditions established by law," and 29 noted "*i limiti stabiliti dalla legge a garanzia dell'unità familiare*" (the limits stabilized by the law to guarantee family unity). The amendments and compromises of working politics meant that women constituents rarely succeeded in getting their own extremely specific language approved. But even as party politics became an ugly battle outside the doors of the chamber as communist ministers were kicked out of the government in May 1947, the male constituents could not disavow the egalitarian and progressive rhetoric that had inspired their task. Their female colleagues were able to act in extraordinary cooperation across party and ideological divisions to hold the line for women's rights. They continually pushed their colleagues to more rigorous formulations of rights that explicitly affirmed the framers' intentions to guarantee equality among all citizens.[33]

Consequences for Democratization and Renewal

The Italian Constitution, then, is an extremely progressive document, given its adoption of human rights discourse, the sense that women's political rights were natural and inevitable as a postwar condition, and the understanding of women's participation as a fundamental guarantee of democratic governments. It is a document that enshrines solidarity, community responsibility, and social citizenship in the fundamental definition of the Italian republic.[34] But it also displays the founders' ambivalence when it came to evaluating and making concrete the ways that asserting women's equal rights would and should affect family law, the rights of labor, and programs associated with social services and social citizenship. In the end it was not so difficult to find approval for women's rights *as individuals*; but in those areas where women's equality seemed to necessitate changing the entire legal approach *to family, to marriage, and to the workplace* there was decided and powerful resistance.

This attempt to uphold both a "logic of solidarity" and a conception of individual human rights as the basic citizenship rights for women highlights the uneven utility of the constitution in providing a new democratic foundation for Italy's republic. In the years to come, its implementation would be a frequent problem, and women parliamentarians would encounter these ambiguities as blocks to their proposals for women's rights legislation. Teresa Noce later had to contend with Article 37's wording that working women have equal rights, but that working conditions must allow women to carry out their "essential role in the family." She was eventually successful in arguing that those conditions must include paid maternity leave and employer-supplied daycare and nursing facilities; Italy's maternity leave law, passed in 1950, bears her name. The law is very generous, if still entirely gendered: there is no parental leave guaranteed for fathers, and women face discrimination in hiring and the threat of dismissal upon marriage or pregnancy from employers reluctant to shoulder the costs.

After constitutional ratification in December 1947 women continued to be barred from the judiciary, the diplomatic corps, and many other civil service careers despite their arguments that Article 51's similar qualifying phrase—"All citizens of either sex are eligible for public office and for elected positions on equal terms, according to the conditions established by law"—abrogated the 1919 Sacchi law rather than upheld it. Benefiting from a strong public campaign by the women's associations (both Catholic and Communist), and repeated court cases in which women sued for discrimination, Maria Cocco (DC) ultimately worked successfully to pass a 1963 law making explicit that the constitution's intention to give women access to *all* careers must be respected. In Italy today women may enter the military and police forces, and sixty percent of top scorers on not only the magistrates' but all State exams are women. Around half of all magistrates are female; the figure is just below one quarter worldwide.[35]

The constitution, through compromise and through the reality of Italian social mores, did not and could not fully confront the contradiction between citizens' *de jure* equality and women's *de facto* inferiority.[36] This both reflected the reality of postwar society and conditioned the future: there were major continuities with Italian Fascism not only in the murky waters of popular memory and memory politics, but explicitly in the *corpus* of the laws itself. The core of the problem was whether the constitution was programmatic or prescriptive; that is, did the constitution set forth principles as ideals to be slowly attained through ever-evolving legislation—or was it immediately enforceable law which automatically invalidated any contradictory laws on the books the moment it took effect on 1 January 1948? The entirety of the women constituents' strategy during the Constitutional Assembly depended on the answer. The constitution established a constitutional court to deal with these questions, but it took until

1956 for the court to come to order. That year the court, in its first historic ruling, affirmed that it had jurisdiction over all laws in force in the Republic, and that all laws, including those from the Fascist era and before, must conform to the principles of the constitution and must be annulled if they did not.

This decision legitimated the constituents' strategy, and pushed the course of women's rights and overall democratization in Italy into constitutionalist movements that emphasized a need to achieve equality and justice by fulfilling the lofty promises of an admittedly flawed and ambiguous document. Today this tradition continues—for example in the encouragement of women's equal representation in political office taking the form of a constitutional amendment, despite the ruling that a parity quota was unconstitutional.[37] The continued incompleteness of women's equality and the instability of government and inefficiency of reforms have proven the initial postwar belief true: women's full participatory citizenship has, indeed, been a precondition for and a measure of the success of full democratization in republican Italy, and both remain incomplete in law and uneven in practice. Have all Italians come to trust politics as "an essential way of life," as the first twenty-one women constituents wished? Probably not; indeed, years of corruption, clientilism, and transitory governments make many Italians despair of such goals. But are they closer to participatory democracy, and are citizens capable of creating important change? The oft-used power of the referendum and the average voting rate of ninety-two percent over the entire postwar period suggests a more positive response.[38] The foresight of the constituents in writing a constitution that did not reflect reality but was activist about changing it was an important force in creating a new political culture and a democratic society in Italy, and women's citizenship was key to that commitment. As Nadia Spano later said, "We were twenty-one, we worked a great deal, and I believe not too poorly [...] We were looking to the future."[39]

Notes

[1] Ada Gobetti was the widow of the philosopher and political leader Piero Gobetti and an author, activist, and important leader of the Partito d'Azione in her own right elected to lead the city of Torino after its liberation. Ada Gobetti, *Diario partigiano* (Turin: Einaudi, 1996), 323. All translations are mine unless otherwise noted. I would like to thank the American Academy in Rome and the German Marshall Fund for their generous support of the research for this project.

[2] Quote attributed to Piero Calamandrei, from P. Vercellone, "The Italian Constitution of 1947-48" in *The Rebirth of Italy 1943-50*, ed. S.J. Woolf (London: Longman, 1972), 124.

[3] The sentiment appears throughout Vercellone, 121-33. See also Pietro Scoppola, *La repubblica dei partiti. Evoluzione e crisi di un sistema politico. 1945-1996,* 2nd ed. (Bologna: Il Mulino, 1997), 211-221. Elio Fameli and Fiorenza Socci, *Globalex Guide to*

Italian Legal Research and Resources on the Web, http://www.nyulawglobal.org/globalex/italy2.htm (accessed 26 June 2007). For full texts of the constitution in Italian and English, see *Italian Studies Web: Politics & Government. Constitutions and Civil Codes*, Western European Section, Association of College and Research Libraries, http://net.lib.byu.edu/~rdh7/wess/ital/constitu.html.

[4] Camera dei Deputati, *Il voto alle donne. Le donne dall'elettorato alla partecipazione politica* (Rome: Camera dei Deputati, 1965), 67.

[5] Lucia Chiavola Birnbaum, *liberazione della donna. feminism in Italy* (Middletown, CT.: Wesleyan UP, 1986), 58; Maria Michetti, Margherita Repetto, and Luciana Viviani, *Udi:laboratorio di politica delle donne. Idee e materiali per una storia,* 2d ed., (Soveria Mannelli: Rubbettino Editore, 1998), 18-19; Miriam Mafai, *L'apprendistato della politica. Le donne italiane nel dopoguerra* (Rome: Editori Riuniti, 1979), 177-8.

[6] Molly Tambor, "The Lost Wave: Constitutional Rights Feminism in Italy, 1948-1963" (Ph.D. diss., Columbia University, 2006).

[7] Paola Gaiotti de Biase, "The Impact of Women's Political and Social Activity in Postwar Italy," in *The Formation of the Italian Republic* eds. Frank Coppa and Margherita Repetto-Alaia (New York: Peter Lang, 1993), 229; Mafai, *L'apprendistato della politica*, 66-67. The most famous of Togliatti's expositions of the link between emancipation and democracy was made to the first women's conference of his party in June 1945: see Palmiro Togliatti, "L'emancipazione della donna," reproduced in *Donne Comuniste. Antologia di scritti e discorsi*, ed. Graziella Falconi (Rome: Claudio Salemi, 1989), 52-80.

[8] Nadia Spano and Fiamma Camarlinghi, *La questione femminile nella politica del PCI. 1921-1963* (Rome: Donne e Politica, 1972), 152-3. Most of these women would also be elected to the first Parliament in 1948, notably Angela Maria Guidi Cingolani (DC, b. 1896), Teresa Noce (PCI, b. 1900), Adele Bei (PCI, b. 1904) Lina Merlin (PSI, b. 1899), Maria Federici (DC, b. 1899), Nadia Spano (PCI, b. 1916), Angela Gotelli (DC, b. 1905), Nilde Iotti (PCI, B. 1920), Maria Jervolino (DC, b. 1902), Maria Maddalena Rossi (PCI, b. 1906), and Vittoria Titomanlio (DC, b. 1899). The twenty-first woman was from the *uomo qualunque* ("everyman" or "common man") party, a particularly Southern phenomenon against the Allies, the antifascist government coalition, and anything that threatened the "common man." It came to be seen as an opportunistic, potentially Fascist, movement, as many ex-bosses who had been refused admittance to the Liberal Party turned to this one. She was the sister of the party founder. For *uomo qualunque* see Paul Ginsborg, *A History of Contemporary Italy: Society and Politics 1943-1988* (London: Penguin, 1990), 99-101.

[9] Rossi-Doria, "L'invisibilità politica delle donne," in *Donne guerra politica. Esperienze e memoria della Resistenza*, ed. Dianella Gagliani, Elda Guerra, Laura Mariana, Fiorenza Tarozzi (Bologna: CLUEB [Cooperativa Libraria Universitaria Editrice Bologna], 2000), 365; idem, *Diventare cittadine. Il voto alle donne in Italia* (Florence: Giunti Gruppo Editoriale, 1996), 10-11.

[10] Victoria de Grazia, *How Fascism Ruled Women: Italy, 1922-1945* (Berkeley: University of
California Press, 1992).

[11] Patrizia Gabrielli, *Il club delle virtuose. Udi e Cif nelle Marche dall'antifascismo alla guerra fredda* (Ancona: Il lavoro editoriale, 2000), 16.

[12] Rossi-Doria, *Diventare cittadine*, 74.

[13] The decree was Decreto legislativo luogotenenziale n. 23 del 1 febbraio 1945, "Estensione alle donne del diritto di voto," passed by the Bonomi government. As Anna Rossi-Doria shows, some women in Italy did participate in activism to agitate for suffrage, and the immediate reappearance of these first wave feminist representatives is an important argument for seeing continuity in the waves of Italy's women's movements. Rossi-Doria, *Diventare cittadine,* 20-26; Gaiotti de Biase, "The Impact of Women's Political and Social Activity," 221.

[14] A fifth woman, Ottavia Penna, dropped out but was later replaced by Angela Gotelli, so that some accounts number the women in the Committee of 75 as five.

[15] Teresa Noce, *Rivoluzionaria professionale* (Milan: La Pietra, Bompiani, 1974), 387, 389.

[16] Nadia Spano, quoted in Erica Scroppo, *Donna, privato e politico. Storie personali di 21 donne del PCI* (Milano: Gabriele Mazzotta editore, 1979), 81.

[17] Centro Italiano Femminile, *Memoria di Donne a cinquant'anni dalla Costituzione* (Rome: Istituti Editoriali e Poligrafici Internazionali, 1997), 98.

[18] Maria Federici, "L'Evoluzione Socio-giuridica della donna alla costituente," in *Le donne nel Parlamento della repubblica dalla Consulta alla VII Legislatura*, ed. Anna Miserocchi, Beniamino Altezza, Daniela Chiassi, Mario Mammuccari (Viterbo: Fondazione Cesira Fiori, Union printing, 1989), 122.; Maria Weber, "Italy," in *The Politics of the Second Electorate. Women and Public Participation. Britain, USA, Canada, Australia, France, Spain, West Germany, Italy, Sweden, Finland, Eastern Europe, USSR, Japan,* ed. Joni Lovenduski and Jill Hills (Boston: Routledge and Kegan Paul, 1981), 185.

[19] Giovanna Ceccatelli Gurrieri and Gabriella Paolucci, *Il Paradigma dell'emancipazione. Donne e politica nella Toscana degli anni '50* (Florence: Edizioni Polistampa, 1995), 22.

[20] M. Federici, "Relazione su Garanzie economico-sociali per l'esistenza della famiglia," Archivio storico della Camera dei Deputati, Archivio dell'Assemblea Costituente, Gruppo di serie 006, Commissione per la Costituzione, Serie 003, Relazioni, studi e ricerche (27-08-1946/ 13-02-1947) busta 74 sottofascicolo 3.

[21] Ibid.

[22] Teresa Noce, Lina Merlin, Michele Guia, "Relazioni su Garanzie economico-sociali per l'assistenza della famiglia," Archivio dell'Assemblea Costituente, Gruppo di serie 006, Commissione per la Costituzione, Serie 003, Relazioni, studi e ricerche (27-08-1946/ 13-02-1947) busta 74 sottofascicolo 3. See also Federici, 126-7, 129.

[23] Miriam Mafai, "Dal diritto di voto ai diritti di cittadinanza," in *Desiderio e diritto di cittadinanza. Le italiane e il voto. Atti del convegno Napoli 6-7 dicembre 1995*, ed. M. Antonietta Selvaggio (Palermo: La Luna, 1997), 46-47; Romano Canosa, *Il Giudice e la donna. Cento anni di sentenze sulla condizione femminile in Italia* (Milano: Mazzotta, 1978), 40-41.

[24] Emilia Sarogni, *La donna italiana. Il lungo cammino verso i diritti, 1861-1994* (Parma: Pratiche Editrice, 1995), 155; *Atti Assemblea Costituente.* Resoconto stenografico della seduta del 22 maggio 1947, 4171.

[25] The salient parts of these discussions are reproduced in Marina Addis Saba, Mimmo de Leo, and Fiorenza Taricone, eds., *Alle origini della Repubblica. Donne e Costituente* (Rome: Consiglio dei ministri, Commiussione nazionale per le pari opportunità, Dipartimento per l'informazione e l'editoria, 1996), 137-44.

[26] The law, number 1176, known as the Sacchi Law, had actually been a victory of the first wave feminist movement in Italy, profiting from its alliance with the Radical Party asserting women's right women to enter the free professions and to civil posts, and abolishing the requirement of spousal approval (*autorizzazione maritale*). Sponsored by Ettore Sacchi, a leader of the Radical Party, this law was commonly known as women's "demobilization reward." See Lucia Motti, *Le donne* (Rome: Editori Riuniti, 2000), 13; and Sarogni, 156.

[27] Maria Sofia Lanza, "La donna e la Costituzione: le giuriste italiane difendono la loro 'giusta causa,'" clipping in CIF National Archives, *Cronache*, June 1955.

[28] Federici, 128.

[29] Discussions of Article 29's impact on women's equality appear in Coppa and Repetto-Alaia, 274; Anna Rossi-Doria, "Il voto alle donne nel 1945," in *Il voto alle donne cinquant'anni dopo, Campidoglio, 6-7 marzo 1995. Atti del convegno*, by the Centro Italiano Femminile with the Ufficio Progetti Donna del Comune di Roma (Rome: Istituto Poligrafico e Zecca dello Stato, 1996), 64; Marta Boneschi, *Santa pazienza. La storia delle donne italiane dal dopoguerra a oggi* (Milan: Mondadori, 1998), 117-8, 260; and Federici, 128.

[30] Boneschi, 260.

[31] Addis Saba et al., 32-3.

[32] Ginsborg, 101.

[33] Renata Micheli, "Voto: 50 anni di democrazia," in *Il voto alle donne cinquant'anni dopo*, 113-4.

[34] See for example Article 2, which refers to the "inalienable duties of social solidarity" and the "social reality within which the personality develops." Gaiotti de Biase, 236.

[35] Ulrike Schultz, "Introduction: Women in the World's Legal Professions: Overview and Synthesis," in *Women in the World's Legal Professions*, ed. Ulrike Schultz and Gisela Shaw (Portland: Hart Publishing, 2003), xlvi-xlviii;
Mafai, "Dal diritto di voto ai diritti di cittadinanza," 48; statistics on numbers of *concorsi* participants are published each year in the *Forze di lavoro* chapter of the Annuario statistico, available for download at www.istat.it.

[36] Ceccatelli Gurrieri and Paolucci, 4; Anna Rossi-Doria, "Le donne sulla scena politica," in *Storia dell'Italia Repubblicana,* vol. 1, *La Costituzione della democrazia* (Torino: Einaudi, 1994), 833, 839.

[37] In 1993 two laws had been passed which set actual quotas for women candidates but were repealed by the Constitutional Court in 1995 on the basis that they went against the equal treatment guaranteed in Article 51. Constitutional Law 30 May 2003, No. 1 then amended article 51 of the Constitution so that it now commits the Republic to the promotion of equal opportunities for women's representation. See the websites of the Constitutional Court, http://www.cortecostituzionale.it/; and of the European Parliament, http://www.europarl.europa.eu/workingpapers/femm/w10/4_en.htm.

[38] This figure applies to national elections between 1946 and 1989. If brought up to 2006, the percentage is eighty-nine percent, as turnouts have dipped into the eighties since about 1994. Giorgio Galli and Alfonso Prandi, *Patterns of Political Participation in Italy* (New Haven: Yale University Press, 1970), 28; International Institute for Democracy and Electoral Assistance, http://www.idea.int/vt/country_view.cfm? CountryCode=IT.

[39] *Il voto alle donne cinquant'anni dopo*, 164.

Intellectual Considerations or Taciturn Eloquence about the Past? The Democratizations of Hungary 1945-1990

Béla Rásky

What is the role of Hungary in a collection treating political culture and democratization in Europe since 1945? Unlike other societies examined here, the country is neither a Western European society in its historical and/or political sense1 nor did it face re-democratization after 1945, since the country—apart from very short interludes in its history—had never been a liberal democracy. Nevertheless Hungary in this context could serve as a kind of control or reference to something which in general is referred to as "Western Europe."2 Most important of all, Hungary is one of the few European societies which after World War II had to come to terms with its extreme-right wing and dictatorial past first under democratic circumstances (1945-1948), under Stalinism (1945-1963), under a "soft" dictatorship (1963-1989) often referred to as "Kádárism" (named after the First Secretary of the Hungarian Socialist Worker's Party János Kádár), and finally again under liberal-democratic circumstances—when after 1990 "coming to terms with a dictatorial past" had come to mean clarification of guilt in and collaboration with the communist regime, as opposed to a fascist one.

Hungary is commonly regarded as a society with a tradition of thinking along pronounced historical lines, endowed with a marked and complex historical memory.3 No matter what political position one espouses, reference to history provides the supposedly real and correct material, although the historical reference points or axes with which each political affinity operates may differ. After all, it is the defeat of two democratic projects which until today unites Hungarian society, in a way creates the nation—namely, the revolutions of 1848 and 1956—while two other instances of democratization still divide the country, namely 1918/19 (marking at the same time the fall of the Habsburg Empire and the territorial dissolution of the historical Kingdom of Hungary) and 1945 (the end of the old autocratic, anti-democratic as well as overt fascist system). As cynical as it may sound, one might add that the only successful democratic project, 1989/90, is buried in neglect, ignorance, and disregard—or maybe it was not a project, it was not democratic, and it was not successful.4

Post 1945

For the majority of Hungarians, 1945 brought not liberation from the Germans, but a new, Soviet occupation. Nevertheless it was clear that with the end of World War II, Hungarian society—just like the German or the Austrian—would face the task of coming to terms with its past. The crucial point for a democratic development was whether meaningful and sufficient portions of the Hungarian public could critically come to terms with their own antisemitic and fascist traditions. As historian Szabó Miklós stated, "[T]he most important problem for Hungarian identity after 1945 was to master its own extreme right-wing past"5; in short, the Hungarians faced the challenge of facing up to "the distorted Hungarian character," to see through the democratization of society and thereby create a new democratic Hungarian identity.

While "the possibility for revolution and democracy did not come from 'below,' but from outside the country,"6 1945 marked what in most respects was a social and political revolution; it marked a clear, even radical attempt to call the country's past into question. The need to integrate the disenfranchised Hungarian masses into the political and social system became evident, and it was clear that the fascist Horthy period and the social bases for its support had to be confronted in the wake of the social, political, and moral catastrophe it had wrought upon the country. After World War II and the Shoah it was clear that the old antidemocratic social elites of the country had to withdraw from positions of influence and assume responsibility for their past actions. It also became clear that the lower classes—albeit to a lesser degree—had to face their involvement in the crimes of the Horthy years. In short, Hungarian society as a whole had to confront its moral, social, and political shortcomings over a historical longue durée. The new national identity was to be one closely associated with modernization; for example, land reform integrated the lower classes in the provinces into Hungarian society virtually overnight, and social movements facilitated the beginning of vertical integration of the lower classes into the ranks of social elites.

In key respects, discussion in the immediate aftermath of 1945 followed lines similar to those in Germany, where on the one hand some posited the need for what Walter Dirks has called Restauration7 (i.e., inventing or reconstructing an understanding of German continuity that preceded 1933 such that the Nazi period could be portrayed as an aberration), and on the other hand there were those who demanded critical analysis of recent historical developments. Friedrich Meinecke's extended essay Die deutsche Katastrophe, published in 1946, was a first step in the latter direction, followed by other more or less important studies of a similar kind.8 As a consequence those who propounded a deutscher Sonderweg (German "special path" of historical development) and those who called for Vergangenheitsbewältigung (confrontation with the past) clashed again and again—culminating in the Historikerstreit ("Historians' Dispute") of the 1980s.9

Similar to circumstances prevailing in (West) Germany, Hungarian political culture sustained both tendencies: one which formed a collective identity out of the critique of the past, and one which sought to build a new political culture out of historical myths. The laltter awakens memories of past ages and the symbols, rituals, and fantasies associated with them, while the former tries to critically analyze processes. The two methods differ fundamentally; moreover, they represent not only different approaches towards history, but also ultimately towards democratization. The critical method confronts itself with sound scholarly history. The traditional method selects out the ideological tropes that fit into the model (regardless if this model is conservative, liberal, or leftist); history here is not a process, but a collection of examples, a gallery of mythologies. This is not "scientific" (i.e., rigorous, academic history). Rather, the past becomes something aesthetic, and its motive power can easily be instrumentalized for ideological purposes.

Thus, in many respects Hungary was in the same situation as Germany insofar as historians and an inquiring public took stock of the recent past. During the immediate postwar years the outcome of the struggle between these two tendencies still seemed open, and one could account for affinities to forget as well as for the need to analyze the past in order to overcome its negative tendencies once and for all.10 Gyula Szekfű, perhaps the leading ideologue of prewar Hungary was the first to provide an analysis of the roots of Hungary's extreme right wing in his essay "After the Revolution," in which he made a sharp turn away from his earlier ideas. In rewriting the foreword to his main oeuvre on Hungarian history, he imparted to us an impressive (though controversial) image of the views and political preferences of a conservative intellectual of the times, not merely revealing the opportunist in him, but also his analytical and self-reflective sides—rather like Friedrich Meinecke's exercise in rewriting the foreword to his Weltbürgertum und Nationalstaat.11

But more importantly, it was the essays of István Bibó that sought to analyze the complexity of Hungarian history and the need for a radical democratization. One of these announced its program quite clearly in its title: Distorted Hungarian Character: The Deadlocks of Hungarian History,12 a kind of Hungarian Sonderweg. No less important for present purposes was his book The Jewish Question: The Case of Hungary after 1944,13 published in 1948 as a kind of a summary of the public discussions concerning responsibility for the extermination of almost eighty percent of the Jewish population after May 1944 and possible restitution measurements in postwar Hungary. The work also tried to outline possible paths for resolving conflicts and ways of remembering the genocide. Bibó's book has stood the test of time, and is in no need of revision. It remains a clear and surprisingly topical analysis, an uncompromising reckoning with Hungarian antisemitism, with clear suggestions on how to overcome and clarify the problem. In his essay he imagined some dialogues between Jews and non-Jews in post-Holocaust Hungary. Hungarian sociologist Éva Kovács suggests that Bibó tried to open up a discursive space in which survivors, resistance fighters, and bystanders should find individual ways to assert sovereignty over previously unclaimed experience and to treat the traumas resulting from it. 14 But these "words did not find any resonance in the Hungarian society, and I am almost sure that these imaginary dialogues—besides some marginalized literary texts, so, once again, fiction—never have been realized." Bibó answers: "The demands for restitution and moral reparations for persecution of the Jews in Hungary were, from their inception, marked by nebulous circumstances and insincere preconditions."15

In certain fundamental ways, after 1945 Hungary found itself in a situation very similar to that of Austria: a society with widespread participation in crimes against compatriots, one that scarcely produced any form of resistance and in many respects had willingly collaborated with the Nazis. But what makes the country rather comparable with Germany is the fact that Hungary was not given the opportunity to cast itself as a victim (as had Austria), evidently for the simple reason that the Allies (in this case the Soviets) did not provide this possibility—and therefore it had to find other strategies.

It was quite clear that any fantasies of a "Greater Hungary" were hopeless, due both to internal factors and the victorious Allies' creation of spheres of politics. It had been this expansionist policy of regaining lost territories that had dominated the interwar period, preventing meaningful social reforms and the establishment of a viable democratic political culture, and had ultimately led the Hungarian government to side with the Axis powers. Thus, a revision of the political conditio sine qua non of the interwar period, the Treaty of Trianon—or, for that matter, the claim for the territorial gains of the two Vienna Arbitraries of 1938 und 1940, when Hungary expanded into Southern Slovakia and Northern Transylvania—were not even raised.

The "number and political importance of those sentenced" in the political trials after 1945, historian István Deak reminds us, "was extraordinarily large."

> In Hungary, four prime ministers, a deputy prime minister, and scores of other cabinet members as well as several generals and high-ranking officials were executed. Three hundred thousand Hungarians, or about three percent of the total population, suffered some kind of punishment [. . .] Remarkably, no collaborationist trial [. . .] became a show trial. Defendants had their say in court, and even though judicial irregularities were legion, no one was forced to plead guilty and none begged to be executed as had been customary during the Stalinist Great Terror and would become customary in Eastern Europe in the late 1940s and early 1950s. [16]

We would do well to remember that nearly all the Hungarians who had died in Nazi camps were Jews according to legislation prevailing in Hungary at the time. The number of non-Jewish resistance martyrs paled in comparison. This important point notwithstanding, the short-lived Hungarian Second Republic of 1945-48 received its legitimacy from a critique of the past. In significant ways it sought to break with the traditions of Hungarian history, and wanted to find—

perhaps invent—new points of reference, new links. Debates concerning the past were painful, but helpful, and, as we shall see, sustainable in the short term.

My account of this short-lived democracy might be too positive and many Hungarian historians might challenge this optimistic view. But beyond its shortcomings—it was rather restricted, since the Soviet occupation power dictated political taboos and the fate of political parties. The German-speaking minority found itself pressured to emigrate and population exchange along the Hungarian-Czechoslovak border was clearly a form of ethnic cleansing; there were riots with antisemitic undertones as late as 1946—the balance of this hesitant, inconsistent, quarrelsome and contradictory democratization process was, on the whole, positive. 17 As historian Miklós Szabó has observed

> In thc critical work of Bibó and Szekfü—and so many others—there seemed to be a chance that this change could be realized. [. . .] [The possibility of a c]oming to terms with the reactionary national past [seemed possible], such that the nation does not experience this accounting as a new conflict between nation and progress, but as a national renaissance, where the nation does not have to give up progress for being able to stay a nation. This very demanding intellectual process was at its very beginning when it was broken up by the political turn of 1948.18

The result was silence . . . a silence that Hungarian society still has not overcome.

Stalinist Take Over, 1948/49

Critical analysis of the past was not to become the ideological leitmotif of the Hungarian People's Republic of 1949. The emergence of a Stalinist regime led to the disruption of democratization processes and any critical examination of the Hungarian past was not in keeping with official mandates. Hungarian Stalinists were quite aware of the strength and power that direct confrontation with the past had meant in Hungarian political tradition. Stalinists, therefore, created their own official mythology—established, in part, as an opposition to the neo-baroque images of the Horthy-era—in which the disenfranchised always had been fighting for national freedom, while the landlords had consistently betrayed the nation. This historiographic school, named the Andics-Révai-School after its founders,19 simply constructed a progressive Hungarian lower class that had always fought for democracy and national values: “In reality it was some kind of substitution. Instead of the ruling classes, now the masses came into the focus of a teleologically interpreted national process.”20 This propagandistic representation did not offer an analysis of traditions associated with the national past, but a rather oversimplified historical method, blurred contradictory phenomena, and denied or disregarded other developments inconsistent with the struggle for independence.21 The communist workers' movement became the custodian of national history and all genuine democratization processes. The old elites were simply excluded from the project.

István Bibó's contribution to confronting the past was banned immediately after the communist takeover, not to be republished until shortly before the fall of the Kádár regime (1987), after his works had already been made available by publishing houses in exile or by underground publications in Hungary proper. The Stalinist system and later Kádárism simply had no need for an uncompromising analysis of the moral neglect of all classes in Hungarian society as expressed in antisemitism. The confrontation with this era became part of a cynical politics of history: the guilty parties would simply be excluded from the Stalinist project for a "new Hungary."

Great official effort was devoted to blocking memory of World War II, effectively checking efforts to come to terms with Hungarians' supporting role on the Axis side. After 1948 the topic was not merely taboo; inquiry into it was forbidden as part of condemnation of a particular politics of the past. The memory of those many Hungarian soldiers, non-Jews, who were simply fed into senseless slaughter, was suppressed and left to the individual level; any public declaration about personal suffering on the eastern front was obliterated. Surviving Hungarian Jews were allowed to recall their suffering only as part of a collective; they were permitted to remember the horrors of Mauthausen or Auschwitz only as martyrs for the whole of Hungarian society. On the other hand, by relegating those complicit in the policies of a "criminal and fascist nation" to a minority who did not really belong to Hungarian society, reinforcing the notions of "them" (fascists, the bourgeoisie, etc.) vs. "us," Hungarians did not have to examine their history; they could easily sequester themselves from a past fraught with moral shortcomings. Sociologist Éva Kovács argues:

> This collective memory handles the Hungarian Shoah as an atypical storage in the history of our society. The Shoah can have its singularity, because—in this form of collective memory—it is not the result of political and social processes of the past centuries. Free speech concerning the Shoah was declared taboo under the communist regime (although we do know that the system itself was not free of antisemitic slips): a meta-narrative was put into its place, which embedded political antisemitism, the events of the camps, and the ghettos in the critique of a society surmounted by communism. This meta-language, responsible for its own atonality, looked for and found delinquents in the past (deceased) generations and foreign countries, introduced the victims as "victims of fascism" and the resistance fighters as "antifascist heroes." The notion "Jew" referred exclusively to a past over and done with and could not be really addressed in public aside from in [the context of] certain literary

works and films. This meta-language also infiltrated private speech and commanded silence not only to all voices longing to remember, but gave deceptive comfort to the survivors and false self-justification for the ones who had been inactive.22

The Revolution of 1956

Paradoxically, it was the 1956 uprising that took ownership of the Stalinist historical ideology regarding national independence. While there is still a great deal of detailed research on the uprising yet to be done, we can interpret the events as the initiative of an authentic workers' revolution with the goal of establishing some kind of a broad, popular democracy through worker's councils23; as a struggle for national independence; or as a simple expression of dissatisfaction. In any case, the fact remains that the deep impact of envisioning a new kind of republic displayed tenacity in the form of this violent democratization project. No one stipulated a return to the Horthy era and the question of Trianon was never raised. The sense of being a small nation, but equal among members of the world community re-emerged; no territorial or other demands against Hungary's neighbors were raised in return for a declaration of Cold War neutrality. The revolutionary symbolism reflected democratic-progressive traditions. But one should add that although the ultimately triumphant Kádár regime's denunciatory White Book could not find any evidence for large scale antisemitic atrocities, recent research points to different possibilities, insofar as it explores the antisemitic undertones associated with the course of the events.24

It is not the social scientific and historical research on the events themselves that still reveal the impact on recent and contemporary democratization efforts, however. More significant is memory of the revolution, or rather least the struggle about who is authorized to remember 1956. In the years of transition after 1990 it has become ever clearer that the anti-democratic radical right has lay claim to the memory of 1956, denying the democratic left the right to remember their version and their victims, although it was the Hungarian working class who had paid most dearly once the revolution's suppression and its aftermath. As was evident in the fiftieth anniversary of the revolution, the radical right has been able to control this discourse; indeed, 1956 has become a part of the radical right's political folklore. For that reason, the revolution of 1956, unlike that of 1848, does not currently appear to offer any viable reference point for understanding a post-fascist democratization process in Hungary.

The Kádár Era: 1963-1989

Once its six-year crackdown against real or supposed revolutionaries ebbed, Kádárism revealed itself as a system that, within the Soviet-style framework, tried to democratize Hungary in a limited, halting fashion. Still, it remained a single party regime that established, then enforced, its ground rules in an authoritarian fashion. Many of the power plays and intrigues of the "liberal" Nomenklatura of the cultural sector still burden today's discussions of Hungarian political culture more broadly.

Early on, the Kádár regime proved able to skirt the historical trajectory of Hungarian political culture over previous generations. If we look at the revolution of 1956 as an enormous democratization project, then Kádárism had to make Hungarian society forget this event25; any historical remembrance of 1956, particularly any that entailed critical analysis, would have revealed the regime's genesis in the 1956 Revolution's bloody suppression. Since the Kádár regime opted not to restore the old Stalinist system once it had consolidated itself, it had to find a different way to legitimize itself in the absence of rule through terror. Some attempts to introduce historical traditions into the new model were attempted, but the concepts of Erik Molnár, presented in his articles "The National Question" and "On Nationalist Remnants in Our Historical Perception",26 proved too complicated for communication to a wider public.27

The new regime took another direction instead, and grounded its ideology on the complete denial of recent Hungarian history. It did not create an opposite concept, it applied a much simpler method: it simply acted as if there was no history to be reckoned with at all. History was relegated into official exhibits in state-controlled museums. Hungarian society also participated in these processes, gaining certain benefits as compensation for acquiescence in the new system. We do not know whether this strategy proved successful in the long run, since Hungarian social scientists are still debating the circumstances of forgetting and remembering 1956.28 However, the fact remains that Hungarian society was never so ahistorical as during the zenith of Kádárism, and neither before nor since have so many taboos characterized public discourse—not necessarily in the form of censorship, but by means of tacit agreements.29 Dehistoricization became part of the foundation for the regime's legitimacy. All the same, the regime did not suppress the Hungarian predilection for mythical history; insofar as it preserved the illusion of freedom of speech, arrived at tacit agreements with compliant citizens, provided escape routes into the relative comforts of everyday life, and championed the myth of Hungary as the happiest barrack in the socialist camp, the regime circumvented a return to calls for democratization beyond spaces where it exercised power.

The Transformation of 1989

Superficially, 1989 is the happy ending vis-á-vis the sufferings and traumas accounted for in the trajectory of recent Hungarian historical narratives: Hungary finally became a free, democratic, and independent state. Thus, 1989—just like 1945—marked a year when roots, points of reference, processes, eras, events, and democratization narratives had to be identified anew. After 1989, though, Hungarian society and the nascent third republic had to cope with antagonistic memories of two dictatorships. Increasingly it became clear that this task was overwhelming, for 1989 represented a smooth transition from something already long in a process of collapse, and the need for coming to terms with the immediate past did not appear as pressing as had been the case in 1945. Further, the parameters for a discussion of the past were different. Some might argue that they had never been established. Consequently, public discourse in 1989 was dominated by a kind of enthusiasm, staged or genuine—but not by analysis.

After 1989/90, Hungary had again to weave its political culture out of historical material, since a marginalized democratic opposition has not been successful in creating new, generally acknowledged democratic traditions from scratch. While in the early 1980s Bibó became a kind of mentoring voice for the democratic opposition, by 1989 the integrating figure of a new and promising democratic political culture had vanished from public political discourse. In a Hungary awash with remembrance there is not a single bridge, street, or park named after Bibó; only in late May 2005 was a monument dedicated to him in central Budapest.30 But among the two alternatives—critical confrontation with two pasts or a return to old, worn-out national myths—this time, unlike in 1945, the young democracy initially chose the latter. In this respect the historical-political references of so many democratically elected politicians were no blunders, they were the simple verbal expression of the path the new, third republic had chosen to take regarding its democratization policies.31 The politics of past history experienced a powerful comeback.

Hungary will always be confronted with the problem, indeed the necessity, of remembering the victims of both National Socialism and Stalinism. Immediately after the 1989 transformation there was an interesting short-term development in Hungary: numerous villages and small towns spontaneously erected memorials to victims of World War II. Soldiers, victims of bombing raids, and Jews were all remembered, the various categories of victims not clearly distinguished. Naturally, a politically sensitive expression of memory should have differentiated more distinctively among victims, but this was a spontaneous process without ulterior motives, simply the expression of a need to commemorate the dead. For a short time after 1990, it appeared as if it might be possible to bring another period in the country's history to a close soberly, without excessive pathos. However, in the course of consolidating Hungarian democracy this memorialization became politicized and reformulated according to political and racist categories. Moreover, debates about excluding certain individuals who were involved in the state security system or in political crimes from the public sphere for a certain time emerged, even if lists identifying the names of those involved in the regimes of 1948 to 1989 were never published. Over fifteen years after the transformation, parts of society can still be blackmailed or falsely accused for collaborating with the old system. Even in this very narrow area the framework for coming to terms with the past was never clearly defined, an omission remaining an obstacle to thorough-going democratization, as long as the country is still deeply involved in chasing down old agents instead of engaging in the clarification of roles in, reasons for participation in, and reactions to the old system.

After an emotional debate about how to remove the physical presence of socialist structures from the cityscape, a decision was ultimately reached to create a monument park at the edge of Budapest.32 This memorial meadow can also be read as a "monumental" illustration of Hayden White's thesis about alternative readings of historical events, including their manifestation as irony. After more than a decade the as yet unfinished park makes it possible for irony to gain the upper hand; the space permits the realization of embodiments of the past in a kind of open-air museum constantly accessible for purposes of memory, an area meant to be a kind of spatial concentration of this past over and beyond the removal of statues and cleansing of public places. Fenced in, the evil spirits petrified in stone, coupled with a rearrangement of the statues chronologically and thematically, a new narrative about socialism came into being. This was facilitated by the exploitation of the park as a marketing of the past for tourism purposes.33 But the park also opens itself up to different memories, for different approaches towards the past, and with the different possibilities to "use" the park it democratizes Hungarian past.

On the whole, though, pathos is once more de rigueur, irony out of style.34 The House of Terror that opened in 2002 is devoted to Hungary's most recent contemporary history, and deals almost exclusively with Stalinism. It is as if the House of Terror's organizers wished to relegate the entire topic of right-wing terror to a Holocaust museum, as though the Shoah were not an integral part of Hungarian history, as one particularly astute observer remarked:

> The museum has attracted controversy and should concern historians because of the exclusions on which the interpretations of history it presents is based. It concentrates in large part upon the crimes against humanity committed during the Stalinist years and minimizes those committed prior to 1945. This "museum" presents an argument that implies that "terror" began with the Arrow Cross in October 1944. This effectively ensures that the deportation of Hungary's Jews to Auschwitz in the summer [of 1944] is given no coverage. [...] Furthermore the "museum" seeks to whitewash the issues of domestic collaboration and responsibility. Few

> historians would disagree that the understanding of Hungary's mid-twentieth century tragedies is impossible without consideration of the antisemitic measures of the interwar and early wartime years.35

Even if the House remains a kind of tourist attraction of Budapest, it is still highly challenged by historians and museum specialists alike. "The manner in which the political past becomes a technical spectacle is all too eye-catching, attention-grabbing, striking," commented Neue Zürcher Zeitung journalist Paul Jandl. "[. . .] the relevant era for the museum, the years between 1944 and 1956, eliminate the question of Hungarian responsibility; German Nazism or Russian communism—both coming from outside—are made responsible for terror."36

Along these lines, the form in which the awarding of the Nobel Prize to Imre Kertész in 2002 was celebrated in Hungary is more than a bit depressing in its implications. It had been the conservatives who repeatedly stressed their cultural traditions, and they were largely not prepared to share in the euphoria of a liberal and left-liberal public.37 But the day after the announcement of the award, the then liberal-oriented Hungarian daily Magyar Hírlap carried the ironic headline: "Imre Kertész, Hungarian author, is a Nobel laureate. Jew." The article predicted that the decision in Stockholm would "tear open a wound that would run straight through Hungarian culture, history and society"38—and that is what indeed has come to pass.

When we reflect on the post-fascist period in Hungary, it should come as no surprise that Auschwitz and Mauthausen were not present in 1989, for they were never present in the public discourse after 1948. The space that might have been occupied by this missing history was filled with narratives of Hungarian suffering during the war and dominated by nostalgia for the old Hungary and the concern for Hungarian minorities living outside the country's borders. The fact remains that Holocaust memory is important neither for the majority of Hungarian society nor for the state-managed politics of contemporary history. In August 2004 the historian Attila Pók raised the question "Why was there no Historikerstreit in post-communist Hungary?"39 In a country that consistently raised numerous questions about its past during the last fifteen years, this question is all the more striking. Pók attempts to address the question why in the years following 1989 Hungarians' (co-)responsibility has not been addressed, and despite offering a wide range of plausible arguments he never satisfactorily arrives at a conclusion. According to Éva Kovács, up to the present there is no consensual and legitimized narrative concerning the Shoah in Hungary. Narratives are fragmented—thus limited to political declarations, commemorative days, and family memory—or they are so generalized that victims lack particular identity and their recollections are swallowed up in collective memory. For Kovács, two sentences are missing in the Hungarian discourse: "The victims of the Shoah are our victims" and "It hurts me so much." Precisely in the discourse of memory, in scholarly debate or the acceptance of certain popular discursive rules regarding the Holocaust, there appears to be a persistent barrier inside Europe. Many rules, codes, texts, images, and tacit compromises and agreements devised in postwar Western Europe are not (yet) valid in the former Soviet bloc. At the same time, memory of the Holocaust in Eastern and Central Europe still retains a democratic potential reminiscent of and nourished by the region's antifascist traditions.

On the other hand, one could assert that the Shoah has become virtually ubiquitous here, but only if one really wishes to see it. The townscape is now marked by innumerable small, quite impressive, honest and therefore moving memorials. All features of European commemorative forms exist in Budapest, and in 2002 the Magyar Holokauszt Múzeum opened its doors almost as a crowning conclusion to this development. However, upon closer examination this staging of a memory remains quite superficial. Sometimes this staging process almost resembles the working off of a debt, an almost burdensome duty, in order to prove that Hungary conforms to the standards and expectations of the European Union. Architectural critics are unanimous in bemoaning the fact that the design of the new Holokauszt Múzeum makes it seem almost a building in hiding, that it is located in a less than representative area of the city and has turned its back on the hustle and bustle of the metropolis. It appears as if the museum is almost ashamed to have to document the fact that it is the memorial and documentation center for 400,000 murdered Jewish Hungarians, and thus seemingly turns its face away from the city in which it stands.

The political culture of the third republic pays the price for communist Hungary's foul compromises, tacit agreements, and small privileges. Some two decades after 1989 it is still unclear which of the two available alternative paths for democratization Hungary has opted for: a critical confrontation with the past or a return to the old national legends. It appears that the country has taken decision for a very Central European solution, which in Austrian German is called fortwursteln, i.e., to carry on, but take no stand. For the foreseeable future, the two approaches will coexist in a conflict-laden relationship in which each side dislikes the other, but requires it to legitimize itself—and thus potentially fruitful or, equally, ruinous for further democratization projects.

Notes

[1] See Jenő Szűcs, "The Three Historical Regions of Europe: An Outline," *Acta Historica Scientiarum Hungaricae*, 29 (1983): 2–4, 131–84.
[2] See Andrea Ellmeier and Béla Rásky, *Differing Diversities: Eastern European Perspectives: Cultural Policy and Cultural Diversity*, Report for Phase 2 of the Transversal Study on the Theme of Cultural Policy and Cultural Diversity. Phase 2. (Strasbourg: Council of Europe Publishing, 2006).
[3] Hilde Weiss and Christoph Reinprecht, *Demokratischer Patriotismus oder ethnischer Nationalismus in Ostmitteleuropa. Empirische Analysen zur nationalen Identität in Ungarn, Tschechien, Slowakei und Polen* (Vienna: Böhlau, 1998), 139f.
[4] Gerő András, "A historikum a politikumban [Historicity in Politics]," in *Csendes? Forradalom? Volt?* [*Silent? Revolution? Was there one at all?*] (Budapest T-Twins and Tipográfiai Kft., 1991), 12–17, here 14.
[5] Szabó Miklós, "Magyar nemzettudat-problémák a huszadik század második felében [Problems of Hungarian National Identity in the Second Half of the Twentieth Century]," in *Politikai kultúra Magyarországon 1896-1986* [Political Culture in Hungary 1896-1986], Szabó Miklós (Budapest: Medvetánc könyvek, 1989), 225–51, 225.
[6] Jenő Szűcs, op. cit., 181.
[7] Walter Dirks, "Der restaurative Charakter der Epoche [The Restorative Character of the Era]," *Frankfurter Hefte* 5 (1950), 942–95; see also A Bushell, "Prescribing for the New Germany: The Journal Frankfurter Hefte in its First Year of Publication (1946)," in *German Life and Letters* (January 1988), 106–20.
[8] Friedrich Meinecke, *The German Catastrophe: Reflections and Recollections* (Boston: Beacon Press, 1950).
[9] See Piper Verlag, *"Historikerstreit": Die Dokumentation der Kontroverse um die Einzigartigkeit der nationalsozialistischen Judenvernichtung* (Munich and Zurich: Piper Verlag, 1987).
[10] Works such as Jenö Lévai's or Imre Hermann's can be seen in this light. Lévai Jenő, *Zsidósors Magyarországon* [*Jewish Fate in Hungary*] (Budapest: Magyar Téka, 1948); Hermann Imre, *Az antiszemitizmus lélektana* [*The Psychology of Antisemitism*] (Budapest: Bibliotheca, 1945) (Reprint Budapest: Cserepfalvi, 1990).
[11] See Glatz Ferenc, *Előszó a "Hóman-Szekfű"-höz* [Preface to the Reprint of Bálint Hóman's and Gyula Szekfű's *History of Hungary*] (Budapest: Maecenas, 1990); Friedrich Meinecke, *Weltbürgertum und Nationalstaat* (Munich: Oldenbourg, 1962).
[12] See in German: István Bibó, "Deformierter ungarischer Charakter, ungarische Geschichte auf Irrwegen," http://www.kakanien.ac.at/beitr/fallstudie/Bibo1.pdf (2002).
[13] István Bibó, "The Jewish Question in Hungary," in *Democracy, Revolution, Self-Determination. Selected Writings* (Boulder, CO and New York: East European Monographs/Columbia University Press 1991), 155–324.
[14] Éva Kovács, "Die nicht in Anspruch genommen Erfahrung. Zwei fehlende Sätze über die ungarische Shoah," in *Zivilisationsbruch und Gedächtniskultur*, ed. Heidemarie Uhl (Innsbruck–Vienna–Munich–Bozen: StudienVerlag, 2001), 209–222, here 217.
[15] István Bibó, *The Jewish Question* op.cit., 231; The word "account" (*Rechenschaft*) in my 1990 translation is replaced here by "restitution," since it seems more applicable in the context of the present debate. See also Emery George and István Bibó, "The Jewish Question in Hungary – A Review Essay," *Cross Currents* 4 (1985), see

http://www.hti.umich.edu/cgi/t/text/text-idx?c=crossc;idno=ANW-0935.1985.001;view=toc

[16] István Deák, "Civil Wars and Retribution in Europe 1939-1948," *zeitgeschichte* (Juli/August 1998): 244–52, esp. 250.

[17] Szabó Miklós, "1945-1947 és 1989-1991: két átmenet [1945-1947 and 1989-1991: Two Transitions]," in *Csendes? Forradalom? Volt?*, 18-21, here 18; see also Fehér István, *A magyarországi németek kitelepítése. 1945-1950* [*The Expulsion of the Germans from Hungary*] (Budapest: Akadémiai Kiadó, 1988); Balogh Sándor, "Az 1946. február 27-i magyar-csehszlovák lakosságcsere egyezmény [The Hungarian-Czechoslovak Treaty on Population Exchange of 27 February, 1947]," *Történelmi Szemle* 1979/1: 59–87; Varga F. János, "A miskolci népítelet [The People's Tribunal of Miskolc]," in *Skandalum. Magyar közéleti botrányok 1843-1991* [*Scandal: Hungarian Public Scandals, 1943-1991*], ed. Gerő András (Budapest: T-Twins, 1993), 194–213, here 194; and Ungváry Krisztián, "Két röpirat – politikai hangulat Magyarországon 1945-1946-ban [Two Leaflets – Political Mood in Hungary, 1945-1946]," *"2000"* (május 2002): 59–63, here 59.

[18] Szabó Miklós, *Magyar nemzettudat-problémák*, op. cit. 226.

[19] Révai József, *Marxizmus, népiesség, magyarság* [*Marxism, Ethnicity, Hungarianness*] (Budapest: n.p., 1955).

Andics Erzsébet, *Munkásosztály és nemzet* [*Working Class and Nation*] (Budapest: Szikra, 1952).

Andics Erzsébet, ed., *A magyar nacionalizmus kialakulása és története* [*History and Development of Hungarian Nationalism*] (Budapest: Kossuth, 1964).

[20] Jenő Szűcs, "Die Nation in historischer Sicht und der nationale Aspekt der Geschichte," in *Nation und Geschichte Studien* (Budapest: Gondolat, 1981), 11–160, 43.

[21] Lackó Miklós, "Révai-problémák. Írások az 1931-34 börtönévekből [Révai Problems: Works from the Prison Years 1931-34]," in *Válságok - választások* [Crises – Decisions], Lackó Miklós (Budapest: Gondolat, n.d.), 265–94, 287.

[22] Éva Kovács, "Die nicht in Anspruch genommene Erfahrung," op. cit., 219.

[23] Bill Lomax, *Hungary 1956* (London: Allison and Busby, 1976).

[24] *Ellenforradalmi erők a magyar októberi eseményekben* [*Counterrevolutionary Forces in the October Events*], Volumes I-IV (Budapest: A Magyar Népköztársaság Minisztertanácsa Tajékoztatási Hivatala, 1957). On antisemitism see Standeisky Éva, "Elmismasolt antiszemitizmus, elhallgatott múlt. Az 1956-os miskolci licselés [Mangled Anti-Semitism, Past Kept as a Secret : The 1956 Lynching in Miskolc]," *Élet és Irodalom* (August 20, 2004): 8/9, and Standeisky Éva, "Antiszemitizmus az 1956-os forradalomban [Anti-Semitism in the 1956 Revolution]," *Élet és irodalom* (February 27, 2004): 14/15.

[25] See Béla Rásky, "Nationale Frage und Arbeiterbewegung in Ungarn," in *Arbeiterbewegung und nationale Frage in den Nachfolgestaaten der Habsburgermonarchie*, ed. Helmut Konrad (Vienna and Zurich: Europa Verlag, 1993), 65–89, particularly 86.

[26] Molnár Erik, "A nemzeti kérdés [The National Question]" and "Történetszemléletünk nacionalista maradványairól [On Nationalist Remnants in our Historical Perception], " in *Vita a magyarországi osztályküzdelmekről és a függetlenségi harcokról* [*Debate on Class Struggles and Independence Battles in Hungary*] (Budapest: Kossuth, 1965), 1–28 and 76–152, respectively.

[27] See Béla Dinnyei, "Molnár Erik a nemzeti ideológiáról – A vita mérlege [Erik Molnár on National Ideology – Balance of the Debate]," presented at the conference "Hungar-

ian Political and Historiographic Discourses in a Central European Context," 13-14 May 2005 at the Central European University.

[28] György Péter, *Néma Hagyomány. Kollektív felejtés és a kései múltértelmezés 1956 1989-ben. A régmúltól az örökségig* [*Silent Tradition: Collective Forgetting and Belated Interpretation of the 1956 Revolution in 1989 — From the Past to Heritage*] (Budapest: Magvető, 2000); and Gyáni Gábor, "1956 elfelejtésének régi-új mítosza [Old-New Myth about Forgetting in '56]," *Élet és irodalom* (9 February 2001); Rainer M. János, "1956 változó emlékezete [Changeable Memory of 1956]," in *Magyar Hírlap* (21 October 2000) and Litván György, "Az elnémult hagyomány," *Élet és irodalom* (April 13, 2001).

[29] See Miklós Haraszti, *The Velvet Prison: Artists under State Socialism* (New York: Noonday Press, 1987).

[30] "Bibó-szobrot avattak. [Bibo Monument Inaugurated]", *Népszabadság* (21 May 2005).

[31] See Kathrin Sitzler, "Ungarn: Im Spannungsfeld von Demokratie und Geschichte," in *Nationalismus in Osteuropa. Gefahrvolle Wege in die Demokratie*, ed. Margareta Mommsen (Munich: Beck, 1992), 96–117.

[32] Szűcs György, "A 'zsarnokság' szoborparkja [The Monument Meadow of 'Tyranny']," *budapesti negyed*, no. 1 (1994): 151–65.

[33] Éva Kovács, "Mythen und Rituale des ungarischen Systemwechsels," *Österreichische Zeitschrift für Geschichtswissenschaft* 2/1999: 210–37, 234f.

[34] Kovács Éva, "Az ironikus és a cinikus. A kommunizmus emlékezeteiről [The Ironic and the Cynic: On Memory of Communism]," *Élet és irodalom* (28 August 2003): 9/8.

[35] See Mark Pittaway, comments on the House of Terror, http://h-net.msu.edu/cgi-bin/logbrowse.pl?trx=vx&list=habsburg&month=0202&week=d&msg=M73roY2C9wVDc7WepQ/ChQ&user=&pw (September 14, 2004).

[36] Paul Jandl, "Terror und Trauer. Ungarns neue Gedächtniskultur," *Neue Zürcher Zeitung* (14 May 2004).

[37] See Kóczián Péter, "Kertész Imre és a jobboldal [Imre Kertész and the Right]," *Népszabadság* (24 October 2002): 12, especially the headlines in the leading Hungarian dailies on October 11, 2002.

[38] Nicolas Pethes, "Nobel-Dilemma. Ist Imre Kertész falsch? Ein Blick in die ungarischen Feuilletons," *Frankfurter Allgemeine Zeitung* (7 December 2002).

[39] Attila Pók, "Why was there no 'Historikerstreit' in post-communist Hungary?" *RFE/RL East European Perspectives*. Vol 6., No. 17 (18 August 2004): no pagination.

Private Occupations: Inter-generational Dialogue on the German Occupation in Denmark and the Netherlands

Isabella Matauschek

In both Denmark and the Netherlands the German occupation remains the most important period in modern national history: no other period in the history of the two countries has been examined, debated and researched as extensively as those five years. The Second World War is omnipresent today not only in school curricula, the media, and public commemoration, but is made topical in contemporary debates as wide-ranging as migration, European integration, the Israeli-Palestinian conflict, and the fight against terrorism. However, to achieve a meaningful appreciation of the tradition of historical consciousness one must look well beyond the public domain. This essay argues that it is necessary to integrate the private sphere to gain a more complete, and complex, perspective. Beyond this, the questions raised here concerns the dynamic interplay between private and official public memories of the past, and explore the influence of family traditions and generational belonging on the formation of historical consciousness.

Strange Bedfellows? Public Commemoration and Family Memory

Research on memory across Europe has expanded continuously over the past decades and has hitherto been dominated largely by interest in public commemoration and national memory.[1] On the other hand official narratives of the past and especially the experience of the Second World War (more often than not, national ones) have been simultaneously challenged by so-called "counter narratives." This was most obviously the case in Central and Eastern Europe, where during the 1990s other narratives were substituted for communist readings of the past. These counter narratives were not invented out of the blue, however; rather, they had long been in circulation within the private sphere. On the other hand, in Western Europe—with the possible exceptions of the perpetrator nations Germany and Austria—everything seemed rather stable and unchanging. This stability instantly begins to crumble upon closer scrutiny, however. Even neutral countries like Switzerland and Sweden experienced heated debates during the 1990s generated by indigenous and international scholars with respect to their relationship to looted Nazi assets, as well as critical investigations of their policy of neutrality.[2] All over Western Europe patriotic national interpretations of the war prevailed, shaped during the immediate postwar period,[3] and have come under rising pressure from globalized images of the past transmitted by films, museums, and other media products.[4] For example, international media played a crucial role in (re)introducing the catastrophe of the Holocaust into Western European historical consciousness.

This essay seeks to address the question of what happens if we shift our perspective from the official culture of commemoration—together with its images, rituals, and narratives—to the private sphere. What can we learn about processes of reception and discursive production of meaning when we observe families talking about the experience of the Second World War? What kind of narratives surface and in what ways do these narratives relate to public commemoration? Communicative memory to borrow the term coined by German Egyptologist Jan Assmann[5] reaches back to the Second World War and has the potential to challenge many of the dearly held myths in Western Europe that represent universal heroic resistance vis-à-vis a brutal German occupational regime.

Just how deep the chasm between official public memory and family traditions can be has been revealed in research into German families' memories of the Second World War. The startling conclusion was that the more people knew about National Socialist crimes—especially young people—the greater was their tendency to exclude family members and relatives from any association with those crimes. Simply put, others were always Nazis, one's own family exemplars of consistent, moral behavior.[6] The German example may be very different indeed from the experiences of people in occupied Western Europe, but by rephrasing the question to include the relationship between actual choices taken during the occupation and the postwar contention of universal heroic resistance similar patterns surface; those (emotionally) closest to the narrators are generally depicted in positive terms. For example, Dutch historian Frieso Wielenga delights in narrating an incident from his school years in the 1960s: asked whose parents had been members of the resistance movement all children had raised their arms.

One should not forget that family memory is strongly interrelated with nationalized representations and discourses even as it is a separate realm, and can at times in turn influence and shape official representations of the past. The questions raised here 1) examine the dynamic interplay between private and official public memories of the past, and 2) explore the role of family traditions and generational belonging on the formation of historical consciousness. This project and the methodology employed form part of a larger research project that investigates family traditions in seven European countries.[7] The fact that the Holocaust today constitutes one of the most important features of memory of the Second World War in Western Europe guided the case selection. Denmark and the Netherlands were chosen to represent the Western European experience; among the occupied countries of Western Europe, the highest percentage of the indigenous Jewish population survived in Denmark and the highest percentage of the indigenous Jewish population perished in Holland. In each country, twenty families consisting of three generations volunteered for qualitative interviews. One family member per generation was interviewed individually, followed by a group interview including other family members.[8] Additionally, group interviews with members of four cohorts (those born before 1934, between 1934 and 1957, between 1958 and 1970, and those later than 1975) were conducted to gain further insight into generational-specific ways of generating and negotiating meaning with respect to their understanding of the war and occupation years.

Turning the Second World War into National History: Victims and Heroes

In both Danish and the Dutch postwar societies, references to World War II and the German occupation have played a central role in negotiating national identities and values. The basic narrative of the five years of occupation was built upon the idea of a resistance movement supported by every "real" Dane or Dutch person. With very few exceptions the dominant post-war narrative turned everyone into a hero.[9]

Following the German invasion, the Danish government submitted to a German ultimatum and opted for a policy referred to as "samarbejdspolitik"; i.e., collaboration with the occupation forces. A coalition government including representatives from across the Danish political spectrum, with the exception of the communists, was formed and remained in office until summer 1943. The acceptance of the status as a "model protectorate" secured a relatively high level of domestic sovereignty at the price of collaborating in the Nazi war effort. Resistance, officially discouraged, was limited and situated at the political margins. A broader resistance movement only gained wider popular support from summer 1943 onwards. Following a popular uprising that culminated in a general strike, the government stepped down in protest against the German introduction of martial law. In autumn 1943, German plenipotentiary Werner Best began to plan the deportation of Danish Jews. However, word of the plan was leaked and a singular rescue operation started: within fourteen days the overwhelming majority of the Danish Jews escaped over the Øresund to neutral Sweden.[10]

Postwar commemoration of the Second World War in Denmark is characterized by the reconciliation of collaboration at the level of the government and state bureaucracy with the resistance movement, to the effect that every member in every layer of society was thought to have done his or her best for the country. On the one hand, by collaborating with the German occupation the state had assured a relatively smooth occupational regime; it had ensured that the Danish population enjoyed comparatively good living conditions throughout the war, and it had saved Danish lives by abstaining from fighting a superior German military force. The resistance movement, on the other hand, was accredited with saving face for Danes vis-à-vis the international community; it had subsequently allowed Denmark to place itself on the side of the victorious Allied nations. The population at large had, so the postwar construction insinuated, given the occupiers the cold shoulder and had thus demonstrated passive resistance. This view of the past allowed the majority of Danes to place themselves in the camp of resisters, who had resisted the Germans—albeit the overwhelming majority not actively. This interpretation of the occupation, emphasized by Danish historians such as Claus Bryld and Anette Warring, quickly turned into a key narrative about central values of postwar society for the Danish public.[11] The paramount importance of this interpretation, in Danish historiography referred to as "basic narrative," is that it has exercised a strong influence on private interpretations of the past.

In contrast to Denmark, the German attack on the Netherlands on 10 May 1940 met with military resistance. After a few days of fighting the Dutch army capitulated to a militarily superior adversary. The most traumatic aspect of the short conflict proved to be the German aerial bombardment of Rotterdam, which destroyed the city on 14 May. The government and the Dutch queen fled to London and remained there throughout the occupation. Unlike in Denmark, the German occupatio regime attempted to introduce strict Nazi measures into the country with the help of the Dutch National Socialist Party, the *Nationaal-Socialistische Beweging* (NSB). These efforts were of little success, and the party failed to mobilize widespread popular support.

Although the majority of the population greeted the harsh anti-Jewish measures introduced by the German occupation regime with disdain, the deportation of Dutch Jews encountered virtually no popular resistance. Collaboration of Dutch authorities and the bureaucracy ensured that deportations went off smoothly, and more than seventy percent of the Dutch Jewish population perished in Nazi extermination camps. The few surviving Jews were subsumed among all other national victims at the end of the war. Only from the 1960s onwards did the extent of the Jewish tragedy begin to enter the public consciousness.[12] Resistance to the occupation only picked up momentum towards the end of the war and was met with brutal reprisals against the Dutch civilian population. From 1944 onwards, increased forced labor conscription drove many Dutch into hiding—altogether about 300,000 people went underground, approximately 25,000 of them Jews. (In the contemporary public imagination, the typical *onderduiker* has turned into a Jew on the model of Anne Frank, however).

Unique to the Netherlands experience was the country's piecemeal liberation. Whereas the south was liberated in September 1944, the north of the country had to endure another hard winter under occupation. This so-called *hunger winter* cost the lives of thousands of Dutch civilians and still features prominently in public and private commemoration. The postwar period was characterized by what Pieter Lagrou describes as the formation of a patriotic national memory, one that included almost everyone in the group of both victim and heroic resister. Only a few were excluded from the national context by being called "wrong Dutchmen" (*foute Nederlander*). This group included members of the Dutch National Socialist Party, women who had sexual relationships with German soldiers,[13] and, to a lesser degree, economic collaborators. The postwar politics of commemoration in the Netherlands anxiously strove to prevent any group from being celebrated at the expense of others. Indeed, the government strictly monitored all commemorative events; for example, monuments could not be erected without approval from an official committee.[14]

The official commemoration of the Second World War in both Denmark and the Netherlands stressed national unity. Each of the small democratic nations had been subjected to a severe trial in dark times, and had emerged from this ordeal morally pure. The five years of occupation are separated from ordinary life and history by what the Norwegian ethnologist Anne Eriksen had designated a dark parenthesis that has bestowed upon those five years a mythical, ahistorical quality. Nazi occupation was turned into national history and decoupled from the history of the Second World War, thus serving the function of a foundational myth that demonstrates and explains who the Danes or Dutch are.[15] However, in comparison to Denmark, the changes within Dutch commemoration of the occupation have been more accentuated. Over the last several decades, more and more groups have claimed recognition as victims and have thus subverted the notion of universal and equal national victimhood. For instance, since the late 1960s the Jewish tragedy and Dutch complicity in it entered public debate. In the 1970s psychological trauma as an effect of persecution was recognized, and help centers and special pension schemes were established. Since then, the Indonesian minority—many of whom had experienced internment in Japanese camps, as well as men who fought in the decolonization wars—have pushed for recognition of their own status as victims. Most recently, children of so-called "wrong" (*foute*) parents—i.e., mostly members of the Dutch National Socialist Party, began to draw attention to their sufferings in the wake of their parents' social exclusion. In Denmark, controversial discussions of the Danish treatment of so-called "German girls" (the girlfriends of occupation soldiers and administrators) and German refugees strongly reverberated in public. In both countries the occupation remains a period of lasting importance, and can become a topic of contemporary debate in various contexts and, often, contradictory circumstances.[16] Today, the classic resistance movement hero is no longer the focal point for identification with the national past, however, and over recent years victims and damaged heroes have increasingly become the subjects of public commemoration. This development is mirrored in the private realm of family memories. The representative samples, below—limited in number in the interest of space, but indicative of the thematic treatment of issues in the wider catalogue of interviews conducted—illustrate the point quite clearly.[17]

Danish Family Memory: The Antonsen Family

The interviews with members of the Antonsen family conducted in March 2003[18] involved Asta Antonsen (age 88), her son Flemming (age 56) and granddaughter Sille (age 31). All family members were native to Copenhagen.[19] What distinguished the Antonsens from other interview partners was the great number of stories that circulated within the family. Granddaughter Sille in particular loved listening to her grandmother's recollections and during the interview with Asta, Sille prompted what appeared to be one of her favorite stories.

Grandmother Asta Antonsen and some of her friends had visited Germany in 1937. To her granddaughter, this story examplified Asta's sense of adventure and daring. Asta was reluctant to speak about her prewar visit to Germany, however; in the context of an interview concerning the occupation it seemed of paramount important to highlight one's anti-German attitude. In the course of the interview Asta told twenty-seven stories, Sille narrated another eleven, and Flemming (who emphasized that they used to talk little about the war and that he left home at the age of seventeen) contributed eight stories. When assess which stories are most important for family memory, it is imperative to look at which stories are handed down over generations. In the case of the Antonsen family, two stories were told by all three generations, both of which fall into the category of war stories. One concerned the bombing of the French school in Copenhagen, which is possibly the most important single event in Danish historical consciousness relating to the German occupation: during a March 1945 British air raid directed at Gestapo headquarters in Copenhagen, bombs accidentally fell upon the French school in Copenhagen, killing ninety-three pupils. Asta recounted that she witnessed this event on her thirtieth birthday from the office building where she worked. She told this story several times during the interview with varying degrees of specificity. Both her son and granddaughter referred to this story in some detail. The story brings together the experience of war with the otherwise unrelated history of everyday life; i.e., narrations of everyday life are anchored within the dramatic events of the War. As is quite frequently the case with such stories, there was a tendency among subsequent generations to turn them into accounts of *victimization* and/or *heroism* involving their family elders.

The other story concerns the bombardment of a block of flats in the harbor region by German warships at the end of the war. The family moved into one of the buildings struck by shells after the war, and the holes in the wall of their own unit were still visible. Whereas for Asta and her son it is the story of a neighbor who would have been killed if he had not by chance repositioned himself during the bombardment, in Sille's account centered on a family story, one in which her family had been or might at least have been indirectly threatened.

<u>Sille</u>: Yes, and then she also told/she lives as I said […] in Østerbro. And they moved in … that was … during the war, that must have been during the war, I think. Or after the war, right at the end. Because, as she told, that there were big holes in the wall of the flat and in the third floor, there, she lives facing the harbor, Nordhavn, and there some German warships, that shot at … that shot at everything. And so they hit through the wall and were about to kill family members, that was quite wild.

<u>Interviewer</u>: That is, indeed […] .

<u>Sille</u>: But that had happened before they moved in, but that had been relatively shortly before that ahh … that that had happened. So there are actually … there are such holes in the wall after the attack.

<u>Interviewer</u>: Was there something—did history report something —as to why there was an attack or [...] ?

<u>Sille</u>: That was something like "now we have to leave the place anyway, so now we ravage everything" or something like that … but I cannot right now remember why, but I think that was it.

<u>Interviewer</u>: But your grandmother did indeed have quite dramatic experiences!

<u>Sille</u>: Yes, that one can really say. (Antonsen family interview, lines 48-65.)

To Sille the occupation was characterized by excitement, thrills, and danger. Further, we can observe a tendency to heroicize her grandmother; a tendency she has in common with many members of the children's and grandchildren's generations.

For her grandmother, many memories of the occupation were of a somewhat more mundane character, however; Asta was already married and had two small children at the time of the German invasion. When we assess her stories it becomes obvious that to her that recollections of the war were primarily linked to the difficulties of organizing everyday life. Indeed, approximately one-third of the stories Asta shared dealt with everyday life, which was not easy either during or after the war for a working mother with a husband disinclined to work. Yet another important issue reoccurred in Asta's stories, namely her association with the resistance and her own engagement in what can be termed small acts of resistance—reading underground newspapers and listening to the BBC, for example. As noted above, the topic of resistance has long been paramount in public commemoration of the war; within the family interview the topic of resistance took on a somewhat controversial quality, however.

> Flemming: (to Asta) [...] there had been extremely many freedom fighters towards the end, weren't there?
>
> Sille: [laughs] The saints of the final days! [everyone speaks simultaneously]
>
> Asta: There were really been many who did much [...]
>
> Interviewer: Was it the case that suddenly everyone was wearing an armband?
>
> Flemming: There was something like a business in freedom[-fighter] bands, wasn't there?
>
> Sille: Wasn't this what one calls the saints of the final days? Those who quite suddenly were so [...]
>
> Asta: I don't know, I have never heard that [...]
>
> Sille: Yes, I think so, because I have heard this expression in *Matador* [a well-received Danish drama series—I.M.]
>
> Flemming: Well, yes I think so [...]
>
> Asta: But yes, there were some of them who did all kinds of things. There had been one who had been fastened under a train, but I don't know that. I shall see if I can find it, because I do have those books about that. (Antonsen family interview, lines 143-157.)

Yet however critical the younger generations, in particular, tend to discuss the myth of widespread involvement with the resistance and the government's role in collaborating with the German occupation, the resistance is still an important feature of Danish identity formation. For example, granddaughter Sille drew a moral distinction between necessity and avarice when asked to judge on collaboration, then concluded boldly: "[...] if this had been now, had we been in this situation, then I think it's totally clear that I would have deeply resisted it [...]". A paradoxical pattern emerges: the more critical the discussion of (alleged) universal involvement of the Danish population within the resistance movement, the more the resistance turns into an ideal norm by which the past is judged.

However convinced Asta was of the importance of the Danish resistance, she assessed her husband's connection with it rather sceptically. He had refused to work with the rationale that he did not want to contribute to the German war effort. Son Flemming shared her misgivings about his father's account. Only Sille, who had a romantic attachment to the period of the occupation and for whom this period was characterized by dramatic events, adventure, and a strong sense of community, told a highly dramatic story of her grandfather's involvement in a shooting incident. Her grandmother was an important source for her—more so than was her father. Moreover, it is evident that her view of the past was strongly influenced by media treatments. She referenced different sources, including films, books, and—most importantly—the Danish televisions drama series *Matador* in order to make sense of the past.[20] How much importance Sille attached to the television series becomes clear when she discussed her plan to show the series she loved dearly to her children once they are old enough to appreciate it.

The Antonsen interview reveals interesting examples of elements consistent with stories told in interviews with other families. It is also representative in that which is absent from family memory: the Jews. Neither the National Socialist persecution of European Jewry nor the rescue of Danish Jews form more than a peripheral part of historical memory in the Danish family tradition. This is not a unique feature of the Danish family tradition, moreover; it has also characterised Danish historical scholarship into the 1980s.[21] When asked what they learned from their parents and grandparents about the persecution of Jews or the Holocaust, the overwhelming majority of interviewees actually cited the media and educational institutions as the primary source of information rather than family members. Not surprisingly, the only story recounted that treated Jews was told by granddaughter Sille; she referred to a Jewish family hiding in a garden house. Her narration was less a story than her attempt to imagine how it would feel to spend the winter in a wooden shed, however. This story gives the impression of having been informed by media: Danish Jews who went into hiding after word of German plans for deportation was leaked were taken to Sweden within two weeks. The experience of hiding for Danish Jews was thus extremely limited. The kind of experience Sille raised is related to hiding in other countries and possibly informed by the image of the Frank family. Not surprisingly, it is *The Diary of Anne Frank* that is the most frequent international media reference in the Danish interviews.

Indeed, the absence of the Jewish experience in narratives was not particular to the Antonsen family. Rarely did stories about Jews and their experience emerge in any of the Danish interviews. The persecution of Danish Jews and their flight to Sweden is not part of the family tradition, but was introduced via the media. The persecution of the European Jews is a topic mostly taken up by the second and third generation, insofar as they reflect on the Holocaust and discuss films and TV programs they have seen or books they have read.

Family Memory in the Netherlands: The Bannink family

The Bannink family, interviewed in May 2003, consisted of Wim Bannink (age 87), son Ab (age 54), and grandson Jeroen (age 29). Grandmother Trui, Wim's wife, also participated in the family interview; despite initial misgivings she took part with great enthusiasm. Wim and his wife both spent their entire lives in a farming community in the so-called Achterhoek (literally "outback corner") in the east of the country, not far from the German border. Before retirement Wim had cultivated a farm inherited from his parents. His son Ab was very interested in history and especially local history and the German occupation. He was active in a local history association. The grandson Jeroen declared himself very interested in the Second World War. He and his father were very close, they watched films together and shared in discussions of them. Jeroen, like the overwhelming majority of the members of the third generation in the Netherlands, was not conversant in the local history of the German occupation.

Many stories circulated within the Bannink family, and not surprisingly the rural background of the family featured prominently in them. For instance, the hunger winter of 1944/45, usually recounted from the perspective of privation and want, was remembered differently; as farmers they profited from the scarcity of food and rising prices. Grandmother Trui made a point of stressing that they never took unduly from the hungry people who made it to her parents' farm. Evacuees living on the farm, forced labor for the Germans, relations with local representatives of the Dutch National Socialist Party, and the resistance are some of the reoccurring themes of their stories.

Three stories stand out as particularly important due to the fact that they are narrated by all three generations of the Bannink family. One of these stories concerns the death of grandfather Wim's sister at the end of the war. An Allied bomb that hit their parents' house and killed her. The liberation that should have been a time of celebration thus turned into a time of grieving for this family. Through this tragic accident the liberators were transformed into murders, whereas the family had not suffered at the hands of the German occupiers. This story added a twist to the standard commemoration of the liberation and therefore requires further explanation; this aim was achieved by including the death of the family member into the construction of an understanding of universal victimhood as a product of war. Indeed, it is the tragic experience of war that was decisive in the family's pacifist outlook. The second story deals with the hiding of an English pilot in Wim's parental home. For both son Ab and grandson Jeroen this was a story that depicts Wim heroically defying the German occupiers.

Interviewer: You have a certificate from Eisenhower hanging here?

Trui (Wim's wife): Oh yes!

Wim: No, this was for the hiding of a pilot.

Interviewer: Hmm. [To Ab and Jeroen:] You knew about that?

Jeroen: Yes.

Ab: Yes, we certainly knew that. Yes indeed, I felt that it was worth the trouble, because we have only recently, or no, that isn't true, well about ten, fifteen years ago I found it so, or found it so important eh, that I thought, I'll have it framed for once. For father always had the thing just rolled up somewhere.

Wim: In the closet, it was in the closet. [...]

Jeroen: But I also think you have something like, wow, that happened. Grandpa possibly saw it more as something ordinary, nothing above the normal. And because of that he also treated it as something normal. But you really think, hop, up onto the wall. And he thinks, hop, into the closet.

Wim: Yes [...] Just something else, the people that had, eh, hung it up, that was then, eh ...

Ab: Oh yes, that was not unique for the Netherlands.

Wim: No, no, no.

Ab: That was non-stop, eh, but well, you have to look how many people ...

Trui: Yes, but that was particularly dangerous. Then with the ...

Ab: Yes, no, but eh ... if they had really found him with an English soldier, or an American soldier, yes then, eh, then you were taken away.

Trui: Yes.

Ab: Then you had the, eh, good chance not to survive it.

Trui: Then you had no more peace, didn't you, if you had someone like that in the house. (Bannink family interview, lines 723-758.)

This sequence brings up some features characteristic of Dutch family memory: heroism and the scepticism of those who openly boasted of their heroic deeds, the difficult balance between an urge to depict one's family heroically and the norm of not risking one's family's security, however limited this risk may have been. During the interview with Wim the story took another, less heroic bend, however. The resistance movement placed a downed English pilot in his parent's house for a night because an evacuated English teacher was living whose services as a translator were required.

The third and possibly most interesting story concerns a monument dedicated to forty-six men who were shot by the Germans in a retaliatory measure designed to curb increasing acts of resistance. The occasion for the execution had been the killing of four German soldiers by resistance fighters. The monument is located close to the Banninks' farm and grandfather Wim was thus a potential victim of the German reprisal action. The village mayor installed by the local branch of the Dutch National Socialist Party managed to persuade the German officials to shoot inmates of a nearby prison instead. Every May 4th the monument is a location for the official commemoration of the dead. To both Wim and his son Ab the monument and the events it commemorates formed an important aspect of their narration. Grandson Jeroen on the other hand, though familiar with the existence of the monument, was to his own acute dismay unable to narrate the story. An awkward moment passed when he was unable to answer the interviewer's question concerning the monument. He emphasized that he had to visit the monument himself in order to make sense of it. He shifted the focus and referred to the reference the interviewer had made to Yad Vashem during an exchange with his father Ab. He then discussed his visit to Yad Vashem in some detail, especially the children's monument that had made a tremendous impression on both the interviewer and himself.

> Jeroen: I have thus also been in Israel in 1999, what I … that was really, eh … one of the most eh, yes, touching and yes, the most emotional event I have ever experienced.
>
> Interviewer: I came out of there weeping. [laughs] (Bannink family interview, lines 181-184.)

The Holocaust is foremost on the mind of many members of this generation when they think about the Second World War. Whereas Wim saw the occupation in a local and national framework and assigned less importance to the Holocaust, his son Ab's view of the Second World War had been strongly influenced by the media coverage of the Eichmann trial and the emergence of the Dutch debate on the Holocaust. However, like his father, Ab was influenced by a national and local interpretation of the past. Universal lessons of the past featured in their narratives but not as prominently as they did in the statements of the member of the third generation, Jeroen. The knowledge that members of the third generation have about their families' experiences during the war may be somewhat vague and diffuse, but the Second World War has not lost importance for them. Thus, all three of them stated that they observe the moment of silence during the May 4th commemoration of the war dead, but though the form may be identical it is obvious that the content of their reflections was quite different.

> Interviewer: And during the two minutes of silence do you then really think about …
>
> Jeroen: Yes, I am there, well, eh … yes, you probably don't think about it all the time but yes, yes, yes, exactly. They're always then, you don't use two minutes eh, eh, really to think back about…about… Anne Frank, or a concentration camp, or the Germans or what do I know, or the war in general. But there are always moments within the two minutes again, that you then realize, that you then stand in silence, that [this] has happened and that this may never happen again. (Bannink family interview, line 292-99.)

Family Memory between "Re-nationalization" and "Universalization"

Through these interviews it has largely been possible to identify the continued effects of the basic narrative of wartime memory in Denmark. This narrative offered an inclusive compromise solution and the possibility of identification for all Danes; resistance thus became both a moral duty and the symbolic core of the Danish nation. Resistance today is made topical in a wide range of areas, and the younger generations in particular see the importance of democracy and human rights as lessons they draw from the German occupation.

Thus, Amalie Fredriksen (age 21), a student from Aarhus, when asked about the lessons of the occupation made an impassioned plea for democracy:

> […] I think more about how the conditions in Germany were, well more in that direction, that it is important that we have a democracy and that it is important that there are many who decide and … even if the people quarrel a lot and politicians squabble and one can get enough of listening to that, then I only think that that is good, that that is fantastic, that different opinions are voiced instead of that absolutism rules and … that the whole becomes black and white. And if this is something that makes people think about how important it is to participate in democracy and that they value freedom of speech and … and also only, that one should be able to live together, because one is a Jew or a Christian or a Muslim. But especially democracy, that is something I think a lot about, because

> that is simply so important.[22] (Amalie Fredriksen interview, line 117-126.)

In addition to the resistance movement and democratic principles, national solidarity in the face of external threat belongs to the standard inventory of Danish constructions of the past. Asked what he perceives to have been positive about the occupation era, Nis Gade (age 21) declared:

> Nis Gade: The solidarity!
>
> Interviewer: The solidarity. . .
>
> Nis: Yes, and that it … that one ... yes, the hell what can one say. That one found out how … how small Denmark is and how much one has to stick together when something so big happens. And I believe that it became much more social afterwards.[23] (Nis Gade interview, line 523-27.)

In the Netherlands many members of the younger generation complained about their families' silence on the war. Most of their knowledge was derived from the media and schools. Universal interpretations of the war are thus omnipresent. They have heard about the icons of Dutch commemoration, such as those in recognition of people who went underground to avoid forced labor for the Germans, the so-called *onderduikers* or hiders. Many members of the younger generations find it difficult to make sense of this, however. One member of the third generation, twenty-three year old student Marijke Groen, even recounted that she thought her grandfather, a farmer's son from the northern Holland, was Jewish because he had to go underground.

> Interviewer: How […] did you get this idea?
>
> Marijke Groen: Well, because he had to go underground and I thought why do you have to, why do you have to go underground if you are not, if you are no Jew, why does this then have to be. But yes, like … I think that, I think that that was just because he didn't want to join the army.
>
> Interviewer: But did you then ask that, something like, were you Jewish?
>
> Marijke Groen: Yes, indeed [laughs] but the, eh, yes, the answer was then no.[24] (Marijke Groen interview, line 397-401.)

Dutch members of the third generation were no less zealous to depict their families on the right side as their Danish counterparts. Dexter Bel, for instance, asked his grandfather during the family interview if he had been on the right side. When his grandfather answered that he certainly had been on the right side, Dexter emphasized that he knew his grandfather had not done anything wrong; he excused himself by stating he had only asked "for the sake of clarity."[25]

Conclusions

Public commemoration in Denmark and the Netherlands during the immediate postwar period have heavily emphasised national victimhood and resistance. Though there are many critical debates in the public that cast these constructs into doubt, they have proved to be of surprising resilience. This finding seems less surprising when we take family tradition into account. Suffering and brave acts of resistance on the part of one's own family members are the dominant trope handed down within families. Informed by images of the war and the Holocaust, the everyday struggle to make ends meet can at times turn into brave acts of resistance in the face of omnipresent danger. Although obvious similarities between Denmark and the Netherlands exist, there are marked differences in the national family traditions: in Denmark, similarities in interpretation of the past among the members of the three generations are strong; in the Netherlands, members of the third generation are more distanced from the interpretations and experiences of their families than their Danish counterparts. In both countries a tendency among members of the second and the third generations to transform members of the first generation into heroes can be observed. Despite the fact that many members of the younger generations take a critical view vis-à-vis national history and commemoration, the stories handed down within families in fact underpin older conceptions of victimization and resistance. Thus, instead of setting the national patriotic interpretation of the German occupation into relative terms, national and international media depictions together with family tradition have served to update these images of the past for the present.

Notes

[1] Henry Rousso, "Das Dilemma eines europäischen Gedächtnisses," in *Zeithistorische Forschungen / Studies in Contemporary History*, Online-edition, 1 (2004), H. 3, http://www.zeithistorische-forschungen.de/16126041-Rousso-3-2004.

[2] For Switzerland see the publications of the Independent Commission of Experts Switzerland – Second World War, http://www.uek.ch. For Sweden the living history project website provides a select bibliography, http://svefor.levandehistoria.se.

[3] For France, the Netherlands and Belgium see Pieter Lagrou, *The Legacy of Nazi Occupation: Patriotic Memory and National Recovery in Western Europe, 1945–1965* (Cambridge UK and New York: Cambridge University Press, 2000).
[4] Daniel Levy and Nathan Sznaider, "Memory Unbound: The Holocaust and the Formation of Cosmopolitan Memory," *European Journal of Social Theory* 5, 1 (2002): 87–106.
[5] See Jan Assmann, *Das kulturelle Gedächtnis. Schrift, Erinnerung und politische Identität in frühen Hochkulturen*, 4. ed. (Munich: Beck, 2002).
[6] Harald Welzer, Sabine Moller and Karoline Tschuggnall, *Opa war kein Nazi. Nationalsozialismus und Holocaust im Familiengedächtnis* (Frankfurt/Main: Fischer, 2002).
[7] The project "“traditions of historical consciousness in Europe" was carried out at the Institute for Advanced Study in the Humanities in Essen, Germany between 2002 and 2005. In addition to Denmark and the Netherlands, the countries included Croatia, Serbia, Norway, Germany, and Switzerland. For a detailed account of the country results in German see Harald Welzer (ed.), *Der Krieg der Erinnerung. Holocaust, Kollaboration und Widerstand im europäischen Gedächtnis*. (Frankfurt/Main: Fischer 2007).
[8] The families interviewed were recruited via "snowball sampling": the research design sought a grandparent born 1934 or earlier, and the grandchild had to be at least twelve years old. These requirements made any approach to representative sampling virtually futile; however, a geographical balance was maintained in order to make the representation of different regional experiences possible. The interviews were conducted by native speakers, all of them members of the third—i.e., grandchildren's—generation. The interviews were modeled as close as possible on an everyday-style conversations. The interviewers asked contemporary witnesses for their experiences during the German occupation; members of the children's and grandchildren's generation were asked what they had learned from their families about the occupation and the Holocaust. For a detailed account of the methodology used see Olaf Jensen, "Zur Methode der vergleichenden Tradierungsforschung," in *Der Krieg der Erinnerung*. 260-74
[9] For the Netherlands see Lagrou, 59–77; for Denmark see Claus Bryld and Anette Warring, *Besættelsestiden som kollektiv erindring, Historie- og traditionforvaltning af og besættelse* (Frederiksberg: Roskilde universitetsforlag, 1998).
[10] Leni Yahil, *The Rescue of Danish Jewry: Test of a Democracy* (Philadelphia: Jewish Publication Society of America, 1969).
[11] Bryld and Warring, *Besættelsestiden*, 460.
[12] J. C. H. Blom, "The persecution of the Jews in the Netherlands: A Comparative Western European Perspective," *European History Quarterly* 19, 3 (1989): 333–53. See also Bob Moore, *Victims and Survivors: The Nazi Persecution of the Jews in the Netherlands, 1940-1945* (London and New York: Arnold, 1997) and Conny Kristel, *Geschiedschrijving als opdracht: Abel Herzberg, Jacques Presser en Loe de Jong over de jodenvervolging* (Amsterdam: Meulenhoff, 1998).
[13] These women are referred to as *moffenmeiden* in the Netherlands or *tysker piger* in Denmark—i.e. literally "Germans' girls."
[14] Frank Van Vree, *In de schaduw van Auschwitz: herinneringen, beelden, geschiedenis* (Groningen: Historische Uitgeverij, 1995), 72f.
[15] Anne Eriksen, *Det var noe annet under krigen. 2. verdenskrig i norsk kollektivtradisjon* (Oslo: Pax Forlag, 1995); see also Bryld and Waring, *Besættelsestiden*, 53–72.

[16] For the Danish debate on immigration and its references to the Second World War see Mette Zølner, *Re-Imagining the Nation: Debates on Immigrants, Identities and Memories* (Frankfurt, Brussels, and New York: Peter Lang, 2000).
[17] The interviews were analyzed combining hermeneutic case studies with computer-assisted content analysis. For a detailed account of hermeneutic interpretation methods in the social sciences see Jo Reichertz, "Objective Hermeneutics and Hermeneutic Sociology of Knowledge," in *Companion to Qualitative Research* ed. Uwe Flick et al. (London: Sage 2004) 290-96. For a discussion of the adaptation of the hermeneutic methodology to the project's scope see Jensen, "Zur Methode der vergleichenden Tradierungsforschung" (note 8, above). In-depth analysis of the interviews generated an inductive category scheme. The categories from the hermeneutic case studies, in turn, formed the basis for the computer-assisted content analysis of the vast body of interview material. Content analysis was carried out with the help of the computer software Maxqda. For a detailed account by the program's developer see Udo Kuckartz, *Einführung in die computergestützte Analyse qualitativer Daten*. Second edition (Wiesbaden: VS Verlag, 2007.) An introduction to computer-assisted qualitative content analysis with the help of Maxqda is offered by Juliet Corbin, *Basics of Qualitative Research Techniques and Procedures for Developing Grounded Theory*, Third Edition, (Thousand Oaks, CA: Sage 2007).
[18] The interviews were conducted in Danish and the names of interview partners were changed to preserve their anonymity.
[19] The experience of the occupation in Copenhagen was in many ways distinct from that of the rest of the country. This difference has been even further developed in historical commemoration. In our material we found frequent references, that there was "no war" outside of the big cities, especially with respect to Copenhagen.
[20] The TV series "Matador" was initially broadcasted in the late 1970s and early 1980s. This quite successful series is the source most frequently referred to among all families interviewed; seventy-five percent of the families interviewed refer to the series. The series can, without exaggeration, be characterized as the Danish historical master narrative.
[21] Sofie Lene Bak, *Forfølgelsen af de danske jøder. Forestillinger om oktober 1943 i forskning og offentlighed* (Copenhagen: Museum Tusculanums Forlag, 2001).
[22] Amalie Frederiksen (*1981, name changed) was interviewed November 11, 2002.
[23] Nis Gade (*1982, name changed) was interviewed June 11, 2003.
[24] Marijke Groen (*1980, name changed) was interviewed April 25, 2003.
[25] Dexter Bel (*1986, name changed) was interviewed December 21, 2003; line 578.

Abbreviations

AGE	*Agrupacion de Guerilleros espanoles*
AN	*Archives Nationales de la France*
BAK	Bundesarchiv Koblenz
BGBl.	*Bundesgesetzblatt der Republik Österreich*
BPA	*Bezirksprüfungsausschuss* (district review board)
BZÖ	*Bündnis Zukunft Österreich* (Alliance for Austria's Future)
CDU	*Christ-Demokratische Union (*Christian Democratic Union)
CGT	Confédération générale du travail
CSU	*Christlich Soziale Union* (Christian Social Union)
DC	*Democrazia Cristiana* (Christian Democrats)
DJV	*Deutsche Zentralverwaltung für Justiz* (German Central Administration for Justice)
DP	*Deutsche Partei* (German Party)
DPs	Displaced Persons
EDC	European Defense Community
FFI	*Forces Françaises de l'Intérieur*
FPÖ	*Freiheitliche Partei Österreich* (Austrian Freedom Party)
FRUS	Foreign Relations of the United States (Series)
FSK	*Freiwillige Selbstkontrolle der Filmwirtschaft* (Voluntary Self-Regulation of Film Industry)
FTP	*Franc Tireurs et Partisans*
GDR	German Democratic Republic
HAD	Dorotheum House Archive
HHstA	Hessisches Hauptstaatsarchiv
HICOG	US High Commissioner for Germany
IMT	International Military Tribunal at Nuremberg
IRO	International Refugee Organization
KPD	*Kommunistische Partei Deutschlands* (Communist Party of Germany)
KPÖ	*Kommunistische Partei Österreichs* (Austrian Communist Party)
LPA	*Landesprüfungsausschuss* (provincial review board)
MLN	*Mouvement de Libération Nationale*

MOI	*Main d'Oeuvre Immigrant*
MRP	*Mouvement Républicaine Populaire*
MUR	*Mouvement Unifié de Résistance*
NACP	National Archives, College Park
NATO	North Atlantic Treaty Organization
NCO	Non-commisioned officer
NFB	National Film Board of Canada
NPA	*Neues Politisches Archiv*
NPD	*Nationaldemokratische Partei Deutschlands* (National Democratic Party of Germany)
NSDAP	*Nationalsozialistische deutsche Arbeiterpartei* (National Socialist German Workers' Party)
OMGUS	Office of the Military Government, United States [in occupied Germany]
OPI	Office of Public Information
ÖStA/AdR	*Österreichisches Staatsarchiv/Archiv der Republik* (Austrian National Archives, Archive of the Republic
ÖVP	*Österreichische Volkspartei* (Austrian People's Party)
OWI	U.S. Office of War Information
PCE	Partido Comunista de España (Spanish Communist Party)
PCF	Parti communiste français (French Communist Party)
PCI	*Partito Comunista Italiano* (Italian Communist Party)
Pg	*Parteigenossen* (NSDAP party members)
POW	Prisoner of war
PSI	*Partito Socalista Italiano* (Italian Socialist Party)
PSOE	Partido Socialista Obrero Español (Spanish Socialist Party)
RM	*Reichsmark*
RS	*Revolutionäre Sozialisten* (Revolutionary Socialists [Austria])
SA	*Sturmabteilung* (NSDAP Storm Troop)
SED	*Sozialistische Einheitspartei Deutschlands* (Socialist Unity Party of Germany [East])
SFIO	Section française de l'Internationale ouvrière (French Socialist Party)
SNP	Subsequent Nuremberg Proceedings

SPD	Sozialdemokratische Partei Deutschlands ([West] German Social Democratic Party)
SPÖ	*Sozialistische Partei Österreichs* (Austrian Socialist Party)
StGBl.	*Staatsgesetzblatt* (der Republik Österreich)
UDI	Union of Italian Women
UNE	*Union Nacional Espanola*
UNESCO	United Nations Educational, Scientific and Cultural Organization
UNRRA	United Nations Relief and Rehabilitation Agency
USDA	US Department of Agriculture,
VdU	*Verband der Unabhängigen* (Alliance of Independents [Austria])
VEAV	*Vermögensentziehungs-Anmeldungsverordnung*
VF	*Vaterländische Front* (Fatherland Front)
VGA	*Verein für die Geschichte der Arbeiterbewegung* (Association for the History of the Labor Movement)
WSchG	Währungsschutzgesetz
ZPA	*zentraler Prüfungsausschuss* (central review board)

Contributors

Matthew Paul Berg is Professor of History at John Carroll University in Cleveland, Ohio. His research focuses on social democracy, reconstruction, and identity in postwar Austria. Among his publications are (with Greg Eghigian) *Sacrifice and National Belonging in Twentieth Century Germany* (College Station, 2002) and (with Jill Lewis and Oliver Rathkolb) *The Struggle for a Democratic Austria: Bruno Kreisky on Peace and Social Justice* (New York and Oxford, 2000); his work has also appeared in journals such as *German History*, *Central European History*, *zeitgeschichte*, *Austrian History Yearbook* and *Contemporary Austrian Studies*. He is currently preparing a monograph entitled *Renewing Red Vienna: The Reconstruction of a Social Democratic Milieu, 1945-1955.*

G. Daniel Cohen is Assistant Professor of History at Rice University in Houston, Texas. He specializes on the history of forced displacement, humanitarianism and human rights in Europe in the aftermath of World War Two and has published several articles on these topics in *The Journal of Contemporary History*, *Immigrants and Minorities* and *Archives Juives*. He is the author of a manuscript entitled *Europe's Displaced Persons and the Making of the Postwar World 1945-1955* currently under review Columbia University Press.

Valerie Hébert is currently a postdoctoral fellow at the Jack and Mae Nathanson Centre on Transnational Human Rights, Crime and Security at Osgoode Hall Law School at York University in Toronto. She has held grants and fellowships from the Social Sciences and Humanities Research Council of Canada, the German Historical Institute, the Holocaust Educational Foundation, and the United States Holocaust Memorial Museum. Her book *Hitler's Soldiers on Trial: The Nuremberg High Command Case and the Politics of Punishment, 1947–1958* will be published by the University Press of Kansas.

Christoph Jahr is Assistant Professor (Wissenschaftlicher Assistent) of Modern History, Humboldt University Berlin. His publications include *Feindbilder in der deutschen Geschichte. Studien zur Vorurteilsgeschichte im 19. und 20. Jahrhundert* (Berlin, 1994) (co-editor); *Gewöhnliche Soldaten. Desertion und Deserteure im deutschen und britischen Heer 1914-1918* (Göttingen 1998); *Die Berliner Universität in der NS-Zeit*, 2 vols. (Stuttgart 2005) (co-editor); *Straftat, Norm, Skandal. Die Debatten über die juristische Ahndung antisemitischer Agitation in Deutschland 1879 bis 1960* (forthcoming).

Robert Knight is Lecturer in European and International Studies at Loughborough University. He has published extensively on Austrian history and on Western policy towards central Europe and served as amember of the Austrian Historians' Commission investigating Nazi property theft and postwar compensation and restitution.

Stefan August Lütgenau is an independent historian living in Austria. His main fields of research have been diplomatic history, Holocaust-era assets, and National Socialism in Austria. He is also active in international development and cooperation projects and international human rights protection. His publications include *Human Rights and a Middle East Peace Process. Analyses and Case Studies from a New Perspective* (Rutgers, NJ and Innsbruck, 2007) and *Esterházy Pál (1901–1989). Az utolsó herceg sorsa a szélsőségek évszázadában* (Budapest 2008).

Sabine Manke studied cultural anthropology, German language, literature and media in Marburg, Washington DC and Athens. She received her PhD in cultural anthropology from Philipps-University/Marburg in 2008. She is a founding member of an interdisciplinary working group on critical hermeneutics. Since 1999 she has served as an editor for a publisher of academic literature and as curator of artistic projects. Her publications are situated in the interrelated fields of gender images, cultural history and politics.

Isabella Matauschek is lecturer in Intercultural Communication at the Johannes Kepler University in Linz, Austria. Her research focuses on international relief efforts, the tradition of historical consciousness in Europe, and cultural encounters between Europe and (Southeast) Asia.

Maria Mesner teaches Modern History at the University of Vienna, is director of the Bruno Kreisky Archives Foundation in Vienna, and serves as co-editor of the *Österreichische Zeitschrift für Geschichtswissenschaften.* Her research focuses on political cultures in the US and Austria, gender relations during the 20th century, and reproductive history.

David A. Messenger is Assistant Professor of History at the University of Wyoming. A specialist in the history of Spain during and after the Second World War, he is author of *L'Espagne Republicaine: French Policy and Spanish Republicanism in Liberated France* (Sussex, 2008). His work has appeared in journals such as *Intelligence and National Security*, *The International History Review*, *French History* and *The Journal of European Studies*.

Sonja Niederacher is a historian at Bruno Kreisky Archives Foundation. Her research focuses on National Socialism and Austria's relationship to the Nazi past, emigration, exile studies, and property and gender in the twentieth century.

Bela Rasky is an independent historian and head of the Austrian Science and Research Liaison Office in Budapest. He has published widely on the First Austrian Republic, Austrian and Hungarian history in the twentieth century and the history of cultural policies in Europe

Alexandra Staub is Associate Professor of Architecture at the Pennsylvania State University. She has written widely on urbanism and postwar German and Soviet housing. Her work has appeared in *The Journal of Urban History*, *Wolkenkuckucksheim*, *Bauwelt*, and *Baumeister*.

Molly Tambor teaches European History at Barnard College and The Cooper Union for the Advancement of the Arts and Sciences in New York City. Her research interests center on women and political militancy in contemporary Europe. She is currently preparing her manuscript *The Active Citizen: Women in Italian Politics, 1948-1963*.

Austria: Forschung und Wissenschaft – Politikwissenschaft

René Cuperus; Karl A. Duffek; Erich Fröschl; Tobias Mörschel (eds.)
The EU – A Global Player?
The integration of Europe over the past fifty years has been a success story. However, considerable disagreement exists today about the future development of the European Union, particularly in relation to the speed and intensity of political integration, but also concerning the role to be played by Europe in the global political system. In this book, renowned European academics and politicians discuss the question of whether Europe should and can be a „Global Player." In particular, the following issues are raised: Has the EU reached the status of an economic „Global Player"? What are common European values, if any? Can Social Democracy be the European Model? Which are the differences and commonalities in the perception of a Common Foreign and Security Policy?
Bd. 1, 2006, 208 S., 24,90 €, br., ISBN 3-8258-9581-5

Oliver Rathkolb (Ed.)
Sweden – Austria: Two Roads to Neutrality and a Modern Welfare State
This volume is organized around Swedish and Austrian models of social partnership, the welfare, economic policies and neutrality policy with special focus on developments since the end of the Cold War. There is a stronger trend towards changes in Sweden within the process of decorporization with a more intensive change into more pluralistic decision making models. In GDP per head Austrian economic performance has been more successful. On the other hand, Sweden succeeded better than Austria in reaching more equal income distribution. Both countries seem to continue the neutrality policy track.
Bd. 4, 2008, 168 S., 19,90 €, br., ISBN 978-3-8258-1311-6

LIT Verlag Berlin – Münster – Wien – Zürich – London
Auslieferung Deutschland / Österreich / Schweiz: siehe Impressumsseite

Cultural Patterns of Politics
edited by Silvia Miháliková, PhD (Bratislava University) and Dr. Andreas Pribersky (Vienna University)

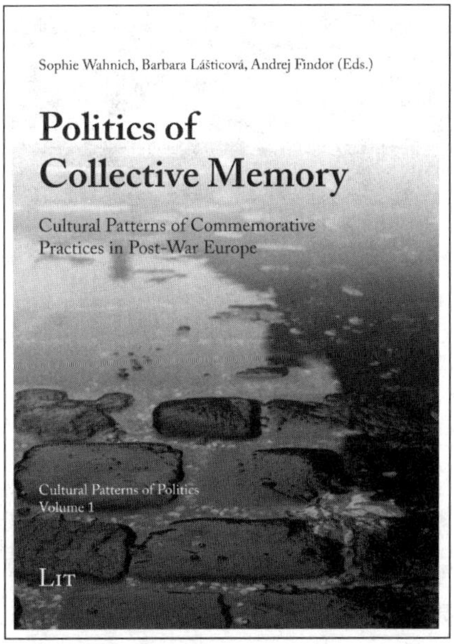

Sophie Wahnich; Barbara Lášticová; Andrej Findor (Eds.)
Politics of Collective Memory
Cultural Patterns of Commemorative Practices in Post-War Europe
The memory is not shared. In a present reconstruction of the past, it rather produces the sharing of the sensible, its cleavages and clashes parallel to the clashes of political sensibilities. To examine the shifting representations of heroes, victims, terror, and oppression of the Great War, Second World War, holocaust and communism in museums, historical monuments, public spaces and buildings, public holidays, and state symbols allows to capture what different countries of Europe are sensible to, to ask whether they share or not a common sensibility, common cultural patterns.
Bd. 1, 2008, 272 S., 24,90 €, br., ISBN 978-3-8258-0226-4

IUS VIVENS
Quellentexte zur Rechtsgeschichte
hrsg. von Prof. Dr. Heinz Holzhauer (Münster), Dr. Wolf-Dieter Barz (Karlsruhe), Prof. Dr. Andreas Roth (Mainz) und Prof. Dr. Stefan Chr. Saar (Potsdam)

Siegfried Moses
Jewish Post-War Claims (Tel Aviv 1944)
With an introduction by Professor Dr. Paul Kirchhof and a bio-bibliographic annotation by Rachel Heuberger. Edited by Wolf-Dieter Barz. Introductory part and appendix translated by Eli Moses
It has been only recently that the long drawn out international negotiations conducted in the U.S. on the subject of the finalization of reparations to be paid by Germany to the, mainly Jewish, forced laborers of the National Socialist regime were concluded. The American-Jewish aspect of the broader subject of involvement with the aftermath of the Holocaust has already evoked an echo of wide-ranging discussions in the recently published works of Wolf Calebow, Peter Novick and Norman Finkelstein.
Bd. 6, 2001, 184 S., 35,90 €, br., ISBN 3-8258-5024-2

LIT Verlag Berlin – Münster – Wien – Zürich – London
Auslieferung Deutschland / Österreich / Schweiz: siehe Impressumsseite